This book should be returned to any branch of the
Lancashire County Library on or before the date

1 9 APR 2014

SKE

2 3 JUN 2015
0 7 NOV 2016

3 0 DEC 2016

1 6 OCT 2018

Lancashire County Library
Bowran Street
Preston PR1 2UX

Lancashire
County Council

www.lancashire.gov.uk/libraries

LANCASHIRE COUNTY LIBRARY

3011812556894 3

D0410545

IRAQ
FULL
CIRCLE

From Shock and Awe to the Last Combat Patrol

COL. DARRON L. WRIGHT

LANCASHIRE COUNTY LIBRARY

3011812556894 3	
Askews & Holts	18-Jan-2013
956.70443 WRI	£20.00
2|13	

NOT FOR FAME OR REWARD, NOT FOR PLACE OR FOR RANK, NOT LURED BY AMBITION OR GOADED BY NECESSITY, BUT IN SIMPLE OBEDIENCE TO DUTY AS THEY UNDERSTOOD IT, THESE MEN SUFFERED ALL, SACRIFICED ALL, DARED ALL, AND DIED.

—Confederate Memorial at Arlington National Cemetery

I dedicate this book first and foremost to my loving wife Wendy and my amazing children Dillon, Chloe, and Kyle, for enduring all the months and years that I was forward deployed doing what I love to do. To my mom, stepfather, brother, sister, and their families, thanks for all your love and support over the years. To all the men and women who wear the uniform both past and present defending democracy abroad and serving as the beacon of freedom for America, you represent less than 1 percent of our nation's population who have stepped forward to serve a cause greater than yourselves. You all are heroes and deserve the highest regard and praise that our nation can bestow upon you. You are America's finest. To the brave and courageous soldiers of 1st Battalion–8th Infantry Regiment, 3rd Brigade Combat Team–4th Infantry Division, 4th Brigade Combat Team–4th Infantry Division, 1st Battalion Airborne–509th Infantry, and the 4th Stryker Brigade Combat Team–2nd Infantry Division, thanks for your service and most of all your sacrifice. You made your mark on this war at different stages and times over the past years, but, most noteworthy, you brought freedom and hope to a country that only knew tyranny and oppression. Finally, to our fallen warriors, you died a hero's death; our nation is forever indebted. You will never be forgotten. May you rest in peace in the big FOB in the sky.

"Greater love has no one than this,
that he lay down his life for his fellow man."

—John 15:13

First published in Great Britain in 2012 by Osprey Publishing,
Midland House, West Way, Botley, Oxford, OX2 0PH, UK
44-02 23rd Street, Suite 219, Long Island City, NY 11101, USA
E-mail: info@ospreypublishing.com
OSPREY PUBLISHING IS PART OF THE OSPREY GROUP

© 2012 Darron L. Wright

All rights reserved. Apart from any fair dealing for the purpose of private study, research,
criticism or review, as permitted under the Copyright, Designs and Patents Act, 1988, no
part of this publication may be reproduced, stored in a retrieval system, or transmitted
in any form or by any means, electronic, electrical, chemical, mechanical, optical,
photocopying, recording or otherwise, without the prior written permission of the
copyright owner. Enquiries should be addressed to the Publishers.

Every attempt has been made by the Publisher to secure the appropriate permissions
for material reproduced in this book. If there has been any oversight we will be happy
to rectify the situation and written submission should be made to the Publishers.

The views expressed by the parties named herein do not necessarily reflect the official
views or policies of the United States Army or any branch of the U.S. Armed Forces.

Darron L. Wright has asserted his right under the Copyright, Designs and Patents Act, 1988,
to be identified as the author of this work.

A CIP catalogue record for this book is available from the British Library.

ISBN: 978 1 84908 812 1
PDF eBook ISBN: 978 1 78200 282 6
Epub ISBN: 978 1 78200 291 8

Page layout by Ken Vail Graphic Design, Cambridge, UK
Index by Zoe Ross
Typeset in Palatino and Helvetica
Originated by PDQ Media, Bungay, UK
Printed in China throught Worldprint Ltd

Cover images © Getty images

12 13 14 15 16   10 9 8 7 6 5 4 3 2 1

Osprey Publishing is supporting the Woodland Trust, the UK's leading woodland
conservation charity, by funding the dedication of trees. To celebrate the Queen's Diamond
Jubilee we are proud to support the Woodland Trust's Jubilee Woods Project.

www.ospreypublishing.com

CONTENTS

PROLOGUE

❝ For courage mounteth with occasion ❞

William Shakespeare, King John. Act ii. Sc. 1

As the smoke cleared during the early morning hours of February 27, 1991, all that could be seen were thousands of burning hulks. Death and destruction littered the landscape and the main roadway running north from Kuwait into Iraq. This was to become known as the infamous "Highway of Death," as it was appropriately coined during the Gulf War. U.S. and coalition forces from more than twenty-five nations either in active or supporting roles had just helped U.S. forces destroy and unhinge Iraqi Army forces that had invaded and occupied Kuwait. However, some remnants of Saddam's war machine, most notably elements of his famed and most feared enforcers known as the Republican Guard, managed to escape and lived to fight another day. U.S. and coalition forces were unable to completely close and seal off the trap door in a maneuver known as the "Right Hook," made famous in briefings by CENTCOM Commander General Norman H. Schwarzkopf.

The operation was a showcase of U.S. military might and prowess, which succeeded in accomplishing stated operational objectives; ultimately, however, Saddam and his government structure remained intact, thus allowing him to declare victory to his people and followers around the world. Over the next ten years, Saddam focused on reconstituting and rearming his war machine, oppressing and terrorizing his citizens through intimidation and denial of basic resources. Saddam, despot that he was, maintained an opulent lifestyle for his family and for the Ba'ath Party Leadership while standing on the necks of the general population. Those who spoke out or rebelled against the regime quickly met their fate.

Bottom line: Saddam reigned as the bully of the region. Despite countless numbers of United Nations sanctions and mandates, he blatantly defied the world. There was clearly unfinished business in the region.

In the fifth century B.C., the great Athenian mercenary general Xenophon led ten thousand Greek mercenaries up the Tigris River valley from Babylon to its headwaters and then on to Sinop on the Black Sea. In March 2003, the United States and its allies returned for round two, the sequel to the Gulf War. The tragic events of September 11 opened the door and allowed us to march back into the cradle of civilization, The Land Between the Two Rivers, and once and for all rid the region of the tyrant Saddam Hussein. Operation Iraqi Freedom had begun.

This story of Operation Iraqi Freedom is written from the inner circle. Events in my life outside of Iraq also profoundly affected me and my perception of the events I was involved in and that were happening around me during my three tours. Every soldier has a personal story, family, and issues that make up the human aspect of war. I will share some details about my personal life in order to paint a more accurate picture of my wartime activities.

You will experience many of the key phases and battles of the operation through the front sight of an M-4 Carbine. I will walk you through the many facets of this campaign, including strategic policies and how these policies impacted operations on the ground. I will introduce you to numerous personalities and key leaders who shaped the outcome, both good and bad. Most importantly, I will share with you the heroic stories and feats of the brave men and women who, under the most austere, life-threatening conditions, stood up to those who sought to do us harm, soldiers who shed their blood and made the ultimate sacrifice so that the citizens and children of Iraq could taste the sweet nectar of freedom.

This is a soldier's story, wrapped in a strategic, operational, and tactical review of operations conducted in Iraq during the past decade. Walk point into the ancient city of Samarra in 2003, then through the hell of the following years, and, finally, on the last combat patrol in 2010.

CHAPTER 1
BACKGROUND BRIEFING

The Army Prior to September 11, 2001

“ You may fly over a land forever; you may bomb it, atomize it, pulverize it, and wipe it clean of life—but if you desire to defend it, protect it, and keep it for civilization, you must do this on the ground, the way the Roman legions did, by putting your young men into the mud. **”**

T. R. Fehrenbach, This Kind of War

The U.S. Army of 2001 was an army in transition. Most of that Army was still designed and equipped to defeat the Soviet Union at the Fulda Gap. Big Kevlar helmets, armored vehicles, and operational rations were the standards of the day.

All of that changed when the U.S. Army opened combat operations in two different theaters in the same geographical region. This was the Army's chance to prove that it could fight a two-front war. Geographical differences impacted the scope of change, but the entire Army morphed around a common enemy. Equipping changes that ordinarily would have taken ten to twelve years were effected in months. No longer did the crews of soft-skinned vehicles have to rely on sandbags to protect themselves. Up-armored High Mobility Multi Wheeled Vehicles (HMMWVs, commonly referred to as "Humvees") and MRAP vehicles became part of the Army lexicon, and the armored carrier began dominating battle space in Iraq.

As the enemy became more and more savvy and grew to understand the value of the roadside mine, the improvised explosive device (IED), vehicle borne improvised explosive device (VBIED), and then the explosively formed projectile (EFP) came into being. Concurrent with these actions were the counters to the IED family of weapons and the technology to combat them.

Each soldier was given an entire issue of go-to-war equipment called RFI (Rapid Fielding Initiative). This included all the items that would better protect the soldier and increase soldier comfort. Ballistic eyewear, heavy body armor, improved ballistic helmet, and fire retardant gloves are but a few of the items in the RFI issue.

Forward operating bases, mayoral cells, clearing barrels, and traffic control points soon crept into the daily operations scope of all involved in the fight in Iraq and Afghanistan. The Army began to rely on contracted services to sustain its combat power, and an entire subculture emerged to support the soldier at war. What follows is the evolution of these changes.

Prior to the tragic events of September 11, 2001, and continuing until 2005, the U.S. Army was governed by the AirLand Battle Doctrine. AirLand Battle concept was written and developed in the late 1970s by General Donn A. Starry, a former corps commander in Germany and Training and Doctrine Command (TRADOC), Fort Monroe, Virginia. In the circle of Army masterminds and strategists, he is one of the most recognized and respected. While serving as V Corps commander in Germany from 1976 to 1977, he was tasked with the responsibility of confronting the mighty Soviet Red Army and preventing it from attacking and penetrating the Fulda Gap, a major avenue of approach that led from East Germany directly to Frankfurt.

Starry's concern was not the initial invasion forces, but rather the flow of follow-on units. The main goal of this strategy was to prevent Soviet penetration of the Fulda Gap while simultaneously attacking behind the lines to disrupt second- and third-echelon forces as well as attacking their logistics supply lines and depots. An army that cannot refuel or rearm cannot fight and maintain momentum. A prime example of this occurred during World War II when General Patton's rapid advance across France got bogged down in Lorraine due to a lack of fuel.

As stated in the Army's bible, Field Manual, *FM 100-5, Operations*,[1] recognizing the inseparability of tactics and logistics, "what cannot be supported logistically cannot be accomplished tactically." By attacking and destroying the enemy's logistics lifeline, we could halt their advance and render them as useless as tits on a boar hog, as the saying goes.

After much debate from within and without the Army, all participants recognized the need for a strategy to counter the technological edge that the Soviet Union was gaining in weaponry and numerically stronger forces opposite U.S. and NATO partners.

AirLand Battle was officially published in March 1981. After months of briefings throughout the military and the highest levels of government, AirLand Battle was adopted as the official Army doctrine and infused into a revision in *FM 100-5, Operations*, published in August 1982 and revised in 1986. This doctrine carried the U.S. Army through the next decade.

The Cold War persisted through the 1980s while America raced to bridge the gap in tactical and strategic weaponry in order to keep pace with the Soviet Union's mighty arsenal. Espionage was paramount on both sides and kept the movie industry in business. American statesmen and diplomats worked tirelessly, applying a full-court press on the USSR. The highlight from these days was the most famous speech President Ronald Reagan ever made. On June 12, 1987, President Ronald Regan, accompanied by the First Lady, toured the Berlin Wall. At 1400 hours in the vicinity of the historical Brandenburg Gate, with two bulletproof panes protecting him from would-be snipers, he delivered this now-famous speech:

"We welcome change and openness; for we believe that freedom and security go together, that the advance of human liberty can only strengthen the cause of world peace. There is one sign the Soviets can make that would be unmistakable, that would advance dramatically the cause of freedom and peace. General Secretary Gorbachev, if you seek peace, if you seek prosperity for the Soviet Union and Eastern Europe, if you seek liberalization, come here to this gate. Mr. Gorbachev, open this gate. Mr. Gorbachev, Mr. Gorbachev, tear down this wall!"

America stood ready alongside its NATO partners. Joint exercises between U.S. forces and our allies, known as "REFORGER" (REturn of FORces to GERmany), were conducted annually to test readiness and validate war plans throughout Europe. AirLand Battle served as the model in the event the balloon went up.

Finally on November 9, 1989, the Berlin Wall came crashing down, paving the way for German reunification and ultimately closing the chapter on the Cold War. The mighty Soviet Army was no longer the viable threat it had been for so many years. As a result, Army planners had to return to the drawing board to revise its doctrine and, most importantly, define the new threat. Meanwhile, technological advances in weaponry and communication systems continued at a swift pace, so much so that it was outrunning the AirLand Doctrine.

The Tyrant Strikes

Before a new edition of *FM 100-5* could be published, an incident broke out in the Middle East whereby a bullish dictator by the name of Saddam Hussein decided to invade his country's neighbor, Kuwait. The reason given by Saddam was to take back territory that rightfully belonged to Iraq. Truth be told, it was more to seize rich and plentiful oil resources to allow for further financing and building of his empire.

In the early morning hours of August 2, 1990, more than 100,000 Iraqi Army forces spearheaded by armored and mechanized divisions invaded Kuwait. The ill-equipped and undertrained Army of Kuwait was no match for Saddam's forces. Within hours, Iraqi forces reached Kuwait City, seizing key governmental buildings and infrastructure.

Fearing escalation, Saudi Arabia called on the United States to assist with defending its border from potential invasion by Iraqi Forces. On August 7, President George H. W. Bush directed the deployment of U.S. forces to the region to initiate Operation Desert Shield. U.S. Central Command (CENTCOM), led by General Norman Schwarzkopf, quickly responded, and within thirty-one hours, U.S. troops were on the ground in Saudi Arabia.

Operation Desert Shield was a two-phase operation. Phase I was the initial deployment of forces to deter further escalation and aggression and to defend Saudi Arabia. The first of these forces was the famed 82nd Airborne Division, based at Fort Bragg, North

Carolina. The 82nd was America's rapid deployment force, which could deploy anywhere in the world in eighteen hours or less. Upon their arrival in Saudi Arabia, they secured an air base, quickly deployed to the border of Iraq, dug in their positions, and defended the border in what is known as the "Line in the Sand."

Considered a mistake by many strategists, Saddam had an opportunity to attack Saudi Arabia and could have done so with relative ease, but as fortune would have it, he never did, though many feared he would. This mistake would prove costly as it allowed for the build-up of coalition forces during the weeks ahead. This build-up of combat power was Phase II of Operation Desert Shield. Its purpose was to build up enough forces to provide the coalition with a counteroffensive capability to attack and destroy Saddam's forces ultimately liberating Kuwait, known as Operation Desert Storm.

Operation Desert Storm also consisted of two phases. Phase I was the air campaign, followed by Phase II, the ground offensive. CENTCOM initiated the bombing campaign using allied air and naval forces on January 17, 1991. The objective was to gain the initiative by attacking critical targets in both Iraq and Kuwait, specifically command and control (C2) sites, air defense weapon and radar sites, Scud missile launch sites, and suspected nuclear, biological, and chemical weapons locations. Once these targets were destroyed, attention turned to the attrition of Iraqi ground forces. This massive bombing campaign lasted thirty-four days and set the conditions for the ground offensive, which commenced in the early morning hours of February 24.

The ground war began with a massive artillery barrage using multiple launched rockets systems (MLRS), 155-mm and 105-mm howitzers supported by attack aviation, and close air support against Iraqi frontline troops. In less than a hundred hours into the ground offensive, the majority of the Iraqi Army in Kuwait was completely destroyed. The remainder of the Iraqi Army fled north back to Iraq, although a lot of them, including Republican Guard forces, were destroyed by U.S. forces, which had advanced into Iraq and executed a maneuver known as the "right hook."

Immediately following the liberation of Kuwait, U.S. forces transitioned to postinvasion operations. Task Force Freedom commenced operations to restore Kuwait. These operations included but were not limited to explosive ordnance disposal, health service support, public safety, water and food distribution, sanitation, conversion of currency, reopening of schools and colleges, and the restoration of telephone, radio, and other communication systems. Within occupied Iraq, U.S. Army forces provided humanitarian relief and assistance to displaced Iraqis and helped to resettle some 20,000 Iraqi refugees into Saudi Arabia. Subsequently, units that were no longer required for the fight began to redeploy back to the United States.

Many question why the coalition did not destroy the government of Iraq and remove it from power as part of operations in the region. At the conclusion of Operation Desert Storm, with the objective of ousting the Iraq Army from Kuwait having been met, the argument was made that our plans and secondary objectives were not to invade Iraq. Specifically, United Nations Security Council Resolution 687, dated November 29, 1990, gave Iraq until January 15, 1991, to withdraw from Kuwait and empowered the United States to use all "necessary means" to force Iraq out of Kuwait after this deadline; there was no U.N. mandate to destroy the Iraqi Army in detail or to unseat the sitting government, thus the decision to terminate the war was made.

This decision meant that Saddam would remain in power to continue his reign of terror in the region for another decade. It also served to validate our doctrine as the blueprint for success for future operations. It is true that this decisive use of air, land, sea, and special operations forces combined with the tenets of AirLand Battle enabled us to defeat a Soviet-equipped conventional army in short order. However, it set us up for failure heading into Operation Iraqi Freedom.

Strategic planners failed to look at and consider postinvasion operations and determine what the environment would be like and who our enemy would be. The premise heading into Operation Iraqi Freedom was that coalition forces could simply overwhelm and defeat the Iraqi Army with the same decisive plan as we had executed during Desert Storm, only this time we would have to completely invade Iraq to do so.

The plan was that once we had completed the destruction of the Iraqi Army and toppled the government, next would be a short period of restoring law and order, instilling a temporary representative democratic government and carrying out a few humanitarian tasks. Then we would depart victorious. Fighting a well-equipped, financed, and dedicated insurgency at the same time was never considered.

The problem was that the Army did not have a dedicated doctrine for prosecuting an insurgency. Therefore, we would execute discovery learning for three to four years, doing a lot of things right but making several costly strategic, operational, and tactical mistakes before we finally figured it out in 2006 with the implementation of counterinsurgency (COIN) doctrine. We were a learning organization that was adaptable, led by great leaders and soldiers; through trial and error we would prevail, but at a cost.

Upon completion of Operation Desert Shield and Desert Storm, the Army revised and published a new version of *FM 100-5, Operations*, dated June 1993, superseding the May 1986 edition. This version incorporated the lessons learned from the Gulf War with a strong emphasis on conducting joint and interagency operations. Furthermore, the revised doctrine reflected Army thinking in a new, strategic era. It recognized that the Cold War had ended and that the nature of the threat, and hence the strategy of the United States, had changed.

This doctrine reflected the shift to stronger joint operations, prompted by the Goldwater–Nichols Act of 1986, which reorganized the command structure of the U.S. military. It also prompted AirLand Battle to evolve into a variety of choices for battlefield framework and a wider interservice arena, allowed for increasing incidence of combined operations, and recognized that Army forces operate across a range of military operations. It is truly a doctrine for the full dimensions of the battlefield in a force-projection environment.

The whole premise behind designing the new doctrine was that the United States had to be capable of fighting and winning two major theater wars simultaneously. The other important factor was that we had to have the right force structure to carry out these wars. "No more Task Force Smith!" became the Army battle cry of the 1990s.

Army Structure

At the time, the U.S. Army operated under a division-based structure whereby army divisions were made up of three maneuver brigades, one artillery or fires brigade, one signal battalion, one aviation brigade, one military intelligence battalion, a main support battalion, and an engineer battalion. All the combat enablers were then subdivided to the respective maneuver brigades to form a brigade combat team (BCT) when the brigade deployed for field exercises or training center rotations and eventually deployed to war or other regional conflicts.

To aid in preparing and training expeditionary brigades for worldwide combat operations the Army established three combat training centers (CTCs): Joint Readiness Training Center (JRTC), Fort Polk, Louisiana; National Training Center (NTC), Fort Irwin, California; and Combat Maneuver Training Center (CMTC), Hohenfels, Germany. It was mandated by Department of Army Chief of Staff that all brigade commanders would be scheduled for a training center rotation at least once during their command tenures. This essentially was their report card of command; how they and their unit performed at a training center could make or break a brigade commander's career. The same applied to battalion commanders and even company commanders. Prior to Desert Storm and in the years immediately after, the United States, for the most part, was a peacetime Army, so the training center rotation served as a dress rehearsal for combat and as a measure of a unit's combat readiness and preparedness.

From 1991 to 1999, the Army would undergo a massive drawdown and reorganization known as Army Transformation, which essentially shifted us away from being a division-centric force to a modular brigade organization. (See Appendix H for details of the drawdown and transformation.) With the drawdown and reorganization came further doctrinal reviews and changes. The most significant of these changes came on the eve of the September 11 attacks, when *FM 100-5* was replaced with a new manual, *FM 3-0 Operations*, published in June 2001. This manual became the keystone doctrine taken to the fights in Afghanistan and Iraq.

While the new doctrine was sound and a far better product than before, it was still inadequate. *FM 3-0 Operations* did allude to the fact that in future conflicts we would face asymmetric threats,[2] such as the terrorist attacks on September 11; however, the doctrine did not address fighting and prosecuting a protracted counterinsurgency campaign that we would end up fighting in Iraq over the next eight years.

Once Operation Enduring Freedom (OEF) and Operation Iraqi Freedom (OIF) commenced, and up until 2005, the Army's strategy still remained focused on defeating national standing armies and combating other small-scale regional contingencies. As units mainly at the division level were alerted and designated for deployment, their assigned brigades would deploy to one of three training centers (geographical location dependent). Meanwhile, the division headquarters and staff would execute a simulated computer battle known as a "Warfighter Exercise" (WFX) to train its staff on processes and ready them for battle. The issue was that the brigades that deployed to one of the respective training centers were still being opposed by a conventional threat known as the opposing force (OPFOR) even though U.S. forces were fighting an insurgency-type battle in both Afghanistan and Iraq. The same goes for division headquarters; they were opposed by a conventional threat in the simulation exercise. The Army needed a new strategy.

Operating under and within the framework of the AirLand Battle Doctrine, tactical operations were centralized. In other words, tactical decisions were being made by divisions and brigade-level leadership and staffs as opposed to decentralized operations in which decisions were made by the units and soldiers on the ground at the tip of the spear. When fighting insurgency or terrorist groups, the fight is at the squad and platoon levels.

The paradigm shift from AirLand Battle to decentralized operations is profound. It meant that commanders who once orchestrated battlefield enablers no longer controlled the overall fight. Instead, they merely monitored and received reports from subordinate units. As a result, the direct firefight conducted by squads and platoons usually would end before a battalion or brigade commander could influence the fight. The company commander has become the new manager of battle space and now controls enablers at his level, often task organizing these enablers to his respective platoons. The concept of decentralized fighting is known in Army circles as the "Three Block War."[3]

The Three Block War is a concept described by Marine General Charles Krulak in the late 1990s to illustrate the complex spectrum of challenges likely to be faced by soldiers on the modern battlefield. In Krulak's example, soldiers may be required to conduct full-scale military action, peacekeeping operations, and humanitarian relief within the space of three contiguous city blocks. The thrust of the concept is that modern militaries must be trained to operate in all three conditions simultaneously, and that to do so, leadership training at the lowest levels needs to be high. The latter condition caused Krulak to invoke what he called "strategic corporals:" low-level unit leaders able to take independent action and make major decisions.

The strategic corporal concept adheres to the notion that leadership in complex, rapidly evolving mission environments devolves lower and lower down the chain of command to better exploit time-critical information into the decision-making process, ultimately landing on the corporal, the lowest ranking noncommissioned officer (NCO), typically commanding a fire team of four soldiers or a squad of seven to nine soldiers. In rapidly evolving mission situations, obtaining mission instructions from remotely located command may result in mission failure or in casualties to both force personnel and civilians. Conversely, misusing this kind of responsibility may result in personal liability for the team leader: a decision executed to respond to situational needs may result in later prosecution as the team leader's actions are reviewed by higher authorities.

In Iraq, as in any guerrilla campaign, decentralized operations are the keys to success. After toppling the Iraq regime and the Iraqi Army from March to June 2003, conventional tactics were no longer needed as there was no longer a uniformed enemy or Iraqi Army to fight. During the invasion, those who were not killed or captured simply ran like cowards and went into hiding, except for the hardcore Fedayeen, which U.S. forces eventually destroyed and dismantled. But the majority of regular army soldiers and other high-ranking individuals stripped off their uniforms and scattered back into the population.

Commonly referred to as Ba'athists, Saddam loyalists, or former regime elements (FREs), these individuals lived to fight again in the months and years ahead. In my opinion, one of the strategic mistakes that U.S. forces made was in designing an ineffective job plan prior to the invasion to promote the fact that it was not the Iraqi Army we were seeking to totally destroy, knowing we would have to rebuild it later and expend a lot of manpower and resources. Rather, the goal was a regime change and a changing of the guard to rid Iraq from the rule of Saddam and his cronies, the Ba'athists or loyalists, and his higher military commanders and security apparatus.

I would argue that one of our strategic goals should have been to lead or start the campaign with an information operations effort by sending a message to the Iraqis prior to the invasion that informed the Iraqi Army that U.S. and coalition forces were not specifically targeting them—only if they engaged our forces or showed hostile intent would we attack. They should have been provided with instructions to lay down their arms and consolidate on the nearest base. By doing so, they would be targeted by neither the initial bombing nor the ground force. All others, such as the hardcore loyalists and Saddam's Republican Guard, who chose to fight or oppose U.S.-led forces, would be destroyed. Those who chose to surrender and cooperate would have been rounded up. A census would have been conducted, and U.S.-led forces would have vetted them as well as possible. Then, units or divisions maintaining unit integrity would have been established from what was left, and the new Iraqi Army could begin to be built.

This method would have provided a starting point versus having to recruit, train, equip, and rebuild the entire thing. We eventually did this at a great cost in lives, money, time, material, and manpower that to a certain extent could have been avoided. I believe we would have been out of Iraq years earlier had we done those things.

This effort would have been led by the Department of State (DOS or State Department), and most likely the Army's task simply would have been to maintain some semblance of law and order, security on key sites, critical infrastructure, and other associated duties while buying time for DOS to establish the new government versus staying for eight years and ultimately fighting an insurgency in a protracted campaign. Furthermore, I believe this approach would have prevented the insurgency from forming in the first place.

As the plan was written and decisively executed, U.S.-led forces dismantled the Iraqi Army, devastated Iraq's security apparatus, and destroyed the infrastructure, which was of third-world quality, but at least it was functioning. If the security apparatus and infrastructure had been left intact, we just would have needed to pick up where the system was and continue to build upon it instead of rebuilding the whole damn country. The rebuilding included all essential services, an army, a police force, and a whole new government while fighting an insurgency as well as an internal civil/tribal war. As it was, we took this strategy and the Powell Doctrine[4] and fought our way through it, learning some tough lessons along the way. But, hindsight is 20/20.

On May 2, 2003, President George W. Bush called an end to major combat hostilities from aboard the flight deck of the USS *Abraham Lincoln*, declaring "Mission Accomplished." In my opinion this announcement was a premature declaration. Once the declaration was made, the strategic focus shifted from combat to nation building or Phase IV: Post Invasion. The end result was that the carrot was introduced way too early;[5] major combat operations were over in some areas but not in all areas of Iraq. More intense fighting was going on in the streets of Samarra, Fallujah, Baqubah, Ramadi, and Balad, where my unit was located. (This region is better known as the Sunni Triangle.) For all intents and purposes, this was the beginning of the insurgency.

The way I look at it is if I am being fired at, it makes sense to bring all assets to bear, such as attack aviation and field artillery cannons on the ground. That is major combat. Period. I do not need to be fighting the Russian horde or the North Korean Army for me to consider it major combat operations. It sure felt like major combat operations, and the soldiers I came in contact with asked me, "Sir, why did they announce the end to major combat operations?" My reply was simply that the decision makers were not here on the frontline with us. I believed the call for the end of major combat operations stemmed from the political climate back home, from people who did not favor the invasion in the first place and wanted a quick, hundred-hour war like Desert Storm. Well, that wasn't to be.

Bottom line: The Army had neither the requisite doctrine nor the necessary training and/or resources for the operations and missions that would be undertaken in Iraq after the initial invasion. The doctrine we did have was the correct doctrine for the initial invasion, allowing us to destroy Saddam's army, his command and control, and the Iraqi government. Had we departed Iraq right after that, there would have been no issues. Once the liberation of Iraq was over, though, our forces switched from an Army of Liberation to an Army of Occupation, changing the whole environment and the complexity of the war. A strategy for fighting and prosecuting a counterinsurgency would not emerge until 2006.

CHAPTER 2
THE ROAD TO WAR
September 2001–March 2003

❝ If there must be trouble, let it be in my day that my children may grow in peace. **❞**

Thomas Paine

As I awoke on a cool, crisp New England fall day, exhausted from reading more than three hundred pages of Clausewitz's *On War* assigned as homework by my Strategy and Policy instructors at the Naval War College, nothing I had done in seventeen years of military service prepared me for the shock I soon received.

I stepped out of the shower, and as per my daily schoolhouse battle rhythm, I turned on the television to the local ABC affiliate out of Boston. A special "Breaking News" banner appeared on the screen. I do not recall exactly who was broadcasting on the national network, but I tuned in while I dressed for the day. It was reported that an airplane, Flight 11 originating out of Boston, had just slammed into the North Tower of the World Trade Center (WTC) in New York City. My first thought was that this was merely an unfortunate accident of some kind. The time was approximately 0846 hours. Outside in the distance, I heard a loud and thunderous roar overhead. I immediately ran outside and looked up in the air to spy two F-15s headed south racing toward New York. Later I would learn that these fighter jets were scrambled from Otis Air Force Base, Cape Cod, Massachusetts. I returned to my room and saw the news reporting live from the scene at the WTC. At approximately 0903, a second plane, Flight 175, also originating out of Boston, slammed into the South Tower against the backdrop of smoke and fire bellowing from the North Tower.

Right then I knew this was no accident. The United States was under attack—a terrorist attack. I discovered later that the fighter jets were scrambled by the Department of Defense (DOD) to pursue Flight 175 and shoot it down before it could hit its target. Major General Paul Weaver, director of the Air National Guard, stated that, "The pilots flew like a scalded ape, topping 500 mph but were unable to catch up to the airliner. We had a nine-minute window and in excess of 100 miles to intercept 175. There was literally no way."[1]

I immediately grabbed my cell phone and called my family to see if they had heard the news. By sheer luck I got through. After confirmation, I let them know I was safe and I would stay in touch. The hits kept coming as breaking news cut in again. "What now? Isn't this enough for one day?" I thought to myself. But there was more to come. At approximately 0938, a third plane, Flight 77 originating out of Washington Dulles International Airport, crashed into the wall of the Pentagon.

"What the fuck? Over," I said to myself. I was in total shock. My mind was racing. I ran back inside the bachelor officers quarters building and knocked on my neighbors' door. Major Roger Carsten quickly answered, as shocked as I was. Next I headed upstairs to my good friend and fellow student Major Keaton Beaumont's room. We watched the news attentively, soon learning that a fourth plane, Flight 93 originating out of Newark, New Jersey, bound for San Francisco, was reported hijacked.

As did millions of Americans, we found out later that Flight 93 crashed in a field just outside of Shanksville, Pennsylvania. Somehow, the passengers on board were able to overwhelm the hijackers and crash the plane before it could reach its target, most likely the U.S. capitol or the White House. "Un-fucking-believable," I said to myself. This clearly was a well-planned and thought-out attack by those who conspired and executed it.

Of course, we were all to learn the truth later when it was revealed that the attack was the work of the terrorist group al-Qaeda led by Osama Bin Laden. Needless to say, classes were cancelled that day as students, faculty members, and the entire nation were in shock and disbelief.

I was 178 miles north of New York City, the epicenter that quickly became known as "Ground Zero." The towers were engulfed in flames, and smoke billowed above New York City, creating a black cloud—the only cloud in the sky that beautiful blue morning, like a smoke signal to the rest of the world: "Send help. We are in distress."

Keaton and I continued to watch the news, while rumors abounded that other hijacked planes were in the air headed for numerous unknown targets. No one really knew what was going on or what threats might still remain. I felt useless and helpless and wished that I could be there to lend a hand to rescuers.

At approximately 0959 hours, the South Tower crashed down. Twenty-nine minutes later, at approximately 1028, the North Tower collapsed. I was speechless as tears streamed down my cheeks.

Suddenly it hit me: a trip I went on to visit friends in New York City. It was my first trip ever to the city. Darlene and Lewis Mahaffey were long-time friends of my ex-wife. They lived in a small apartment on the Upper West Side of Manhattan. Lewis was an avid fan of aeronautics who liked flying helicopters. He had worked his ass off day and night outside his normal job as a bartender and finally obtained his pilot's license. Timing is everything. As luck would have it, I got an exclusive tour of New York City, riding copilot in a Robinson, R-22 helicopter. We flew along the Hudson River, getting an up-close view of lower Manhattan. I was snapping pictures frantically.

One of the many pictures I took that day twelve years earlier was of the World Trade Center. It would prove to be the most memorable photo of the trip and would accompany me on my first tour to Iraq, a source of inspiration reminding me why I was there. To preserve it from the grueling heat and sweat, I laminated the picture to another; on one side was a photo of my kids, and on the other was the Twin Towers. The picture was kept in my helmet under the main webbing and accompanied me wherever I went. When times got really tough or when I was feeling sorry for myself and needed extra motivation, I would pull it out and be reminded first of my family, then flip it over and instantly be served the reason why I was fighting in this God-forsaken country. This was just one of the small items that got me through twelve months of grueling combat, but the most significant.

Keaton and I watched the news for hours. The images from people jumping out of the highest floors had a chilling, mind-numbing effect on me. My stomach was on edge, and my appetite was lost or, in military speak, it was absent without leave. I desperately wanted to help, but there was not much either of us could do. Finally, President George Bush appeared on television from the oval office in a sobering brief to the nation. What I remember most was stated at the end of his speech:

"The search is underway for those who are behind these evil acts. I've directed the full resources of our intelligence and law enforcement communities to find those responsible and bring them to justice. We make no distinction between the terrorists who committed these acts and those who harbor them."

At that instant, I knew that I would soon be in harm's way based on the unit that I was being assigned to following school. I was on orders to Fort Carson, Colorado, for assignment to the 3rd Brigade, 4th Infantry Division, a heavy mechanized brigade equipped with M1 Tanks and M2 Bradley Fighting Vehicles (BFVs), meaning I would most likely end up in Iraq if we invaded. The possibility of deployment to Afghanistan was slim as the rugged mountainous terrain was not conducive to mechanized infantry troops and armored vehicles.

Deep down, what I really wanted and needed was to get to my unit, train up, and get my ass in the fight, as if I was going to miss it or something, which is what happened when Desert Strom passed me by. During Desert Storm, I was completing my undergraduate degree at University of North Texas. I was six months from making the show. As graduation came in summer 1991, troops were on their way home, being welcomed with ticker-tape parades. Desert Storm, better known as the "100 Hour War," went by so fast that even had I graduated early, I am not sure I would have been able to make the fight anyway.

It's not that I am a bloodthirsty warmonger. The mark of every good infantryman and the reason they choose to join the infantry is because they want to fight. That is what infantrymen do: they kick ass when called upon and they have their numbers on speed dial. In correct doctrinal terms in accordance with Chapter 1, *Field Manual 3-21.8, Infantry Rifle Platoon and Squad* (former FM 7-8), the sole purpose of the infantry is to close with and destroy the enemy by means of fire and maneuver in order to destroy or capture him or to repel his assault with fire, close combat, and counterattack.

Regrettably, I missed Desert Storm. Based on the world outlook at that time, I thought I would never see combat. I figured I would simply serve twenty years in a peacetime army conducting tough, rigorous training, always being prepared for the show, but without an official reservation for the table. I equate it to being on the second string of a varsity football team: you practice hard and take all the snaps but never get on the playing field during the game unless it is a blowout, and then it is simply about running out the clock and not turning over the ball.

As the day progressed amidst the chaos, I attempted numerous phone calls to family and friends, but to no avail. Phone lines across the United States, particularly the upper east coast, were jammed. The fallout from the aftermath continued for days. All the while, the U.S. Army, specifically U.S. Central Command (CENTCOM) led by General Tommy Franks, was dusting off and drafting new invasion plans for both Afghanistan and Iraq. The war machine was churning.

Classes at the Naval War College continued in earnest a week later. All conversation centered on the 9/11 attacks, and fear of the unknown, set in for most officers as they all knew that, depending on where their follow-on assignment was, they soon would have a date with destiny—and that date was rapidly approaching. I lacked concentration and focus on the task at hand. Most of my days in class were spent drafting up engagement and invasion plans of my own for Afghanistan and strategizing as to how our military would prosecute this battle. My plan was fairly accurate, knowing immediate bombing of Afghanistan would be first, followed by a ground/airborne invasion by ground forces including Army special operation forces (SOF), conventional units, Marines, and other coalition partners such as the United Kingdom.

Then, on October 7, 2001, the United States and forces from the United Kingdom launched military operations in Afghanistan after the continued refusal by the Taliban regime to cease harboring of al-Qaeda and its leader Osama Bin Laden. Coalition special forces and the Central Intelligence Agency teamed up with the Afghan United Front, also known as the Northern Alliance, and began attacking several targets. They primarily focused on Taliban strongholds and other key command and control facilities located throughout the country, including the key locations in Kabul, Kandahar, and Jalalabad.

The attacks were supported by massive airstrikes signifying the beginning of Operation Enduring Freedom (OEF). I remember well the night this all commenced as my classmate Keaton and I watched President Bush address the nation, confirming that joint forces had begun the assault on Taliban targets in Afghanistan. President Bush stated the aim and objective of the invasion was to find Osama Bin Laden and other high-ranking al-Qaeda members and bring them to justice, as well as to destroy al-Qaeda and remove the Taliban from power.

As the battle in Afghanistan continued to wage during the next few weeks, strategic planners were working behind the scenes diligently drafting branches to the overall operations plan (OPLAN) for Iraq. I was drafting my own plans for the invasion of Iraq as well. Rather than sketching it out on paper, I addressed it in a required essay for my Strategy and Policy Class. My argument centered round the question posed by our instructors of whether sanctions would work against Saddam and whether the United States could win without fighting. I argued emphatically that sanctions would not work. I cited countless examples of United Nations sanctions and resolutions that Saddam had repeatedly defied. My conclusion was that the United States would inevitably fight a second go-round of the Gulf War, only this time to finish what should have been done years ago.

October 2001 through June 2002 passed by rapidly as operations in Afghanistan were progressing and near misses of capturing Osama Bin Laden happened regularly. Meanwhile, the build-up and final plans were being made for the invasion of Iraq as Saddam remained in defiance of U.N. sanctions and weapons inspectors.

Behind the scenes, the National Command Authority and DOS were working feverishly to form a coalition to support and assist in the invasion of Iraq if sanctions did fail. At the outset of the war, thirty-five nations were contributing in a variety of ways. It seemed that the invasion into Iraq was all but inevitable. According to Secretary of Defense Donald Rumsfeld, a "smoking gun" was not required and need not be disclosed to the world to justify the invasion. He believed that sufficient justification lay in Iraq's long pattern of thwarting inspectors and their failure to disclose weapons to be destroyed.

Days spent in class were uneventful, and the tempo moved at a snail's pace. It was difficult to focus on the required reading, writing essays, and the like, so much so that my papers lacked substance from the required research. I simply lacked the motivation and inspiration to put forth maximum effort; needless to say my grades suffered as a result. I didn't want to be in the classroom. I wanted to be on the battlefield.

Graduation came and went in June 2002. I said my goodbyes to friends and instructors, wishing them all the best in their future endeavors. My favorite was Professor Jim Giblin, my National Security Decision Making course small-group instructor. He was surely the most down-to-earth person and most approachable instructor on the NWC staff. Giblin took to me most likely due to my shoot-'em-straight, no-holds-barred attitude. What I liked and respected most about the man is the fact that he would provide honest feedback and constructive criticism on work or essays in a manner that was not abrasive yet direct and to the point with the intent to make you a better writer and officer. That was a tough goodbye. Upon graduation, he gave me a copy of Michael Handel's book *Masters of War*. Inside the cover was a hand-written note addressed to "Sunshine" (that was me): "This is a good read, remember the only easy day was yesterday. Fight, Win & Come Home Safely. Jim."

I still have that note, and it accompanied me along with the book to Iraq. From time to time when there was a break in action, I would read it and find encouragement. That note and his teachings and mentorship left a mark on me, so much so that it served as the inspiration to write this book.

My late-model Ford Bronco was loaded down along with a U-Haul trailer as I set out on my journey back to Fort Carson, Colorado. The weather was beautiful that June day as I crossed the border of Rhode Island into Connecticut heading south along I-95. I was in a hurry to get to and through New York City before rush hour. A couple of hours went by, and soon I was on the outskirts approximately 15 miles outside of New York City. I could see the skyline in the distance, but this time it was different from the last time I passed by. The skyline had changed. The twin towers of the World Trade Center were no longer there. I was quickly reminded that this journey leading me home to family would soon draw me closer to prosecuting and serving justice to those responsible for changing the profile of New York City and, in fact, the profile of America. As I passed by downtown, I bowed my head and said a prayer for all those who perished that day, reminding myself that we would never forget them or the cowards who did this.

I finally arrived home in Colorado Springs around July 1, 2002. My children, Dillon and Chloe, were elated to see me. We spent a couple minutes embracing as tears fell from our eyes. The next few days were spent catching up on things I missed during the past year. The one question I could not dodge was the one that loomed heavy on everyone's mind: "Dad, are you headed to war?"

I replied that I would most likely deploy, but I was not exactly sure about the time frame. At night we spent time watching Fox News and CNN, getting updates on the situation, events in Afghanistan, and, more importantly, events in Iraq. Things were not going well as Saddam was still being defiant toward the U.N. weapons inspectors and the international community President Bush, Secretary of State Colin Powell, and others urged the United Nations to apply pressure to encourage Saddam to comply with the resolutions. Bush said that Saddam had repeatedly violated sixteen U.N. Security Council resolutions, including the main one calling for Iraq to "disarm its chemical, biological and nuclear weapons programs."

Saddam laughed in the face of the international world. It seemed as if the inevitable—the invasion—was fast approaching. Meanwhile, orders had already been issued putting 4th Infantry Division on notice to prepare for deployment. In April 2002, Major General Raymond T. Odierno, Commanding General of the 4th Infantry Division, was summoned to a meeting along with the commanders of the 3rd Infantry Division, 1st Cavalry Division, and 1st Armored Division with CENTCOM Commander General Tommy Franks. Also attending was General Eric Shinseki, Army Chief of Staff. During this meeting, all were told to prepare for future combat operations in Southwest Asia.

I signed into my new unit, 3rd Brigade Combat Team, 4th Infantry Division, located at Fort Carson, Colorado, right after the 4th of July. Prior to arriving, I knew that I would serve as the brigade personnel officer (S-1). Duties included managing all personnel transactions to include awards, efficiency reports, and pay issues. Based on the

Army's professional development and job growth model, as an infantry major, I was to be assigned to an infantry battalion to serve as an operations officer (S-3) or an executive officer (XO). However, these jobs were filled at the time, so I would have to wait my turn, hence the job assignment as the S-1. As any good officer does, I gladly accepted the assignment and jumped right in. Deep down, I knew that my time in purgatory would be short lived and that I would eventually get to an infantry battalion.

The immediate task at hand was to train and prepare the brigade for future deployment to Iraq. We already knew that our unit, along with the rest of the 4th Infantry Division, would deploy soon, but in what order was the million-dollar question.

When the orders officially came down, I had just finished conducting some rigorous physical training, and as I was walking into the headquarters building, I was approached and met by Brigade Executive Officer Lieutenant Colonel Paul Welsch, who informed me that we were having a staff meeting at 0900 hours. At 0900 sharp, the entire staff was assembled and Brigade S-3 Major Dan Barnett broke the news to the staff that we had received unofficial notification that we were deploying and would be part of the initial invasion force into Iraq. Along with the remainder of the 4th Infantry Division, we would be invading Iraq from the north out of Turkey, while the 3rd Infantry Division, 82nd Airborne, 101st Air Assault Division, and the Marines invaded from the south out of Kuwait.

The first order of business for the brigade staff was to immediately draft a "Road to War" plan by phase, outlining all the tasks and requirements to be accomplished for deployment. This first phase was the train-up, starting with local individual and team training in the Fort Carson training area, followed by squad- and platoon-level training, such as conducting live-fire exercises and command post exercises to work out command and control systems. The culminating event was our validation or mission rehearsal exercise at the National Training Center (NTC) located at Fort Irwin, California. The NTC rotation was our showcase or dress rehearsal event whereby the entire brigade, along with a host of supporting assets, would deploy to "the sandbox," as NTC was called, and execute a force-on-force exercise (FOF) against a conventional opposing force (OPFOR), known as the Krasnovians. The Krasnovians were a formidable force that would out-think and out-gun the most seasoned units. Rarely if ever did any unit stand toe to toe with them. A typical rotation would net a

20:1 casualty rate against this foe. If a unit was successful at achieving anything less than that rate, it was considered successful.

In September 2002, we readied the force at Fort Carson; our collective level train-up was complete as we loaded equipment on railcars bound for the Mojave Desert. The brigade, along with all its organic units (i.e., all units such as infantry, armor, artillery, maintenance, supply, and medical needed to sustain combat operations) arrived at NTC in late September on contracted buses.

That was one hell of a road trip: eighteen hours from Fort Carson to the NTC reception station. I remember debarking the bus and feeling the blistering heat melting my face. Sweat was pouring from my brow at an alarming rate, so much so I could not drink enough water. It had been several years since I last trained at NTC; the majority of my training center rotations based on assignments to light or airborne divisions were conducted at the Joint Readiness Training Center at Fort Polk, Louisiana.

As it was, the brigade would be "in the suck," a term of affection referring to the location and dusty environment that was the NTC. Our task was to train for combat and endure the pain associated with it for the next two weeks. The initial phase of NTC is the "Reception, Staging, On-ward Movement and Integration" (RSOI) phase. This phase included receiving and downloading equipment from the railhead, personnel in-processing, and combat preparation tasks to ready things for movement into the "box" or competitive area for execution of the FOF fight. The RSOI portion lasted approximately three to four days and ended with the brigade staff receiving our final operations order from the NTC operations group and executing our planning phase known as the Military Decision Making Process (MDMP). This planning effort is the most intense, stressful, and difficult task a brigade will execute. It also is the most important task because of the end product that it developed.

Derived from MDMP is the operations order (OPORD), which is issued to all subordinate elements defining the threat, missions to be accomplished, key tasks, commander's intent, and end state. The OPORD puts everything in motion and initiates the movement of subordinate units into the competitive box or battle area, officially signifying the start of the battle. The brigade staff spent more than twenty-four hours straight planning and crafting our order. Sleep was at a premium, and most staff officers went without it until the order was issued.

The observer controller (OC) is the external set of eyes you have watching over you 24/7 and breathing down your neck, which provides additional stress. OCs are assigned to an operations group (OPS Group) and are broken down by task forces. Certain task forces cover down (i.e., observe and provide evaluation and feedback) on rotational battalions and the brigade staff. For this rotation, the Bronco Team was responsible for covering down on our brigade staff. The primary function of an OC is really to serve as an external set of eyes to evaluate and provide constructive feedback on staff processes, both in the planning and execution phase. The intent is for units to take these evaluations and lessons learned and apply them where applicable to better enhance a unit's effectiveness and efficiency in combat. Primary focus is placed on things that units should sustain and those things that need improvement. Depending on the OC, the evaluation could be a blessing or a curse. It all depends on the level of experience of the OCs that are covering down on you. The Army handpicks the highest caliber officers and NCOs for these assignments, but sometimes a few incompetent ones slip through the cracks. This was certainly the case with the overzealous OC that covered down on my admin section. Rarely was the critique I received constructive; mostly it was damning. It was almost as if this guy thought he was the modern-day version of Patton and had possessed all the answers. Personally I think the joker was a dud and further he was jealous of the fact that he was not heading off to war and would miss out on the action. You certainly could glean that impression from the enormous chip he carried on his shoulder. Needless to say I was smothered the two weeks we were there and departed NTC thinking we must have been the most "ate up" unit in the Army. Finally about two days into the FOF fight, I got fed up with this guy and his constant criticism and sarcasm, so much so that I pulled him aside and gave him some pointed feedback and specified guidance.

Basically I threw him out of my command post and told him to take his little green notebook and shove it, being the polite Texas gentleman I am. I kindly thanked him for his services rendered and told him that while his services were appreciated, they were no longer welcome. The issue at hand was that his personality and critique methods were so abrasive they became an obstacle to progress; the last time I checked there were no OCs in combat.

This situation I encountered does not apply to the general population of OCs, especially today. Before the invasions of Afghanistan and

Iraq, rotations at combat training centers were a brutal experience for units and soldiers alike. The OPFOR would absolutely destroy your entire force in simulated combat, and the OCs would critique you, pointing out how fucked up you were, rarely identifying anything done right. It was mainly highlights of all the things you screwed up and needed to fix. Basically, you walked away with your tail between your legs, thinking you were the lowest form of life on earth. This practice continued until 2004 when training centers were overhauled and made a paradigm shift from conventional fights to stability and support operations and subsequently to COIN-centric operations. This shift brought on a whole new breed of OCs, and a new training methodology to go with it, all to serve the war fighter headed down range. The OCs' new role was not simply to critique units, but to be hands-on and serve as coaches and mentors to all soldiers and leaders in the formation. The Army assigned OCs, both officers and NCOs, who had recently returned from the fight to capitalize on their experiences and firsthand knowledge of the fight.

Nevertheless, we planned and issued our order on time to our subordinates and executed our FOF operations against the Krasnovians, which included a deliberate attack against a dug-in fortified enemy, including obstacle breaches, conduct of a deliberate defense, and a movement to contact. We fought them gallantly, but in the end, if keeping score, the OPFOR would have won, as per the norm.

Prior to the rotation ending, Odierno visited us in the field at our tactical operations center (TOC) and provided some insight into what the Army was thinking at the strategic level and where we fit into the plan. He also informed all key leaders who were assembled to "take this training seriously, and get your troops ready." Odierno's visit was short and sweet, as he had to hurry off to a trip to Germany, summoned by Lieutenant General Scott Wallace, V Corps Commander.

From this meeting, we learned that 4th Infantry Division would be a separate command under V Corps called Task Force Ironhorse (TF Ironhorse). The force package included the 173rd Airborne Brigade based out of Vicenza, Italy, and a host of other selected reserve and National Guard support units. Altogether, TF Ironhorse would total around 32,000 troops, double the typical size of any Army division.

As for NTC, our brigade and battalions learned some valuable lessons at the tactical level when prosecuting a campaign against a conventional threat. The overall scenario and fight at NTC was solely kinetic. The value of the NTC experience manifested itself with leaders and staff agents at every level. Whether writing and publishing orders or communications or reporting, the process at the NTC is the same as it is in combat. The NTC experience exposed the soldiers of TF Ironhorse to every war experience short of actual combat. This training and experience gained proved invaluable for Phase I of the invasion into Iraq, but in hindsight, the rotation did little to prepare us for the mission we would undertake in Iraq during Phase II, or postinvasion. Most notably, it failed to prepare us for the enemy we ultimately would encounter and, subsequently, for the nation-building tasks we had to accomplish while fighting against an insurgency.

After returning to Fort Carson, we refitted and executed a two-week recovery plan, ensuring all equipment was accounted for, serviced, and prepared to load for deployment. The brigade continued on the typical glide path for deployment. To date we had conducted individual and team-level training, followed by platoon- and company-level training, and battalion command post exercises (CPX). Our rotation to NTC served as the brigade culminating training event (CTE). The last thing to accomplish before being mission ready was the division culminating event known as the "Warfighter Exercise" (WFX), executed in November 2002 at Fort Hood, Texas.

The WFX was a simulations exercise (resource intensive) whereby all TF Ironhorse units including 173rd Airborne Brigade, 555th Engineer Brigade from Fort Lewis, Washington, and other attached units came together to participate in a computer war game conducted virtually on the same terrain and location we would eventually be fighting on in Iraq. The central training audience was all division-, brigade-, and battalion-level staffs. For a two-week period, we worked on systems including communications, reporting, command and control, and other staff processes. This exercise served as the dress rehearsal and validation of our plan to invade Iraq from Turkey.

Much like our rotation at NTC, we learned several valuable lessons, categorized into things to sustain and things to improve. However, the overall scheme and scenario was kinetic in nature, focused solely on our attack south from Turkey into Iraq; no sequels or branch plans were addressed, certainly as was the case with our NTC rotation. Nor was any forethought paid to fighting a long, protracted campaign against an insurgency or to the associated tasks that nation building demands.

The brigade staff returned home from the WFX and continued on its glide path to war. We took time out to celebrate Christmas, spending time with family and friends, but the celebration was short lived as the inevitable continued to draw near. As 2002 came to a close, my simple New Year's resolution was to deploy over there, kick some ass, and return home safely to my family in one piece, along with every other soldier. Meanwhile back at Fort Hood, the division staff worked tirelessly around the clock finalizing the OPLAN. Finally, after a week or so, the plan was completed and ready for implementation once the official order came.

During this time, parallel planning and coordination was occurring at all levels between brigade staff and division staff counterparts. The OPLAN was sound and solid. The mission of TF Ironhorse was to stage in Turkey, then attack south into Iraq in order to destroy enemy forces, and secure lodgment in the north. Supporting this attack was the 173rd Airborne Brigade, whose mission was to conduct an airborne assault into the vicinity of Bashur Airfield, located 75 miles east-northeast of Mosul. Their objective was to secure the airfield and establish a lodgment to expedite the flow of tanks and BFVs and subsequently secure key oil facilities located in and around Mosul and Kirkuk. This attack from the north would facilitate the rapid destruction of the elite Adnan Brigade, Saddam's heavy armored forces, and prevent their repositioning and interdiction against the main effort attack from the south. As the attack advanced south, it would ultimately encircle Baghdad by linking up with forces advancing from Kuwait.

European Command (EUCOM) established a forward headquarters in Ankara, Turkey, while 1st Infantry 1st SUPCOM and other elements began establishing satellite command post positions across Turkey. EUCOM set up shop in the JUISMAT, Turkey's equivalent of the Pentagon. EUCOM leaders negotiated the land rights to move across Turkey and attack Iraq from the north. In addition, overflight rights for fixed wing, rotary wing, drones, and cruise missiles were being negotiated in earnest. As the weeks wore on without achieving much headway, it became apparent that the Turkish government had no intention of granting permission to work through Turkey, let alone mass forces for a major attack.

By March it was obvious that we were only meeting with Turkish officials to establish a credible threat of a northern attack to pin down as many Iraqi forces north of Baghdad as possible. Initially, as many as three Iraqi Corps were situated north of the capital. By the time the attack from the south developed, only one large Iraqi Corps remained in the north. To those in EUCOM forward headquarters in Ankara, the dead giveaway was depicted on our common operational picture. The ships loaded with 4th ID equipment previously holding station in the Mediterranean Sea off the coast of Turkey were now on the move heading south to the Suez Canal. The north was now just a ruse.

Thoughts and plans on the flank attack continued, though, with the planning of the largest heavy metal, air mobile operation in history. Eight M1s and an equal number of M113 armored personnel carriers married with the 173rd Airborne Brigade and made for a credible threat and combat force that General Burwell B. Bell III was looking for. C17s landed at a remote northern Iraqi airfield; the M1 tanks and armored personnel carriers off-loaded and headed out at rapid pace toward the only remaining Iraqi Corps defense in the north. While the armor helped lend credibility to this attack, the real instrument of destruction would be the hundreds of sorties called in by the special forces teams and 173rd Airborne Brigade spearheads attacking south. Eventually the Iraqi defensive line crumbled and ran.

While 4th ID would not play a significant role in the initial attack, the Army's follow-on force was within comfortable reach, ready to execute a flawed Phase IV plan.[3]

As for the overall invasion plan, elements of 3rd Infantry Division, 82nd Airborne Division, and 101st Air Assault Division, along with Marine forces, would attack north into Iraq from Kuwait to destroy enemy forces and secure key lines of communication and other critical oil and key infrastructure. From there, the final objective was to attack to seize Baghdad, ultimately toppling Saddam and the Iraqi Government. This two-prong attack from the north and south would allow for the quick destruction of Iraqi Army forces and security of key infrastructure and would apply a stranglehold on Baghdad, forcing the surrender and fall of Saddam.

My brigade's specific mission was to attack south in the vicinity of Kirkuk to destroy enemy forces and secure key oil infrastructure to prevent its destruction. The follow-on mission was to attack south to isolate Tikrit from Baghdad.

As we continued to hash out details and logistic challenges, our soldiers continued to train hard and focus on personal readiness issues such as finances, life insurance policies, and legal matters, including powers of attorney and wills. The toughest challenge for most soldiers, specifically those who were married, was whether to move the family back to their hometown near a support network of family and friends or leave them near base. For single soldiers, this amounted to packing up all of their household goods and other personal belongings from the barracks to include their cars, known in army jargon as "personally owned vehicles," and placing it all in storage. Somewhere in the back of their mind, a question lingered: "Will I ever see any of my stuff again?"

On Friday, January 17, 2003, Odierno received official notification that he would be deploying the 4th Infantry Division to combat. Two days later, all brigade commanders and staff were summoned by the commanding general to receive the official order. Those of us at Fort Carson participated in the brief via a secure video teleconference from our headquarters basement. The Mighty 4th Infantry Division, TF Ironhorse, which had not seen action since the Vietnam War, was headed to Iraq. The preparation and waiting was finally over. It was game on.

In the remaining weeks leading up to deployment, we continued with final preparations. The most important task was readying equipment for rail load and movement to several port facilities located along the Texas coast, including Beaumont and Corpus Christi. All across Fort Carson, Colorado, and Fort Hood, Texas, troops assigned to the 4th Infantry Division continued to refine load plans, eliminating equipment and tools not required for the fight while adding new and more advanced items as mission requirements became known.

Railcars began showing up around the clock at the Fort Carson rail yard. M1 Abrams tanks, BFVs, fuel tankers, bulldozers, and thousands of Humvees were loaded and prepared for movement. Empty flat cars pulled in, vehicles were loaded and moved out—all during a wicked snowstorm that hit us as temperatures dipped into the teens. Despite hazardous and unsafe conditions, our soldiers persisted and worked around the clock without incident, ensuring every vehicle was loaded. Soldiers worked in shifts. Those who were not on the line gathered around fires or warming barrels to warm their hands and bodies for their respective turn on the line. Soldiers could usually pull an hour then rotate to the warming barrel. By week's end, they had mastered the art of rail load operations in extreme adverse conditions, so much so that it became second nature.

The Army had already deployed units based in Germany to Turkey to prepare the assembly areas and establish several logistics bases for receipt of TF Ironhorse.

As the final week of February passed and the deployment neared, the brigade staff continued its refinement of the operations order, working a branch plan in the event that we were rerouted to Kuwait for our attack. This decision—Turkey or Kuwait—was being considered at the highest levels of government. This was not our job to worry about as we had little impact on the decision; we would simply plan for either course of action and follow orders when they were issued.

Meanwhile, as the deployment loomed, the Department of the Army had sent out a handful of news reporters and journalists who descended on us and would embed with our units and brigade staff to cover the invasion. The reporters came from all walks of life, men and women who represented all types of national, regional, and local news teams. We took them under our wing as if they were our own. We housed, clothed, and fed them, and our medics provided them the required immunizations. It was basic media "Indoctrination 101" into our ranks, and the Army held them to the same standard as any other soldier who joined our ranks. Finally, we put them through a series of training events consisting of likely scenarios they and we would face in combat.

The most critical and perplexing of these tasks was teaching them how to don their protective masks and chemical suits in case we encountered some type of chemical or biological attack. This task captured their attention and focus, sending the message that the threat we faced was real and that we were ready for any and all dangers. Based on the seriousness of the threat and conditions faced, a lot of the representatives from smaller media outlets departed and opted out of the contract; others were recalled by their higher affiliates because their parent companies could not provide the required insurance coverage.

I met each and every media person who entered our ranks, ensuring they were in-processed and that we captured all their pertinent information such as their next of kin notification contact lists. I gathered that the majority of these press folks were sincere in word and deed and wanted to cover the war as part of their profession and provide the American and international communities an honest and forthright story. In contrast, several others seemed to have personal agendas depending on which way they slanted in their political make-up, though this was the exception and not the rule.

Embedded media was a new phenomenon the Army was trying out. During World War II, the press was censored and reported only what the military approved. By the time Vietnam came around, a strong disagreement developed between the media establishment and the Army as to what should and should not be reported. Operation Desert Shield and Desert Storm in 1991, with the vast coverage by CNN, changed how news was reported. Reporting was uncensored and immediate. The flash to bang time was a matter of minutes compared to hours and days as in past conflicts. But what remained was the general stigma associated with media types based on biased, negative reporting. Regardless of the stereotypes, all press members were treated with dignity and respect. Respect was a two-way street; in most cases it came back two-fold from them knowing that their lives and well-being were in our hands.

As I dealt with integrating the media and other commander issues, my personnel section was busy integrating and assigning the last handful of new soldiers arriving fresh out of basic training and advanced individual training (AIT). As these soldiers in-processed, the look on their faces was so innocent; their eyes wide open, not really knowing what was ahead of them. They were green to say the least. They had missed out on so much of the individual and collective training we had completed to date. But as any great unit does, they would be assigned to a squad, platoon, or section whereby a good NCO immediately took them under wing and got them trained as quickly as possible to ensure they were ready for the mission and challenges ahead.

The Army, specifically the Department of Human Resources Command, had done a great job of ensuring we were manned and filled to a prescribed level of 110 percent aggregate. Factored into all this was a list of approximately 500 to 600 (equivalent of an infantry battalion's strength) nondeployable soldiers who remained at Fort Carson. When personnel were totaled and planes loaded, we arrived in theater at about 95 percent manned.

Another critical task I had to accomplish as part of the preparation was to draft the casualty estimate report. This was a grim but necessary task. Before all combat missions, unit personnel officers, logisticians, and medical officers get together during the planning phase and draft up the initial casualty estimate report.[4] This report, provided to the commander, provides a forecast of potential losses that his formation will sustain from anticipated fighting and provides a snapshot to higher headquarters so they can anticipate numbers for medical care and replacement operations once the flow began. As a reference, we used *Field Manual 101-10-1/2, Organizational, Technical, and Logistical Data Planning Factors*. This was the logistician's bible for operational planning all things logistics.

This manual assists logistical planners as a tool for figuring out things such as water consumption rates, bulk fuel expenditures based on terrain and distance traveled, and ammunition expenditures based on type of expected fighting and intensity. It is strictly a forecast. The issue with the manual is that it was outdated for the current fight. All the tables, numbers, data, and charts were based on previous wars or engagements that the United States had fought. When it came to casualty estimation, the numbers were really inflated since the manual did not factor in new equipment, body armor, and vehicles or other additional force protection equipment worn and measures taken by units to protect the soldiers and the unit. It also failed to factor in the tactics we were using. Finally and most notably, it failed to factor in the degradation the enemy would suffer from the initial wave of air attacks prior to the ground offensive that would deplete their force and will to stay and resist.

This was the case during the ground offensive during Desert Storm when scores of Iraqi Army soldiers surrendered. But as it was, based on the enemy we were facing, the elite Adnan Armored Division, an entrenched or dug-in fortified force equipped with Soviet T-72 tanks and armored personnel carriers and chemical weapon capabilities, fighting on their home turf, my estimation was that our brigade would sustain approximately 8 to 10 percent force degradation. As a breakdown, our force strength at the time was approximately 4,000; a 10 percent hit would be approximately 400 casualties. Of that number, I estimated that approximately 150 would be killed in action (KIA), another 200 wounded in action (WIA), and the remaining 50 would be degraded due to some type of illness or injury not caused by combat actions, referred to in Army circles as a nonbattle loss.

The estimate I drafted covered the first thirty days of combat, with the majority of anticipated losses occurring during the first forty-eight to seventy-two hours of the ground invasion, during which we predicted the heaviest fighting would occur. During the deployment, these estimates were continually refined and updated. For historical context, during Operation Desert Storm, casualty estimates were well over 20 percent anticipated across the board.

The Army Medical Department had more than 13,000 beds in forty-four hospitals available in theater. These estimates proved to be grossly overstated because only 357 were WIA and another 145 KIA based on reports from the end of the war.[4] Casualty estimation is not an exact science as many variables factor into the equation on both the friendly and enemy side.

During our last staff update at home station on approximately March 15 to the brigade commander; I presented the casualty estimate report. He thought it seemed pretty sound and detailed and accepted the forecasted numbers. Only time would tell as the invasion neared. I hoped that my calculation was too high for the sake of our soldiers who would soon embark on the largest invasion since the Allied invasion of France (Operation Overlord, commonly referred to as "D-Day") on June 6, 1944.

The final decision for TF Ironhorse in order to initiate movement was whether we would invade Iraq south out of Turkey or north from Kuwait. The decision was still up in the air. At this point it did not matter to us. We were ready.

CHAPTER 3
SHOCK & AWE

The Invasion Begins, March–May 2003

❝ From time to time, the tree of liberty must be watered with the blood of tyrants and patriots. **❞**

Thomas Jefferson

On March 19, 2003, bombs were descending on Baghdad and throughout Iraq. Thousands of Tomahawk cruise missiles and other precision-guided munitions littered the night sky, launched nearly simultaneously from U.S. attack bombers flying overhead and Navy ships and submarines positioned in the Persian Gulf and Mediterranean Sea, as if Xerxes himself had once again amassed his Persian archers in the valley, firing arrows to blot out the sun in his quest to conquer Greece and eliminate the Spartans at Thermopylae in 480 B.C.

Within hours of the operation commencing at approximately 2215 hours eastern time, President Bush addressed the nation from the Oval Office:

"My fellow citizens. At this hour, American and coalition forces are in the early stages of military operations to disarm Iraq, to free its people and to defend the world from grave danger.

On my orders, coalition forces have begun striking selected targets of military importance to undermine Saddam Hussein's ability to wage war. These are opening stages of what will be a broad and concerted campaign.

In this conflict America faces an enemy that has no regard for conventions of war or rules of morality.

A campaign on the harsh terrain of the nation as large as California could be longer and more difficult than some predict and helping Iraqis achieve a united, stable and free country will require our sustained commitment.

We come to Iraq with respect for its citizens, for their great civilization and for the religious faiths they practice.

We have no ambition in Iraq except to remove a threat and restore control of that country to its own people.

For your sacrifice you have the gratitude and respect of the American people and you can know that our forces will be coming home as soon as their work is done.

Our nation enters this conflict reluctantly, yet our purpose is sure. The people of the United States and our friends and allies will not live at the mercy of an outlaw regime that threatens the peace with weapons of mass murder.

My fellow citizens, the dangers to our country and the world will be overcome. We will pass through this time of peril and carry on the work of peace. We will defend our freedom. We will bring freedom to others and we will prevail.

May God bless our country and all who defend her."

At home in Colorado Springs, my son and I were glued to the television watching live coverage broadcasted on NBC and CNN news as events unfolded. The images of "Shock and Awe" are forever embedded in my mind. The Baghdad skyline lit up like a scene out of the movie *The Day After*. Explosions rocked the capital. Amidst smoke and flames, the rubble of weakly constructed buildings littered the landscape. Iraqi Army Air Defense Forces engaged blindly out of desperation, filling the night sky with thousands of tracer rounds that seemed to vanish in the night, never coming close to hitting their intended targets. This was reminiscent of the images from the first Gulf War when CNN reporter and war correspondent Peter Arnett broadcasted live from atop of the Al-Rasheed Hotel in Baghdad showing the thousands of tracers being fired over Baghdad amid the loud explosions and air raid sirens blaring in the background.

Following President Bush's address, at approximately 2200 hours EST (0600 hours in Baghdad) on March 20, 2003, the ground invasion of Iraq, led by U.S. Army General Tommy Franks, CENTCOM Commander, began under the codename "Operation Iraqi Liberation," later renamed to "Operation Iraqi Freedom." U.S., U.K., and Australian Forces, combined with forty other nations, formed the "coalition of the willing" led by the United States. They participated by providing troops, equipment, security, and special forces, with the United States providing 248,000 soldiers. Another 45,000 from the United Kingdom, 2,000 from Australia, and 194 Polish special operation forces were staged in Kuwait on D-Day. The invasion force also was supported by Iraqi Kurdish militia troops, estimated to number upward of about 70,000.

The stated objectives of the invasion were first and foremost to put an end to the brutal tyrannical regime of Saddam Hussein; to eliminate whatever weapons of mass destruction could be discovered in order to prevent their use against coalition forces; to find, capture, and/or destroy leaders and military forces of the Ba'athist regime while minimizing civilian casualties and collateral damage; to obtain intelligence on militant networks; to distribute humanitarian aid; to secure Iraq's petroleum infrastructure to prevent ecological disasters; and, finally, to assist in creating a democratic representative government to serve as a model for other Middle Eastern nations.

The ground invasion was spearheaded by the storied 3rd Infantry Division "Rock of the Marne" based out of Fort Stewart, Georgia. The division was comprised of approximately 20,000 soldiers, armed with more than 300 M1 Abrams tanks, a similar number of BFVs, and self-propelled Howitzers. The division attacked along an avenue of approach in the far west, flanking the other forces, its main objective to destroy all Iraqi Army Forces and seize Baghdad. Adjacent units supporting the attack included the 1st Marine Division and the 1st Marine Expeditionary Force, whose main avenue of attack led through Nasiriyah, continuing on a path between the Tigris and Euphrates rivers en route to its major objective: Baghdad. In addition, one U.K. division attacked the key port and oil infrastructure in the vicinity of Basra.

Follow-on and supporting forces included 101st Airborne Division, which air assaulted and seized key terrain and facilities in An Najaf, and the famed 82nd Airborne Division, whose mission was to seize and secure key routes and terrain in As Samawah to facilitate the attack of the main effort and the uninterrupted flow of follow-on forces (mainly logistical supplies) and eventually securing the passage of the 4th Infantry Division as they were introduced into theater and commenced their advance through Baghdad to objectives beyond there to the north, mainly Saddam's hometown of Tikrit. All the while, SOF operating in secrecy infiltrated deep into northern Iraq and out west prior to March 19, 2003, attacking to destroy likely Scud missile launch sites and key command and control facilities. The goal was to neutralize both these sites and the threat of Scuds being fired into Israel to provoke a response by the Israeli Defense Forces, which was certain to inflame the Arab World and further gain popular support for their cause.

The combination of precision air strikes and SOF operations wreaked havoc on Iraqi forces' capabilities. The air campaign quickly destroyed Iraq's integrated air defenses and command and control apparatus. Air superiority was gained instantly, thus preventing any Iraqi aircraft from ever flying to this day in contest of its airspace. Likewise, at no time during the war was a missile ever fired into Israel. Based on the success of these attacks, conditions were set for the ground invasion. By contrast, during the first Gulf War in 1990–91, the bombing campaign lasted more than a month before the ground invasion commenced. The campaign was prolonged because it took several strikes to destroy a target known as a sortie.

During the Gulf War, approximately 7 percent of missiles launched from land-based aircraft were precision bombs; most fired were laser guided. The difference this time was that approximately 65 percent of munitions fired from sea and air were all precision GPS guided, meaning it took one to two bombs to destroy a target, as opposed to multiple bombs as was the case during Desert Storm. The overall result was a significant change in our technology and capabilities. In previous conflicts, the measure of effectiveness was calculated based on the number of sorties it took to destroy a target; in this campaign, it was reversed so that effectiveness was measured on the number of targets destroyed by a single sortie.[1]

The ground attack followed the same course of action and attack routes as discussed previously, with the exception of the 4th ID attack from Turkey.

Meanwhile back in the United States, frustration had set in amongst the leadership of TF Ironhorse located at Fort Hood, Texas, and Fort Carson, Colorado. The war had started, but we were still sitting at home, waiting for the call. The decision finally came on Saturday, March 22. All attempts at political persuasion failed to convince the Turkish government to grant the United States permission to use its country as a staging base in order to invade Iraq from the north. The Turkish parliament voted unanimously to reject the notion, most likely for fear of reprisal in the years ahead. Based on this decision, General Franks on March 22 ordered the 4th ID to shift from the eastern Mediterranean south to Kuwait. As it happened, the thirty-seven ships carrying our equipment stationed just off the coast of Turkey were diverted to Kuwait by way of the Suez Canal, and it was expected that they would port in Kuwait by March 30. The work of hundreds of European-based U.S. troops who had been mobilized in southern Turkey preparing for TF Ironhorse's arrival was wasted effort, but in retrospect the plan did provide the United States with an operational and tactical advantage. The build-up in Turkey and our initial intent to use that country to open up a northern front most likely kept two Republican Guard Divisions postured in and around Kirkuk and Mosul and out of the fight and defense of Baghdad. The disadvantage for the United States was that the most technologically advanced and equipped division in the Army was not available for the initial ground campaign.

The Army still had a plan to counter the threat in the north and open up the desired front, which was essential to ensuring that the enemy stayed at bay and would not move to reinforce Baghdad. Four days into the invasion, at 2000 hours on March 26, the 173rd Airborne Brigade based out of Vicenza, Italy, parachuted into northern Iraq in the vicinity of Bashur Airfield, located approximately 150 kilometers (about 93 miles) north of Kirkuk. Their objective was to execute a parachute assault and link up and reinforce SOF and Kurdish forces in the north and assist in the defeat of enemy forces (see Chapter 2 for the details of this assault).

Their follow-on mission was to seize and secure the air base in Kirkuk in order to allow its use for bringing in follow-on second-echelon forces. After that was achieved, their final objective was to secure and gain control of the rich oil fields in and around the city of Kirkuk. The actual combat jump was executed flawlessly; there was no enemy resistance as the SOF unit secured the drop zone. From March 27 to April 9, the 173rd fought hard and seized the Kirkuk air base relatively quickly. Upon seizing it and defeating enemy forces, they commenced to conduct air–land operations to allow for the build-up of combat power, most importantly the introduction of armor and mechanized forces.

TF Ironhorse Arrives in Kuwait

As the 173rd was taking the fight to the enemy in Kirkuk, the 4th ID and remainder of TF Ironhorse began arriving in Kuwait. Lead elements of the division from Fort Hood arrived on March 27 to establish C2 nodes in order to receive the flow of main body troops. Based on the flow of forces, my brigade arrived between April 3 and 5. I remained behind at Fort Carson, as it was my task as the brigade personnel officer to ensure that all soldiers were accounted for and manifested on their respective flights. I finally arrived with the trail party on April 4 after a grueling eighteen-hour flight that made one layover stop at Rhein-Main Air Force Base located in Frankfurt, Germany.

The trail party consisting of the remaining soldiers of the brigade departed out of Peterson Air Force Base located in Colorado Springs on a chartered United Airlines Boeing 747. I actually got a great seat in first class. "What a way to deploy to war!" I thought. "First class. Unbelievable!" Based on the necessity of getting our division to the war, the Pentagon spared no expense, and it showed. What I recall most about the flight was the hospitality and generosity of the crewmembers, in particular the flight attendants. A few hours before the flight landed in Kuwait, airline crewmembers handed out writing tablets, pens, and envelopes to all 270 soldiers on board. They gave us the opportunity to write letters to family and loved ones left behind, and they collected the letters and mailed them free of charge for us.

I also recall some of the movies we watched en route to Kuwait. One in particular was somewhat disturbing: *Unfaithful* starring Richard Gere and Diane Lane. Here we were, hundreds of other soldiers and I, having just departed and left our beautiful wives and girlfriends back at home, heading off to war for who knew how long.

Any time soldiers head off to war, there's always the fear that some of our better halves, in particular younger spouses or girlfriends, may venture off and seek out other romance while their husband, wife, boyfriend, or girlfriend is away. Watching *Unfaithful* certainly left soldiers with dark thoughts in the back of their minds. I personally knew a few soldiers who received "Dear John" letters while deployed. War is hell, even on the home front at times. Support from loved ones, especially significant others, is a key combat enabler and motivator for all soldiers and leaders. You simply trust and pray that you left your relationship in good order built on a solid rock.

When we arrived in Kuwait, operations were well underway throughout surrounding locations. It is standard operating procedure (SOP) that when any unit arrives into a new theater, they execute reception, staging, onward movement, and integration, referred to as RSOI. This happens in peacetime training as well as war. During the reception phase, soldiers are accounted for and in-processed into theater by their respective unit representatives or designated personnel clerks, ensuring soldiers receive their pay and benefits for being deployed. The next step is for units to move to the port facility to receive and account for their equipment. This can be time-consuming, especially if equipment was loaded and spread across several ships.

The ships had made a relatively quick transit from the Mediterranean Sea through the Suez Canal and were waiting when we arrived. Port operations were executed as smoothly as could be expected. Tanks, BFVs, self-propelled Howitzers, and all other equipment and containers were downloaded quickly and moved to a staging area located adjacent to the ship yard. From there, units opened containers and vehicles, laid out all the equipment, and took inventory, ensuring 100 percent accountability of all items. Vehicles and containers then were reloaded and prepared for onward movement through the desert to outlying base camps via commercial line haul trucks.

While that was happening, I headed to base camp on contracted buses, along with several hundred other soldiers from the division. The drive to the outlying base camps was uneventful. As we headed north from Kuwait International Airport, we passed several herds of camels. Scattered throughout the desert were thousands of Bedouin tents. These tents played a major role in middle-east history and culture, and they can be found throughout the region.[2]

The Kuwait highways were packed with hundreds—even thousands—of U.S. military vehicles, mainly logistics convoys carrying our sustainment load consisting of ammunition, fuel or Class III petroleum, repair parts, and thousands of pallets of bottled water and food rations known as Meal, Ready-to-Eat (MRE; aka "meal rejected by everyone" or, less elegantly, "meals rejected by Ethiopians"). All the convoys and buses carrying soldiers were escorted by Kuwaiti Highway Patrol, which was significant because the Kuwaiti Royal Government feared that local third-country nationals or free radicals posed a threat, hence they wanted to guard against it.

Our brigade finally arrived in total with all personnel and equipment at Camp New Jersey, approximately 75 miles northeast of Kuwait International Airport. Upon arrival, we met several soldiers from the 3rd ID, 101st Airborne Division, and Marines who stayed behind as the rear echelon from their respective units that were fighting it out up north in Iraq. Overall the 4th ID occupied five camps: Camp New Jersey, Camp Pennsylvania, Camp Virginia, Camp New York, and Camp Udari. These camps had been constructed soon after Desert Storm ended and were used on a rotational basis by units practicing and conducting joint training with Kuwaiti Army forces in preparation for possible future conflicts. This exercise was known as "Operation Intrinsic Action." By design these camps were built to house battalion-sized units, but the occupation by 4th ID would soon fill them with brigade combat teams (BCTs). These brigades included about four times the number of soldiers and equipment than the camps were designed for. Space was at a premium.

As we entered the gate of Camp New Jersey, the first thing I noticed was the appearance of soldiers walking around the camp. They all were wearing chemical suits and protective masks. Apparently a base alarm had sounded, signifying an attack of some kind. As it turned out, an internally initiated test drill was being executed; no real attack was imminent. Units were merely rehearsing in the event a real attack occurred. These drills were a matter of routine and occurred frequently.

Prior to the commencement of the ground war as U.S. troops staged in Kuwait and prepared for combat, the greatest fear facing our forces was the threat of weapons of mass destruction, specifically missile-borne chemical attacks. As the ground invasion grew closer, the tension and stress increased. General (Ret.) Montgomery Meigs described actions on the ground in the introduction he wrote for the NBC News book *Operation Iraqi Freedom: The Insider Story*:

> *"Soldiers and Marines in assembly areas and Airman on bases sweated out the danger of missile-borne chemical attacks. They withstood frequent alarms requiring frantic donning of chemical suits and masks and long, anxious stays in hot, crowded bunkers. Men and women at sea agonized over mines and the likelihood of shore-to-ship missile attacks. All deployed personnel remained continuously wary of terrorist attacks, but frustration and inactivity bred determination."*

During our two-week stay at Camp New Jersey, these activities continued even after the initial invasion force had commenced the attack into Iraq. Alarms sounded daily at all hours. All of them were false alarms, but even so we always took precaution as if it was real. We fast became well trained in the drill of donning chemical masks and protective suits. The drills usually lasted about ten to fifteen minutes; in extreme cases, we stayed suited up anywhere from forty-five minutes to an hour, packed like sardines into tight concrete bunkers in temperatures exceeding 90 degrees. The overcrowding of the camp did not help. We would stay suited up under cover until the "all clear" signal was sounded.

Executing this drill over and over again really got old quickly. Frustration grew, evident in the eyes and verbal expressions of soldiers. In reality this drill really pissed us off and motivated us even more to get in the fight and on the move as opposed to staying cooped up inside a base camp executing the cry-wolf drill over and over. But drill or not, every soldier had to remain alert and vigilant, at a constant state of readiness. Despite the fact that every alarm proved false, the enemy only had to be right once. As leaders, we had to impress upon our soldiers to always assume the alarm was real, never taking for granted that it was not. Bottom line: We could never let our guard down.

The thing that saved us was the long, hard days we had spent at home station at Fort Carson training on these battle drills in subzero temperatures. Oftentimes, soldiers got frustrated during this training, but once in theater they soon realized how invaluable it was, especially when facing an imminent threat.

The final phase was integration. During this phase, soldiers acclimated to the environment and continued preparation for combat. Activities continued at an accelerated pace; individual and crew served weapons (weapons requiring two or more soldiers to operate them) were zeroed and test fired; digital computers and communications equipment was tested; and, finally, vehicles were loaded with personal and other mission-essential gear (mainly ammunition).

Our stay at Camp New Jersey was short lived and ended sooner than expected. What commanders had estimated would take three weeks to complete enabling 4th ID to move north took only ten days. Credit had to go to the soldiers and leaders for busting their tails, ensuring all combat vehicles were prepped and loaded with ammunition and other supplies and made ready for the move north. The war had commenced, and we were not wasting any time getting in on the fight.

4th ID, Task Force Ironhorse Enters the Fight

At 0200 hours on April 14, 2003, lead elements of 4th ID spearheaded by 1st BCT, "Raiders" led by Colonel Don Campbell crossed the border. The 1-10 Cavalry Squadron was the first unit followed by 1-8 Infantry (IN), which was chopped from 3rd BCT and attached to 1st BCT. This change was based on the fact that 1-22 IN, an organic unit assigned to 1st BCT, had issues unloading their equipment at the port as it was dispersed across several ships, while 1-8 IN's equipment was consolidated on one ship and off-loaded quickly. All the tracked vehicles, including M1 Abrams tanks, BFVs, and other mechanized vehicles, were carried into Iraq by large semitrucks known as heavy equipment transporters (HETs). These vehicles would be manned by their respective crews and armed for combat if the need arose. HETs were used to haul assets organic to Army logistical units. Meanwhile, the wheeled fleet of Humvees and other trucks followed and were intermingled in the column.

The truck assault, at that point a one-of-a-kind operation, was undertaken thanks to a decision made by Combined Forces Land Component Commander (CFLCC) Lieutenant General David McKiernan and 4th ID Commander Maj. Gen. Raymond Odierno in order to speed up the process to allow 4th ID to advance north beyond Baghdad as quickly as possible.

The objective assigned to the division was to conduct a passage of lines through 3rd ID in the vicinity of Baghdad, maneuver north in order to destroy remaining enemy forces, and seize Taji and Balad airfields. The follow-on objective was to seize Tikrit (Saddam's hometown), the city of Samarra, and the main airfield in Baqubah. The division would accomplish this by leading with 1st BCT, whose mission was to attack Taji and Balad airfields and then move north and seize Tikrit. It would be followed by my brigade, 3rd BCT, which would move along the east side of the Tigris River to seize Samarra. 2nd BCT, following in trail as the division reserve, would later be ordered to attack and seize the airfield in Baqubah, located in the Diyala Province.

This decision was tactically sound and made operational sense given that the route to Baghdad was secured as 3rd ID and Marines had cleared everything in their path and seized and controlled Baghdad and all the major routes leading into the capital city. The other factor affecting this decision was the importance of getting north of Baghdad to counter the potential threat of three Republican Guard Divisions that could easily maneuver and counterattack us. Of equal importance was the necessity to seize Taji, Balad, and Baqubah airfields. These airfields housed Saddam's Air Force and other Army units and also were large ammunition depots. When the invasion commenced, these bases were abandoned and the ammunition bunkers were left unsecured, thus inviting looters and free radicals to pilfer tons of ammunition such as rockets, artillery rounds, SA-7 surface-to-air missiles (SAMs), AK-47s, RPK machine guns, and thousands of tons of small-arms ammunition. You name it—it was all there for the taking. If we did not seize and control this, we would certainly see it fall into the wrong hands and eventually be used against us.

Based on these factors, the plan called for a truck assault to occupy a tactical assembly area (TAA) known as TAA Ironhorse located in the desert approximately 20 miles south of downtown Baghdad. Once there we would stop, download vehicles, form into our fighting formations, and continue the attack north. Mounted in our fighting formations, units maneuvered north and attacked to seize their follow-on objectives. On April 20, Odierno, along with his division tactical operations center, arrived in Tikrit. The remaining headquarters elements arrived on April 23, occupying an extravagant palace complex where they established the main command post and remained there until the end of the deployment. Last in trail was 2nd BCT, commanded by Colonel Jim Hickey. They followed in trail as the division reserve, attacked east, and seized the airfield in Baqubah. As we maneuvered north, the fighting had all but ceased en route to Baghdad. Coalition forces had done a great job destroying any and all viable threats.

I made the trip north in my Humvee, which I had stripped the doors off to allow a cross breeze to circulate as temperatures hit 95 degrees. My serial was last in the order of movement as we fell in with our logistics battalion, 64th Forward Support Battalion, commanded by Lieutenant Colonel Gustave Perna. Perna was well suited for the job; in army circles and throughout the military community, he is highly regarded as the premier logistician.

Prior to our brigade's movement, one of my supporting tasks was to establish a command post (CP) known as the administrative logistical operations center (ALOC) outside the base camp in the middle of the Kuwaiti desert that would serve as the movement control node for staging and uploading our combat vehicles and placing units into march formations known as serials. It is customary in accordance with our doctrine that the brigade adjutant (S-1) and the brigade logistical officer (S-4) collocate together and run this CP. As ordered on April 14, the S-4 and I established the ALOC and began making preparations for the arrival of HETs and our unit's equipment and personnel. The staging and uploading operation went smoothly, mainly due to the fact that senior NCOs took charge of their formations by providing leadership, supervision, and at times extra motivation to their assigned soldiers to accomplish the tasks. The ALOC stayed in place, ensuring that all units moved in accordance with the movement matrix. When the uploading was completed, we would break down the CP and move with the trail element.

Just as we completed upload of 1-12 IN and as they departed the staging area en route to the Iraq border, out of nowhere came a single Humvee scurrying across the desert at a high rate of speed headed straight for us. As the Humvee pulled up adjacent to our CP, three male passengers exited the vehicle. To my surprise one of the gentlemen was none other than Lieutenant Colonel (Ret.) Oliver North, who was there as a journalist embedded with the Marines. I had heard about this man my entire career, and here I was meeting him for the first time in the middle of the desert. The first thing I noticed about him and his crew was that their faces were severely sunburned and somewhat blistered. Their eyes were bloodshot and sunken in to the back of their heads as though they had not slept for days. They looked hungry. I introduced myself and offered them some fresh cold water, which they accepted without hesitation.

North stated that they were returning from the front lines where they had covered the invasion riding along with the Marines.

He described a few of the contacts they had been involved with and stated that the Marines and other coalition forces were doing a great job taking the fight to the enemy. As we continued to talk, another vehicle pulled up with our evening chow. I offered the first plates to North and his crew. We dined on T-rations and swapped a few more war stories. My young soldiers were inquisitive about what to expect as we moved north. After about an hour, North and his team moved out and continued their mission. He kindly thanked us for the hospitality and said "Kick some ass, and we will see you on the front lines." We ended with a group picture and his crew sped off heading back to the fight.

The day finally came for my section to move north. The ALOC had completed its task, packed up, and readied for movement north. On April 17, we crossed the border out of Kuwait into Iraq. We soon entered a village approximately 10 to 15 miles north of the border. The village of Safwan was very small, a poor community made of ten or twelve shanty mud huts. All its occupants were most likely related, belonging one tribe. As we entered the village, children and adults alike straddled both sides of the narrow roadway, cheering us as we drove by. In some cases, the kids were holding out their hands begging for water and food or whatever they could get their hands on. Some went so far as to rip duffle bags off vehicles that were strapped to the side. We felt a sense of euphoria and elation, as this was certainly a surprise welcoming. We were seen as heroes or, in this case, liberators. This type of treatment would last for at least a month and was a frequent occurrence throughout Iraq as soldiers entered villages and major cities.

The site in Baghdad was even more intense as Iraqi citizens, young and old alike, turned out to the streets in mass, celebrating the fall of the regime while cheering coalition forces as liberators. The most noteworthy of these events was a massive gathering in Firdos Square located in downtown Baghdad whereby Iraqis, assisted by U.S. Marines and equipment, toppled the famous statue of Saddam Hussein.

As we continued north to Baghdad, I monitored the radio and received reports over our command net from our forces forward of sporadic gunfire. There were several small engagements, but the enemy direct fire was never effective.

Along the route, I could see hundreds of burning hulks, remnants, and hollow shells of Iraqi Army tanks and other equipment that had been destroyed by elements from the 3rd ID and Marine forces. Likewise, hundreds of U.S. vehicles had been damaged or broken down, simply abandoned and left on the sides of the road. Every U.S. or coalition vehicle that we passed had been completely stripped of tires and any other equipment Iraqis could get their hands on. This scene along Highway 1 (the major route that runs from Kuwait through Baghdad north beyond Mosul) was reminiscent of the "Highway of Death" during Operation Desert Storm.

The journey to Baghdad took more than twelve hours, covering 350 miles, with one stop in between to refuel at a location approximately 75 miles south of Baghdad. When our brigade finally reached TAA Ironhorse, lead elements of the division, namely 1st BCT, had already executed the passage of lines with 3rd ID and Marine forces, seized Taji Airfield, and were in the process of seizing Balad Air Base. Behind us by several days was the last 4th ID element, 2nd BCT, the division reserve. Once we arrived and consolidated at TAA Ironhorse, our three maneuver battalions quickly downloaded their combat vehicles, issued last-minute changes to orders, and continued their tactical maneuver en route to Baghdad and on to our follow-on objective of Samarra. My serial followed in trail. As we reached the outskirts of Baghdad, we could see that the skyline of Baghdad was burning. Our route took us on a bypass route around the city, similar to beltways around major U.S. cities. As we reached downtown Baghdad, the death and destruction became more evident.

The stench of death combined with gunpowder, burning rubber, and smoldering debris permeated the air. This odor would never subside the whole time we were deployed. As we drew closer, we could see the vast and widespread devastation marred the city. Government structures, including Defense Ministry buildings, Ba'ath Party headquarters, and every palace that Saddam owned, were targeted and destroyed by precision-guided bombs and munitions fired from fixed-wing aircraft and Navy ships and submarines during the initial wave of attacks. Seeing all of this, my driver and I quickly gained an appreciation of the awesome firepower that U.S. and coalition forces could bring to bear.

Thousands of locals were running amuck, looting every shop and store, stealing everything from basic food items to washing machines to extravagant plasma televisions. Although it seemed as if the entire city had been destroyed, the military made every attempt to avoid collateral damage and did not deliberately target anything outside of approved military or government targets. "Shock and Awe" was as advertised.

By the time we passed north of Baghdad, the ground invasion had ultimately ceased for all intents and purposes, save for the work left to be done by the 4th ID in defeating small pockets of resistance in the north vicinity of Taji, Balad, Samarra, and Tikrit.

The ground invasion was a quick and decisive operation encountering heavy resistance, most notably in the vicinity of Nasiriyah, where the Marines slugged it out with Iraqi Army regulars and took some of the first casualties of the war. Overall, the level of resistance was not what U.S. and U.K. forces expected. It seemed the Iraqi regime had prepared to fight simultaneously both a conventional and guerrilla or irregular war, basically conceding territory when faced against superior forces, mainly our armor and mechanized forces. To counter this, they chose to execute smaller-scale attacks in the rear areas using troops dressed in paramilitary garb or civilian clothing. This technique achieved some military success and created unexpected challenges for coalition forces. By dressing in this type of clothing, these fighters were able to blend into the population and fight amongst civilians, reducing the risk that invading forces would engage for fear of causing unexpected or unintended civilian casualties and collateral damage.

If in fact this occurred, which in several cases it did, then immediately it was reported by the embedded media or other nonsanctioned media such as Al Jazeera and would serve Iraq's cause, allowing them to exploit the situation in the media, further advancing their cause, and alienating the West, as though we were executing an all-out blitzkrieg against any fighter or civilian in our path. The flash to bang time on news hitting the international wire and daily broadcasts was almost instant, contrary to the news cycle during World War II or even as recent as Vietnam when news of various battles and engagements took days to report and often was censored by the Army. Moreover, there were not as many news journalists covering those wars, which the Army frequently censored. This was not the case in Iraq; any and all events—good or bad—could be reported.

The enemy's technique of fighting amongst the population is nothing new. Throughout history, inferior forces when faced against a numerically conventional foe often resort to this tactic, knowing that any incident involving civilian casualties would be a black eye against us. The best example of this in recent times was the Vietnam War, whereby the guerrilla force known as the Viet Cong predominantly lived and fought amongst the population. Eventually, the bloodshed of civilians—innocent or not—scarred our Army and led to massive antiwar protests back home in the United States. American soldiers returning home from the fight were greeted by large crowds and in extreme cases were spat on and called "baby killers."

War is nasty business. It is not fair. Best efforts to minimize civilian casualties and collateral damage can sometimes hamstring the fight. The Rules of Engagement (ROE) are set in place, first and foremost to protect soldiers and to provide the rules and guidelines for engaging an enemy target in certain conditions (see Appendix B). I can say unequivocally that the U.S. Army took every precaution necessary to avoid killing or wounding innocent civilians and causing collateral damage. In all precombat training and preparation leading up to the war, the ROE were constantly beat into our heads. But, despite training, mistakes happen in peacetime and are prone to happen in war. It is the nature of the business. What makes the U.S. Army stand out from others is that we train the way we fight, and when incidents or mishaps occur in training, leaders stop and execute an After Action Review (AAR) and immediately rectify the situation. Then we retrain and get it right. This same process occurs in war, with the difference being that a mistake in war usually means someone was wounded or killed unnecessarily. By the time 4th ID got involved in the action, most enemy resistance had been destroyed; many had abandoned their posts and went into hiding.

We continued on our route through Baghdad north along Highway 1 heading toward Taji approximately 20 kilometers (about 12.5 miles) north of Baghdad. On April 18 at approximately 1000 hours, we arrived on the outskirts just south of Taji. 1st BCT had already attacked, destroyed leftover enemy remnants, and seized control of Taji Airfield. Resistance was sporadic, with the hardest task being that of clearing all buildings and structures on the base room by room. This was taxing and time consuming. However, the soldiers of 1st BCT, including soldiers attached from 1-8 IN, had executed this task with precision. Based upon this successful mission, 1st BCT continued the attack north with a mission to seize Balad Airfield.

According to 4th ID historical accounts, Balad Airfield was a bigger and more strategic objective than Taji had been. With a larger physical space, an ammunition storage area, and airfield buildings, it was destined to become a major strategic supply area for Combined Joint Task Force 7 in Iraq, soon to evolve and become known as Logistical Support Area Anaconda (LSAA). Before 1st BCT made their advance onto the airfield, unmanned aerial platforms flying overhead showed that enemy soldiers were moving ammunition and other military equipment out of bunkers and off the airfield. Civilians and enemy soldiers were looting, taking whatever they could salvage. The ROE in this case were clear, and our forces were well within their right to fire, but the decision at the time was made not to shoot indirect artillery fire onto the base to stop the looting for risk of inflicting civilian casualties. In hindsight, this was probably a mistake because as time passed, these weapons and munitions would be used against us.

1-8 IN spearheaded the attack with forty-four BFVs and twelve tanks, using the attack plan that was successful at Taji. By nightfall on April 17, 2003, the airfield was under 4th ID control with no U.S. casualties. The next objective for 1st BCT was to maneuver north to seize Saddam's hometown of Tikrit. In doing so, 1st BCT deliberately bypassed the town of Samarra, leaving this objective for my brigade.

3rd BCT Arrives in Samarra

My brigade arrived in Samarra during the morning hours on April 18. Brigade headquarters occupied an abandoned electrical plant located in the town of Ad Dawr (the village where Saddam was later captured), approximately 15 kilometers (9.3 miles) north of Samarra. Upon occupation, we established local security and command posts and then commenced operations to clear Samarra.

The scene in Samarra was similar to that in Baghdad: chaotic and lawless. Thousands of local residents were running wild through the streets, looting and stealing everything they could get their hands on. The first priority was establishing security in the city and returning it to some semblance of law and order. The issue at hand was that there was no one to turn to: All the local police and government officials had fled. Since we had the biggest guns, we were the law.

Recognizing this, our units quickly established patrol bases and then commenced offensive operations to establish security. The first action was to establish checkpoints on the outskirts of all major routes leading in and out of the city. Then they began around-the-clock patrols. One of our units, 1-12 IN, seized and occupied a large walled compound that housed the Ministry of Pharmaceuticals. 1-68 Armor (AR) Battalion occupied a similar compound, which housed an electronics plant. Upon searching these facilities, several bunkers were discovered filled with tons of top-secret Iraqi documents, weapons, ammunition, and 55-gallon drums of unknown chemicals. It seemed that in anticipation of the bombing campaign, Iraqi Army officials had moved and hidden all this material in order to avoid destruction and capture.

On April 29, 1-12 IN executed a raid based on intelligence and captured a high-ranking Fedayeen general. Integration of and intelligence gleaned from the general and other sources led to the capture and killing of other enemy targets, known as former regime elements (FREs).

The final step taken to quell the chaos and establish law and order was the institution of a citywide curfew from 1800 to 0600 hours. This was put in place with orders given that anyone seen on the streets after these hours would be detained by U.S. forces. During the three-week period following our entrance into Samarra, this action, combined with persistent patrolling, all but brought a halt to the chaos and local violence. Other steps were taken to locate and reach out to local leaders and sheiks to gain their support, but this really came to no avail.

On a midafternoon a few days into our occupation, I drove into downtown Samarra. As I entered the city, it seemed like martial law was in existence. The streets were all but abandoned. On every corner, a tank or BFV was surrounded by concertina wire and sand bags. A persistent stream of soldiers patrolled the streets. The city appeared to be in a state of relative calm. Based on existing conditions, our brigade was ordered to maintain a small presence in the city. We also received orders from Odierno to execute another mission to our direct south.

Disarming the Mujahadeen-e-Khalq (MEK)

The mission we received was one of the first highly visible operations to occur following the initial invasion. Our task was to conduct a political–military operation to disarm the Mujahadeen-e-Kalaq (MEK, aka People's Mujahidin Organization of Iran [PMOI], National Liberation Army of Iran [NLA]).

According to 4th ID historical files, the MEK were reputed to be the trainers of Saddam's Republican Guard. They were a well-equipped and highly disciplined Iranian terrorist organization that had previously operated in central Iraq. The MEK consisted of an armored division's worth of tanks, artillery pieces, and armored personnel carriers concentrated at several camps in northeast Iraq near the Iranian border. Before the war began U.S. SOFs worked with MEK leaders and agreed to a cease-fire. As part of the agreement, they were able to keep their weapons and move to four separate camps north of Baghdad near Hamrin Lake, where they would be safe from bombing and targeting by coalition warplanes. The camps, named in honor of their female leaders, were Camp Alevi, Camp Ashraf, Camp Zora, and Camp Zekari.[3]

U.S. commanders faced a challenge with the MEK's presence. They could not allow an organization that operated freely under Saddam Hussein and that was identified by the State Department as a terrorist organization to continue to operate in Iraq. MEK commanders had an equally difficult task at hand. Colonel Fred Rudesheim, commander of 3rd BCT, noted that one of the female commanders told him that she had fought with the MEK for twenty years and had seen a lot of her friends martyred. She said that surrendering was the toughest thing she had done in her life. The MEK feared that turning over their weapons to coalition forces would leave them vulnerable to attack. The Badr Corps, an Iranian-backed Shiite militia, had been their adversary for years and was still moving freely in the area.

On Thursday, May 8, 2003, before negotiations began, Rudesheim told them we would take control of the four areas by the end of the day. The MEK wanted us to wait until Friday. Rudesheim refused and said we would take over the areas in one hour. They seemed surprised, but 3rd BCT was able to achieve the end state. Further supporting our cause was the ultimatum given by Odierno, who during negotiations told MEK leadership to "throw down your arms—or be destroyed." The notion of surrendering did not sit well with MEK leadership. In the end, however, they agreed to come under U.S. control. Our units, including 1-8 IN (which came back under our control from 1st BCT), 1-12 IN, and 1-68 AR, quickly located MEK positions, took control, and moved all soldiers and equipment into designated camps without incident.

This mission could have turned south and gotten ugly quick, but the show of force and the threat to use it most likely convinced the MEK leadership to give in. Upon consolidation of MEK forces into the base camps, we turned the mission over to 2nd BCT and departed en route back to Samarra.

As we returned to Samarra, our brigade was again ordered to move. This time we were given new mission orders to head north to the vicinity of Kirkuk to conduct a link-up with 173rd Airborne Brigade and assist with offensive operations. As we departed, we were replaced by 1st Battalion, 66th Armor Regiment, "TF Iron Knight," led by Lieutenant Colonel Ryan Gonsalves. His unit had been detached from TF Ironhorse and had been operating with the 101st Airborne Division in Mosul. It was brought back under TF Ironhorse control and assigned the mission to relieve our brigade in place and assume control of Samarra.

3rd BCT Arrives in Kirkuk

We arrived in Kirkuk around the time President Bush delivered his "Mission Accomplished" speech announcing the end to major hostilities. We had reached Kirkuk and linked up with the 173rd Airborne Brigade, which was based out of an old Iraqi Airbase seized during the initial invasion. 173rd Airborne Brigade controlled the area from Kirkuk north to Irbil and as far east as Al Sulaymaniyah near the Iranian border. To its immediate north, the 101st Airborne Division based out of Fort Campbell, Kentucky, then led by Petraeus, had control of the far northern region known as Kurdistan, which included such major cities as Mosul, Tal'Afar, and Dahuk.

For the most part, fighting was sporadic at best, an occasional skirmish here and there, only to see the enemy run and hide when faced by overwhelming firepower and lethality. Upon link-up with the 173rd Airborne Brigade, space and housing on the base was at a premium as most of the hardened structures had been destroyed by coalition bombs and direct fire. All that was available was occupied by units of the 173rd. We finally found an old, abandoned factory and took refuge there, just west of the air base, approximately 10 to 12 kilometers (6 to 7.5 miles) from 173rd's headquarters. The factory offered some protection against direct fire as it was surrounded by a 20-foot-high brick wall. The enemy rarely attacked a base directly;

instead they chose to stand off at a given distance and fire mortars or indirect fire at us. This was smart on their behalf, as this course of action offered them the greatest probability of survival all the while achieving their goal of simply attacking and harassing us. It was an even greater bonus if they actually wounded or killed one of us.

Evolution of Forward Operating Bases

Inevitably, our action, along with those of our sister units, in establishing these small bases in a semihardened facility ultimately started an evolution and served as the catalyst to pave the way for the establishment of larger hardened facilities and bases known as forward operating bases (FOBs). This was the trend all over Iraq. As the years passed and the war endured, these bases grew in magnitude and scope, and often were referred to in Army circles as "Über-FOBs." The most well known of these bases was Victory Base Complex (VBC), located 7 kilometers (about 4.3 miles) west of Baghdad. The base was established and constructed around Baghdad International Airport upon the seizure of the facility during the invasion.

As time passed, VBC grew into a massive, sprawling base camp, adding several other clusters or camps within the perimeter fence, including Camp Liberty, Sather Air Base, Camp Slayer, Camp Striker, and Camp Cropper, which was built to serve as the new U.S. detainment facility replacing the controversial Abu Ghraib Prison after the fallout surrounding the maltreatment of detainees in 2003–04. Also within the confines of the base is the Al Faw Palace, which served as the headquarters of the Multi-National Force–Iraq (MNF–I) since 2004 and also serves the joint operations center (JOC), which controls Operation Iraqi Freedom.

VBC consumed the majority of terrain of southwest Baghdad with a troop strength of approximately 50,000 soldiers and airmen and an equal amount of civilians and contractors. The base was larger than the Fort Hood garrison. This base became an easy target for enemy mortars and rockets due to its enormous size. The enemy could simply fire in the general direction and in most cases cause serious damage and even inflict casualties. Commanders went to great extremes to enhance force protection and mitigate the risks presented to soldiers and civilians, but it was not a fail-safe plan. The enemy got lucky at times.

Our brigade's stay in Kirkuk was short lived and for the most part uneventful; not one direct- or indirect-fire attack occurred during the three weeks we were there. At this stage in the campaign, there really was no defined threat, nor enemy to pursue. The majority of Iraqi Army regulars had fled the scene or had already been killed or captured. That would change drastically in the weeks and months ahead. As it was, 173rd Airborne Brigade had Kirkuk under control. Our brigade was not needed there and would soon move again.

Meanwhile, the 4th Infantry Division staff, in particular the G-2 or intelligence officer, had received various forms of intelligence that there was an area along a peninsula immediately to our south vicinity of Balad where several high-ranking Ba'athist officials and Iraqi Army officers on the U.S. kill or capture list were taking sanctuary. As a result, Odierno decided to dispatch our brigade to execute and spearhead the operation.

Operation Peninsula Strike

Around June 1, the brigade was ordered to move south to Samarra East Airfield (SEAF) and prepare for the first major postinvasion operation, codenamed Operation Peninsula Strike. Our brigade as a whole minus one of our sister battalions, 1-12 Infantry Battalion, and the addition of elements from 173rd Airborne Brigade reformed and consolidated operations at SEAF to prepare for the operation. Planning lasted for a week. Then on June 9, 2003, during predawn hours, our brigade task force conducted numerous near-simultaneous raids along the peninsula bordering the Tigris River to the northeast of Balad in order to eradicate former Ba'ath Party Loyalists, former high-ranking Iraqi Army leaders, and other government officials. One of the most famous on the target list was none other than "Chemical Ali" Ali Hassan al-Majid himself.

Official 4th ID files report that Operation Peninsula Strike was a two-phased operation. The first phase of the operation involved moving soldiers and equipment into strike positions, intelligence gathering, and coordinating with local police. During the second phase, raids were conducted within the area of operation via land, air, and water to capture or destroy subversive elements. Air assault teams, ground attack squads, raid teams, river patrol boats, and local security combined forces to block escape routes and operate checkpoints to ensure success.

The operation incorporated a variety of units, utilizing the overwhelming firepower and effects of a joint and combined arms team. Army infantry, armor, artillery, aviation, and engineers, along with Air Force elements, worked together to accomplish the mission. Thousands of soldiers from 3rd BCT, 173rd Airborne Brigade, and 3rd Squadron, 7th Cavalry Regiment, 3rd Infantry Division were involved in the operation.

When it ended on June 12, Operation Peninsula Strike had captured 377 detainees and seized numerous weapons systems and ammunition. The seizure of illegal weapons was in support of the national weapons policy implemented on June 1. Four soldiers and two hostile civilians were wounded during the operation.

Specially trained soldiers screened the detainees to determine who was to be released and who was to be retained for further questioning. The soldiers also collected information that might lead to the future apprehension of hostile groups. Two former Iraqi generals turned themselves in during the raids. Abul Ali Jasmin, secretary of Defense Ministry, and Brigadier General Abdullah Ali Jasmin, head of the Iraqi Military Academy were detained.

It was reported through intelligence channels that Ali Hassan Abd al-Majid al-Tikriti, better known as the infamous Chemical Ali, Saddam's first cousin, who served as Iraqi Defense Minister and head of Iraqi intelligence, was one of the detainees who was questioned by U.S. troops and subsequently released as his true identity could not be determined. He was later captured on August 17, 2003, by U.S. forces in a raid and was tried several times and found guilty by the Iraqi High Tribunal Court. His trial started in 2006, and numerous trials followed through 2010. After eight total convictions and death sentences were awarded, he was finally executed by hanging on January 21, 2010, for various crimes committed against the Iraqi people, most notably for ordering the use of chemical weapons against the Kurds in northern Iraq.

Operation Peninsula Strike's success was a significant step forward in the ongoing journey of TF Ironhorse toward providing a safe, secure and free Iraq.

After Operation Peninsula Strike ended, I was released from the brigade staff and reassigned to 1st Battalion, 8th Infantry Regiment, "Fighting Eagles," to serve as the Operations Officer (S-3). Weeks earlier, Lieutenant Colonel Nate Sassaman had taken command of 1-8 IN from his predecessor, Lieutenant Colonel Phil Battaglia, while the battalion was staged at Samarra East Airfield. As S-3, I was responsible for overall planning, synchronization, and management of all combat operations. I fell in with a crack staff and adjusted quickly to the mission at hand. My first mission was to draft a plan that moved the battalion from SEAF to LSA Anaconda (LSAA) just west of Balad, approximately 15 kilometers (9.3 miles) from SEAF. This was a simple operation that would take less than two hours to accomplish. We drafted and issued the order to subordinate companies, and within hours we occupied real estate within the confines of LSAA. This move was shaping up to be one of our last and would ultimately be our final set for the remainder of the deployment.

LSAA was a sprawling airbase located in central Iraq that served as the theater's strategic logistics hub. It also served a large Special Operations unit and Air Force contingent, and was home to several high-ranking U.S. military officers representing all branches of the military. The majority of logistics that arrived in theater by strategic airlift was flown directly into LSAA, and from there materials were sorted, packaged, and distributed to their respective units.

Over the ensuing years, LSAA would expand to more than 40 square kilometers (25 square miles) and house more than 28,000 soldiers and airmen and 8,000 civilians. Its facilities included a movie theater, fast food courts, dance studio, an Olympic-size swimming pool, and an indoor swimming pool.

1-8 IN was responsible for the area outside the perimeter mainly to the north and west. Due to its population density of soldiers and airmen, the base was a lucrative target for enemy fighters. Our number one task was to protect LSAA from both direct- and indirect-fire attacks. The majority of attacks against the base were by means of indirect fire, as it afforded the enemy the greatest opportunity for survival as well as maximum infliction of casualties. Indirect-fire attacks against the base came in the form of rockets and mortars ranging in sizes from 60 mm to 120 mm. Attacks occurred randomly but almost daily. LSAA was attacked so much that soldiers referred to it as "Motarittaville" after Jimmy Buffett's classic song "Margaritaville."

Sassaman realized that if we were going to be responsible for the protection and security of this base, we could not do it from being on the inside. Recognizing this, he decided and all leaders concurred that it was time to look outside the base and find a new home for the battalion whereby we were living amongst the population as opposed to having to commute to work from our FOB.

This notion of living on or inside the large base complex was a technique widely used by a lot of units, but it was not the most effective. The advantages of living off the base and out amongst the population was that units were more prone to gain real-time actionable intelligence from local Iraqis seeking to provide information about known or suspected enemy activity. Moreover, troops were living and sleeping in their area of operations and thereby could quickly respond to anything that happened and recognize any changes in the environment and the dynamics of the battle space. On the contrary, local nationals who wanted to seek out U.S. forces in order to provide intelligence tips would rarely if ever approach a large base; gate guards unfamiliar with units living on the base often would simply turn would-be informants away because it was easier to do than tracking down the respective unit and linking them up with the informants.

The other factor that contributed to this decision was the mass traffic congestion that occurred on the base at all hours day and night. There were only three access gates in and out of the base during this time, and attempting to negotiate and maneuver off the base presented quite a challenge. First, as we attempted to leave, the guards at the gate would stop us and ask twenty questions, such as for our gate pass, our route, etc., all valid questions but not required when dispatching units for an emergency mission to react to enemy contact or running to the aid of an ambushed logistics convoy, which happened at an alarming rate.

Even during routine exits such as simply leaving to conduct a daily patrol, it was difficult to get off the base. The main gate would be bottlenecked with semitractors and trailers carrying loads of sand, lumber, and other materials purchased from the local economy simply for the upgrade and what I refer to as the "luxuration" of the unit headquarters. There were tons of other nonmission-essential items bought that should have been last on the priority list. At that time, our unit was under the impression that we only had a few months left in the country before we departed and returned home victorious. Hell, I guess others knew better based on the tens of thousands of truckloads of supplies that were shipped in daily, which certainly gave the impression that we were there for the long haul.

Final Set

By the middle of June 2003, Sassaman dispatched our battalion executive officer, Major Rob Gwinner, giving him orders to find us a suitable headquarters near Balad that were large enough, easily defendable, and offered protection. Gwinner set out with a patrol from our headquarters company and within a few hours located a suitable building in the village of Baldah approximately 4 kilometers (about 2.5 miles) from LSAA in between Balad and the base. The building was the former town hall or former mayor's office. Upon arrival there, Gwinner met with the former mayor and bartered a deal that would allow us to use the facility as our new headquarters under one condition: our unit would allow the mayor to work there and provide protection for him. We could have taken the place by force, but opted not to and agreed with the deal.

Gwinner returned to the base and informed Sassaman and me of what he had found, and within hours we had occupied the building and were converting it into a small FOB for our headquarters and command posts. Meanwhile, our five subordinate companies had occupied smaller structures similar to ours throughout the area surrounding LSAA. Being that this was our area of operations assigned to us by the brigade commander, it made sense.

This was our home for the foreseeable future. Our sister units throughout 4th ID were busy occupying FOBs the same as we were. Locations that were merely dots on maps a few weeks earlier were now permanent homes and areas of operations (AO) for the 32,000 troops assigned to TF Ironhorse. As for the disposition of TF Ironhorse units, 1st BCT remained in Tikrit along with the 4th ID Division Headquarters, which had occupied a large palace complex owned by Saddam; 2nd BCT was directly to our southeast across the Tigris River occupying an AO in Diyala Province and established FOB Warhorse in Baqubah. Our brigade established their headquarters on LSAA and controlled the AO surrounding the base in each cardinal direction. In addition, 1-66 AR operating in Samarra was attached to the brigade, meaning that we had the largest area within the 4th ID footprint covering approximately 700 square kilometers (about 435 square miles) from as far north as Samarra, south to Taji, east to Baqubah, and west to Fallujah.

Within the 3rd BCT Area of Operations, 1-8 IN was assigned the majority of battle space covering more than 600 square kilometers (nearly 373 square miles) with a mixed population of approximately 500,000 Sunni and Shia.

Our brigade had fought hard and traversed most of Iraq from Kuwait as far north as Kirkuk. We traveled approximately 700 miles in the first thirty days from the time we crossed the border out of Kuwait into Iraq. We were always on the move and never really settled down in a given area for more than two weeks. As the dust settled, we were rewarded with an extended stay in the heart of the volatile Sunni Triangle.

CHAPTER 4
TRANSITION TO PHASE IV

Postinvasion Operations, June–August 2003

❝ The owl of history is an evening bird. The past is unknowable; only at the end of the day do some of its outlines dimly emerge. The future cannot be known at all, and the past suggests that change is often radical and unforeseeable rather than incremental and predictable … ❞

Macgregor Knox,
What History Can Tell Us About the New Strategic Environment

Our relocation and occupation in Baldah came on the heels of the May 1, 2003, "Mission Accomplished" speech delivered by President Bush. While gathered in front of sailors aboard the deck of the USS *Abraham Lincoln*, President Bush officially announced the end to major hostilities. Weeks earlier, we had completely dismantled Iraqi Army forces and other remnants of irregular resistance. This announcement ended major combat operations in theater and officially signified the transition to Phase IV of the strategic operations plan (OPLAN): the postinvasion plan.

At the strategic level, the postinvasion plan called for the establishment of the Office for Reconstruction and Humanitarian Assistance (ORHA). ORHA was intended to act as a caretaker administration in Iraq until the creation of a democratically elected civilian government. Retired U.S. Army Lieutenant General Jay Garner was appointed as the director of ORHA, along with three deputies, including British Major General Timothy Cross. The plan was that when major combat operations were completed, a senior civilian administrator would be appointed in Iraq as head of the Coalition Provisional Authority (CPA) and ORHA would report to that administrator. Upon the creation of the CPA, Garner became the first chief executive of the CPA. Due to Garner's past military experiences in Iraq during Operation Desert Storm in 1991 and his reconstruction efforts in northern Iraq during Operation Provide Comfort,[1] Garner's credentials (and close ties to Secretary of Defense Donald Rumsfeld) made him an obvious choice for the task. His term, however, lasted only from April 21, 2003, until he was replaced abruptly less than a month later by L. Paul Bremer on May 11, 2003.

Garner's swift dismissal from his post by U.S. authorities came as a surprise to many within the CPA. Prior to his dismissal, Garner publicly stated in an interview with the BBC program *Newsnight* that his preference was to put the Iraqi people in charge as soon as possible and to do it with some form of elections. Privately, there was intense pressure from the U.S. government to begin a process of removing members of the Ba'ath Party from their positions within the Iraqi government and military. Garner's refusal to implement this "de-Ba'athification" of Iraqi society as a matter of public policy infuriated several senior members of the U.S. government and led directly to his dismissal.

Upon assuming his post in May 2003, Bremer also assumed the title of U.S. Presidential Envoy and Administrator in Iraq. He was frequently referred to as "ambassador" by numerous media organizations and the White House, because the highest government rank he had achieved was ambassador to the Netherlands. However, Bremer was not the ambassador to Iraq as there was no U.S. diplomatic mission present in Iraq at that time. The CPA was created and funded as a division of the Department of Defense, with Bremer reporting directly to the Secretary of Defense. Although troops from several of the coalition countries were present in Iraq at this time,

USCENTCOM was the primary military apparatus charged with providing direct combat support to the CPA to enforce its authority during the occupation of Iraq.

Many of Saddam Hussein's ornate palaces were looted in the days immediately following the invasion, though most of the physical structures survived relatively intact. It was in the numerous palaces situated throughout the country that the CPA chose to set up offices. Several of these palaces were retained by the U.S. government even after the transition of power back to the Iraqi people. The administration was headquartered in the central district of Baghdad, known as the Green Zone, which eventually became a highly secured, walled-off compound surrounded by more than 50,000 12-foot-high, portable, steel-reinforced concrete walls (T-Walls), which cost $1,000 each. The concrete business was clearly the most lucrative economic business sought after by local Iraqi businessmen. During my second tour (2005–06), my brigade, the 4th Brigade, 4th Infantry Division, based out of Fort Hood, was assigned the security mission to protect this critical area.

The CPA was responsible for administering the development fund for Iraq during the year following the invasion. This fund superseded the earlier U.N. Oil-for-Food Program and provided funding for Iraq's wheat purchase program, currency exchange program, electricity and oil infrastructure programs, equipment for Iraq's security forces, Iraqi civil service salaries, and operation of various government ministries. Basically, the CPA ran everything during this period of transition.

The way it handled these programs, implemented policy, and undertook other decision making brought heavy scrutiny on the organization as a whole; the criticism centered on perceived mismanagement and misappropriations of funds. Moreover, a lot of the policy decisions seemed to favor Shiites, which enraged the Sunni population and former Sunni government leaders. Eventually this became a contributing factor that brought the country to the brink of all-out civil war in late 2005.

The first act of the CPA under Bremer was the order for the de-Ba'athification of Iraqi society. On May 23, CPA Order Number 2 formally disbanded the Iraqi army. This was a mistake made during preinvasion planning. From my vantage point, it seems as though not one thought was ever given by strategic planners, nor was a course of action proposed, whereby the Iraqi Army could be kept somewhat intact at least so that a baseline organization was available to start the rebuilding. Instead, the CPA opted to completely dismantle it and start from scratch.

I would argue that there was a better way to approach this and in turn save a lot of time, energy, and taxpayer dollars in the process. My plan would have been to alert the Iraqi Army prior to the invasion through broadcasts or the dropping of leaflets that gave instructions for these units to move to the closest base and consolidate their arms and combat vehicles; if they complied, they would not be targeted by coalition bombers and ground forces. A better option would have been to follow the same plan that was executed with the disarming and relocation of the MEK.

Instead, disbanding the entire Iraqi Army meant that it had to be rebuilt from scratch, including the recruiting of soldiers and officers; providing basic and advanced training; equipping them with weapons, vehicles, and uniforms; feeding and paying the soldiers; and so on. You name it—we did it all, and we are still doing it. It is estimated that more than $100 billion of taxpayer money has been spent in rebuilding the Iraqi Army.

Furthermore, if it was so important to rid the Army of Sunni influence (a plan that did not work), why are a lot of former Sunni Iraqi officers serving as Iraqi Army battalion, brigade, division, and corps leaders today?

Granted, it was important and wise to get rid of Saddam's inner circle and top military leaders, but I still firmly believe that we did not have to completely disband the entire Army. Today we have come full circle in rebuilding the Iraqi Army and police forces, but the same corruption that existed then still exists. It will always exist in that culture. Of course, they are better equipped and better trained and can function on their own today, but we could have taken an easier path to get there.

On July 13, 2003, the CPA formed the Iraqi Governing Council and appointed its twenty-five members. The council membership consisted largely of Iraqi expatriates who had previously fled the country during the rule of Saddam Hussein as well as of outspoken dissidents who had been persecuted by the former regime. This group's sole charter was to guide the nation toward free elections and establishment of a constitutional government. Another group created by the multinational force in postinvastion Iraq was the 1,400-member international Iraq Survey Group (ISG), which conducted a fact-finding mission to find Iraqi weapons of mass destruction (WMD). In 2004, the ISG's Dueler Report stated conclusively that Iraq did not have a viable WMD program.[2]

At the operational level during this period of transition, division commanders were busy establishing their headquarters and taking ownership of their assigned AO. Simultaneously, they were issuing orders and guidance to subordinate brigade commanders, assigning sectors and new mission orders based on those received from Coalition Forces Land Component Command (CFLCC) and directives published by the CPA. Even as new mission orders came down, division commanders and staffs were somewhat puzzled about exactly which tasks needed to be accomplished during Phase IV of the OPLAN. This was evident by the lack of details provided in the base order received through brigade headquarters.

At the tactical level, Phase IV signified the transition from ground combat to stability and support operations (SASO). As we, the 1-8 IN, occupied our new AO headquartered in Baldah, we did in fact receive a new operation order and mission statement sent from 4th ID headquarters through our brigade, originating from the CFLCC, commanded by Lieutenant General David McKiernan. Our new mission was as follows:

1-8 IN (M) conducts stability and support operations in AO Eagle to destroy remaining Former Regime Elements, (FRE)/Terrorists in order to provide a secure and stable environment for Iraqi people and allow a seamless transition to Iraqi Government.

1-8 IN Occupies Baldah

We established our headquarters in the small town of Baldah on June 23, 2003. Baldah was located approximately 4 kilometers (about 2.5 miles) from the northwest gate of LSA Anaconda, essentially straddling the only paved road leading from the LSA to the city of Balad. In typical military fashion, the route was given an operational American name, Alternate Supply Route (ASR) Linda. This route would play a significant role in our combat operations over the next six to eight months, during which we were plagued by direct-fire ambushes and roadside bomb attacks, commonly known as improvised explosive devices (IEDs).

During our occupation and establishment of our headquarters and subordinate forward operating bases (FOBs), things were relatively quiet throughout our sector. It seemed as if the enemy and local citizens were in a wait-and-see mode. This period of calm was a plus for the battalion as it afforded the opportunity to get our command post established, including the critical tasks of establishing radio and other digital communications nets. Moreover, it allowed us to bring our staff and company commanders into the headquarters to conduct mission analysis and lay out the plan for operations covering the next few months.

There was no longer a standing Iraqi military to fight, and our initial plan only covered the invasion; we had not, nor did anyone else below brigade level, addressed or drafted a plan for Phase IV. This plan and new mission was issued to us while we were in the process of moving into Baldah and came as somewhat of a shock to Sassaman and myself. The mission of SASO and the key tasks associated with it were not clearly defined. During the planning process, battalion staff struggled at times to fully grasp the concepts, tasks, and timeframe associated with accomplishing it, and there was no clear end state.

Part of the mission statement—finding and killing or capturing the enemy—was clearly understood. This was the easy part; it's what infantry battalions do. Executing SASO (in actuality better termed "nation building") forced our organization to redefine itself. As a matter of fact, we all were under the impression that we would be home by year's end. In my opinion, based on past experience, SASO meant long-term commitment and required resources which at the time were absent from theater. Nation building is the charter of key agencies such as the Department of the State and other subset agencies such as United States Agency for International Development (USAID), which were not yet in theater.

In fact, it would take three years for these resources and agencies to show up and be integrated into operations. The key enabler was the addition of enhanced provincial reconstruction teams (ePRTs). These were ten- to twelve-man teams made up of subject-matter experts who specialized in nation building. Each of them had a unique skill set covering such areas as governance, rule of law, agriculture, and economics. These teams were governed by the DOS and were assigned one to each brigade. I worked with and managed one of these teams during my last tour (2009–10).

As I understood the tasks at hand from what I derived from the brigade OPORD, we were to continue to hunt down and kill or capture the enemy, establish local law and order, and launch projects such as building, repairing, and restoring roads, schools, medical clinics, basic infrastructure, and essential services such as water, sewage, and electricity. Also, we were tasked to recruit, train, and stand-up a whole new police force and army, known at the time as the Iraqi Civil Defense Corps.

Sounds easy right? Bullshit! This was a massive undertaking of daunting tasks. We did not have the subject-matter expertise or skill sets to plan and execute nation-building tasks. The one thing we did have at our disposal was a large pot of money, U.S. cash, tens to hundreds of millions of dollars known as the Commander's Emergency Response Program (CERP), which we could request and issue at a moment's notice based on submittal of plans to get these projects started. Local contractors were coming out to our FOB in droves selling us on their company's capabilities and placing bids for work. We took full advantage of the CERP money, though in some cases we were scammed as work was left uncompleted. Over time, we vetted these companies and paid out in small increments based on milestones achieved.

Nevertheless, things were quiet and we used the time commencing with planning attempts to codify and produce a simple plan that infantry troops could relate to and execute on the ground. This planning process is known as the Military Decision Making Process (MDMP). In short, it is a seven-step process used by Army units at all levels as a tool that assists commanders and staffs in developing estimates that lead to an overall plan being published for execution (see Appendix C). The plan includes an analysis of the environment, the likely enemy that will be encountered, and key tasks to be accomplished. Once this information is captured, it allows a commander to develop courses of action to achieve the mission based on the unit's capabilities.

Time was on our side, and staff worked around the clock to produce a quality product that would serve as the base for SASO for the foreseeable future. Moreover, we were ahead of the game as our organic companies had already moved to and occupied their assigned portion of our AO. These same operations were being mirrored across Iraq as every unit was presented the challenge of figuring out what SASO really meant in their given area.

The most important information derived from the MDMP is known as the Intelligence Preparation of the Battlefield (IPB). The IPB identifies and analyzes who you are fighting and the overall environment you are fighting in. A lot of this information was unknown; one would think this information would be included in the OPORD, but it was not. Lieutenant Dave Gray, our battalion intelligence officer (S-2), did a phenomenal job scratching and clawing his way through multiple echelons of command and sister governmental agencies in attempts to obtain information regarding our AO. These included numerous sources such as our immediate brigade-, division-, and corps-level headquarters and other external agencies including National Security Agency, Defense Intelligence Agency, and Central Intelligence Agency. Each of these agencies had representation in theater and provided a wealth of information to assist in understanding every facet and dynamic surrounding our environment or AO, including information about the enemy.

AO Eagle

As for the environment, terrain, and population classified as our AO makeup, we were located and centered in the heart of the Sunni Triangle. Our AO covered more than 675 square kilometers (about 420 square miles) of terrain extending from as far north as Sammarra, east to Lake Thar Thar, south to Taji, and west to Baqubah. Our battalion covered the largest AO in the brigade. Furthermore, our AO had a population density of more than half a million inhabitants. Even more challenging, it was a mix of Sunni, Shiite, and other tribal affiliations. We were located at the epicenter of a Sunni and Shiite fault line, a fault line that was tenuous at best and would ultimately fracture in the months and years ahead.

There were several towns and villages ranging in size throughout our AO. Balad was the largest city, a predominantly Shiite town of approximately 100,000 people. One day during a routine patrol, Sassaman and I had tea with one of the local Shiite tribal sheiks, using the opportunity as a means to better gain a thorough understanding of our surroundings. During the meeting, Sassaman asked the sheik why it was that Balad was the only Shiite town in this predominantly Sunni area. The sheik explained that years ago Balad was by itself and basically ruled Yethrip Municipality, a township that governed Balad under Saddam. He also told us that Balad had been a thorn in Saddam's side, so much so that he surrounded it with numerous Sunni enclaves and villages to keep the Shiites in check.

We soon discovered a thorn of our own: the village of Albu Hishma.

Albu Hishma was a small village of approximately 7,000 Sunnis, located approximately 2 kilometers (about 1.25 miles) east of Baldah along ASR Linda, the last town you ran into while traveling east before reaching the friendly confines of LSA Anaconda. A small farming community, its residents generated income by growing and selling dates and other crops. The entire village was surrounded by palm orchards. Upon our occupation of Baldah and the continuing establishment of LSA Anaconda, these orchards were used less for farming and more for conducting mortar attacks against the bases. The orchards were thick and provided excellent cover and concealment for the enemy to conduct attacks. Moreover, the orchards also supported direct-fire and rocket-propelled grenade attacks of U.S. convoys traveling along ASR Linda. In many cases, these attacks were successful in killing and wounding U.S. soldiers.

During our tenure there, our battalion spent the majority of our time patrolling the streets and scouring the orchards in search of enemy mortar teams. Attacks of this kind increased dramatically both in lethality and complexity in the weeks and months ahead. Each new attack brought newer and stricter measures. Albu Hishma manifested itself as the hub for terrorist activity in our AO. The majority of enemy activity (about 90 percent of attacks, based on the data we tracked while operating in the area) originated from this village. Daily contact with enemy fighters from this village was the norm, and drastic steps were needed to subdue it before we could ever focus on stability operations and nation-building tasks.

Of the $20 million we spent in our sector, less than one third of the funds were spent on Albu Hishma. We used the money as an incentive to garner support from the local sheiks and community leaders. It was a risk/reward system. The option was simple: stop the violence, control your people, and/or turn them in, and by doing so you will see much-needed projects and new construction in your village. This plan worked well in some instances; overall the local citizens, especially the future generation of Albu Hishma, suffered because of the Sunni bad actors who lived amongst them.

Enemy Disposition

Initially, enemy resistance stemmed from Fedayeen (Saddam's hardcore irregular forces) and Ba'ath Party Loyalists. It took a while for the intelligence community to coin a name for these groups. In the beginning of Phase IV, all enemies were classified as former regime elements (FREs); around mid-June 2003, the name changed and all enemy resistance was coined "Anti-Iraqi Forces" (AIF). Regardless of what they were called, bad guys were out on the street trying to kill us and derail any of the gains we obtained. Moreover, these groups were supplied by hundreds of weapon caches scattered across Iraq, put in place by the Republican Guard prior to the invasion by orders of Saddam or obtained by looting Iraqi bases abandoned during the onslaught of the invasion. The main weapons of choice were IEDs, mortars, RPGs, and machine guns. In extreme cases, all of these would be integrated into planned ambushes against us. As the war persisted, enemy tactics continued to evolve and advance. With each new attack came increased complexity and lethality.

As time went on and offensive operations continued, more and more information was learned about the enemy, mainly from the capture and interrogation of these individuals. Specifically in our AO, based on numerous raids conducted and subsequent captures, we learned that enemies were nothing more than peasants or local farmers who had been paid through a local financier (typically a former Ba'ath Party official or designee) to carry out attacks against us.

In late July 2003, I was returning to our FOB from having been out conducting battlefield circulation. I was traveling in my BFV along with two scout Humvees on ASR Amy, a route just south of Balad, when my section was ambushed by enemy personnel armed with AK-47s and RPGs. There was no moon that night, and we were traveling in blackout drive using night observation devices in order to conceal our movement.

All of the sudden, an explosion and a barrage of intense machine gunfire appeared to be coming from the east side of the road. Another explosion rang out. A flash and trail of smoke whipped over the top of my BFV. It was an RPG round that went astray and missed my vehicle by inches. I immediately screamed at my gunner, Sergeant Cory Blackwell, and told him to scan right, identify targets, and engage with 25-mm high-explosive rounds. Blackwell did as ordered and laid down a base of fire so intense it seemed as if we had melted the barrel of our 25-mm cannon. This suppressive fire enabled the scouts traveling in unarmored Humvees to maneuver behind us and out of the kill zone.

My Humvee driver, Specialist Jason Testa, dismounted the Humvee along with the other scout soldiers, took up cover, and continued to engage the enemy. While the engagement persisted, I got on my FM radio and called for attack aviation support. I also called for reinforcements from Charlie Company, commanded by Captain Karl Pfutze, who had an element nearby that had been manning a check point on Highway 1, known as MSR Tampa.

The squad from Charlie Company got there within minutes, and I gave them orders to flank the enemy, close in, and destroy them. Within minutes of their arrival, two Apache helicopters showed up and immediately spotted the enemy attempting to flee through an irrigation ditch. The pilots vectored in the soldiers from Charlie Company, and I shortly received a call over the radio that they had detained two enemy personnel; one was still holding the RPG in his hand. I moved quickly to their location. The soldiers of Charlie Company had the two enemy personnel subdued and flex-cuffed. I ordered my driver to escort the two detainees to my vehicle and informed Charlie Company that we would take them to our FOB for processing. We mounted up and returned to our FOB without incident.

After processing these two detainees, we brought them one by one into our interrogation room and asked them a series of questions through a translator. These detainees were Sunnis, local farmers who had been paid $500 by some unidentified male to attack us. Further intelligence gleaned the value for different attacks carried out against us. He stated that an RPG attack was worth $500, an IED attack was worth $700, and if you actually killed an American or other coalition soldier(s) or destroyed a vehicle, it garnered $1,000. So that was the price on my head.

Luckily for my fellow soldiers and me, these untrained hacks could not shoot; they were simply poor farmers trying to make money to feed their families. Attacking coalition forces paid more than the going rate for a fifty-pound bag of dates. At that point in time, farming had been put on hold, and they really had no alternative to make money. Enemy attacks like these were being carried out all over Iraq, but luckily for all of us, we were fighting local farmers with no previous military experience or training. That would all change in the months ahead.

On the evening of July 1, 2003, our battalion staff had wrapped up the planning and subsequently issued the OPORD to all subordinate companies (see Appendix C). Our companies took the plan and customized it to their given sectors within AO Eagle, as every area was unique and had its own demographic makeup and challenges. What worked well in one village or sector often did not work in another. In the meantime, we continued setup and took prudent measures to harden our facility and execute other force protection measures, taking nothing for granted.

On the night of July 4, 2003, we celebrated Independence Day. Sassaman had gathered the troops in front of our headquarters and addressed them about the importance of this day, relating it to the current situation. Moreover, we had erected a makeshift flagpole, and every half hour starting at midnight for the next twenty-four hours, we changed the American flag. These forty-eight flags were saved and mailed back home to friends of the battalion and other groups or local businesses that had supported us by providing care packages and other necessities during our time away from home.

Our headquarters company had trucked in chow from the field trains located at LSA Anaconda. As customary, chow was delivered in mermite cans, which were rugged containers used by all Army units to ship chow to the troops during field training exercises and combat operations. Being that it was a special day; the troops were served hamburgers, hot dogs, and an assortment of vegetables and drinks. We tried to mirror events back home as best we could under the circumstances and conditions. We completed the celebration at 2000 hours local time, all the while maintaining security as troops rotated off the perimeter so they, too, could participate in the festivities.

Then all hell broke loose.

At approximately 2100 hours, just after nightfall, a large explosion rocked the building, followed by a few bursts of gunfire. Soldiers searched frantically for any available cover. Soldiers pulling guard on the roof were shouting about enemy to the north, all the while returning fire in that general direction. We all braced for another explosion, but nothing happened. From the outset, we thought that we were under some sort of mortar or rocket attack. A quick search inside the perimeter revealed no such evidence. Sassaman and I rushed to the rooftop to get a bird's-eye view of the situation; the building we chose was the highest structure in the town and dominated the landscape, allowing for a clear line of sight in all directions. Soldiers on guard duty informed us that they had witnessed several suspicious individuals and a car speed off from the north but did not actually witness them attacking the base.

Sassaman quickly dispatched our scouts to mount their vehicles and gave them orders to establish traffic control points or blocking positions around the roads exiting the town. Lieutenant Brian Barber, our scout platoon leader, and Sergeant First Class Timothy Bolyard, the scout platoon sergeant, rallied their troops, mounted their vehicles and departed the base perimeter in less than five minutes. The scout platoon did as ordered and sealed off the town minutes later.

Sassaman huddled with the key leaders inside the TOC and issued a hasty plan, basically stating that all available soldiers of HHC would form into squads of seven to nine soldiers and execute a cordon and search of the entire town of Baldah. Our mission was to locate, kill, or capture those responsible for the attack. In the process, we would detain all military-aged males and consolidate them at our TOC for questioning to see if we could find the perpetrators. Sassaman's intent was to send a loud message to all in the area that our battalion, the 1-8 IN Fighting Eagles, meant business and that we would not tolerate this type of violence or any attack. Period. Moreover, he wanted our action to set the tone for the remainder of our time in theater.

Before we moved out to execute the cordon and search, I tasked our Engineer Company, Bravo Company, 4th Engineers, led by Captain Eric T. Paliwoda, whose company was located blocks away occupying a structure similar to ours, to assist us in the mission. Paliwoda rallied his troops, and upon his arrival we provided him a schematic of the area his company would be responsible for searching. At 2200 hours, we moved out of the perimeter with approximately forty-two HHC soldiers divided into six squads of seven personnel each. Paliwoda's company took the east side of the town, and our group took the western side. We used the main north–south road running through the town as the dividing line and control measure to deconflict direct fires (that is, to delineate and coordinate the limits of direct fire). I took my makeshift squad of four personnel consisting of Testa, Blackwell, Captain Matt Capobianco, our battalion fire support officer, and BFV driver Specialist Matthew Francis and methodically began searching for the perpetrators.

We worked one side of the street while Sassaman and his team paralleled us on the other side. Baldah was rather small in comparison to other major Iraq towns or cities; there were approximately seventy-five to a hundred dwellings to search. As I approached the first house on the block, we used the technique of kindly knocking first on the front door. In my best Arabic, I asked if we could search their premises. In the beginning of the war, all units were short on translators across the board; we were no exception. For this operation, we only had two: one was with Sassaman and his group; the other accompanied Paliwoda. Regardless, we managed to get our message across either through broken Arabic or simply by the mere fact of displaying our weapons at the ready, which signified to all locals that we meant business. We were not there for evening tea.

As we entered the first house, our reception was met with anger and disgust by the occupants: men, women, and children of all ages. We quickly separated males and females into different rooms, with the exception of the children, who were kept with the women. We left a guard posted on each group and continued to execute a thorough search of the premises, looking for weapons and other illegal contraband. The first house turned up empty. In accordance with orders from Sassaman, we detained all military-aged males, flex-cuffed them, and consolidated them in the street with designated guards until the operation was complete and we could escort them to the base for questioning.

As we progressed from house to house, based on the initial reception, our technique for entry became more deliberate and aggressive. It was clear that the locals (innocent or not) did not want us searching their homes, and as a result they locked their doors and gates to prevent our entry. Based on this action, we formed a three- to five-man stack and deliberately breached the gate or door to gain access and executed the basic squad battle drill known as "enter and clear a room;" in this case it was multiple rooms. By the time we reached the fourth house, we had the battle drill down to a science. We continued this process at a rapid pace, house by house, block by block.

After the fifth or sixth house, everyone began to look the same. Every household contained a random number of military-aged males, all of whom were detained. After two hours of door kicking and exhaustive searching, we had rounded up and detained more than 150 military-aged males, but the one thing that was lacking was the "smoking gun." It was like looking for a needle in a haystack, and we could not find any evidence that would support the attack against our base. That is not to say that we did not have the person(s) responsible; a lot of these males looked shady and any one of them could have been the perpetrator. Moreover, we discovered and seized several weapons (mainly AK-47s), but none of them appeared to have been recently fired. No explosives or RPGs discovered, either. We had hit a dead end. The only option remaining was the tactical questioning of each and every detainee to see if any evidence turned up.

Around 0200 hours on July 5, 2003, the search was over and we began our movement back to the base. Prior to leaving the area, we accounted for all our personnel and equipment. Then we consolidated and tagged every weapon and detainee, specifically marking the house number and location of all material and personnel seized in the event that items were to be returned or if we had to return to the house based on information and intelligence obtained from the tactical questioning of detainees.

We marched down the street with more than 150 Iraqi male detainees in a single-file line, each blindfolded, their hands flex-cuffed behind their backs. Soldiers armed with weapons at the ready flanked the formation on both sides, ready to act if a threat presented itself. Family members and other residents took up positions on their rooftops and along the street to observe our actions. Some of the females, either wives or mothers, were screaming at us to release their sons or husbands, pleading for mercy, not knowing whether they would see these men again. This fear and desperation was understandable.

While under the brutal rule of Saddam, Iraqi males were often rounded up by his henchmen and carried away, never to be seen or heard from again. In many cases, they were executed on sight depending on the severity of what they had been accused of. As we escorted the men away that night, their families obviously wondered if this was the beginning of another brutal regime, whether the Americans simply conquered Iraq and were picking up where Saddam left off. Based on our actions and first impressions, this certainly gave cause for Iraqis to believe this was the case.

Upon returning to the base, the detainees were lined up against a wall and told to sit on the ground. Guards were posted, and we started tactical questioning. One by one, detainees were escorted to an area away from the group and presented several basic questions, such as name, sect, and tribal affiliation. After answering these basic questions, they were asked specific questions about the attack on our base. Every interview was conducted by Sassaman, along with Gray, our intelligence officer, and one of our translators. Each session lasted approximately fifteen to twenty minutes. Gray recorded the detainees' answers.

Based on body language, demeanor, and answers provided, each detainee was either released to return home or placed into a group for further questioning. As it turns out, some of the information provided to us had nothing to do with the attack on our base, but was otherwise credible information about other planned future attacks as well as the whereabouts of former Ba'ath Party members on our target list. This information was logged and served as actionable intelligence that led to subsequent raids and captures.

The operation came to a close at 1200 hours on July 5, 2003. Of the 150 males detained, all but three were released, kept for further questioning and processing based on their intelligence value. Although we did not capture the perpetrators who attacked us, the message we sent was loud and clear. Word spread quickly that anyone who messed with us or attacked us would pay, if not with their lives then with years locked up in confinement.

After the dust settled from this operation, Sassaman brought the leadership together to conduct an AAR to capture the lessons learned from the operation as well as to analyze the intelligence gathered from it. The first questions we tried to answer was why we were attacked and by whom. Best we could figure out was that it must have been conducted from outsiders who did not reside in the town of Baldah and that they were most likely former FRE/AIF who lived in the surrounding area, probably from the nearby village of Albu Hishma. In the weeks and months ahead, Albu Hishma became the focal point for probably 80 percent of all our combat operations as the majority of enemy attacks were predominantly carried out by enemy fighters who lived there.

Next, we looked at our overall tactical execution of the cordon and search. Based upon input from leaders at all levels, they all agreed that our execution was tactically sound and that the violence of action with which we carried it out clearly sent the intended message, even though our search did not capture those responsible.

But we actually missed the most significant lesson learned, and we didn't discover the mistake until a few years into this war. As a matter of fact, units operating throughout theater were making this same mistake and failed to realize it, too. The mistake made was tied to the lesson just discussed, whereas we as leaders thought that our execution was sound and the violence of action was measured, this was true for the conduct of tactical level operations. However, while it seemed we met the overall intent, our mistake was that we failed to consider the strategic implications or impacts that our actions had in the eyes of the overall population.

At the time, we never considered the impression we were making on the locals. We were simply doing what we thought was right based on all of our training in the months and years leading up to this war. The sense among our soldiers and leaders was that we were at war and that we were going to do whatever it took to find the bad guys who attacked us. This was the first true attack against us since the initial invasion. We were the new guys in the area, and it seemed we were being tested. How we responded would set the tone for whether we would be attacked in the future. We wanted to hedge our bet in that regard. Based on the underlying intent, our battalion went into the town of Baldah strong and heavy-handed. We suspected but were not 100 percent certain that the actual perpetrators were even there. We kicked in every door, screaming at everyone inside—men, women, and children alike—to get down on the floor, while we ransacked the house looking for weapons and other contraband. Upon discovery, we seized every weapon and detained every military-aged male. Once the operation culminated, we escorted at gun point more than 150 detainees through the streets en route to our base, certain that out of all those detained we had got our man.

Therein lay the problem. While we did nothing illegal or immoral—nor did we violate the ROE or any other laws of war— our mistake was in not considering the strategic message we were sending. At the tactical level, our actions were spot on and made sense. But at the strategic level, our actions fueled resentment and hostility and basically served as a recruiting poster for the evolving insurgency.

The strategic costs of capturing two or three attackers certainly did not cross our minds that day. Moreover, these types of operations would continue to occur throughout the theater of operations for years to come until collectively as a military and nation we finally figured it out. This ultimately led to the introduction and implementation of our new doctrine: "Counter Insurgency Operations (COIN)," authored by General David Petraeus. Though these mistakes were unintentional, it was a costly oversight that came back to haunt us, and we would pay dearly in blood and treasure. This attack was only the beginning, a small and subtle sign from the enemy of what was to come in the weeks and months ahead.

As it turned out, our stay in Baldah was short lived. Days after the attack, we got a visit from our brigade commander, Col. Fred Rudesheim. This was his first visit to our headquarters, and he wanted to see our setup and receive a back brief on the attack that had recently occurred. Upon arriving at our base, our entire staff, including all five of our company commanders, were in a meeting discussing future operations. We were all seated around a conference table when all of the sudden Rudesheim stormed in and without hesitation immediately started chastising and berating Sassaman. He went off on a ten-minute tirade about how screwed up our base was.

The main point of his contention was that he did not like the location being in the middle of town. Sassaman tried repeatedly to explain our reasons for selecting the location, but Rudesheim was having none of it. With a stern look and a deafening voice, he screamed at Sassaman and ordered us to find and move to another location within forty-eight hours. Sassaman acknowledged, and Rudesheim stormed out of the room to the friendly confines of his headquarters located at LSA Anaconda.

This rather rude and untimely encounter was seen as very unprofessional in the eyes of Sassaman and every junior leader who was there. It could have been handled differently, whereby Rudesheim could have requested Sassaman to step outside for a minute or go to a separate location versus berating him in front of all his subordinates. Instead, that testy meeting set the tone for the rest of our tour. The brigade commander and Sassaman got off on the wrong foot, and it stayed that way the entire time, actually worsening as time went on. There was certainly no love lost between the two, and it would magnify in spades. Ultimately, it had a detrimental effect on our daily combat operations.

Against our better judgment, based on the orders received, we executed accordingly. Sassaman instructed Gwinner to conduct a reconnaissance patrol into Balad and find us a suitable location. He executed the mission the following morning. Upon return to the base, he reported that he had found the perfect location. The building, an elementary school prior to the invasion, was unoccupied. It would make a suitable location for our new base.

Gwinner linked up with the headmaster and offered to rent the facility for the foreseeable future. The headmaster agreed, and the deal was sealed.

1-8 Infantry Establishes FOB Eagle in Balad

On July 6, 2003, we departed Baldah and immediately began our occupation and establishment of the new FOB Eagle. It was located in the heart of Balad, about a mile east of downtown proper, 20 kilometers (about 12.5 miles) west of LSA Anaconda. During the next two weeks, our soldiers worked tirelessly, modifying the structure into a hardened, well-fortified base. Life on the FOB was ever-evolving and tough at times. When the battalion initially arrived to our final destination in Balad, we took up refuge or camp in a school located on the eastern side of the town. We purchased the building from a family who lived directly behind the building as the caretakers for a grand total of $50. They really thought they were getting a great deal, so they took the money and ran.

When we first arrived, there was no power, running water, or other essential services. Gwinner was in charge, responsible for building the FOB from the ground up. When we started there were no bathrooms, no hot showers, and no running water. The showers that we very rarely took were from a canteen or blivet bag strung up by a rope and poured over our heads. The water was certainly hot, thanks to the scorching 120-degree heat. We also had bottled water trucked in from our logistical base, but there was no ice. We purchased ice from a local vendor. We eventually found a local icehouse and purchased it from the town. Who knew the truth about the people we were buying it from and where the money was going? We feared it was funding local insurgents, but the ice-cold water was a luxury, and the men enjoyed it in the blistering heat.

As time went on and weeks passed, we slowly began to purchase massive generators to provide power for lights and electricity. We also hired local Iraqi contractors to come in and install plumbing for running water. Later, the brigade provided ready-made shower and bathroom trailers. We had showers, individual stalls in the bathrooms, and even a small dining facility. The highlight of FOB life was when we finally purchased an AFN satellite and big-screen TV so we could enjoy football.

Gwinner also made arrangements for thousands of concrete barriers (the infamous "T" walls) to be delivered, and these barriers were placed around the base for added protection. He also arranged a deal with a heavy engineer company located on LSA Anaconda and had them deploy their bulldozers to the FOB to construct a large dirt mound approximately 8 feet high around the entire facility.

The base grew in size over the next few weeks. Eventually we took in the adjacent compound next door that Alpha Company, 1-8 IN, commanded by Captain Matt Cunningham, had occupied weeks earlier upon relieving in place a unit assigned to 3rd Infantry Division. This facility previously served as a training base for Saddam's elite fighters prior to the invasion and was more than suitable to serve as a FOB. By the end of July, all exterior improvements were complete, guard towers were constructed in every direction along the perimeter wall, and a detention facility known as "Eagle Jail" was constructed.

The only improvements left to make were those needed to improve the quality of life for our soldiers. These additions included lights, ceiling fans, air conditioners, bunk beds, running water for shower trailers, and other creature comforts. Later, we would add an Internet café, a basketball court, and a soccer field where we would host matches. Most importantly, it was well fortified and offered maximum standoff for defense in the event of a direct attack. When all was said and done, FOB Eagle, which had started out as a twenty-acre compound, had expanded to more than 200 acres of land, an area equivalent to four city blocks. FOB Eagle would become one of the first enduring FOBs in all of Iraq and would serve as a base for U.S. presence long into the war.

Stability and Support Operations Commence

By the middle of July 2003, our battalion had settled into a routine of steady state operations. These included daily, around-the-clock combat patrols of our entire AO, including all towns and villages. Sassaman mandated to our subordinate companies that we would maintain a 24/7 presence throughout the AO at all times. His intent was that if something went down, we would be there to react. Moreover, it would show an overt presence in the hope of deterring aggression, and it also would signal to the population that we were there to support and protect them.

During this period of steady state operations, the battalion was assigned two specific tasks from our brigade headquarters that had strategic overtones. The first and most important mission we had was the protection of LSA Anaconda, to keep it and all its occupants safe from indirect-fire attacks. This task was assigned to Bravo Company, which owned this portion of AO Eagle, including Albu Hishma. Due to its strategic importance, this mission became an enduring task for the battalion, known as Operation Eagle Howan.

This was not an easy mission. In fact, it was a daunting task, to say the least. LSAA was clearly the number-one high-value target for enemy attacks—and the most lucrative. The sheer size of the facility, along with its dense population, made it an attractive and easy target.

Throughout the month of July, LSAA was attacked by indirect fire in the form of mortars and rockets on a daily basis, usually in the early morning and evening hours. The majority of attacks originated from the orchards located in Albu Hishma. On July 6, 2003, the base was attacked by a mortar barrage. The attack hit the hospital area where the 915th Forward Surgical Team was established, wounding sixteen of the twenty-man team, including six who were critically wounded. During the attack, Captain Noel Pace, deputy brigade surgeon, 3rd Brigade, 4th Infantry Division, rushed over to the scene and assisted with treatment and evacuation of casualties. He later said, "When your vascular surgeon needs a vascular surgeon, the shit has hit the fan!"

Captain Robert "Todd" S. Brown, commander of Bravo Company, 1-8 Infantry, was there conducting change of command inventories from the outgoing commander:

> "LSA Anaconda took more mortars last night. You can see them from our bunker complex. It's reminiscent of the scene in Band of Brothers where they are in the back of the truck watching the artillery in the distance. Anaconda remains a very easy target, 18,000 people who don't patrol, I guess we had eighteen casualties—that is unacceptable."[3]

This was the norm until Brown took the reins from Captain Will Bryant of Bravo Company and immediately implemented an aggressive plan to eliminate this threat. During the first week in command, Brown inserted small hunter/killer teams into the orchards where these mortar teams operated and fired from. These teams established ambush patrols that were highly effective, resulting in killing or capturing more than twenty insurgents and confiscating more than a dozen mortar systems. This was the best technique for eliminating the threat. We had to keep a presence in the orchards. If not, the enemy would simply erect the mortar systems, lob a few rounds, and use the thick cover to evade and escape, living to fight another day.

For a short period, at interim rates, LSA Anaconda got a reprieve. However, attacks persisted. It seemed there was an endless supply of mortars and rockets at the enemy's disposal. With each new attack, we devised stricter measures and repercussions to eliminate it. In the end, we were out of options. Our battalion resorted to draconian measures by encircling the town with triple strand concertina wire and maintaining a 24/7 armed presence to ensure that no further attacks would occur.

The tactic of isolating this village, new to U.S. Army doctrine, gained international media attention and scrutiny. *New York Times* reporter Dexter Filkins was embedded with us and observed the operation. In his article "Tough New Tactics by U.S. Tighten Grip on Iraq Towns," Filkins claimed that we deliberately adopted this tactic from the pages of the Israeli counterinsurgency manual:

"ALBU HISHMA, Iraq—As the guerrilla war against Iraqi insurgents intensifies, American soldiers have begun wrapping entire villages in barbed wire.

In selective cases, American soldiers are demolishing buildings thought to be used by Iraqi attackers. They have begun imprisoning the relatives of suspected guerrillas, in hopes of pressing the insurgents to turn themselves in.

The Americans embarked on their get-tough strategy in early November, goaded by what proved to be the deadliest month yet for American forces in Iraq, with 81 soldiers killed by hostile fire. The response they chose is beginning to echo the Israeli counterinsurgency campaign in the occupied territories."[4]

In our eyes, nothing was too extreme. We were at war, and our goal was to save the lives of U.S. soldiers. We spared no expense and took no chances.

The second strategic task from brigade was securing and protecting the corps' main supply route, known as MSR Tampa or Highway 1. Highway 1 was the main highway running two lanes in both directions north and south from the border in Kuwait north through Baghdad continuing north to Mosul. Given the operational name MSR Tampa, this route was the primary route for all theater logistics including fuel, repair parts, food, ammunition, and other critical commodities. Approximately 20 kilometers (about 12.5 miles) of this route was in our AO. It was vital that the route stay secured, and we maintained freedom of maneuver to allow the uninterrupted flow of logistics throughout theater. If not, operations would come to a halt and be shut down for days. Due to its strategic importance, this, too, became a named operation: Operation Eagle Bandit.

Prior to our battalion's occupation in Balad, MSR Tampa was plagued by daily IED attacks, drive-by shootings, and direct-fire ambushes targeting logistical convoys. On a daily basis beginning in July 2003, there were more than eight to ten IED attacks in the 20-kilometer stretch that ran through our AO. At the time, these attacks were the number one casualty producer of contractors and coalition troops.

These supply convoys were contracted haul assets operated by Kellogg, Brown, and Root (KBR), the main logistics and life support materials provider in theater. Knowing the contents and value of these convoys, the enemy began targeting these at an alarming rate. The tactic used by the enemy was to attack the lead vehicle with an IED, halt the convoy, and hijack at gunpoint the remaining elements and associated goods. The enemy targeted KBR convoys as they were lightly armored and did not have the combat power or heavy weapon systems to sustain a prolonged fight. Therefore, they were easy targets. The enemy knew that if they were successful at destroying and interdicting our supply trucks, they would hamper our operations. Typically, a logistical convoy had one armored Humvee or gun track per every ten to fifteen trucks. Once the convoy was ambushed, the enemy would kill the drivers, hijack the supply trucks, drive them to an alternate location, strip them down, and sell the goods on the black market to finance future attacks. This tactic ultimately became the number one source for funding the insurgency. Likewise, any ammunition seized, particularly artillery rounds, would be used against us in future IED attacks.

To counter this threat, we placed Charlie Company, 1-8 Infantry, "Rock," commanded by Captain Karl Pfutze, in FOB Rock, located directly south of Balad straddling Highway 1. Charlie Company was given the tough strategic mission of securing the MSR. Upon assuming the mission, Pfutze and the soldiers of Charlie Company immediately made their presence felt on the highway. First and foremost, they maintained a constant presence along the route by placing BFVs in overwatch positions (i.e., observation positions or vantage points). Second, they established a series of dismounted flash checkpoints along the route and randomly stopped and searched vehicles for illegal contraband. Finally, they established squad ambushes on known and likely IED emplacement sites. These aggressive methods bore fruit right away as enemy fighters were being killed or captured at a rate of three to four a day.

With each new capture came more collected intelligence. Soon the enemy cells responsible for these attacks began to fall like dominoes. During the following months, Charlie Company either killed or captured more than fifty enemy fighters and dismantled several IED/hijacking cells. During the remainder of our stay in Balad, attacks along MSR Tampa decreased sharply, from thirty attacks per week to almost zero, and the portion of MSR Tampa that ran through the Eagle AO became the safest route in Iraq.

These two named operations consumed the majority of our time and resources, better known as combat power. Based on our MDMP of the new mission set, these were the critical offensive or lethal tasks we had to undertake. In support of these named operations, we used our engineer company to clear the key routes in our sector to allow us freedom of maneuver. Bravo Company, 4th Engineer Company, commanded by Paliwoda, was essentially our fourth maneuver company. They were assigned battle space as a landowner responsible for the terrain surrounding Baldah and their essential tasks of clearing routes and reducing the IED threat. As each new day passed, more and more IEDs were being discovered along the key routes in our AO. The engineers had the difficult task of clearing these routes at a time when assets were limited. Unlike later route clearance operations, there were no up-armored vehicles such as the Mine Resistance Ambush Protected Vehicle (MRAP), nor did they possess the sophisticated Buffalo or Husky mine detection/exploitation vehicles. These vehicles arrived in theater later and were created by DOD solely to counter the IED threat and mitigate risk and damage to our troops.

Back in July, our engineer company was equipped with old legacy equipment such as the M1113 Armored Personnel Carrier. These were leftover Vietnam-era relics (troop carriers) that were lightly armored and open on the top, exposing troops to the effects of IED blasts. The only mine detection equipment they had were the old Vietnam-era hand-held mine detectors. Soldiers had to walk along the route carrying these hand-held devices in search of IEDs, exposing themselves to the danger of the blasts and shrapnel, snipers, and direct-fire ambushes. Soldiers did not have advanced body armor either.

Each day these engineer soldiers cleared more than 20 kilometers of road, operating in extreme temperatures, often under attack. Lessons about how the enemy operated and weapons used were being learned at an alarming rate. However, it took a while for these lessons learned to catch up to the leaders at the Pentagon and the policymakers in Congress who controlled the purse strings that would lead to technology advancement and fielding of new equipment.

Bottom line: engineer soldiers had the toughest and most dangerous job in theater, and they were worth their weight in gold.

The one advantage if any that we had operating in Balad was the fact that the IEDs that were being emplaced were not to the level of sophistication and did not carry the same lethality of those being emplaced in Baghdad. Catastrophic IED technology had not migrated north to Balad. The explosive material, artillery rounds, and all the deadly components were there, but missing was the expertise and skill to build them. We were fortunate in that regard—but our luck was short lived.

By late August, the catastrophic IED made its appearance in the Sunni Triangle and quickly gained everyone's attention. The attack occurred just to our north, approximately 8 kilometers (nearly 5 miles) across the Tigris River, near Baqubah in 2nd Brigade Combat Team, 4th ID sector or AO. It was an armor battalion equipped with M1A1 tanks that had been operating in the given area for a couple of weeks. Their mission was to establish an observation post (OP) to observe and interdict enemy mortar teams that were operating in the area. There was only one main trail leading to the location where they established the OP. After approximately a week of executing the same mission over and over, using the same route over and over, they began to pattern themselves, and it became clear that the enemy was watching and taking notes.

On July 2, as the M1A1 tank was headed to establish its OP position, a large blast occurred. I heard and felt the shock 8 kilometers away. It was a deeply buried IED, a 500-pound, old Iraqi Air Force bomb left over from the invasion. Somehow the enemy had dug in and wired it to detonate when the tank crossed over. The devastation was horrific: the 72-ton M1A1 tank was completely destroyed. The turret and engine were blown over a hundred yards away from the strike. All crewmembers were killed instantly, discovered several yards away from the vehicle, unrecognizable in some instances.

Several lessons were learned that day, and tactics changed based on that event. We learned that the enemy was always watching and that we could not pattern operations by doing the same thing over and over again. That was a recipe for failure. Second, we learned that remaining stationary at a given location was simply inviting trouble. Finally, we learned that the enemy possessed the skill and expertise to build and emplace catastrophic IEDs in our AO. This was one hell of a way to learn a lesson, tragic to say the least. However, the great soldiers who perished that day did not die in vain. This incident paved the way and served as the catalyst for the Pentagon to immediately start the research, testing, and, ultimately, the fielding of up-armored vehicles and other critical force protection equipment that directly saved the lives of a countless number of soldiers.

Operations Eagle Howan and Eagle Bandit were the offensive or lethal operations that we had to accomplish to achieve stability during the postinvastion period. Frankly, these were the easiest to plan and execute as tasks such as these formed the baseline Mission Essential Task List associated with infantry battalions. These types of missions were our bread and butter. Likewise, in some form or fashion, we trained on these tasks at the squad, platoon, company, and battalion levels prior to the invasion.

The toughest mission or challenge for our battalion staff was figuring out a plan to accomplish the other half of the new mission set: nation-building tasks. These tasks were not clearly defined in the Phase IV OPORD. Basically, we were told to go out into the local towns and villages to conduct assessments of basic utilities, schools, medical clinics, roads, and other infrastructure and draft or initiate projects to address the repair or new construction of these based on community needs. These operations were classified as civil military operations (CMOs), also referred to as nonlethal operations. Furthermore, we were told to recruit, train, and stand-up a local police force and army, known as the Iraqi Civil Defense Corps (ICDC). In order to set the conditions for these operations, our primary task was to establish security and restore some semblance of law and order.

The security piece was easy. We did this by conducting daily presence patrols both mounted and dismounted. During these patrols, company commanders and platoon leaders engaged local citizens in order to identify community leaders, known as spheres of influence, including former town mayors, tribal sheiks, and spiritual leaders, known as imams. Once these leaders were identified in each company AO, weekly council meetings were arranged. We used this forum, similar to town hall meetings, to put out our message and receive feedback from the community about concerns and issues. This proved an excellent forum to gather intelligence about enemy cells operating in the area.

The challenge with getting all this organized was that there was no local government structure. The local, district, provincial, and even national government architecture was destroyed during the invasion. Most of the key leaders, both at the national and local levels, fled to neighboring countries such as Syria, Jordan, Saudi Arabia, and in some cases Iran, depending on their sect. As it stood, we were the government, we were the law, and, as it had been in the past whereby Saddam provided everything to include basic services, it was our job to fill the void. Company commanders served as de facto mayors, police chiefs, and city managers until local government could be reestablished. Our plan was to follow the same path and guidelines established by the CPA, simply at a lower level.

Community outreach lasted for about two weeks and ended around the end of July 2003. Commanders had done an admirable job in reaching out, locating, and identifying key Iraqi leaders. On August 1, we started conducting local council meetings in each company's respective area. On a monthly basis, the battalion held an executive provincial council meeting hosted by Sassaman, which all the local representatives from each village, tribe, and outlying area would attend. At times these meetings were contentious, especially when a mix of Sunni and Shiites showed up. Regardless, security measures were in place so forces could react in the event a tribal fued erupted or other incident occurred. These meetings laid the groundwork for the first democratic-style local elections ever conducted in Iraq.

As part of our task organization, two civil affairs teams were assigned to us, largely comprised of reservists who had been mobilized for the deployment. Reservists brought a unique skill set to the battalion. In their ordinary everyday civilian jobs, they worked as city managers, police officers, and other professionals, which prepared them for executing the same tasks that challenged us. They were truly a combat enabler to us, and we relied heavily on them in planning and executing projects.

By the end of July, new paved roads were being constructed in areas that had never seen asphalt. Schools and medical clinics were being renovated and constructed from the ground up. The majority of these projects were built in Balad, the one city in our AO that actually had law and order. Our battalion used the carrot-and-stick approach. Our message to the masses was "If you, your citizens, or your tribe did not attack us, then projects would come to your area." In the case of Albu Hishma, not one dime was spent in the village the entire time we were there due to the persistent violence. The community and citizens suffered because of it.

This approach enraged the Sunni population and actually backfired on us. A day after we opened one of the first newly constructed primary schools in Baldah, it was attacked and destroyed by explosives, most likely from insurgents residing in Albu Hishma. No matter the circumstance, we stood our ground and simply rebuilt the school. This time, we had the population take ownership and pull security on it.

The other major undertaking was the recruiting, training, and formation of the Iraqi police and army. This obviously would take time because there was no plan or template to follow. We knew what had to be done, but we lacked the expertise to do so. Our first priority was the establishment of the local police force. It was imperative to stand up this organization first so they could provide local law enforcement and take responsibility in enforcing rule of law and investigating local crimes. Likewise, it was better to put Iraqis in charge to do Iraq's bidding. Alpha Company, 1-8 IN was the lead company for this initiative as the city of Balad was our highest priority, known in military terms as the center of gravity, and was their responsibility.

Recognizing this, Cunningham searched his ranks and discovered a soldier who, prior to entering the Army, served as a police officer back home in the United States. Through his own initiative, this soldier contacted his former police colleagues and had them send their police organization and training manuals. This took a couple of weeks to be delivered through the Army postal system. Meanwhile, we continued to recruit and vet all those who volunteered. Once the manuals arrived, Alpha Company used them as reference to form and train the first local police force in theater postinvastion.

By the middle of August, five different police forces were operating on the streets in every major town and village in the AO. These forces were a great asset to have on our side. Moreover, they were able to infiltrate the local population to gather and collect intelligence about the enemy, which led to several captures of valued individuals on our target list.

The recruiting, training, and formation of the ICDC required more detailed planning and coordination. Likewise, it took more assets and resources, which we did not have at our disposal. Finally in late August, directives implemented by the CPA were sent down from higher headquarters and a plan was issued stipulating the requirements. CPA Order Number 29, dated September 3, 2003, established a temporary security and emergency service agency for Iraq to complement operations conducted by coalition military forces. The ICDC was tasked with the following missions: fixed site security, route security, natural disaster aid, general assistance, and joint patrolling with coalition forces. The ICDC was to be composed of 15,000 men, divided among 18 battalions of 846 men. Soldiers serving in the ranks were issued solid brown uniforms and baseball-type caps in red, blue, and black embroidered with "ICDC' in block letters. They were issued and armed with AK-47 assault rifles and were equipped with two jeeps and twelve trucks per battalion. They were recruited and hired under a one-year renewable contract and trained by U.S. forces.

Upon receiving this plan, Sassaman appointed Lieutenant Patrick Bradley, the battalion chemical officer, as the head officer in charge and ICDC coordinator. Bradley did a phenomenal job organizing and standing up our program. Within weeks, more than 800 candidates had been recruited, vetted, and placed in training. To assist with training, the army sent two drill sergeants from Fort Sill, Oklahoma, to serve as trainers and subject-matter experts. They quickly established an aggressive six-week training program of instruction that covered a variety of topics including first aid, marksmanship, drill, and ceremonies. Once these milestones were achieved, the Iraqis received advance training on the conduct of tactical operations to include establishing checkpoints, cordon and search, route security, patrolling, and map reading. After two months of training, these soldiers graduated and were assigned to one of four battalions in our AO.

The first class graduated in August 2003. These soldiers were assigned to Charlie Company, 203rd ICDC Battalion, and based in

Balad. We continued to cycle and train a new class of recruits every eight weeks. By November, four companies were operating in every major city and town, including Ad Duluiyah, Dijayl, and Ishaki. At that point, we recruited and trained a battalion staff and appointed a battalion commander. 1-8 Infantry was light years ahead of every other unit in Iraq. Through the feats of Bradley and his staff of NCOs, we were credited as the first to achieve the full organization, training, and implementation of the first ever ICDC battalion in theater: 203rd ICDC Battalion.

These units immediately joined us on the streets, assisting in conducting joint patrols, raids, and other missions. By December 2003, a new milestone was achieved: Each ICDC company had established its own traffic control points throughout the city and along MSR Tampa, operating independently of U.S. forces. These achievements served as the catalyst for the future formation of the new Iraqi Army. Finally, in June 2004, Multi-National Security Transition Command–Iraq (MNSTC–I) was established by the CPA as the catch-all agency responsible for developing, organizing, training, equipping, and sustaining the Iraqi Security Ministries made up of the Ministry of Defense, Ministry of Interior, and their associated Iraqi Security Forces (ISF; i.e., the military and the Iraqi Police).

Lieutenant General Petraeus was appointed as the head man to lead this organization and serve as the architect for the eventual formation of the new Iraqi Army. He commanded this organization from June 2004 through September 2005. By the time his tenure ended, the Iraqi Army and Police Force totaled more than 600,000 strong. Of that number, five divisions consisting of ninety or more battalions had been trained well enough and were deployed independently throughout Iraq but were mainly concentrated in Baghdad, the strategic center of gravity for Iraq.

Both of these initiatives, police and ICDC efforts, were monumental. It was difficult at times to vet and screen the applicants. The overall intelligence databases had not been fully implemented in theater. Therefore, we relied on instinct and detailed questioning to determine whether we were recruiting the right individuals. In some cases we got it wrong and eventually captured complicit police and army soldiers who days prior were in the ranks training and on our payroll. It was not a failsafe system; we simply did the best we could with the resources and personnel we had.

By the end of August 2003, we had fully grasped the mission and tasks associated with executing SASO. We were still operating with limited resources and manpower, and our daily operation tempo was increasing. This was mainly due to an increase in enemy activity and other factors beyond our control, such as policies and decisions being made by the CPA that affected operations on the ground. It seemed that the majority of decisions favored the Shiite population. Likewise, the CPA issued a policy to remove all weapons from Iraqi homes and started a weapons buyback program whereby local citizens would show up at the gate of our FOB with a truckload of weapons, such as AK-47s, RPGs, and mortar systems, some of which were unserviceable. We had the funds, so we bought them all, ensuring that those weapons were removed from the street and would never be used against us again. At one point, more than two tons of weapons and explosives were consolidated and stored in our FOB; engineers destroyed all of them. Serviceable weapons were issued to police and ICDC soldiers.

But it was impossible to remove all the weapons from the enemy. The whole country was a damn cache; weapons of all sizes, small and large caliber, were readily available on the black market. This weapons removal policy would come back to haunt us later on, especially during the height of the sectarian violence in 2005 and 2006. Local law-abiding citizens, Sunni and Shiite alike, did not have weapons for self-defense. As a result, they could not defend themselves from would-be attackers or the death squads that would show up in the middle of the night to kill them.

Basically it came down to this: postinvasion operations were in flux because we did not have an overall, succinct, unified plan. Resources were scarce except for money; there was plenty of that. When we had a problem we could not solve, we simply threw money at it. In some cases, if we could not win over the population through our actions, we could buy them through projects.

Iraqis were scared about the apparent bleakness of their future. The enemy got out in front of us on their messaging and recruiting efforts. The message sent to the public was that the U.S. military was no longer an army of liberation but rather an army of occupation for the foreseeable future. Based on this message, local, provincial, and national sentiment grew stronger as each week passed. By September 2003, enemy attacks increased dramatically, both in lethality and complexity, throughout Iraq, but most prominently in the Sunni

Triangle. IEDs were killing U.S. soldiers at an alarming rate, so much so that we exceeded 147 combat-related deaths, the benchmark established during our first go-round with Iraq during Operation Desert Storm. Moreover, Saddam had avoided capture and remained at large. His sons, Uday and Qusay, however, were killed on July 22, 2003, in Mosul by soldiers of the famed 101st Airborne Division. The tell-all sign of what was to come was the capture of a Somali national during a predawn raid. Based on intelligence gathered from the interrogation, foreign nationals from across the Middle East were rallying to the cry of "Jihad," destination Iraq.

The Growing Insurgency

At the tactical level, the nature of the war was changing, as evidenced by the spike in enemy attacks, not just in our AO, but throughout Iraq. The most concerning of these attacks was an outbreak of never-before-seen suicide car bomb attacks known as vehicle borne improvised explosive devices (VBIEDs). On August 7, 2003, a car bomb killed eleven people outside the Jordanian embassy in Baghdad. Jordan numbered among the Arab nations attempting to be significantly helpful with the reconstruction. On August 19, suicide bombers destroyed U.N. headquarters in Baghdad, killing envoy Sergio Viera de Mellis and twenty-four others while injuring more than a hundred. On August 24, a car bomb killed three security guards at Ayatollah Mohammed Baqir al-Hakim's office. On August 29, another killed al-Hakim himself and eighty others outside a mosque in the holy city of Najaf, located approximately 60 miles south of Baghdad.

Al-Hakim cofounded the modern Islamic political movement in Iraq in the 1960s. He was seen as dangerous by the ruling Ba'ath regime, largely because of his agitation on behalf of Iraq's majority Shia population (the ruling regime was mostly Sunnis). This led to his arrest in 1972 for promoting Nikah Mut'ah, a legal form of temporary marital relationship in the Shia sect, but he was released shortly thereafter. Due to the intense pressure and frequent arrest by Saddam, he fled to Iran in 1980.

Al-Hakim returned to Iraq in May 2003 following the invasion and soon emerged as one of the most influential Iraqi leaders. At the time of his death, he remained distrustful, but urged Iraqis to abandon violence, at least for the time being, and give the interim government a chance to earn their trust.[5]

The insurgents seemed to be turning their attention from U.S. soldiers, who were proving difficult and dangerous to kill, to the process of reconstruction and reconciliation itself. The choice of technique suggested foreign assistance and involvement. From this point on, a Jordanian al-Qaeda affiliate named Abu Musab al-Zarqawi would gain infamy as the leader of al-Qaeda in Iraq.[6]

Expert analysts, both uniformed military members and civilian, surmised that the suicide VBIED attacks were intended to derail the reconstruction efforts, push the Iraqi population into despair, and exacerbate tension among the ethnicities and allies in Iraq.[7] Based on arrests of suspected insurgents involved in these attacks, it was discovered during interrogations that al-Zarqawi was responsible for these and many other attacks that had been taking place. Furthermore, it was discovered that the insurgency was much more than just a movement to oppose our occupation. Al-Qaeda in Iraq, led by al-Zarqawi, had a strategic objective of reestablishing an Islamic Caliphate, which was last seen during the Ottoman Empire in 1919.[8]

It was a war of ideologies; western democracy pitted against radical Islam or Wahabism. Al-Qaeda in Iraq executed its strategy through "Jihadism." This Sunni-based insurgent group and other Shiite insurgents had organization and substantial financial backing from numerous terrorist states, including Yemen, Syria, Lebanon, and Iran, and terrorist organizations such as Hezbollah, Hamas, and the Taliban. These attacks had second- and third-order effects across the country beyond fueling increased tension between Shiite and Sunni population. The war was taking on a sectarian undertone, no longer focused solely on attacking coalition forces and ridding them from the country. Shiites, recognizing that they were being targeted, started a movement and formed their own militia force to protect their population and other Shia Holy sites. Shiite men by the thousands, mainly in the city of Najaf but elsewhere as well, joined the newly formed militia of radical cleric Muqtada al-Sadr, the emerging and eventual leader and political voice of Shia opposition.[9] Ultimately, the Shia militia would take up arms against us, further expanding and complicating the problem set.

From my vantage point at the tactical level, it seemed that all indicators signifying the evolving insurgency were missed by senior leadership, specifically the civilian leadership that occupied the

Pentagon. On June 18, 2003, Secretary of Defense Rumsfeld dismissed the notion altogether, basically stating that the enemy was a pocket of "dead-enders" trying to reconstitute the country in their image.[10]

Granted, in the two months following the invasion this was true; it was amateur hour. The enemy was nothing more than peasants trying to earn a dollar to feed their families. We quickly disposed of them and removed these amateurs, who often were leftovers from the battlefield. Over time, as attacks increased and the insurgency gained momentum, Rumsfeld remained in denial and dismissed the notion, as evident by a comment he made on March 14, 2004, whereby he dismissed the insurgency altogether stating that, "any remaining violence is due to thugs, gangs, and terrorists."[11] This statement was patently false.

The insurgency continued to grow, as evident from an intense battle waged two weeks later in April 2003 between Sunni hardcore insurgents and U.S. Marines in Fallujah. The event that triggered the siege of Fallujah was the killing of four U.S. contractors in the middle of town. These contractors worked for the security company then known as Blackwater Worldwide and were conducting security operations when their patrol was ambushed by insurgents. After the ambush, insurgents grabbed the four corpses and paraded them through the streets, similar to the events in Mogadishu in 1993. The bodies were taken to a nearby bridge that crossed over the Euphrates River and suspended from it for the world to see. These gruesome images were captured and broadcasted over every major news network.

During the succeeding battle, Marines fought hard for two weeks in what really was the most intense fighting in the war. Going house to house, block by block, they were able to root out and kill or capture the majority of insurgents. Death and destruction littered the streets. Embedded reporters and journalists captured the carnage. The broadcasted images of dead civilians and battle damage in Fallujah triggered solidarity uprisings across Sunni areas. Because of this, the battle was suspended.

This battle and events leading up to it served notice to all, specifically to leaders in Washington, D.C., that the insurgency in Iraq was legitimate. Even after the battle of Fallujah had ended, however, there were those who were still not convinced, some of which were military leaders on the ground in Iraq. One of them was Lieutenant General Ricardo Sanchez, once the top U.S. commander in Baghdad, who in late 2003 was still describing the brewing insurgency as "strategically and operationally insignificant."[12]

I had briefed Sanchez on a couple of occasions during visits he made to our FOB. The only thing I recall him telling us was to "stay after these bastards and keep taking the fight to 'em," a direct quote I captured in my journal after the visit. There was never an acknowledgement that we were fighting an insurgency.

Contrary to belief, the enemy we were fighting was a well-organized, determined foe motivated by a radical ideology, not simply a "gang of thugs." The battle for Fallujah simply validated that our senior civilian leadership in the beltway was out of touch with reality on the ground. Even before the invasion occurred, the White House and Rumsfeld were warned in advance by General Eric Shinseki, Army Chief of Staff, that this war and in particular the postinvastion phase would be a challenge and massive undertaking requiring far more U.S. troops and resources than currently allotted. On February 25, 2003, testifying before the Senate Armed Services Committee, Shinseki stated:

"Something on the order of several hundred thousand soldiers, are probably, you know, a figure that would be required. We're talking about post hostilities control over a piece of geography that's fairly significant with the kinds of ethnic tensions that could lead to other problems. And so, it takes significant ground force presence to maintain safe and secure environments to ensure that the people are fed, that water is distributed, all the normal responsibilities that go along with administering a situation like this."[13]

This estimate was spot-on. However, Shinseki's comments fell on deaf ears as his testimony was dismissed immediately by Rumsfeld's office. On February 27, 2003, Paul Wolfowitz, deputy defense secretary, went on the offensive and stated publicly "that the recent estimate by General Shinseki was wildly off the mark." The smear campaign continued on March 19, 2003, when a senior Pentagon official dismissed Shinseki's comments as "bullshit from a Clintonite enamored of using the Army for peacekeeping and nation-building and not winning wars."[14]

The political infighting at the national level amongst top decision makers had begun to impact operations on the ground throughout Iraq. This bickering and lack of understanding by senior leadership was evident down to the lowest private. They clearly knew whom we were fighting. The inability to make the paradigm shift from force-on-force combat to fighting the emerging insurgency was not lost on the Army's tactical leaders. Moreover, operational-level leaders who disagreed with Rumsfeld's assessment understood that speaking ground truth about the war was not the key to success or career progression based on the rebuke of senior leaders in the Army. Therefore, key leaders often remained silent. The last dissenting voice in the Army was Shinseki. After speaking the bald and unvarnished truth in 2003, he was sanctioned into retirement. In 2006, Shinseki was vindicated with the approval and deployment of the "surge" force.

All the while, as this political bickering and strategic chess game played out, operations were in full swing in Balad, and the Fighting Eagles were getting after it. Our leaders knew that despite frustrations and resource shortcomings, we still had a mission to do. We knew there was little we could impact at that level, other than voicing concerns and needs to our superiors.

As the insurgency was evolving, we had yet to witness any of these spectacular car bombs or VBIEDs in our AO. Clearly, however, we were aware of the threat and took every precaution to guard against it. To mitigate the threat of such attacks, we instituted an armed watch and observation on critical holy sites and other infrastructure deemed valuable throughout our AO. The most important of these sites was the Shiite holy shrine known as the Sayyid Mohammed Mosque located on the eastern edge of downtown Balad.

Sayyid Mohammed, son of Imam Ali Alhadi, was born in the city of Sayra near Medina in 228 BC. At age thirty-four, he traveled to Samarra to see his father and brother. On his way back, he became gravely ill and died at the site of the mosque that now houses his tomb. It was believed amongst Shiites that he would be the next holy Shiite Imam succeeding his father. Shiites from around the Middle East participate in an annual pilgrimage to visit and pay homage to him. Following the invasion, the number of pilgrims who came to visit was drastically reduced out of fear of violence like what had occurred earlier in Najaf.

Our days in August 2003 were consumed by constant patrolling throughout our sector, mainly along MSR Tampa. Sassaman and I spent anywhere from twelve to sixteen hours a day outside the wire patrolling, sometimes with subordinate companies and sometimes independently. Essentially, the battalion was conducting a movement to contact; in other words, we were trying to seek them out in order to destroy them. By our presence alone, we were tempting, almost begging, the enemy to attack us. In a sense we felt invincible as we traversed the hinterlands and urban areas in our heavily armored BFVs. If nothing else, they were intimidating to the population and sent a clear message to the masses that this was one unit you did not want to mess with. The real intent and goal was that we Fighting Eagles were going to stop the insurgency before it could get started.

Civil military operations continued at a steady pace. Every week we were hosting and conducting grand opening ceremonies for new schools and clinics. Likewise, Iraqi police training and ICDC basic training was progressing better than expected. These events showed signs of success and provided a light at the end of the tunnel. As leaders we knew that training a capable police force and army, one that could take over security operations, was our ticket out of Iraq. However, the battalion had other worries and distractions that diverted our attention and resources away from this vital nation-building effort.

Two enemy events still plagued the battalion and were increasing. Mortar attacks on LSA Anaconda, in addition to IEDs, increased at a rate of three to four attacks per week, and direct-fire ambush attacks along MSR Tampa and other routes occurred at a rate of about eight to ten attacks per day. What concerned us most was the spike in IED attacks and direct-fire ambushes. Somehow it seemed the enemy was emboldened to carry out these attacks. Moreover, it seemed like there was an influx of enemy fighters, ones who were better trained and more experienced. Attacks had become more complex in nature and were more lethal than previous attacks. The spike in enemy activity became evident to me while leading a mounted patrol on ASR Linda.

On the night of August 17, 2003, I received a call from Major Troy Perry, our brigade operations officer. He informed me that the brigade had received actionable intelligence that a couple of high-value targets (HVTs) with close ties to Saddam were hiding out in an isolated home in our AO. Furthermore, the mission to raid the home was passed off to a special operations task force known as Task Force 20 (TF 20). It was customary in theater for TF 20 to execute these priority missions depending on the value of the individuals involved. Priority targets were made famous in a deck of cards called "The Top 52 Bad Guys" (the ace of spades was HVT #1: Saddam Hussein).

Our mission was to serve as the supporting effort and provide the outer cordon and security so TF 20 could execute the raid on the house. I was told to get to LSA Anaconda right away and link up with leaders from TF 20 for planning and execution of these time-sensitive targets. I informed Sassaman of the orders received; he acknowledged and I quickly organized a patrol to escort me to LSA Anaconda. Some of the customary elements that I patrolled with were not available. As a result, I had to organize an ad hoc patrol, which basically meant taking troops available right then and there who could quickly ready themselves for movement and get me to LSA Anaconda within thirty minutes so I could conduct this time-sensitive planning with TF 20. Soldiers of our HHC who were based on LSA Anaconda and other elements from our Scout Platoon happened to be there at the time.

I quickly selected the group, assembled them, and issued mission orders. Within ten minutes, we were exiting the FOB gate. One of the critical tactical decisions I made was that we would travel along ASR Linda with all vehicles using white lights (headlights on). I felt this was necessary at the time based on two factors. First, speed was needed to get us there quickly due to the time-sensitive nature of the operation and the priority targets we were going after. Second, this was not the group that I regularly patrolled with; as such they were not accustomed to the way I fought and maneuvered with my organic scout element. Another factor that led to this decision was the fact that a patrol from our HHC had preceded us by approximately ten to fifteen minutes. My thinking was that the route was proofed and enemy contact was not as likely.

I was the third vehicle in the order of movement traveling in my BFV. In front of me were two scout gun Humvees, and behind me were other elements from our HHC, consisting of a mix of cargo trucks and Humvees. As we headed east at a quick pace, I radioed ahead to the patrol from HHC and asked for an update on the route and if they had seen anything suspicious. The reply was negative: the route was clear. Within minutes, though, a frantic call came across the radio, "IED! IED! IED!" followed by an immediate explosion. The scout Humvee in front of me was hit. I witnessed the explosion and saw a bright flash from my commander's hatch on my vehicle. The scout vehicle came to a stop.

I ordered all other elements to scan south and immediately open fire to suppress the wood line, being that this was the most likely area from which the enemy had detonated the IED. A heavy barrage of .50-caliber machine gun, 7.62-mm coax machine gun, and 25-mm HE fire was laid down across the canal into the wood line, sparking a fairly large brush fire. We also fired illumination flares in the area so we could clearly see the kill zone and identify and kill insurgents fleeing the area.

The suppressive fire was necessary to provide a window to reach the injured scouts, treat them, and evacuate them if required. The suppressive fire continued for at least twenty minutes. Meanwhile, Brown had arrived, having departed FOB Eagle minutes behind us. He rushed over to the damaged Humvee and started treating the two wounded scout soldiers. Both soldiers had shrapnel wounds to their legs and arms, and both were conscious and talking, a great sign that their wounds were not life threatening.

It was our SOP to medically evacuate all wounded soldiers by air, referred to as a MEDEVAC. Based on the first report of casualties, the aircraft was called and issued a 9-line MEDEVAC request (a standard radio report for requesting medical support). Within twenty minutes of the initial blast, the aircraft arrived. Soldiers from Bravo Company and HHC quickly secured and established the landing zone. The two scouts were escorted to the aircraft and flown to the combat support hospital (CSH) located at LSA Anaconda.

As they departed, we executed a quick search of the area to see if we had in fact killed the attackers and if any evidence was left behind. No bodies were found; the only piece of evidence was the electrical wire they had used to command detonate the IED. The wire ran from the road, south across the canal, and into the wood line—exactly where we had suspected. Based on our initial barrage of fire, either the insurgents were really fast and escaped the scene or they were wounded and escaped. The one good thing that came from this was that the heavy vegetated wood line was completely burned down from the fire started by the tracer rounds we had fired. This meant that it was highly unlikely that this area would be used to perpetrate another attack like this one. There was no available cover or concealment for them to use.

From there we consolidated the patrol and continued movement without incident along ASR Linda to LSA Anaconda. Upon arriving at LSA Anaconda, I conducted a link up with the TF 20 operations officer. He provided details about the raid to be executed the following morning and outlined what our tasks and responsibilities were. The overall plan was fairly simple: Alpha Company would secure and seal off the outer cordon, and TF 20 would arrive by helicopter, fast rope in on the target house, execute the raid, kill or capture the targets, and then move out and return to base. We arranged for a link-up at our FOB for execution and then departed LSA Anaconda and headed back to FOB Eagle for mission planning with Alpha Company.

We returned to the base using the alternate route of MSR Tampa without incident. Upon arrival, I was informed that the two wounded scouts were alive—good news to say the least. The bad news was that one of them, Private First Class Joseph Kashnow, had suffered injuries more severe than originally suspected. The shrapnel wound sustained to his lower right leg would require amputation below the knee. He would soon be flown to Landsthul Regional Medical Center in Germany for this procedure, followed by further evacuation to a treatment facility in the United States.

The other wounded soldier would stay at the CSH for a couple of weeks for recovery; ultimately he was returned to duty.

We got lucky that night. It could have been far worse. These soldiers and others on the mission could have been killed. Until then, catastrophic IEDs had not migrated that far north. In this case, the IED was constructed out of a 60-mm mortar round packed with less than 8 pounds of explosives. The quick reaction by the scouts to immediately stop upon hearing the alert over the radio allowed the engine compartment to absorb the brunt of the blast. A direct hit underneath them could have been fatal.

Upon return to FOB Eagle, I immediately assembled the staff and provided them and Sassaman a summary of the mission we would execute in support of TF 20. We had twelve hours until execution. Being that the target house was in Alpha Company's sector, I called Cunningham and had him walk the short distance over to the headquarters to be a part of the planning. While the staff continued to work the mission analysis and course of action development, Sassaman and I stepped out of the TOC and went to his office in order to discuss the IED attack that had occurred during our trip.

As we stepped into his office, I could sense that he was very upset, and understandably so. We had just suffered our first serious casualty following the initial invasion. Sassaman wanted to know one thing. He pointedly asked me why it was that the patrol was traveling in white lights as we maneuvered along ASR Linda. I, too, was pretty shaken up about the event and its outcome. I actually had tears in my eyes, more out of frustration that anything else. I told him first and foremost that I took full responsibility for what happened. I told him that I made a command decision as the patrol leader to use white lights because the group was an ad hoc element from three different subordinate organizations that had never patrolled together with me and were not accustomed to the tactics, techniques, and procedures I used while traveling with my assigned scout team. I also cited other factors influencing the decision. First was the fact that speed was of importance based on the time-sensitive nature of the target we were going after and the organization (TF 20) that we were supporting. Second, I added that the route was previously traveled without any reported incidents minutes before we departed and that enemy contact was not likely.

But all of my reasoning was falling on deaf ears. Sassaman was not having any of it. He essentially ordered me to never disobey one of his orders again or else I could depart the battalion.

There were times throughout the deployment that I did not see eye to eye on everything we were doing operationally. This was one of them. Regardless, I would never challenge the decision in front of our subordinates. We would usually go behind closed doors, I would share my opinions, and then I would support whatever decision was made. In this specific case, I felt that Sassaman was way too close to the fight, and too upset about the wounded soldier. Commanders and leaders alike are supposed to be upset and concerned for our soldiers' well-being. However, this was a gray area, and I think he let his emotions get the best of him. Rather than challenge him on it, I acknowledged and let it go. The one thing that I should have mentioned, but that I applied the old adage of "discretion is the greater part of valor" to, was the fact that our battalion did not have a standing policy on the forbidden use of white lights. The theater and environment was still immature as such we were working to develop sound tactics, techniques and procedures (TTPs) and had yet to settle on a definitive technique, as this one.

On numerous patrols I made while conducting battlefield circulation, I would often see patrols operating at night in white lights while patrolling MSR Tampa. Upon review of this, it was acknowledged by Pfutze, C. Co 1-8 IN commander, that the mission dictated whether to use white lights. He also stated that when his forces were operating along MSR Tampa, they used white lights the majority of the time due to the congestion created by Iraqi civilian traffic. It goes to show that this was simply a technique that units could use or not, though it was never a standing order or policy in our brigade or otherwise. The white lights issue would resurface twenty-four hours later, this time with the role reversed and Sassaman as the patrol leader.

Planning for the TF 20 mission wrapped up around 0500 hours on August 18, 2003. Alpha Company linked up with special operators from TF 20, and collectively they staged out of our FOB until execution time at approximately 1000 hours. At 0930, elements from Alpha Company infiltrated the objective area and established the outer cordon. There was one late change: it was determined through satellite imagery and other reconnaissance assets that the target house could not be accessed by air due to thick vegetation that surrounded it. Also, it was discovered that a brick wall surrounded the house. The plan was adjusted, and the TF 20 operators that were to fast rope in would now ride in the back of one of A. Co 1-8 IN's BFVs.

The BFV would drive up to the target house and breach the wall, and the special operators would dismount and execute the raid. At 0955, conditions were set. Special operations helicopters known commonly as little birds were flying overhead in circles, providing close in fire support and sniper cover. At precisely 1000 hours, the BFV carrying the TF 20 raid team slammed through the wall and actions on the objective were underway. Sassaman and I took up a vantage point from our BFVs on a nearby bridge that overlooked the target house below and provided excellent observation of the operation. Once the team was inside the house, explosions could be heard, followed by short bursts of gunfire. This lasted for approximately two minutes and then TF 20 operators exited the house. The mission was complete. It was a "dry hole:" the intended targets were not there. There were a couple of enemy casualties, armed bodyguards or associates of the targets who posed a threat and were killed in action.

Based on my observation, having jointly planned this operation and subsequently observed its execution, the special-forces soldiers from TF 20 executed with skill and precision; clearly they were masters of their craft. As the dust settled, there was no time to relax or reflect to analyze lessons learned from the operation, in particular the attack that occurred the night prior. As for the enemy that attacked us, based upon the tactics they employed with some success, I ascertained that this was a new breed of fighter. We were no longer being engaged merely by local farmers. All previous attacks against us had been ineffective, but these were no amateurs. The number one question still to be answered was not why we were attacked, but rather by whom. Was this enemy part of the emerging insurgency?

Maj. Darron L. Wright, Operations Officer for 1-8 IN, back briefs key leaders of
4th Infantry Division on the mission for Operation Ivy Blizzard, December 2003.

Lt. Col. Darron L. Wright hands candy to a local Iraqi child during a visit to the Taji Qada
Council Meeting, Taji, Iraq, September 2009.

ABOVE 3rd Brigade, 4th Infantry Division readies for movement north into Iraq, April 2003. Picture taken in the staging area in desert in Kuwait, April 2003.

LEFT Destroyed Iraqi Army Vehicles lay in ruin on the side of MSR Tampa. The vehicles were destroyed by advancing coalition forces, April 2003.

BELOW A picture of the Said Muhammad Mosque ("The Mother of All Battles Mosque"), located in Baghdad, taken from above during a night reconnaissance flight, May 2010.

Lt. Col. Darron L. Wright conducts a key leader engagement at the Said Muhammad Mosque, October 2009.

Maj. Gen. Ahmad, Commander of the 6th Iraqi Army Division, and Col. John Norris, Commander of 4-2 SBCT, walk together while executing combined offensive operations in Abu Ghraib, October 2009.

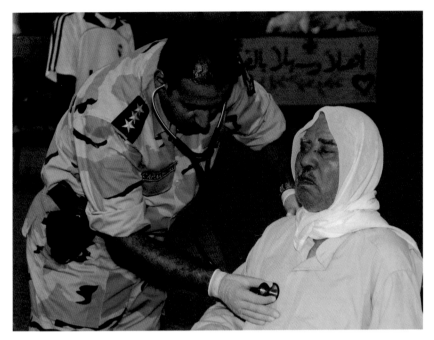

A local Iraqi Army physician examines an Iraqi man during a combined medical engagement in Abu Ghraib, June 2010.

Iraqi citizens take cover outside of Baghdad during the initial invasion, April 2003.

Local Iraqi citizens cheer on U.S. Troops as they enter Baghdad during the initial invasion, April 2003. *(U.S. Army, 2003)*

3rd Infantry Division Troops continue the advance into Baghdad, April 2003. *(U.S. Army, 2003)*

LEFT An Iraqi male surrenders to invading U.S. Forces as they continue the advance to Baghdad, April 2003. *(U.S. Army, 2003)*

BELOW An Iraqi mother takes cover in a ditch with her children as coalition forces continue the attack into Baghdad, April 2003. *(U.S. Army, 2003)*

RIGHT A destroyed Iraqi BMP smolders on the side of the highway as coalition forces continue the attack into Baghdad, April 2003. *(U.S. Army, 2003)*

RIGHT An M-88 Recovery Vehicle destroys a mural of Saddam Hussein during the initial wave of the invasion, April 2003. *(U.S. Army, 2003)*

ABOVE Landmines put in place by Iraqi Army cover the road in an attempt to stop invading coalition forces, April 2003.

LEFT U.S. Troops discover a billboard of Saddam Hussein celebrating the September 11 attacks, April 2003.

LEFT U.S. Forces capture gold-plated AK-47s during the initial invasion, April 2003.

This bombed-out palace was located at FOB Prosperity, Baghdad, Iraq, November 2005.

Picture of the "fugas" explosions set in place by 1-8 IN during combat operations in Albu Hishma, November 2003.

That very question would be answered later that evening. On August 18, 2003, at approximately 2100 hours, Sassaman and I were conducting battlefield circulation on our way to the town of Ishaki approximately 8 kilometers north or twenty minutes away. We were heading there to check on a platoon from Charlie Company, which we had sent to gain control of the area as violence was on the increase. That morning, we had picked up a journalist and his cameraman from ABC News. He was sent down to us from brigade to embed with us for the next five days to cover our operations. Sassaman invited him to join us for the patrol that evening.

It was a crystal clear night with a bright moon. Our patrol consisted of two BFVs and two scout Humvees. I was the lead vehicle that night, followed by the two scout gun trucks in the middle. Sassaman was trailing in his BFV. We departed FOB Eagle and proceeded south on ASR Amy, a route that led directly to MSR Tampa. As we turned on ASR Amy, I got the call to go to white lights as the lead vehicle in order to spot IEDs that were planted along the route. My first thought was, "Are you kidding me?" Less than twenty-four hours earlier, I had my ass chewed out over this very issue. But, rather than challenge the boss over the radio, I did as ordered.

The trip along ASR Amy was uneventful. As we approached the intersection of ASR Amy and MSR Tampa, known to us as Check Point 5, I noticed that there was not a lot of civilian traffic out on the road. This was unusual.

We proceeded by turning north on MSR Tampa and were about a kilometer away from the gate of FOB Rock. Near there is a small marketplace that parallels both sides of the road. The market is made of a couple of convenient stores, a restaurant, and a lot of roadside fruit stands. On most days, the market is crowded, even at night. This particular evening it was deserted. I informed my crew over the radio to be alert. I sensed that things were not right. Next I called Sassaman and asked him if he had noticed what I was witnessing.

That's when the explosion hit.

We were under attack. My BFV was rocked by a large explosion. "I fucking knew it!" I exclaimed. We were struck by an IED.

"Son of a bitch!" I yelled out loud. The explosion was followed by an intense barrage of machine-gun fire that persisted for at least ten minutes.

This was serious shit. I immediately asked my crewmembers if they were hit. Frustration combined with adrenaline was setting in because I could not talk to anyone over our internal radio. Our communications net had been knocked out. My driver, Francis, was scratched by shrapnel. An additional passenger that night who was riding in the back yelled to me that it was an RPG that struck us, but that he was not hit. At that time, 25-mm ammunition specifically armor-piercing (AP) rounds stored in the ready box began cooking off; this was even more dangerous than the RPG hitting us. The RPG had penetrated the left side of my BFV and struck the ammunition boxes that contained extra AP ammo.

The machine-gun fire continued at a steady pace. The halon fire suppression system inside the vehicle was activated, spraying halon everywhere. My eyes were burning as if they were on fire from the gunpowder and halon. Meanwhile, the machine-gun fire persisted. All the while, I was yelling at my gunner, Blackwell, to scan left and engage. "Let's kill these bastards!" I exclaimed.

Blackwell noticed a couple of insurgents running through the field where the enemy fire was coming from and immediately opened up on them with 25-mm high-explosive rounds. I began to engage from atop my commander's hatch with my M-4, a 5.56-mm carbine, a standard-issued weapon carried by the majority of soldiers.

I went through five magazines pretty quickly. Blackwell continued to engage. The fire from our 25-mm cannon was so intense I could see the barrel glowing. Blackwell yelled that we were running low on ammo, switched over to our 7.62-coax machine gun, and continued to engage the fleeing enemy.

As I was firing from my M-4, I heard some of our scouts yelling from the rear, "Man down! Man down!" Someone was hit. I gave instructions for Blackwell to continue engaging and, if there was nothing to shoot at, to continue to scan and maintain security. I dismounted the BFV and headed over to the wounded soldier.

One of the scout drivers, Private First Class Larry Bagley, HHC, 1-8 IN Battalion, had been shot in the neck and was bleeding profusely (he returned to Iraq in November 2009 to continue to fight with us). As I approached the scene, I noticed that fellow scouts and Sassaman were applying treatment. Another scout had been hit as well, shot in the leg, though this wound was not as serious. Fellow scouts trained as combat lifesavers were treating him as well.

All the while, other soldiers and scout gunners continued to engage the enemy. After approximately ten minutes, the firing ceased. At that point, we established a Landing Zone and called in a MEDEVAC for our two casualties. The scouts established the LZ and within twenty minutes, the aircraft was on sight and the soldiers were evacuated to the CSH located at LSA Anaconda.

At 2200 hours, we placed our BFVs in overwatch positions, and the remainder of the group formed a fighting wedge and maneuvered across the median and into the field where the enemy had attacked us. Either the enemy was dead or wounded, or else they had been wounded and escaped, but they were no longer firing at us. We searched the area for two or three hours.

We had called for attack aviation support as the fight ensued. The Apache helicopters did not make it for a while because they were busy supporting other troops in contact. But when they arrived, they circled the entire area, to no avail. Having them overhead was a good thing. We continued the search, and I came across a couple of RPGs and a few extra rounds that had been left behind. What stood out about these rounds is that they were new. As a matter of fact, they were armor-piercing rounds, which had never been seen in our area.

At that moment, our scouts were yelling to us: they had located a couple of trails of blood that led to an irrigation canal. We knew then we had wounded some of them. We followed the blood trail, but discovered no one. From there we policed up the enemy weapons and departed the scene. Rather than going to visit the Charlie Company soldiers as originally planned, we returned back to headquarters.

Upon arriving at the base, I inspected my vehicle along with everyone else to survey the battle damage. It was in fact an RPG that had hit us. A small hole was discovered in the side skirt where it entered, and inside was all the damage. The round penetrated the entire track. As we traced its path, it had traveled right under our feet maybe 2 inches below where the gunner and I sat. We were lucky that the round did not hit up front or more toward the rear where my driver and our passenger sat.

Upon further inspection, all of the extra stored ammunition was completely destroyed and had cooked off. We were lucky that the rounds did not strike one of us.

Our luck continued when we learned that the soldiers who were wounded would be okay. One, suffering from a neck wound, would be evacuated from theater; the other would ultimately be returned to duty. Bagley, after raising hell during his recovery to get back to his platoon, showed up at the FOB out of the blue in November 2003. We welcomed him with open arms.

The following day, we conducted an AAR of the attack, and we surmised that this was a complex ambush, well-coordinated, and most likely executed by at least five to seven Sunni al-Qaeda in Iraq-affiliated insurgents. These were true professionals who had planned this engagement for some time. It was obvious that they had coordinated for no locals to be in the area, and they had spotters tied in to alert them when we were coming. Moreover they were well resourced, as evident by the armor-piercing RPG rounds they fired at us. And, it was evident that these guys could shoot accurately and hit what they aimed at. This entire attack was captured on film by the journalists who accompanied us. The attack aired the following morning on the ABC News program "Good Morning America."

Two days later, we were informed by local nationals that a couple of men had died in the Balad hospital of apparent gunshot wounds. They had been brought there on the night of the attack. Based on the complex nature both in planning and execution of this attack, we knew the insurgency had arrived in the Eagle AO.

CHAPTER 5
AN INSURGENCY TAKES ROOT

August 2003–March 2004

❝ Whenever death may surprise us, let it be welcome if our battle cry
has reached even one receptive ear and another hand reaches out to
take up arms. ❞

Ernesto "Che" Guevara, Cuban Revolutionary

As we entered September 2003, insurgent attacks continued to mount,
as did the U.S. death toll. Enemy mortar attacks persisted against LSA
Anaconda and migrated to our base. We were being attacked by
mortars at least twice a week. On one occasion, I came close to being
added to the casualty statistics.

On Saturday, September 13, 2003, Sassaman and I returned from
patrolling all day and settled in to watch college football on the
Armed Forces Network broadcast, which was piped into our
headquarters via satellite. The Texas Longhorns were playing the
Arkansas Razorbacks. The game was going great; Texas had taken

the lead by half time. I was pumped up and doing all I could to will the Longhorns to victory.

All of the sudden, the FOB was rocked by an explosion and the television screen turned black. It was a mortar attack (clearly, the insurgents were not sports or college football enthusiasts). I was pissed: This time it was personal. We quickly donned our equipment, rushed out to our BFVs, and within minutes were out of the gate rushing to the point of origin. Sassaman took the lead, followed by two scout Humvees, my BFV in trail. Based on a radar bearing, the point of origin was north of us. In order to save time and increase the likelihood of capturing these bastards, we took a shortcut across an open field via an unimproved dirt trail. The speeding vehicles in front of us were kicking up quite a bit of dust. My BFV driver, Specialist Matthew Francis, complained that his driver's scope was impaired due to the thick dust. In the next instant, I felt the vehicle plummeting into a 20-foot-deep ditch. Somehow we lost visual with the lead vehicles, which had made an abrupt right turn, avoiding the obstacle.

As we entered the ditch, I felt the back end of the vehicle coming forward. It seemed like it was happening all in slow motion. We flipped completely over and were upside down inside the ditch. I was riding in the commander's hatch and was fortunate enough to have gotten down inside the turret, avoiding being thrown out and crushed by the vehicle. But we were not out of danger yet. As we were lying upside down, I yelled to my crew and asked them if they were okay. Everyone was fine, but now we were faced with the challenge of getting out.

We were trapped. We could smell fuel. I could see sparks flying from the radio. This was a "face of death" experience. Through some miracle of God, I managed to find a small space of light underneath me. We were racing against time. We needed to evacuate the vehicle before it burst into flames. My driver, Specialist Jonathan Brown, and I managed to get our equipment off, and I was able to dig out enough room for us to crawl out of my hatch to safety. Once out, Brown crawled up on the back and opened the troop door, and we were able to extract Francis from his driver's compartment. Once we were all out, we found ourselves alone in enemy territory, armed with only our M-4 carbines and one magazine; the rest of our ammunition was inside the vehicle. To add to our desperation, we had lost all radio communications and could not contact anyone. At that point, we formed a perimeter and waited for our forces to show up. We hoped the others would realize that we were no longer following them and that we were in trouble.

After about thirty minutes, Sassaman and the scouts showed up. We were lucky that night. We survived another near-death experience, which, in this case, was self-inflicted. After they arrived, we climbed aboard Sassaman's BFV, and he escorted us back to FOB Eagle so we could be examined by our physician assistant, Major Wayne Slicton. Bolyard and the other scout section stayed on site and secured the vehicle until recovery vehicles arrived. Maj. Rob Gwinner led the recovery team to the site and extracted the vehicle back to FOB Eagle.

In the end, my crew and I were all okay and returned to duty. The worst part of the whole night was that we did not capture or kill the insurgent mortar team. They lived to fight another day. To rub salt into the wound, the Texas Longhorns blew the lead in the second half and lost to Arkansas. My morale meter dipped to an all-time low.

In most cases, insurgent attacks were ineffective, though at times the enemy got lucky. Every time we were attacked, we would return counterfire with 120-mm organic mortars. We attempted on several occasions to call for fire and engage the enemy with 155-mm fires from our sister field artillery battalion, only to be denied by brigade headquarters.

These larger-caliber rounds packed a serious punch. Moreover, they were faster and more accurate and had a larger kill radius (approximately 150 meters [492 feet] compared to 75 meters [246 feet] for a 120-mm round). The denial to use these assets by brigade headquarters was based on the fear of causing collateral damage to nearby homes and other structures. These denials happened on other occasions, too, even when troops were in direct contact in rural areas without homes or structures. We were well within the ROE to fire, only to be denied. Ultimately we became seriously frustrated over the lack of support. As a result, Sassaman made a command decision that we would only fire our organic mortars, assets that we controlled and would no longer request support from brigade.

In my opinion, having been on the receiving end of these denials, the real issue at hand was that Rudesheim did not favor our aggressive stance and was reluctant at best to provide critical enabler support when required. This was simply another friction point in the ongoing strife between him and Sassaman. Soldiers suffered because of the conflict between them.

Our standard operating procedure for employing counterfire was for every one round the enemy shot at us, the enemy was to get twenty-four in return, sometimes more depending on whether incoming mortar fire persisted. To initiate the counterfire, we relied on sophisticated radar systems located on LSA Anaconda. These systems would pinpoint the location of enemy mortar fire, and then the location would be sent instantly to us so we could input the data and process the call for fire. As the counterfire was being processed, we would dispatch units to the suspected location to close with and destroy the enemy mortar team in the event they were fleeing the scene. Early on we were successful in killing or capturing a lot of these teams. We ridded the area of them, as these were not hardcore, well-trained insurgents.

That all changed in September when insurgents traveled from outside our AO and began attacking us on a regular basis. The enemy become a lot smarter, too; they had gotten the drill of shooting mortars down to a science. It was a battle drill for them. They would quickly erect their mortar tube(s), fire off a few rounds, and then displace to avoid counterfire or capture. On a couple of occasions, the enemy coordinated simultaneous mortar attacks against us from three different locations. It was likely that a spotter dispatched somewhere with eyes on our FOB to ensure accurate fires.

An old Army adage states that there are no atheists in combat. This could not be truer. During one particular mortar attack, an enemy mortar round had struck the makeshift chapel located behind our headquarters building. It just so happened that Protestant services were taking place when the attack occurred. On hand in the chapel were a few soldiers, including myself. When the round impacted the chapel, we could feel the shock and impact on the roof. We all shouted "Incoming!" and sought cover. Several mortar rounds impacted our FOB; however, the one that hit the chapel had no effect. There was no explosion as we had anticipated. Once the barrage stopped, Chaplain Leaf Espeland, a few other soldiers, and I stepped outside to view the damage. What we saw shocked us. Sitting beside the right side of the chapel was an unexploded mortar round. It was the mortar round that had just hit the building. Turns out that, perhaps through divine intervention, it was a dud. Word about this miracle quickly spread throughout our FOB. To everyone's amazement, the chapel was full of soldiers attending church for the rest of our tour.

On most occasions, such attacks were ineffective; however, in a couple instances the enemy got lucky, inflicting a couple of serious casualties, even though they had yet to kill anyone. That would change in the new year.

Recognizing that the insurgency was in full bloom, our battalion countered by turning up the heat and intensity throughout the AO. Bottom line: We were going to seek out and destroy the insurgency before it truly gained momentum in AO Eagle.

At the direction of Sassaman, the battalion adopted and applied new tactics in prosecuting the fight. Our goal, based on guidance given to us by division commander Odierno during a visit in September 2003, was to "increase the lethality." Furthermore, we were instructed by Sanchez to "be aggressive and go after these guys, with a purpose to deny sanctuary to insurgents and ensure that any momentum gained was halted."

Upon receiving this guidance from Sanchez and Odierno, we took and applied the literal translation. First, to counter the prominent IED threat, we devised and implemented a plan whereby our engineers would clear the shoulders of every major route we traveled. In doing so, they utilized heavy armored D-7 bulldozers to clear out all vegetation, trees, and any other obstacles in our path, pushing them back from the road at least 50 meters (164 feet) on both sides. The enemy would often hide in the thick brush close to the road to carry out attacks. Clearing roadsides made this no longer possible. We did the same thing to counter mortar attacks.

At every known or previous point of origin, i.e., where the mortar was fired from, we removed vegetation and trees from that area. In addition, we dropped 500-pound Air Force precision-guided bombs at each one of these sights. These bombs assisted us in clearing operations, destroying everything in a 250- to 500-meter (820- to 1,640-foot) radius. Moreover, it sent a strong message to the perpetrators that we meant business and would respond with more than just counterfire. The enemy could no longer hide, as the targeted areas were wide open now and did not afford cover and concealment.

One of the most drastic measures we took was detaining tribal sheiks. This mainly occurred in Albu Hishma. We had warned all tribal sheiks weeks in advance that if they did not stop the attacks originating from their villages and give up the individuals responsible, we would arrest them until the insurgents came forward and turned themselves in. In late September 2003, mortar attacks originating in Albu Hishma began to spike; these attacks targeted LSA Anaconda and our headquarters. We had finally had enough.

Sassaman and I organized a patrol and traveled to Albu Hishma accompanied by a platoon from Bravo Company with the sole purpose of detaining Sheik Ahmed Abdul Latif. Sheik Ahmed was the tribal sheik for this village and had been warned on numerous occasions to stop the attacks. Upon arrival, he was detained in front of his four wives and twenty-seven of his forty-one kids. As evidenced by the size of his family, this sheik was a true player, a lady's man to say the least. I could not believe my eyes when I saw kids of all ages running around the yard playing. I asked him if these were his kids or grandkids. He stated with a grin that they were all his children.

We placed flex cuffs around his wrist and escorted him away. As we departed, his wives and children begged for mercy. We returned to base and placed the sheik in our detention facility. This tactic, while some would consider harsh, was effective. During the six weeks he was detained, we were never attacked. The day we let him go, we were rewarded by three mortar rounds—as if they were thanking us for his release. We detained him again, and, sure enough, the attacks stopped.

Another tactic we implemented to deny sanctuary was that of destroying insurgent homes. Bottom line: If you were an insurgent who attacked us from your house or nearby and we captured you, we demolished your home and relocated your family.

The premise was that the particular home would never be used for an attack again. The same policy also applied to vehicles and motorcycles. If used for an attack against us, it was destroyed.

These extreme measures were very unpopular amongst the Sunnis in the area, so much so that they started painting anti-American graffiti on walls and buildings throughout the towns and villages denouncing President Bush and calling on Iraqis to kill Americans. Recognizing this, local leaders were asked to remove it; if they did not, we destroyed it and detained those responsible.

These heavy-handed tactics, while extreme and overly harsh in some eyes, were also highly effective: We witnessed immediate results. These tactics also were one-sided, mainly targeting Sunnis. But the fact is that it was Sunni insurgents who were attacking us, not Shiites. We had very little trouble from the Shiite population.

This aggressive offensive action had immediate results: indirect-fire attacks decreased from four attacks a week to one. IED attacks decreased from eight a day to two per week. Moreover, the insurgents stopped targeting our battalion altogether as they were having little success and suffering more casualties than they were inflicting. Because we were a formidable foe proving difficult to kill, they turned their attention to and started attacking Iraqi police and ICDC forces. This tactic was used to send a message to the local populace that Iraqi Security Forces could not protect them and to further undermine the authority of the interim Iraqi government. These attacks did little to sway us, however, and we simply applied more pressure.

We had figured out that Iraqis respond to authority. Under the rule of Saddam, that was all they knew: fear and violence. Whoever had the strongest fist and was most lethal in its application was king; all others would succumb. During our tenure in Balad, we were certainly feared by the population and the enemy. So much so that the enemy placed bounties on our heads. This was validated during an interview conducted by *New York Times* journalist Dexter Filkins of villagers in Albu Hishma. When he asked a local man about unit 1-8 IN, the man said that everyone feared them, so much so that "When mothers put their children to bed at night they tell them, if you are not a good boy, Colonel Sassaman is coming to get you."[1]

While these tactics proved effective on the ground at the tactical level, we had overlooked the strategic impact they had. We were doing more to fuel the insurgency than we were doing to defeat it. For every insurgent we killed or captured indirectly, we were recruiting three more. Most importantly we were losing the population. As leaders, we were doing what we thought was right and what we had been trained to do. We had no formalized training in insurgency or nation building prior to our arrival. Moreover there was no doctrine written governing counterinsurgency operations. According to Colonel John Waghelstein, U.S. Army (retired), a former Army Special Forces officer who helped to conduct the American backed counterinsurgency campaign in El Salvador, "The Army has never taken counterinsurgency seriously."

At the Army Command and General Staff College in Fort Leavenworth, Kansas, attended by all American officers hoping to rise above the rank of major, students must pass a rigorous program consisting of roughly 700 hours of instruction on Army operations and tactics. Of that, however, not a single required course focused on how to fight guerrilla wars. This was true at the beginning of both Afghanistan and Iraq wars. As I was coming up through the ranks, all the tactical battles we studied and dissected were from the Civil War, such as the Battle of Gettysburg. Rarely was there any discussion about battles fought in Vietnam, for example. It wasn't until Lieutenant General (retired) Hal Moore and Joe Galloway published their book *We Were Soldiers Once ... and Young*,[2] an account written on the battle for LZ X-ray during Vietnam, that the Army examined guerrilla warfare. But even then it was strictly from a tactics perspective focused on one battle and not on the root causes of the war and strategic failures.

All of our training leading up to this war was focused solely on fighting a conventional fight. Soldiers had not received any form of cultural awareness or language training to help deal with the population. Cultural considerations and customs are a huge factor in a Muslim country. Simple gestures, such as showing the bottoms of your feet to Muslims during a seated engagement, while unintentional by soldiers, were a sign of disrespect. Through no fault of our own, we were doing more to disrespect and alienate the population than we were to garner their support. Bottom line: We were figuring out this war on the fly.

Ultimately, we would begin to figure out how to combat the insurgency, but that didn't really happen until 2006 with the implementation of our new COIN doctrine, Army Field Manual, *FM 3-24, Counterinsurgency*, coupled with the deployment of surge forces. During this three-year span, our mistakes outweighed our gains.

The U.S. Army continued to conduct offensive operations based on a flawed paradigm. The insurgents morphed their operations to successfully attack and kill U.S. soldiers at every opportunity. They understood that the key currency was the media and ultimately dead Americans. They made every attempt to exploit this.

October and November 2003 were more of the same. We continued to apply heavy pressure across our AO. Pressure was relative. For instance, areas that persisted with violence, such as the village of Albu Hishma, got more "love" than areas that were quiet and relatively stable, such as Balad. For the most part, Balad was the model city for stability. Projects were flourishing, basic essential services had been restored to a suitable standard (often referred to by us as "Iraq good enough"), and local police and ICDC forces were taking control of security. Based on achieving these historic milestones, conditions were set for establishing a local government. With that, Sassaman, key leaders, and I decided to take a leap of faith and hold the first-ever free democratic-style elections in the history of Iraq.

This was truly cutting-edge stuff. We were doing graduate-level COIN work before it became legitimate doctrine. Soldiers from Alpha Company, along with local officials and other civilians, forged ahead, hitting the streets to register citizens for the election. After two weeks, more than 45,000 citizens had registered as voters.

The most amazing thing was the ingenuity and initiative demonstrated by the candidates. More than a hundred Iraqis were competing for sixty seats on the council. As soon as the election was announced, Shiite and Sunni candidates commenced making posters with their pictures containing messages about why they sought election. This had small-town America written all over it.

Just prior to the election, news got out about our plans for it. The news reached the highest levels of military and civilian leadership. We had pissed off Paul Bremer and the CPA because we were way ahead of them on the idea. And, our plan ran counter to theirs, which was to hold national elections followed by provincial elections, and so on, down to the local level. We finally received permission by agreeing to call the balloting a "selection" and not an election.

The "selection" took place on October 17, 2003. Voters turned out en masse. Every voting site was walled off and secured by Iraqi police, ICDC, and our forces. Voters were searched outside the buildings by police and ICDC forces. When it came time to cast a ballot, they checked boxes with the names of the candidates they were voting for based on one of twelve districts in which they lived. Each district was able to elect five representatives for a total of sixty council members. Once voting was complete, they placed their ballot in a locked box. Once the council was formed, a mayor was elected.

Overall the selection was an overwhelming success. More than 30,000 people (80 percent of registered voters) turned out to cast their ballot. Enemy insurgents attempted to alter the course of history through intimidation attacks, emplacing IEDs on roads leading to the three different voting centers. But there were no direct attacks against the voting centers as security was extremely tight and insurgents could not penetrate the outer perimeter. Bottom line: The citizens of Balad and the surrounding area would not be deterred.

Hussein Ali, a forty-three-year-old farm owner who ran as a candidate put it best: "I won an election without threats or intimidation.

The people know me in this town. I've pledged to do my best for them, to improve city services."[3]

That was a great day for me, a day that stands out as the one single event that gave me and many others hope that Iraq and Iraqis would prosper. In subsequent tours, I would witness similar events when the stakes were a lot higher. Once again, in the spring of 2006 and later in March 2010, Iraqis took to the streets, braving insurgent violence and intimidation to cast ballots for their future. I was fortunate enough to have a front-row seat.

This kind of progress and good fortune in Balad was the exception. The same could not be said for Albu Hishma and other troubled hot spots throughout Iraq where the insurgency was in full bloom. Insurgent attacks increased across the country in October 2003. Ramadan by its nature is supposed to be a period of spiritual reflection and worship. In 2003, it was anything but. Insurgents used this period of tranquility as a rallying point for their operations throughout the country. With each new attack came greater complexity and sophistication.

October 27, 2003, was the bloodiest day since the fall of Saddam Hussein, with thirty-five people killed and twenty-two injured in suicide attacks on the Red Crescent headquarters and three police stations in Baghdad.[4] Insurgents were even successful at shooting down a couple of our AH-64 Apache attack helicopters.

In our AO, orders originating at division level were sent down from brigade headquarters that, as a sign of respect and good faith, we would lift the curfew and limit active patrolling of towns and villages during Ramadan. Sassaman went a step further by inviting all area sheiks and tribal elders to headquarters for dinner, which ended with the signing of a "cease fire." I attended the dinner that day along with approximately fifty to seventy-five Iraqis. The sheiks and elders went all out, wearing their customary robes with gold trim and starched white dishdashas underneath them. In their left hand, each man carried customary prayer beads. The dinner, catered by a restaurant located near Baghdad, included lamb, chicken, carp, rice, and several vegetable dishes as well as flat bread and hummus.

At the end of the dinner, Sassaman stood up and addressed the group: "We come in peace and all want the same for Iraq. Out of a sign of respect to allow Iraqis to enjoy Ramadan, we will scale back our offensive operations as long as we do not come under attack. If we do, then all hell will break loose."

It was frank and to the point. There was no sugar-coating it. I can't be sure about how it was delivered in translation, but after the interpreter concluded, all the sheiks nodded their heads as if in agreement. As the event ended, the agreement was inked as the sheiks formed a single line and signed the makeshift peace accord or cease-fire agreement. This peace negotiation, much like the local election we held, was doctorate-level COIN. We were well out in front of our sister Army units and our government. It was as if we had a crystal ball and could see into the future. We felt like prophets who could prescribe the text to be written in the eventual COIN doctrine.

Truth be told, however, this peace accord was not worth the paper it was written on. Within two days of signing this agreement, violence erupted. One of our HHC logistics convoys came under attack, wounding a couple of soldiers. Within a week, rockets instead of mortars were landing on LSA Anaconda. All bets were off. The last straw came on November 17, 2003. A patrol from Bravo Company, 1-8 IN was returning to LSA Anaconda during the early morning hours. They had just finished a night patrol in Albu Hishma when their patrol came under attack. They were ambushed by insurgents hiding behind a dirt mound on the outskirts of Albu Hishma.

The insurgents engaged the patrol with direct machine-gun fire and RPGs. One of the RPGs struck a BFV and fatally wounded Staff Sergeant Dale Panchot, who was a dismounted rifle squad leader in Bravo Company. The round penetrated the track and struck Panchot in the chest, killing him instantly. Upon receiving this report on the radio, Sassaman and I mounted our BFVs and rushed to the scene. At that same instant, Captain Todd Brown was on sight with his entire company.

The decision was made to launch an all-out assault on the village of Albu Hishma. Sassaman and I maneuvered our BFVs to a ridgeline overlooking the entire village and affording the perfect spot for commanding and controlling the battle. Meanwhile, Brown deployed his entire company along with Alpha Company and cordoned off the village, establishing blocking positions on all routes in and out. This ensured that the insurgents who executed the attack could not flee the area. Simultaneously, Brown deployed his dismounted platoons and began a door-to-door search of every dwelling. He also deployed troops to conduct a thorough search of the field where the attack had taken place in order to find any evidence that might lead to the perpetrators.

As I was taking up position on the ridge, incoming mortar fire landed near us and in the field where the Bravo Company soldiers were searching. Luckily no one was hit. I finally made it to the ridge, while Sassaman maneuvered with Bravo Company. Based on his guidance, I placed a call for indirect-fire support from our brigade, targeting the location that had just fired on us. We brought in ten to twelve rounds of 155-mm artillery on the suspected location. I then called our mortar platoon to execute the same mission. Next I requested attack aviation support, which was approved. Within five minutes, AH-64 Apache attack helicopters were overhead. I came up on the FM radio net and had them execute a strafing run in the field where the enemy had fled the scene.

The Apache pilots did as instructed and executed several iterations, firing Hellfire missiles, 2.75-inch rockets, and 30-mm cannon fire, strafing an area of approximately 300 meters long and 100 meters (about 984 feet by 328 feet) wide. I even had Air Force F-16 attack fighters stacked up at altitude wanting to get into the fight. (They were never employed because our troops were "danger close," meaning they were dispersed on the ground and were too close to the target where a potential 500-pound bomb would land; we could not risk fratricide.)

The entire town and surrounding orchards were smoking from the intense artillery barrage raining down on it. For a moment, I was controlling five different combat platforms, synchronizing them to deliver timely effects of several different target locations. I felt like Lieutenant Colonel Hal Moore standing in the middle of LZ X-ray in Vietnam giving the "Broken Arrow" call to bring in all available fire on that immediate location.

I was fortunate enough to have Captain Matthew Capobianco, better known by his call sign "Eagle 14 Tango," as my fire support officer. Capobianco was controlling the artillery fires while I managed the close-in support of the attack aviation. In all my years of training, planning, and executing countless numbers of live-fire exercises at battalion through squad levels, I had never witnessed or participated in a combined-arms live-fire exercise (CALFEX) that equaled this event. It was an impressive display of U.S. military might.

When all was said and done, we had completely hammered Albu Hishma with everything in our arsenal or at our disposal. In the process, we eliminated four or five likely insurgents who were killed in their vehicle while trying to run a blocking position that Alpha had established on a road leading from the village. Bravo Company located a large cache containing all types of mortar rounds, including 120-mm, 82-mm, 60-mm, and numerous RPG rounds. It was too large to move, so they destroyed it in place using C4 explosives. Operations continued deep into the night and the following day.

That night I accompanied Sassaman and a platoon from Bravo Company as we patrolled the streets for several hours. Accompanying us was the tactical psychological operations (PSYOPS) team, which had a loud speaker on top of their vehicle playing prerecorded Arabic messages notifying the population that an immediate curfew was being emplaced starting at 1700 hours until 0600 hours. It would be emplaced indefinitely. Furthermore, we stated that anyone who was out on the streets after these hours would immediately be detained. As we patrolled the area, in between the curfew message being broadcasted, we rocked the village with loud music by Metallica. If anything, it was a nonlethal tactic to harass the population in an attempt to frustrate them and ultimately come forward and tell us who killed Panchot. We maintained around-the-clock patrolling and harassment for at least a week.

That was not the worst of it. There was more to come. The day following the attack, we deployed all of our engineer assets to orchards where the recent attack occurred. Heavy bulldozers began to reduce and level all the dirt mounds in the area. The dismounted soldiers of HHC, Bravo Company, and the remaining engineers erected triple-strain concertina wire around the entire village. Next, we constructed tank ditches and blocked off all access routes in and out of the village, leaving only one way in and out. Once the wire was emplaced, we placed signs in Arabic and English that read: "Danger! Stay away! Anyone caught removing or around the wire will be shot."

After the village was totally isolated, we registered every adult military-aged male from sixteen to eighty years old. As part of the registration, we took their picture and made identification cards for all of them, much like a driver's license. As mentioned previously, these draconian measures drew a lot of unfavorable media attention, comparing our tactics to those used by the Israelis against the Palestinians in the Gaza strip. The articles claimed that the U.S. Army was being heavy-handed in the prosecution of this fight, mistreating the population. Not one of the articles cited the violence that was perpetrated from this village.

The final measure we took was the most extreme of all. The orchard that was used regularly for mortar attacks and ambushes was proving difficult to clear by our engineers. The project was too large in scope. Sassaman decided to destroy the orchard using fugas, a thermo fuel, improvised munition similar to napalm. This plan was derived by one of the NCOs, Staff Sergeant Templeton, who worked in our TOC. Templeton had a wealth of knowledge and experience in chemistry. He took more than a hundred 55-gallon drums of diesel fuel or JP-8 and mixed it with laundry detergent and some other shit (I didn't know exactly what). We loaded all the drums of fuel on trucks and hauled it to the orchard. From there we linked it together with detonation cord and C4 explosive sticks.

This massive undertaking took approximately ten hours. Once complete, we moved everyone out of the danger area, approximately 500 meters away, and watched with bated breath.

A massive fireball and huge smoke cloud filled the air. The fire burned for more than three hours. Once the smoke dissipated, everyone could see that the orchard was gone. The area was completely clear of foliage. It was as though a tactical nuke had been dropped there. Nothing but black ash remained. We never again were attacked by mortars or direct fire from this area.

The aggressive tactics we used were not happening throughout the entire theater. There was no unified plan. From one battalion sector to the next, from one brigade sector to another, things were vastly different. Most areas were contested. The attitude and aggressiveness of the battalion commander determined how his unit would fight, which determined whether the enemy would have success. Areas where commanders were not aggressive ultimately became safe havens for insurgents. According to Todd Brown, "Insurgents were sufficiently mobile and could easily relocate to areas where the coalition had relaxed its grip. A certain 'whack a mole' aspect began to characterize operations."[5]

That was certainly not the case in Eagle AO. If anything, we forced insurgents to flee the area, the majority of whom fled to surrounding cities such as Samarra, Baqubah, Ad-dulujah, and Taji. 1-8 IN was one of the two most aggressive battalions in theater. The other was 1-22 IN Battalion, commanded by Lieutenant Colonel Steve Russell. This battalion had the responsibility for Saddam's hometown of Tikrit, where some of the most intense fighting and attacks took place. 1-22 IN was known for taking the fight to the enemy using whatever means necessary to defeat him. Most notably they are the unit that supported Operation Red Dawn, which led to the capture of Saddam in December 2003.

Due to our aggressiveness and the fact that our area was tamed, our battalion was called upon numerous times by Odierno to serve as the main effort during several named offensive operations. These operations actually pulled us out of our own sector, only to go into some other battalion's or brigade's battle space and execute it (i.e., implement our tactics).

For instance, Operation Black Flag was executed during the first week of September. We received mission orders based on intelligence telling us that Saddam, HVT #1, and Al-Duri, former vice president of Iraq (he was #6, the King of Clubs), were hiding out in a small, isolated village located along the Jamal Hamrin Ridge, approximately 30 kilometers (18.6 miles) northeast of Tikrit. This village was known to be home to the tribe Saddam's mother was from. Supposedly credible intelligence was provided, so we had to act on it. Leading up to this mission, we had executed raids on two other occasions that targeted Saddam. We referred to these as "Elvis Sightings." They were both dry holes, meaning that the target was not there and there were no signs signifying that he had been there.

This particular mission got a lot of hype, so much so that Dan Rather from CBS News joined us. He was dispatched to Iraq to film a documentary about the war to be aired in autumn 2003. The challenge facing us was that the terrain was very rugged and hard to access by vehicle. If executed by heavy armored vehicles like the BFVs, we would have lost the element of surprise, allowing Saddam to escape and evade capture. Therefore it was decided by division planners that we would execute an air assault utilizing Chinook Helicopters (CH-47) right onto the objective area and immediately exit the aircraft and execute the raid on the village. In addition, we would convoy BFVs 80 kilometers (nearly 50 miles) to be on hand if needed for supporting fire and other contingencies.

The mission went off without a hitch. We landed on the village at approximately 0500 hours, just before sun up. Both Bravo and Alpha Company executed the raid with precision, but as usual it was a dry hole. Upon arrival of our BFVs, led by Gwinner, we searched the entire ridgeline and every village in between.

It was such a desolate place. These villagers had not seen U.S. forces prior to this. They were poor, living in mud huts. It was clear that we had scared them, a large formation descending upon them out of the skies as they awoke. It as was if we were aliens invading earth. We provided them with MREs and water, departing the area after about eight hours of exhausting house-to-house searching. The mission was necessary in the event Saddam was there: For all the times we missed, we only had to be right once.

The second and most significant operation our battalion conducted was the siege of Samarra, known as Operation Ivy Blizzard. Samarra, an ancient city of approximately 250,000 people and home to the Golden Dome Mosque, was the largest city in Salah ad Din province, located approximately 20 kilometers (about 12.5 miles) north of Balad on the Tigris River. U.S. forces had operated in Samarra since April 2003. Our brigade was replaced in June 2003 by TF 1-66 Armor Battalion, commanded by Lieutenant Colonel Ryan Gonsalves. From June to December 2003, Samarra slowly became infested with hardcore Sunni insurgents. Insurgent attacks occurred daily and steadily climbed as each month passed. Attacks came in the form of RPG ambushes and indirect-fire attacks targeting not just U.S. forces, but ICDC troops and political leaders as well. TF 1-66 AR had responsibility for the city but were ineffective and did a poor job of maintaining security and any semblance of law and order. To their credit, though, it was a tough and difficult mission due to the fact that they did not have the dismounted personnel to effectively patrol the city.

With just 550 personnel, these soldiers mainly served as crewmembers for manning M1 Abrams tanks. In contrast, an infantry battalion like ours had a total end strength of approximately 750, of which 350 were dismounted rifleman. Bottom line: 1-66 AR could not put an efficient number of boots on the ground in Samarra to patrol the streets for a sustained period, nor could they conduct the door-to-door fighting required to defeat the insurgents.

Instead, they mainly patrolled the area mounted using their M1 Abrams Tanks. While intimidating to the population, these vehicles, due to their size, were restrained to the outer periphery of the city and could not patrol along the interior streets. Moreover, when enemy contact was made, they could not close with and destroy the enemy, which was elusive and would simply run away and blend into the population.

By November 2003, insurgent attacks had reached an all-time high. Casualties for both coalition and Iraqi Police and ICDC forces mounted.

To compound the problem, 1-66 AR simply vacated the area. Originally they had occupied two FOBs, FOB Daniels and FOB Stoddard, within the city limits in order to maintain a presence, but that was short lived as the commander made a decision to move the entire battalion out of the city after several soldiers were killed in action or wounded from indirect-fire attacks. As a result, the battalion relocated to an industrial warehouse on the outskirts of Samarra approximately 15 kilometers (9.3 miles) away. This meant they would have to commute to work.

The real impact was that there was no presence in Samarra, and insurgents had free reign of the place. Moreover, insurgents viewed the move as a victory for their cause. They were able to exploit this move in the media and with local citizens, claiming that they had defeated U.S. forces and forced them out of the city. In the public's eyes, there was no one left to protect them or the local leaders. Samarra had become a sanctuary for insurgents, and something needed to be done to regain control.

In December 2003, we received orders from Odierno that we were to be the main effort for Operation Ivy Blizzard. Once again, they called on the Fighting Eagles, dispatching us away from our AO to take back a city that had become a sanctuary for insurgents. This mission was the culminating event for our battalion, and it was truly our finest hour. In the end, however, the success of the operation was overshadowed by a series of events laced with controversy that led to our darkest day, casting a bad light on a tour of honor and sacrifice.

Prior to departing our AO, we were relieved in place by 2-3 Infantry Battalion commanded by Lieutenant Colonel Gordy Flowers. The "Patriots" of 2-3 IN were assigned to 3-2 Stryker Brigade Combat Team (SBCT) based out of Fort Lewis, Washington. This was the Army's newest premier fighting force, formed as part of the Army's modularization plan under former Army Chief of Staff General Eric Shinseki. Operation Iraqi Freedom was the showcase event to test it. The remainder of 3-2 SBCT would participate in Operation Ivy Blizzard and would be responsible for the eastern side of Samarra.

2-3 IN showed up at our FOB on December 6, 2003. Because of a tight timeline for us to be in Samarra, we were unable to conduct a traditional battle handover between battalions. Under normal circumstances, all units from corps level down to company level have at least a two- to three-week transition to allow the incoming unit to gain a feel and lay of the land, past and current operations, the enemy situation, including past and recent attacks, and finally an introduction to all the Iraqi key leaders known as spheres of influence (SOI).

In December, several strange-looking space ship-like vehicles showed up at our FOB. Out stepped soldiers dressed like storm troopers. All were outfitted with the latest combat gear and high-tech equipment. Sassaman and I greeted the commander, Lt. Col. Flowers, and his command team, which included his command sergeant major (CSM), XO, and S-3. They were unloading cases of Starbucks coffee, which they had gotten from corporate headquarters in Seattle; it sure beat the Folgers Crystal shit we were drinking at the time.

As for a transition, that was it—nothing more than a greeting, welcoming the "Patriots" to the Sunni Triangle, followed by a one-hour PowerPoint operations and intelligence brief. On December 12, 2003, we handed over the keys to our gate and control of our AO. Then we mounted our BFVs and departed for Samarra. The one thing that was comforting for 2-3 IN was the fact that our AO was tame and relatively quiet. However, the lack of a thorough transition would play a major factor upon our return in January 2004.

Operation Ivy Blizzard, the Siege of Samarra

Our Finest Hour

We arrived in Samarra at FOB Brassfield-Mora on December 12, 2003, around dusk with two rifle companies, Alpha and Charlie Companies, headquarters (or TOC), and support elements from our headquarters company. Bravo Company a month earlier had been detached from us and attached to 1-66 and were waiting when we arrived. In addition, we left behind and attached our Engineer Company, Bravo, 4th Engineers to 2-3 IN so as to provide subject-matter expertise for 2-3 IN and maintain continuity of our AO, knowing we would return after completion of the operation. We had already executed MDMP for the operation, issued the Operations Order, and conducted our battalion rehearsal over a large sand table or mockup of the city.

Our mission statement given to us by our brigade headquarters, taken directly from the brigade operations order, was as follows:

"1-8 IN (M) ATTACKS at H-Hour (TBD) TO ISOLATE AND THEN CLEAR ENEMY FORCES IN WESTERN SAMARRA TO REMOVE FORMER REGIME ELEMENTS AND TERRORIST CELLS AND ALLOW IRAQI SECURITY FORCES TO MAINTAIN CONTROL IN SAMARRA."

The operation kicked off around December 17, 2003, right on the heels of the capture of Saddam, which occurred on December 13 during Operation Red Dawn by units of 1st BCT/4th ID and other joint forces. Prior to the assault on Samarra, Charlie Company executed a raid of a farmhouse based on an informant tip that HVT Kais Hatem was hiding in an old farmhouse just south of Samarra, along with several members of his attack cell. Hatem was a notorious Fedayeen attack planner and financier of insurgent operations, who had eluded several attempts of capture in the past. There was no telling how many attacks he executed against coalition forces or how much blood he had on his hands.

We put the plan together and Charlie Company executed. This operation took place in the predawn hours of December 17, and the enemy was totally caught off guard. Charlie Company, with precision execution, maneuvered BFVs to block all escape routes to and from the objective area. Simultaneously, they dismounted and infiltrated several infantrymen to conduct the actual raid. The enemy had no chance as the soldiers were able to sneak up on the farmhouses using stealth movement techniques and capture more than thirty insurgents, including Hatem. While on the objective, the company conducted a thorough search of the area. What they discovered was a treasure trove.

Altogether they found more than 250 AK-47s, tons of explosives, and detonation cord used for the making of IEDs. The unit also discovered a large cache during the tactical site exploitation, including several RPGs, more than a hundred warheads, and several surface-to-air missiles used for engaging fixed-wing and rotary-wing aircraft such as Apache attack helicopters. These were a crucial find because if these weapons stayed in the hands of the enemy, they could be used to shoot down large cargo and passenger aircraft in what we refer to as "spectacular attacks," thus leading to further exploitation by insurgent media such as Al Jazeera and Jihadist-oriented outlets. This was a textbook operation and one more example of the tenacity and success of our battalion.

We used the success of this operation as a springboard to kick-off the siege of Samarra. Operation Ivy Blizzard commenced at approximately 0100 hours the following morning. Final rehearsals from the individual soldier, squad to platoon level and company to battalion were complete. Soldiers did their final preparations, known as "Pre-Combat Checks" and "Pre-Combat Inspections." These steps included camouflaging oneself and loading up of ammunition with the intent of carrying as many extra magazines, machine gun belts, and grenades as possible. This was certain to be the toughest fight yet against a formidable force.

All the commanders were gathered around the hood of the battalion commander's Humvee with maps spread out, reviewing the final plan and execution checks. The final step before launching the assault, as was customary before any assault, was the gathering of troops around the commander for a fiery speech, followed by reciting of the "Eagle Prayer" led by Chaplain Captain Leif Espeland. All soldiers removed their Kevlar helmets, took out their "Eagle Prayer Cards," bowed their heads, and prayed.

"Almighty God, the author of liberty and champion of the oppressed, hear our prayer. We the soldiers of the 1st Battalion, 8th Infantry Regiment 'Fighting Eagles' acknowledge our reliance upon you as labor to defend our nation with honor and dignity. Protect and strengthen this 'band of brothers' as we endeavor to do your will. Grant us the wisdom by your mind, courage by your heart, and strength by your hand. It is for you that we battle, and unto you the victory. Our Nation's freedom and heritage is built on our faith in you. We are the 'Fighting Eagles.' In God we trust."

There we stood, shoulder to shoulder, man to man, ready to face a determined threat, not knowing what danger and hazards awaited us in the streets of Samarra. I could sense by the steely-eyed killer look in the soldiers' eyes that we were ready. It was midnight on December 17, 2003 (hit time, or "H-Hour," on the objective was at 0200). Troops were mounting up on the BFVs that would carry them into battle as if they were Roman Legionnaires riding chariots in the ancient days in the kingdom of Babylon.

The irony is that Samarra contained several ancient ruins that dated back to the empire of Babylon. But rather than chariots, we would ride BFVs into battle. I donned my battle attire, secured my weapon, climbed up on my BFV (referred to as Headquarters 33), and stepped down into the commander's hatch. I donned my communications helmet and asked my crew if they were ready. Both my driver, Specialist Matthew Francis, and my gunner, Specialist Jonathan Brown, acknowledged with "Yes, sir. Let's go kick some ass."

The rest of the companies were starting to roll out of the FOB in accordance with the published timeline. Alpha Company 1-8 IN, or "Attack Company," would be the main effort for this operation. Attack Company was led by Captain Matt Cunningham, a thin West Point graduate from Michigan, who like Captain Todd Brown, was a competitive triathlete and competent infantryman and officer. He was the right man to spearhead the assault into Samarra.

Attack Company was given the mission to raid several target houses suspected to contain a number of insurgent cell leaders and financiers. These target houses were located in proximity to each other throughout the city, so they made a common-sense objective for them. Cunningham's company would follow Bravo Company 1-8 IN, known as "War Machine," which was the supporting effort under the command of Brown. Just like Attack, they had several target houses as well located south of where Cunningham was attacking. Finally Charlie Company 1-8 IN, known as "Rock," fresh off the raid that captured Hatem, would be the trail element behind Attack Company and would conduct a follow-on operation to seize the remaining houses and provide the reserve force if needed.

My task as the operations officer was to command and control the operation along with the battalion commander, whose call sign was "Eagle Six" (my call sign was "Eagle Three"). We would establish and operate from a vantage point about a kilometer on the outskirts of the actual city sprawl. For additional protection, we brought our customary scout section, led by Staff Sergeant Timothy Bolyard, a tall, lanky hillbilly from Thornton, West Virginia. If there was anyone I wanted to fight beside it was him; there was none better, and everyone knew it.

Bolyard, "Saber 24," always traveled in scout Humvees with his wingman, Staff Sergeant Adam Tymensky, and provided the security and additional firepower and formed the Fighting Eagle tactical command post (TAC). Our TAC traveled and operated together and served as a mobile command post with a sole purpose of providing C2 for our major operations. Our TOC was the secondary command post from which the remainder of the staff worked. For operations in Samarra, the TAC controlled the fight, and the TOC monitored and battle-tracked events as they unfolded. In the event something happened to the TAC, they could quickly pick up and take command of the fight.

The TAC occupied our position on the Samarra dam at 0130 hours, H minus 30 minutes. To add to the fog and friction, a term coined by Carl von Clausewitz, Brigade Commander Col. Rudesheim, call sign "Striker 6," and Operations Officer (S-3) Major Troy Perry, call sign "Striker 3," flew overhead in a UH-60 Blackhawk helicopter to monitor the operation and receive reports from the Eagle TAC on the progress of the operation. This helicopter was a special C2 helicopter unlike any other in that it had special radio communications equipment that allowed commanders to C2 operations from the air versus being on the ground. I called in all the reports as Sassaman focused on commanding and controlling companies on the ground. A radio check at 0150 hours from company commanders acknowledged that they were ready. I reported to the brigade commander and informed him that we were REDCON 1: We were ready to begin the attack.

It was hit time. Three large explosions and bright flashes of light erupted over the Tigris River. As soon as that happened, Eagle Six, the battalion commander, screamed "Yeah! Get some!" over the radio.

These explosions were planned as the initial breaches of the three main target houses that Alpha and Bravo Companies were going after. After a delay of a few minutes, more loud explosions jolted the city, knocking out all the power and lights. It was pitch dark. But we were outfitted with high-tech night-vision devices, which gave our forces a distinct advantage.

The brigade commander screamed at me over the brigade net about the explosions. "Eagle Three this is Striker 6. What the hell were all those explosions? Are you guys in contact?"

I replied, "Negative. Those were planned breaches at the target houses."

The radio went silent. I knew the commander was pissed. The reason behind this was that earlier in the day, back at FOB Brassfield-Mora, our staging base while we were conducting rehearsals and preparations, the brigade commander was walking around the area, checking on things and came across a platoon from Bravo Company preparing demolition charges to be used in the operation that night. He was displeased with this and immediately sought out Brown to inquire about why we were using them. Brown informed him that the demolition charges were needed to breach gates or entrances to houses to prevent forces from having to scale high walls and exposing themselves to potential enemy gunfire.

Brown stated that "You must go in hard or else you accept a huge risk for our soldiers."[6] The demolition charges also would provide an element of surprise and audacity (all tenets found in most Infantry Training and Doctrinal manuals).

Later, Rudesheim sought out Sassaman to ask were we using demolition charges. Sassaman replied, "We made a conscious decision to use the demo charges based on a leader's recon using satellite imagery and our discovery that every planned target house in Samarra had a large, 12-foot-high wall surrounding the house courtyard and they all had large heavy steel gates that were locked from the inside. I am not willing to risk the lives of our soldiers by knocking on doors."

Iraqis who could afford it had constructed walls for self-protection from any outside government forces or henchmen of Saddam during his reign. That made sense, but our decision to use demolition charges to breach them made sense as well. We were at war, and it is textbook to use a demolition breach when conducting a planned, deliberate raid on a known enemy target. Regardless of our explanation and calculated rationale, Rudesheim did not support this decision or the technique; he felt we should knock before entering. As it turned out, however, we were never given a direct order not to use them, so we executed with the demolition charges as planned.

These were hardcore insurgents we were going after based on vetted intelligence. We were not Sheriff Andy Taylor of Mayberry looking for petty thieves who stole candy from the local five-and-dime. We were at war. This was serious shit. In no way, shape, or form were we going to put soldiers at risk by knocking on doors. Are you kidding me!?

At 0245 hours, operations were going smoothly. Two target houses had been raided, and two targets were detained. There was surprisingly little gunfire, signaling that we had caught the enemy off guard and unprepared. As operations continued, situation reports (SITREPs) from company commanders down on the front lines indicated that operations were going as planned. Each time I received a report, I would relay the SITREP to the brigade commander flying overhead. He was pleased, encouraging us to keep the momentum going, which we did. The reports were coming in fast and furious from our different companies, each one confirming or denying capture or killing of the target. After a complete, detailed search of the objectives, numerous stockpiles of weapons and assorted ammunition and explosive caches were discovered.

This is just what Samarra needed: an old fashioned ass kicking in order to restore law and order and rid the city of insurgent groups. It also helped to instill confidence in the local population that coalition and Iraqi forces were in charge and could provide protection.

The sun was beginning to rise, and Sassaman decided to move into the city and follow Bravo and Charlie Companies as they conducted the next phase of the operation, which was to conduct a raid on the industrial park in the southern end of the city. This area was an operating and staging base for the insurgents; many local car dealers, mechanics, and machine shop owners were known active cell supporters and financiers of attacks. We had hard intelligence that tons of weapons and explosives were cached throughout the area.

As the sun rose, we were full up with two companies with BFVs and dismounted infantrymen moving tactically along the street, going from shop to shop, building to building searching for weapons and explosives. I dismounted my BFV along with Eagle 6, and we began to walk the streets with our units. I went with Bravo Company, and Eagle 6 was with Charlie Company a few blocks over. The stores were closed, and all the buildings were locked up tight. Steel doors or steel bars with large heavy-duty padlocks protected most of them, and we used sledgehammers and demolition in some cases to breach the doorways. We searched more than 300 shops and turned up some sort of weapons, ammunition, and other explosive or communication devices used for making IEDs in the majority of them. Heavy transport (5-ton equivalent) trucks followed us as we took out truckloads of seized property to be transported to the FOB and destroyed by engineers and the explosive ordinance demolition team.

The search of the area continued well into the evening. More than thirty hours had elapsed since the beginning of the operation. Fatigue began to set in. Once we were sure we had thoroughly searched every shop, we called "end of mission," and Eagle Six gave orders to execute the retrograde of forces. We then consolidated, and each company accounted for all personnel and equipment and started back to FOB Brassfield-Mora for some much-deserved rest.

Operation Ivy Blizzard was a true success. We detained more than a hundred insurgents and twenty to twenty-five HVTs and seized more than 200 weapons and approximately 2 tons of ammunition and explosives. We did not lose a single soldier during the complex operation. For the time being, Samarra was secure. This was truly our finest hour as 1-8 IN (M) executed the largest complex attack since the invasion by 3rd Infantry Division, 101st Airborne Division and Marine Forces.

The next phase was constant-presence patrolling with Iraqi police and ICDC forces. Samarra, for all intents and purposes, was under martial law, for lack of a better term. The streets were empty, stores were abandoned, and a citywide curfew was put in place from 1800 to 0600 hours. There would be no vehicular movement or personnel movement for approximately two weeks while we worked to reestablish law and order and bring a sense of normalcy to this place. Within this phase was the immediate transition to civil military operations as we began to inject more than $3 million worth of restoration projects into the city and attempt to get local shops back in business and other industries up and running. New police stations and other public service and health facilities were built. We restored the local city council building and appointed a new mayor and city council representatives. Schools were reopened. Samarra was getting a makeover following our assault.

The intense patrolling would last through the rest of December and into the new year until the end of January 2004. We left Alpha Company in place attached to TF 1-66 Armor, the "Iron Knights," as the rest of the battalion moved back south to Balad in order to take over our old AO from 2-3 IN. They in turn moved to Mosul, where they would conduct operations for the remainder of their deployment.

Our Darkest Day

It was during this time of transition that our unit endured its most tumultuous period. An incident that occurred at the Samarra Dam would quickly eradicate all the successes that the unit earned fighting in some of the most dangerous and contested areas of Iraq. The incident was the suspected drowning (never confirmed) of an Iraqi male who, along with his cousin, supposedly was thrown off the side of a bridge into the Tigris River.

The truth behind the incident is that at about 0100 hours on January 24, 2004, two military-aged males were caught violating the established curfew. They were out late, acting suspicious in an area that had seen a lot of IED and other enemy activity. The two Iraqi men were arrested and detained for curfew violation and suspicion of emplacing IEDs. Upon their detention, the two men were placed in the back of an Alpha Company BFV and were to be escorted to FOB Brassfield-Mora for questioning and possible long-term confinement. En route, a strategic lapse in judgment occurred. Lieutenant Jack Seville decided to stop in the vicinity of the Samarra Dam and force the detainees to jump into the water. This was clearly an error in judgment on his behalf. Once the patrol stopped, soldiers from Alpha Company escorted the two men down to the bank of the Tigris River. Once there, they removed the flex cuffs from the detainees and forced them to jump into the cold water of the Tigris River. The purpose of this, as explained during questioning of Seville, was to "teach them a lesson."

Soldiers from the platoon involved all claimed that both Iraqi males were seen getting out of the water and walking away. Two weeks later, some local fishermen discovered a body floating in the river. The body was recovered, and the family of the man claimed that it was one of the men that the Alpha Company patrol had detained. This allegation was never confirmed, nor was an autopsy conducted, as it was viewed by most of our battalion and brigade senior officers to be a ploy to extort money from the U.S. government; this extortion tactic was somewhat a matter of routine in Iraq during this period.

This event drew a lot of media scrutiny, airing around the world on news networks. Based on the report, Rudesheim ordered a Criminal Investigation Division (CID) investigation of our battalion and the events surrounding the incident.

When the Samarra Dam incident occurred, Sassaman and I were away from Samarra. We had traveled back to Balad in order to check up on Paliwoda and his engineer company. Basically, we made a house call to visit him and see how operations were going with 2-3 IN. We arrived at FOB Eagle the morning of January 4, 2004. After dismounting our BFVs, Sassaman and I walked to the front entrance of our headquarters building and were met there by Paliwoda. We had a brief conversation during which Paliwoda relayed to us how tough the previous month had been. The FOB had been under constant attack by mortars and, to make matters worse, the Balad Iraqi police chief had been killed by an insurgent IED attack. Moreover, it appeared that the AO had a setback as insurgent attacks were on the rise. It certainly was not the way we left it. Sassaman said a few more words and departed to meet with Flowers to get an update on issues 2-3 IN was having in the AO. I talked to Paliwoda for a few more minutes about football and some other things. As he was walking away, he told me that he had received some new ammunition pouches in the mail and he had one for me that he would return with shortly.

He then put on his Kevlar helmet and headed to his trailer to retrieve it. These would be the lasts words that he and I would ever exchange. Within minutes, mortar rounds were landing on the FOB. I yelled "Incoming!" and sought cover inside the building. Explosions rocked the FOB. It appeared they had landed over near where the engineer company was located.

After the third round landed, I waited for a few minutes to ensure it was clear and I raced to my BFV along with my crew. We were executing our countermortar battle drill we had so many times before: mount up and head in the general direction of where the mortars were fired from. My crew was mounted, engines were running, and we were ready. We were delayed a few minutes waiting for Sassaman to mount up so we could move out together. Then I got the news: one of the rounds had struck Paliwoda. A piece of shrapnel had penetrated his armor vest and pierced his lung.

Eagle Six, upon hearing the news, rushed over to the sight and provided first aid to Paliwoda. Simultaneously a 9-line MEDEVAC call was placed. Paliwoda was bleeding pretty badly. But, thanks to the quick response by our combat lifesavers, he was treated and believed to have been stabilized. Ten minutes later, the MEDEVAC helicopter touched down on the cement landing pad in front of our headquarters. Paliwoda was placed on a litter and rushed to the helicopter. From the time Paliwoda was wounded until the aircraft departed, approximately twenty minutes had passed. We all thought that we had gotten him treated and evacuated within the critical window known as "the golden hour."

As the aircraft lifted off, Eagle Six rushed over to his BFV, which was parked next to mine. I could clearly see he was distraught. Before we departed, we talked briefly, and he was optimistic that Paliwoda would survive. We raced out of the gate, en route to the point of origin from which the enemy mortars were fired. We were joined in the search for the would-be mortar team by Flowers and his Tactical Command Post. While all this activity occurred, our 120-mm mortar section was busy firing counterfire.

To assist us with finding the point of origin, I gave instructions for them to fire white phosphorus, better known as "Willy Pete" during the Vietnam era. These rounds were great for marking locations as they sent out a cloud of white smoke when they impacted, and usually a fire ensued. Upon reaching the suspected site, no one was in the area. We stopped our formation and dismounted to search the area. Within a few minutes, I came across a 120-mm base plate that was dug into ground, but there was no tube. Clearly this was the spot where they had recently erected the mortar tube and fired from. We were too late. Somehow the enemy had escaped with the mortar tube and ultimately would live to fight another day. We continued our search, but to no avail. While in the process of searching, a chilling call came across the radio.

"Eagle Six, this is Eagle TOC. Over."

"Eagle TOC, this is Eagle Six. Send it. Over."

"Eagle Six, this is Eagle TOC. We have some bad news."

There was complete silence. We all knew the outcome: Paliwoda was dead. We had just suffered our second fatality.

Paliwoda was a great soldier, leader, and, most of all, a friend of mine. We had worked for several months on the brigade staff prior to being assigned to 1-8 IN. He was by every measure one of the most remarkable human beings and officers I had ever served with. Intimidating in appearance with his 6'5" frame, a former West Point football player, yet grounded in his heart, he was known by peers and subordinates as a gentle giant. By every account, he was one of if not the best company commander in our brigade. He was a true combat leader, so much so that he departed from solely focusing on his role as an engineer unit and transformed his company to fight as an infantryman. We actually referred to his company as Delta, 1-8 IN, a credit to him and his soldiers.

It was truly a dark day for the battalion as well as for the Army. But we had no time to pause and catch our breath. Upon returning to the FOB, Sassaman received orders from Rudesheim to report to Samarra as soon as possible.

What now?

What could be so important that we were summonsed immediately to Samarra in light of what had just occurred?

Before we departed, Sassaman exploded emotionally. He reached his breaking point. He confronted Flowers in the middle of the hallway and started screaming at him, obviously upset that Paliwoda had been killed and that the security situation in the area had deteriorated during the time we were in Samarra. Moreover, during their watch, the local Balad police chief and several other Iraqi Police officers had been killed. Sassaman placed the blame on the shoulders of 2-3 IN. At the time, this blame seemed justified, but the true fault or blame was due to the poor transition between the two units. As for Paliwoda's death, while tragic, little could have been done to prevent it. Dozens of rounds had impacted on our FOB in the past months with a few minor injuries; we all dodged death. On this given day, the enemy got lucky.

Flowers and his subordinate companies were simply serving as caretakers. They were the victim of a poor handover of responsibility of the AO simply because 1-8 IN was called into Samarra so quickly. Furthermore, during the hasty transition, 2-3 IN did not get the opportunity to travel outside the wire to see our battalion in action and how we conducted operations, nor did they get to meet any key Iraqi leaders. Despite missing out on these key transition tasks, the battalion was doing as best they could throughout our AO. Bottom line: this battalion was set up for failure by decision makers at echelons above our level.

I personally believe they should never have been sent to Balad. Instead, they should have stayed with their parent brigade and conducted operations with them, as opposed to being sent to relieve us to serve as simple caretakers for an interim period. They did not have a vested interest in Balad, knowing they would soon move on for operations in Mosul. Had there been an opportunity for a thorough transition covering several weeks, we most likely could have prevented the incidents that happened while they were there. This is simply another example of how the U.S. military was fighting this war on the fly; there truly was no unified plan during this period.

Sassaman and I returned to Samarra the night of January 2, 2004. As soon as we arrived, we were greeted by Gwinner. As we dismounted, Gwinner informed us that Rudesheim was angry and wanted heads to roll. No sooner had we finished our conversation when Rudesheim showed up and began screaming at Sassaman, poking his finger in his chest. I heard him shout at Sassaman, "Nate, it was reported to me that a platoon from Alpha Company threw two Iraqi males into the Tigris River. If any of this is true, I will relieve everybody in the chain of command."

Sassaman acknowledged the report and told the commander that he would have to conduct a commander's inquiry to find out the facts before he could offer the commander any findings and recommendations.

The issue I took with this was that Sassaman was under extreme emotional distress as he had just lost one of his best company commanders. Sassaman still had Paliwoda's blood on his hands from treating him. This whole discourse could have happened differently, and more professionally. Rudesheim should have acknowledged and recognized Sassaman's state of mind at the time. He could have shared his condolence over the loss of Paliwoda. But none of that happened. Instead, Rudesheim gave Sassaman an outright tongue-lashing.

These were the rocks in our rucksack at this moment in time. The death of Paliwoda fresh in our hearts, we sought catharsis during the tumultuous quest for answers to events that occurred at the Tigris River. Events in combat are relentless and often terminal. These are the daily dilemmas and challenges of combat leaders.

After the conversation between the two ended, Sassaman and I departed to find Cunningham and Seville to get the full story of what happened at the Tigris River. Seville acknowledged and informed Eagle Six that they had indeed detained two Iraqi males who were out after curfew. He also acknowledged that a squad of soldiers from his platoon based on his direct orders did in fact take the two detainees down to the bank of the Tigris and had them jump in the water. He concluded by stating emphatically that he personally saw the two detainees get out of the water and walk away as the platoon was departing the area.

At that moment, a tough decision had to be made. Sassaman—and the rest of us—had had a tough day. Paliwoda's blood was still literally on his uniform. It was not the best time to make a decision, but he did anyway. Addressing Cunningham and Seville, he said "Matt, Jack, if anyone comes and asks about this incident, I want you to tell them everything, but do not mention anything about the water."

Sassaman's rationale at the time was that he did not want the chain of command, in this case the brigade commander, relieving anyone based on the conversation that took place earlier. Personally, I felt that the statement by Rudesheim was undue command influence insofar as Sassaman had yet been afforded an opportunity to investigate the incident. Likewise, Sassaman viewed the incident as a nonlethal action that was taken to teach the two Iraqi men a lesson, basically looking at it as "no harm, no foul." At the time, under an extreme set of circumstances and given Sassaman's state of mind, as well as the ass chewing that took place, I supported the decision and most likely would have made the same decision had I been in command.

Two weeks elapsed since the incident at the bridge took place, and the entire battalion returned to FOB Eagle and reassumed our AO from 2-3 IN as they moved north to Mosul. During that time, we conducted a memorial service for Paliwoda. We renamed our FOB from Eagle to Paliwoda in his honor. No sooner had we finished his memorial service when all hell broke loose: CID investigators descended on us to investigate the bridge incident.

It was true that fishermen had discovered a body floating downstream in the Tigris River near Samarra. Purportedly, it was one of the two detainees who had been forced by the soldiers from Alpha Company to jump into the water. The CID agents interviewed all soldiers and leaders involved, including Sassaman and Gwinner. Every one of them, to a man, denied throwing or forcing the detainees into the water. They all corroborated that they took the two men to an ICDC checkpoint and released them to their control.

A week later, a soldier in the platoon cracked and actually came forward to speak the truth, stating that he was there and that they did in fact force the two men to jump into the water at the orders of Seville. The investigation changed in an instant, becoming a witch hunt focused on an alleged conspiracy or cover up by the chain of command. This investigation lasted through the remainder of our deployment and culminated in March 2004. Ultimately the fallout over this would not conclude until we redeployed home to Fort Carson, Colorado. In the end, Sassaman, Gwinner, and Cunningham all received General Level Article 15s (Nonjudicial Punishment) from Odierno.

Seville was charged with murder, obstruction of justice, and detainee abuse, among others. The alleged victim's body was never exhumed to substantiate identification or cause of death. Seville was found innocent of all charges except obstruction of justice, for which he was sentenced to twenty-nine days in jail. Sassaman remained in command until November 2004, when he changed out and subsequently retired. Gwinner and Cunningham have since departed the Army.

January through March 2004 saw more of the same from the enemy. The battalion continued steady state offensive operations, and civil military operations (CMOs) continued at a steady pace in areas that had cooperated with us. As each week passed, more and more Iraqi police and ICDC troops joined the ranks and were visible patrolling the streets and manning checkpoints throughout the AO. We conducted a few more named operations. One in particular led to the capture of a couple of insurgents who were responsible for the death of Paliwoda.

As we entered February, elements from 1-77 AR, 1st ID started showing up (they were the battalion that was replacing us as our tour came to an end). The relief in place lasted approximately three weeks. We conducted a right seat ride/left seat ride (RSR/LSR)[7] with key leaders at every level and introduced them to key Iraqi Police, ICDC, and local leaders, including tribal sheiks. This transition was thorough, unlike the transition conducted with 2-3 IN. For the most part, we transitioned without incident and 1-77 AR took the reins.

I departed Iraq on March 17, 2003, from LSA Anaconda on a C-17 military aircraft bound for Fort Carson. Three days prior, I had departed the gate of FOB Paliwoda for the last time. As I departed, I was overcome with emotion. I was elated to be leaving the country of Iraq. I traveled in my BFV along with my crew intact, Specialists Matthew Francis, Jason Testa, and Jonathon Brown. I was thankful to have them with me. After months of heavy fighting and near-death encounters, we survived and were headed home together. But one obstacle still remained. Before we arrived to the safe confines of LSA Anaconda, we had to travel along ASR Linda. I wondered if this would be the day that the enemy would get lucky. Would an IED be their parting shot as they bid us farewell?

The trip along ASR Linda was so surreal. As we passed through Balad, the locals, mainly Shiites, lined the street and waved good-bye. They certainly did not want to see us leave and even begged us to stay. We continued east, and as we entered the outskirts of Albu Hishma, we sensed that the local sentiment had changed. We were in Sunni territory now. Locals on the streets, including kids, were staring us down. Some threw rocks at us, and others gave us the thumbs-down sign. In extreme cases, kids and adults slashed their index fingers across their throats. Needless to say, they were not bidding us a hero's farewell. We had clearly not won the hearts and minds of these folks.

The one thing that stood out the most was how different the Albu Hishma landscape had changed from when we first arrived eight months earlier. There were fewer dwellings, fewer trees, and fewer orchards. Unlike its thriving neighbor to the west in Balad, there were no new schools or medical clinics. All that was visible was a wide path of destruction. As we exited the town nearing the gate of LSA Anaconda, Sassaman was traveling behind me. I said to him over the radio, "This place had a chance. It was a lost opportunity, mainly for the kids standing alongside the road. I do not think it will ever prosper. Maybe the next unit will have better luck. Inshallah, Inshallah."

The soldiers and leaders of 1-8 IN performed superbly, far beyond what was expected as we executed operations outside of our customary role. But the incident at the bridge over the Tigris in Samarra overshadowed and cast a dark cloud over the twelve months of hard work and numerous accomplishments our battalion had achieved. Absent an overall unified plan or national strategy to counter the insurgency, we executed relentless combat operations while conducting cutting-edge COIN or nation-building operations. We formed local councils, served as provincial mayors, held the first citywide elections, and formed and trained police and army forces, all while fighting insurgent cells, Saddam loyalists, and other fighters.

Due to our aggressiveness and our commitment to stay on the offensive, we all but defeated the insurgency in our AO. But we also pissed off a lot of people and alienated the Sunni population. They were reluctant to support us, choosing instead to harbor and support insurgents from their respective villages, who were predominantly responsible for the majority of attacks against us.

Regardless of the second- and third-order effects resulting from our actions or tactics, we never lost a single enemy engagement at the tactical level. Every attack initiated by the enemy ended on our terms. We were simply conducting operations as best we could based on training and experience.

Throughout the deployment, because of our aggressiveness we lost two great warriors: Staff Sergeant Dale Panchot and Captain Eric Paliwoda. More than eighteen of our soldiers were wounded in action. Their sacrifice—and all the sacrifices made by the men of 1-8 IN— ensured that our battalion accomplished every mission assigned to us. In comparison, other sister units that were less aggressive and took up a defensive posture sustained a much higher casualty ratio.

Our aggressiveness and lethality was often viewed as too extreme, which certainly was the case for Rudesheim. On numerous occasions, he reprimanded us for using heavy-handed tactics. In extreme cases, we were blatantly denied combat enabler support while in contact with the enemy. It was a major dilemma that Gwinner and I struggled with throughout the deployment.

On one hand, Odierno told us to turn up the heat against the insurgents. This ran counter to our brigade commander's guidance. It was truly a leadership challenge. In the end, we simply did what we thought was right by our soldiers and what it took to win this war.

On a personal level, this was by far the worst brigade-level command climate I had ever served under or been associated with. It was one thing to be outside the wire fighting the enemy on a daily basis, but it was another thing to have to return to the FOB only to fight internally with your higher chain of command and staff. It was truly a toxic environment, and I am not sure others outside the brigade knew how toxic it was. Despite all the challenges—no unified strategy, no formal training in COIN, limited subject-matter experts on nation building, a toxic command climate, and the fact that we were operating along a Sunni/Shiite fault line—we were able to stay the course, and, ultimately, we persevered.

The soldiers 1-8 IN were a true band of brothers. They fought hard and gallantly for all they believed in and, most of all, for one another. We were the Fighting Eagles, soldiers whose blood and sacrifices ultimately paved the way for success for a free and stable Iraq, which would evolve seven years later ending with the drawdown of U.S. forces in August 2010.

As the plane finally lifted off the runway headed for the United States, it was more than evident to me that if we were going to win this war, things would have to change drastically—at all levels. Somewhere in the back of my mind, I knew in all likelihood that I would be back in Iraq sooner rather than later to see it play out.

CHAPTER 6
ON THE BRINK OF CIVIL WAR
March 2004–November 2006

> ❝ Some people don't believe in reconciliation—they're just keen to settle scores and break the back of the other side. ❞
>
> *Muwafaq al-Rubaie, Iraq National Security Advisor*

We arrived home to a hero's welcome, unlike the reception that was given to returning veterans during the Vietnam War. As the C-17 plane touched down at Peterson Air Force Base in Colorado Springs, Colorado, I peered out the window and saw hundreds of families and patriots waving U.S. flags waiting anxiously to greet us. The moment I stepped off the plane was surreal, the massive crowd and constant cheering enough to bring a tear of joy and elation to my eye. My chest was filled with pride and honor, and my body was covered with goose bumps. One by one as we filed off the plane, we were greeted with a firm handshake by the Fort Carson commanding general and the command sergeant major, who were positioned at the bottom of the stairs. Several soldiers kissed the ground as they exited the staircase. It was a proud day to be an American soldier.

As I exited the plane, a thought crossed my mind: "Will what we sacrificed in Iraq over the past year last? Or was it all in vain?" That thought was short lived as I quickly came back to my senses, knowing that I would be united with my family within the hour.

We filed from the plane into a large building where soldiers were waiting to process us in and receive our weapons and other sensitive items. Once that process was complete, we were loaded onto buses and escorted to the main post gym at Fort Carson, where families and loved ones were standing by to unite with us. Once the buses arrived, we filed off, formed into a large mass formation, and marched into the gym. As the gym doors opened and we marched in, I caught a glimpse of my family seated on the front row. Tears were streaming down their eyes. My precious children, Dillon and Chloe, were cheering frantically, though it blended in with the din of patriotic music that was blasting over loud speakers scattered throughout the gymnasium.

It was all I could do to hold back my emotions. I had been away for more than thirteen months, but it seemed like several years had gone by as my children had changed drastically. I felt sorry for them and every other family seated there; sorry for them having to endure a year of pain and constant worrying about their loved ones. Somehow my children and my wife Angela had persevered.

I spent every waking hour of my leave with my children, basically getting to know them all over again. Kids are so resilient they simply endure and carry on. My homecoming was mixed with emotions. On one hand, I was elated to be home and united with my family. On the other hand, I went from fighting one war to another. In this case it was a "domestic war:" I was smack-dab in the middle of a separation that would ultimately lead to a divorce in autumn 2004. I tried to put the inevitable on the back burner and simply focus on spending time with my children. They were truly the innocent party in this matter. My wife and I made it a priority to shield them from any of the personal issues surrounding us.

The formation lasted approximately twenty minutes and then we were dismissed to our families. I immediately ran over to unite with mine and was mobbed with hugs and kisses from Dillon and Chloe. I felt extremely proud to be a soldier and a father that day. But I also felt sad that I had potentially failed as a husband. Being a military spouse is a tough role for anyone. I commend all who have stepped up to the challenge. Not enough credit is given to spouses who selflessly dedicate their own lives to service members.

Angela and I had been married for twelve years at that point. During that time there had been constant deployments for training, and a lot of hours spent at work all to better myself as an officer. Bottom line: time spent away was time unavailable to my family, and the constant departures from home slowly put more than physical distance between us. I admit up front that my priorities were out of line at times. Being an officer in the Army in the early 1990s was different. In order to succeed, you had to be dedicated to your craft. Doing so allowed you to stay competitive for advancement amongst your peers. The majority of times, your family came second, if not third.

As the old Army adage says, "If the Army wanted you to have a wife or family they would have issued you one!" This couldn't be truer. We attempted to work things out, but it was not meant to be and, in the end, we divorced in October 2004. Through it all, I am indebted to her for the sacrifices she made ensuring our children had a great, stable home environment, were cared for, and were raised to be remarkable students and human beings. I am amazed at the resiliency my children have shown despite all they have endured.

After a well-deserved break, I returned to duty four days later. Upon our return, my team and I had to execute what was referred to as "reintegration training." This program was essentially a pilot program the U.S. Army was testing across all installations for units returning from overseas. The Army had established a series of round-robin classes aimed at preparing soldiers who had been away at war to decompress, adjust to garrison life, and reunite with their families. We all had to attend several mandatory classes, including anger and stress management, alcohol and drug abuse, and family coping.

Topics that should have been addressed but unfortunately were not were those on traumatic brain injuries (TBIs), post-traumatic stress disorder (PTSD), and suicide prevention. The reason they were not was that there was little information available about the effects because the war was so new. No data had been collected nor case studies completed by which the Army could establish a baseline from which to attack these issues from a diagnosis or treatment standpoint. It would take a couple of years for these programs to be established.

Inevitably these problems would plague the Army as a record number of suicides would follow. Countless soldiers who have returned from the war, wounded or not, have been diagnosed with TBI and PTSD. In the early stages of the wars in Iraq and Afghanistan, reintegration classes were given little attention by soldiers as the majority simply wanted to get away for a while and enjoy their leave. That all changed once the issues started surfacing and soldiers realized they needed help. At that point, Army leadership got busy and focused time and resources on these pressing issues. Since 2004, the Army has come a long way in how it views and treats soldiers diagnosed with TBI and PTSD.

Likewise, they have added a plethora of programs and resources focused on soldier and family well-being. The Army has acknowledged and recognized that the family is a true combat enabler; strong families led to success on the battlefield. I can attest to this. After returning stateside from two subsequent tours, the reintegration programs had evolved immensely from when they first started. The classes wrapped up after a week, and after that we departed for a well-deserved two-week block leave.

During that leave, I spent every minute I could with my family. After returning from block leave, we returned to steady-state operations. The Army had developed a new training regiment known as the Army Force Generation (ARFORGEN) cycle. Basically it was a three-year plan, whereby upon return from deployment, you fall into the reset phase. During this phase, each a unit undergoes reequipping and remanning of the force. Phase II is a train-up phase, which starts with training at the individual level, is followed by collective-level training, and ends with a four-week rotation to one of the combat training centers (CTCs). This rotation serves as the validation training event for future deployment. By Phase III, each soldier is considered an available force and programmed for deployment to either Iraq or Afghanistan.

This newly developed model was a great start to the Army's attempt to establish a coherent strategy for force generation that provided predictability to commanders and their units. Moreover, it also provided predictability to soldiers and their families. Bottom line: if things went as planned (in a perfect world), a unit and soldiers who had recently returned from deployment would not deploy for at least eighteen to twenty-four months, known as "dwell time."

Reset started on April 1, 2004. During this phase, all of the commands switched out, including the brigade commander and all subordinate battalion commanders. Also, a mass exodus of soldiers departed the brigade en route to other assignments based on the needs of the Army. In many cases, these soldiers returned to units that were on a glide path to battle, notified and scheduled to deploy within six months of their arrival depending on where that particular unit was at in the ARFORGEN cycle.

It was a good start, but not a perfect solution. Mainly this phase was aimed at resetting all unit systems to include its soldiers and their equipment. By that time I had switched out as the operations officer and was assigned as the battalion XO. From April 2004 through October 2004, my time was spent ensuring equipment was maintained, serviced, and prepared for the eventual training phase. I also had a lot of time to reflect on the recent deployment. I was able to come to grips with all that had transpired. The lesson I learned revolved around leadership, in particular leadership during extreme combat conditions. I had the opportunity to serve with some of the best and some of the worst leaders and soldiers in our Army at all levels.

Sassaman was one of the best senior officers with whom I had ever served. He was a consummate professional, a warrior, loyal to those in his charge, almost to a fault. Was he without flaw? No he was not. We all have our faults, and no one is perfect, especially under combat conditions. His most important attribute is that he always did the right thing by the soldiers he led. He stood up for them, right or wrong, and he shielded them from the second- and third-order effects that occurred because of a toxic command climate established by our brigade commander. The greatest testament I can give Sassaman is that he was a true warrior who simply did everything he could to win this fight and attempt to bring every soldier home alive. There is no one else out there I would rather fight with or alongside.

As for the soldiers of 1-8 IN, they were all warriors who displayed courage and tenacity in the toughest and most challenging conditions. I have never witnessed or served with a finer group of soldiers. This group took the fight to the enemy daily and was relentless in their quest to defeat him. Likewise they were innovative in their approach to executing the required nation-building tasks. Despite a lack of training in this area, they found a way to make it happen. Simply put, they were a true band of brothers who fought hard for what was right but most of all for one another.

My time in 1-8 IN ended in November 2004 as I received orders to move to Fort Hood. I was reassigned to 4th Brigade/4th Infantry Division. This brigade was the Army's newest brigade combat team, formed under the transformation initiative which sought to add a fourth maneuver brigade to every modular division. 4th Brigade/4th ID was the latest brigade to activate under this program and was being formed from scratch. I was selected to serve as the Brigade XO, and it was my responsibility to assist with building up the brigade, including manning, equipping, and training it in order to prepare it for deployment to Iraq in fall 2005.

I departed Colorado Springs in December 2004 and set off for a 900-mile journey to Killeen, Texas. I was excited for the new beginning, essentially a fresh start having just returned from a controversial deployment and more recently a divorce that completely broke my spirit. The change of scenery and new mission set was a welcome change.

The trip to Fort Hood took four days. The winter weather was rough in spots, but my family and I made it safely without incident. Once we arrived, it was "all-hands on deck" as we were under a time constraint to unload the U-Haul truck so I could turn it in on time and avoid additional charges. Within a couple of hours, all my household goods were unloaded as boxes were stacked and scattered throughout the house. From there we left the mess in place and departed for Mesquite, Texas, to celebrate Christmas with my siblings.

On January 15, 2005, I reported for my new duty assignment following three days of in-processing the division. As I arrived at brigade headquarters, I was met and welcomed by the brigade commander, Colonel Mike Beech. He was delighted to see me, as prior to my arrival only a handful of officers and soldiers had been on hand. Being that this was a newly formed brigade (two months from its inception), it would take time to fully man and equip it before it resembled a true brigade combat team.

The good thing is that all six subordinate battalions had their command teams in place and were slowly filling out the subordinate companies below them. During my in-brief with Beech, I was tasked to work all equipment and maintenance issues to increase our operational readiness rate. This task was daunting to say the least. As any good infantryman does, I tackled it head on. At that time, the brigade was right in the middle of its BFV and M1 Abrams Tank fielding. Combat vehicles were arriving daily in droves. As vehicles arrived, soldiers and mechanics from the brigade inspected them and ensured they were operational and ready for training.

Meanwhile, the same influx was happening on the personnel side of the house. Soldiers of all ranks were arriving en masse daily. As they arrived, they were processed and assigned to one of six subordinate battalions depending on their skill set, known as their military occupational skill (MOS). I noticed that a lot of the soldiers had recently returned from Iraq and/or Afghanistan, as evidenced by the combat patch they wore on their right sleeve. There were a lot of "cherry" soldiers as well, young privates who had just arrived to the unit fresh out of basic and advanced individual training who had yet to see combat.

Once the brigade was fully manned, it was comprised of approximately a 60/40 mix, combat/noncombat experience. The good thing is that we had key leaders, namely NCOs at the platoon and squad levels with combat experience who could take the young soldiers under their wings and train them on the critical tasks to prepare them for future combat.

By March 2005, the brigade was fully equipped and at least 90 percent manned. Achieving this milestone meant that we could transition to the training phase, starting with individual training followed by collective-level training. Once collective-level training was complete, the brigade ended the training phase by executing our mission rehearsal exercise (MRX). The MRX was the culminating training event for the brigade, and, once complete, we would execute final preparations for deployment to combat. The training phase by design of the ARFORGEN cycle was to last a year.

Because we were a newly formed brigade, it was crucial that we take advantage of the allotted time and ensure the brigade was fully integrated and trained. The stakes were too high to cut corners; doing so could mean the difference between lives saved versus lives lost. Based on these facts, our brigade operations officer, Major Rich Morales, and the entire staff drafted a succinct and cohesive training plan that would allow the brigade to accomplish all the required training gates for a March 2006 deployment to Iraq.

As the old Army saying goes, "no plan survives first contact," and that was certainly true in this case. In April 2005, we were informed by division headquarters that we were being accelerated in the ARFORGEN cycle and would deploy four months earlier, in November 2005 rather than March 2006. Although a shock, we adapted and adjusted the plan to meet the requirements. If we could pull this off, it would be the first achievement of its kind for a newly formed unit to stand up from scratch and deploy just eleven months later. To put this feat into perspective, the first Stryker Brigade Combat Team, 3rd Brigade, 2nd Infantry Division was officially activated at Fort Lewis, Washington, on March 7, 2000, as the newest Army brigade formed under the transformation initiative put in place by Army Chief of Staff General Eric Shinseki. This brigade did not deploy or see combat until November 2003, some three and a half years later when they deployed to Samarra, Iraq, and participated in Operation Ivy Blizzard, in December 2003.

The one advantage to being accelerated in the deployment sequence is that all the Army's resources were focused on us. The brigade received an influx of personnel, bringing us to a total of approximately 105 percent strength. We received the newest equipment and personal protective gear. Moreover, we had access to funding for the purchase of specialized mission equipment based on the commander's discretion and mission analysis. Resources were plentiful, and we took full advantage of them. One day at Fort Hood, I saw at least four semitrucks unloading thousands of cases of Oakley sunglasses, chemical lights, and other equipment. This was a routine occurrence for every unit assigned to the brigade. The Army spared no expense ensuring we were manned, equipped, and readied for battle.

In March 2005, we began an intense training cycle. In the beginning, all training was focused at the individual level, centered around small-arms qualification and other associated weapons ranges. April through August 2005 was focused on collective training, starting at the team level, then squad, followed by platoon level, and ending with company-level training. This training included everything from basic battle drills to a live-fire exercise. Soldiers and leaders alike were busting their tails to ensure we were ready for the challenges ahead.

Finally, in September 2005, the brigade executed its final training event before our deployment, the MRX. Based on the fact that we were on a condensed timeline, Army senior leadership approved a home station MRX for us. In most cases, units who are based in the United States deploy to the National Training Center located at Fort Erwin, California, or the Joint Readiness Training Center located at Fort Polk, Louisiana.

Originally we were slated to deploy and execute our MRX at JRTC, but based on the acceleration, the operations group at JRTC exported the training to us at Fort Hood. The MRX serves as the brigade's final dress rehearsal before deployment to theater. The ten-day training event was tough and rigorous as we executed around-the-clock operations against an adversary known as the opposing force (OPFOR). This was the most realistic training short of combat. Every key leader from squad through brigade level had an observer controller/trainer (OC/T) assigned to cover down on it. OC/Ts are nothing more than an external set of eyes that provide feedback about things done well and things that need improvement. They also serve as mentors. All OC/Ts have previous combat experience, and the majority have recently returned from combat. Based on their experience, they are able to provide the most current information about tactics, techniques, and procedures that work best in theater. Bottom line: OC/Ts are true combat enablers worth their weight in gold.

Credit must be given to the Army senior leadership for the overall training our Combat Training Centers provide and the OC/T selection process. As mentioned in previous chapters, a rotation to one of the major training centers prior to 2003 was a brutal experience, and units normally departed dragging their heads between their tails with the perception that they were the worst combat unit ever. However, that all changed. Once the wars in Iraq and Afghanistan commenced, the Army was populated with experienced combat soldiers, NCOs, and officers. The best and brightest of these leaders were hand-selected to serve as OC/Ts. Moreover, the experience turned more hands-on and constructive in nature versus simply being a critique.

Our MRX was a quality training event and overall success. We tested and trained all of our systems focused on battle command and reporting. I got a better grasp of our staff's strengths and weaknesses. Likewise, I knew talent levels and who were the go-to guys, known as "Iron Majors." Leaders and soldiers at all levels were fatigued and experienced the stress and rigors they would face in combat in the coming months. This was most critical for the new soldiers who had just arrived from basic training and those who had yet to deploy. Overall it was a quality event whereby every unit achieved the stated training objectives and desired end state.

As the MRX was nearing conclusion, it was interrupted by Hurricane Rita, which followed on the heels of Hurricane Katrina a month earlier. For two days, we were hammered by torrential rain and high winds. We were fortunate that no one was injured and that our equipment stayed intact. After a forty-eight-hour delay, we executed our final attack. After four hours of heavy fighting against the OPFOR, the MRX ended, concluding with the final after-action review (AAR). The AAR focused on the overall sustains and improves (i.e., strengths and weaknesses) for the brigade and our subordinate battalions. Once the AAR was complete, we redeployed from the field and executed recovery operations.

The recovery operations lasted two weeks and consisted of cleaning all vehicles and weapon systems and accounting for all assigned property. Following this event, we executed final preparations for deployment. This phase included loading containers with all equipment to be shipped into theater and the more difficult tasks of loading vehicles onto trains at the rail yard for shipment to the port facility, followed by the loading onto cargo ships for transport to Iraq. Again, facing a tight timeline, the soldiers and leaders of the brigade executed these tasks in a flawless manner without any major incident.

By October 31, 2005, our equipment departed the Texas ports of Beaumont and Corpus Christi bound for Iraq. Once this was complete, the entire brigade was granted a two-week block leave, a well-deserved break from the rigor and stress from months of intense training.

I spent block leave mainly traveling to Colorado Springs to visit my kids for a week; the other time was spent with my lovely girlfriend and future wife, Captain Wendy Scott. Block leave came to an end on November 15, 2005, which meant that there were two weeks remaining until we departed for Iraq. I spent the last two weeks moving out of the rental property, placing everything I owned into storage for the foreseeable future.

During that time, I was able to introduce Wendy to my family, and they immediately took to her. This willing acceptance was comforting to me, knowing that she would have a support network if needed while I was away. Before deploying, we took in a Texas Longhorn football game. The Longhorns beat the Kansas Jayhawks that day 66–14. How my Texas Longhorns faired each Saturday determined my overall level of morale, good or bad. My morale meter was off the charts: I was in love with a beautiful woman, and the Longhorns were undefeated. Life could not be any better.

The big day finally came: Saturday, December 2, 2005. The majority of the brigade and subordinate units had departed a few days prior.

I was to deploy with the trail element, as it was my job to ensure the brigade was manifested and deployed from Fort Hood on schedule. We were actually delayed by twenty-four hours due to poor weather.

Good-byes are always emotional and difficult, especially for those who are left behind. The evening of December 2, 2005, was quite emotional for me; goodbyes always are. We arrived at the brigade headquarters and had approximately thirty minutes to chat and say our goodbyes. The half hour seemed like an eternity, but when it finally ended, I kissed Wendy and told her not to worry and that I loved her. I departed for the accountability formation, and the clock started ticking on the countdown to my reunion with my family. It could not come soon enough.

My team and I departed a couple of hours later on a chartered Boeing 737 en route to Kuwait International Airport. This time around there was no first class seating, and space was at a premium. The flight lasted approximately eighteen hours from start to finish, with one stop in Germany for refueling before arrival in Kuwait.

We arrived in Kuwait on December 4 at approximately 0800 hours local. It was daylight outside. As we stepped off the plane, the blistering hot Kuwaiti wind hit me. It was more than 80 degrees Fahrenheit—in December. I expected milder temperatures. It was certainly a change from the 40-degree weather in Texas. It took a few days to acclimate.

As we filed off the plane, we shuffled over and loaded onto buses that would carry us out to the desert to Camp Buehring some 70 miles away. The one thing that changed from 2003 was that all the local camps, such as Camp New Jersey and Camp Pennsylvania, had been decommissioned, leaving four camps: Camp Virginia, Camp Buehring, Ali al Salem Airbase, and Camp Arifjan. Camp Virginia was occupied by units departing theater. Camp Buehring was for units deploying into theater, and Ali al Salem was the air base where all soldiers staged and flew into and out of Iraq. Camp Arifjan was the main garrison for theater operations and served as the central logistics hub for all of the Middle East.

Once we loaded the buses, we departed on the hour-long trip to Camp Buehring. One thing had not changed from my last trip: we were still escorted by the Kuwaiti Highway Patrol. Along the way, we passed a few camels. All the towns and villages looked the same. The highways in Kuwait are very similar to the Autobahn of Germany.

Locals drive the roads at speeds in excess of 100 mph (200 km/hr). I really never grasped what the rush was all about. As we passed through the desert once again, the landscape was covered with thousands of Bedouin Tents. It was déjà vu all over again.

Once we arrived at Camp Buehring, Kuwait, I met with the commander and S-3 (Training and Operations officer) who provided a lay down of current operations in Kuwait and up north in Iraq. My main focus was on logistical operations in Kuwait. My number one task was to supervise port operations and ensure that all combat vehicles were downloaded in an expeditious yet safe manner and prepared for onward movement to Camp Buehring. Once there, the units would quickly ready them for baseline training in Kuwait and, more importantly, for onward movement into Iraq. Port operations were easy as I placed our best man, Major Gary Martin, the support operations officer (SPO), in charge of the port node. Martin is by far one of the best Army logisticians I have ever served with or have known. He is a protégé of Brigadier General Gustave Perna, with whom I served with during my first deployment. Bottom line: he is a workhorse and is clearly the subject matter expert on all things logistics. His selection as the officer in charge (OIC) of port operations was a no-brainer. My life as the overall supervisor was pretty easy given the cast of great soldiers, NCOs, and officers working for me at the port. As the ships arrived into port, they were downloaded in record time and were quickly loaded for transportation to Camp Buehring. After a week's time, every single piece of rolling stock (800 vehicles total) had been downloaded and moved to our outlying camp.

Once all equipment was on hand at Camp Buehring, our subordinate battalions commenced with their training plans. This training included a limited gunnery for all M1 Tanks and BFVs. The artillery battalion executed numerous live fires to certify crews and verify functionality of their Howitzers. Finally all soldiers, NCOs, and officers had to confirm their zeros (sighting in) of their individual weapons and receive training classes on IED recognition, vehicle rollover drills, first aid treatment, and other associated issues. This training lasted approximately ten days and was beneficial to all.

The Army had come a long way from a year earlier. Prerequisite training had been revamped and improved drastically. This new and improved training was a welcome change from the previous deployment. Lessons learned from units departing theater were being captured by the Army and applied for the betterment and welfare of soldiers and units heading into the fight. It seemed that the Army was turning the corner from OIF 1. Only time would tell if the training was paying off in theater.

Once all the prerequisite training was completed, I was summoned to Baghdad by Beech. He had recently departed with our deputy commanding officer (DCO), Lieutenant Colonel Troy Smith, the operations officer (S-3), Maj. Rich Morales, and other key staff members and was already in Baghdad getting a jumpstart on the transition with the outgoing brigade. Our mission was to relieve 4th Brigade, 3rd Infantry Division in place and assume their AO, which included security of the Green Zone and two highly contested districts in West Baghdad: East Rasheed and West Rasheed, including the volatile neighborhoods of Dora and Risala. Also within our area of operations there were several key routes, including Routes Irish, Jackson, Senators, and Red Wings. These key routes would play a significant role as far as friendly casualties we sustained from IED attacks on them during our tenure.

Securing the Green Zone was our priority mission and received the most attention and oversight from the higher chain of command based on the strategic importance and value if breached by insurgents. The Green Zone is a 9-square-kilometer (about 5.5-square-mile) area in Central Baghdad that is the main headquarters for the coalition and Iraqi government in Iraq and the U.S. embassy. Its official name is the International Zone (IZ).

The contrasting Red Zone refers to anything outside the Green Zone. It is in my estimation by far the most secured area in the world. It is surrounded by more than 150,000 18-foot concrete walls known as T-walls and more than 200 miles of concertina or razor wire strewn across the top. An infantry battalion comprised of more than 800 heavily armed soldiers equipped with M1 Abrams Tanks, BFVs, and heavy machine guns is there with the sole purpose of manning the guard towers and check points surrounding it. Within the perimeter is a highly advanced video surveillance system that allows for 24/7 coverage of all key areas. Finally, around-the-clock combat patrols run the perimeter to ensure there are no breaches.

Prior to our arrival, there had been more than twenty attacks by insurgents attempting to breach the perimeter. Some of these attacks were perpetrated by insurgents attacking the checkpoints using VBIEDs. Thanks to the complex security array and lethal reaction by U.S. soldiers, all attempts failed.

I arrived in Baghdad on the evening of December 14, 2005, at approximately 1700 hours. We landed at Victory Base Complex located at Baghdad International Airport (BIAP), where I was met by First Sergeant Reimer and other soldiers from the brigade headquarters company. I uploaded my equipment and we departed en route to the Green Zone, approximately 12 kilometers (about 7.5 miles) east of BIAP. One obstacle stood in our way: the 12-kilometer stretch of Route Irish.

Route Irish was the only major road that connected Victory Base Complex/BIAP and the well-fortified Green Zone. Because it was the only route to and from, there was a large concentration of military and government-related traffic that used the route on a daily basis. Due to the military traffic density alone, Route Irish instantly became a priority target for insurgents. Insurgents attacked convoys using various means including IEDs, direct-fire ambushes, sniper attacks, and VBIEDs. According to military records, between November 1, 2004, and March 12, 2005, there were 135 attacks or hostile incidents on Route Irish. These included nine complex attacks (i.e., a combination of more than one type of attack such as an IED followed by small-arms fire or mortars), nineteen explosive devices found, three hand grenades, seven indirect-fire attacks, nineteen roadside explosions, fourteen rocket-propelled grenades (RPGs), fifteen VBIEDs, and four other types of attacks. Of these attacks, 66 percent occurred between the hours of 1900 and 0000. Up to that point, insurgent attacks claimed the lives of more than a hundred U.S. and coalition service members, Iraqi government officials, and other civilians. Based on the persistent and lethal attacks, Route Irish was coined "the most dangerous road in the world" by soldiers, commanders, and journalists.[1] So dangerous was the road that an extortionist Baghdad-based security firm offered bullet-proof taxi rides charging up to $3,000 one way.

I kind of knew how bad Route Irish was before making the trip based on horror stories I either read, saw on the news, or heard about from friends previously stationed in Baghdad. Before I climbed inside the Humvee that would transport me to the Green Zone, a soldier told me to "Be ready. At any moment, we could be hit." As we exited the gate of Victory Base and turned east on Route Irish, the point was hammered home as I was looking out the window and noticed numerous road craters created by IED blasts along the shoulders of the road. In some spots there were dried pools of blood. This night we were fortunate. We made it to the Green Zone without incident, but it was truly the most gut-wrenching, white-knuckled, thirty-minute road trip I had ever taken.

Our headquarters in the Green Zone was located right inside the west gate at a sprawling palace complex known as FOB Prosperity. The name of the place shocked me at first because based on what I experienced during my last tour and given the current state of violence and or conditions in Iraq now, there was no prosperity. If anything the FOB got its name based solely on the optimism of the commander who first occupied the place.

The complex that was now my official home for a year was known prior to the invasion as the As-Salam Palace, located on the site of the former Republican Guard headquarters, which was destroyed during Operation Desert Storm in 1990. Construction on the new palace began as the war ended and was completed in September 1999 at a cost of approximately $100 million. The four-story palace was surrounded by orchards of lime, orange, date, and other fruit trees.

A series of artificial pools, lakes, and ponds dotted the 814,000-square-foot complex, which had been used primarily by Saddam and the Ba'ath government to house foreign dignitaries and other VIPs. During the "Shock and Awe" bombing campaign in 2003, the palace took several guided-missile hits fired from coalition aircraft. These munitions are known as joint direct attack munitions (JDAMs), but are more commonly referred to as smart bombs. The evidence of these strikes is readily visible from both outside and inside the palace structure. After the bombings took place, looters stole everything from furniture and carpets to light fixtures and electrical wiring and even the gold-plated toilets. Based on the extensive damage sustained, it was a wonder that the palace was still standing and serviceable enough to serve as a brigade headquarters.

After a quick orientation and layout of the complex, I headed upstairs to the second floor to link-up with the commander and operations officer for an update on the transition. When I arrived at Tactical Operations Center (TOC), a meeting was taking place. Known as the commander's update brief (CUB), this meeting took place daily at 1700 hours. The purpose of the meeting was to allow the brigade commander to receive an update from all subordinate commanders on operations and events that occurred in their assigned AOs during the past twenty-four hours. In this case, the brigade we were transitioning with was still in charge of the area until we officially took over, hence they were the ones doing the briefing.

At that time we were four days into a twenty-five-day transition. All of our equipment and troops were still transiting from Kuwait into Iraq. After the meeting concluded, I talked for a few minutes with Beech, providing him an update on activities in Kuwait. I let him know that the subordinate battalions had completed all prerequisite training and that they were in the process of loading up and moving north. He was elated with the news and eager to get the entire brigade up here safely with all its personnel and equipment so we could get on with the transition and ultimately assume the mission. He told me to focus strictly on force generation.

From there I linked up with my counterpart and fellow XO, Major Ross Coffman. Coffman and I had met about two months earlier when I traveled to Iraq for the predeployment site survey (PDSS). The PDSS is a two-week trip during which key leaders of the brigade and subordinate battalions travel to Iraq and link-up with their counterparts in order to conduct initial coordination for the eventual transition. This process includes receiving several briefings focused on current operations, enemy activity, logistics, civil military operations, and a host of other topics. It is death by PowerPoint.

In addition to all the briefings, we traveled throughout the brigade's assigned AO, visiting every subordinate FOB in order to gain an appreciation of the terrain and mission. The PDSS is the one single event that puts everything in motion and allows for a smoother transition versus units conducting discovery learning upon arrival. I was the senior representative from our brigade during the trip and upon return was responsible for briefing the entire brigade leadership on the results and outcome. Based on that back brief, our brigade and subordinate battalions were able to complete their plans before deploying into theater and knew what to expect.

The Army had finally got this process right. During my first tour, the transition between 1-8 IN and 2-3 IN was a mess. There was no PDSS; nor was a proper transition conducted. They simply showed up and we handed them the keys to our FOB and departed for Samarra.

The two months that had elapsed since I last met Coffman seemed like a lifetime. A lot had changed in theater. Regardless of the changes, it would be our responsibility to tackle the issues head-on as we would have responsibility of the AO in less than three weeks.

During the next week, our equipment began to flow in, and convoy after convoy was arriving at all the outlying FOBs. By week's end, all equipment and personnel had arrived safely without incident. From there the brigade began executing the remainder of the transition phase referred to as right seat ride/left seat ride (RSR/LSR). During this phase, the incoming unit links-up with the outgoing unit and executes operations outside the wire with them over a two-week period. The first week is when the outgoing unit executes operations using their own equipment as they are in the left side driver's seat and the incoming unit occupies the right side passenger seat as a spectator of sorts. This allows the incoming unit and its soldiers to see how operations are conducted in order to gain situational awareness and understanding of the complete area they will be in charge of. After that, the two units switch and the incoming unit takes charge using their equipment and the outgoing unit rides along, serving as a mentor. After RSR/LSR was completed, the transition concluded and our brigade officially assumed responsibility of the AO as the outgoing unit redeployed stateside.

The RSR/LSR occurs at all levels of command, from squad to battalion. All battalion- and brigade-level staffs execute the same type of operations and battle handover with their respective staff counterpart. For me the transition was rather easy. Coffman and I wrapped up the transition in four days versus the two weeks allotted as he had to depart to run redeployment operations in Kuwait for his brigade.

I was promoted to lieutenant colonel the following day. And, lucky for me, the Texas Longhorns had just defeated the University of Southern California Trojans for the college national championship. Things were going well.

On January 14, 2006, we executed the Transfer of Authority by conducting an official ceremony during which 4th Brigade, 3rd ID, "Vanguards," folded and cased their colors and we uncased ours. On hand to preside over the event were both commanding generals of their respective units, Major General William Webster, 3rd ID Commander and Major General James D. Thurman, 4th ID Commander. The ceremony lasted approximately thirty minutes. In barely an instant, the AO and all the challenges that went with it switched from Vanguard AO to Cobra AO. It was our watch now.

The mission assigned to us by the 4th ID, which had assumed command for all of Baghdad known as Multi-National Division–Baghdad (MND–B), was as follows:

"4th Brigade/4th ID on 14 January 2006 secures the International Zone (IZ) and critical infrastructure, partners with Iraqi Security Forces (ISF) to enable forces to assume lead in counter insurgency operations and neutralizes the Anti-Iraqi Forces, (AIF) in AO Cobra in order to allow the unhindered development of the Government of Iraq (GOI) and set conditions for self-reliance."

AO Cobra

As for our AO, in addition to the criticality of securing the IZ, we also had responsibility for most of southern Baghdad. Five districts (similar to counties) comprised southern Baghdad: Mansour, Karkh, Karradah Peninsula, East Rasheed, and West Rasheed. Each district was subdivided into areas known as "hayys" (similar to towns), including key areas such as Aamel, Bayaa, Risalah, Shurta, Amiriya, Yarmouk, and the volatile Dora.

Within the hayys were neighborhoods known as "muhallas." Each muhalla was assigned an identification number (comparable to a ZIP code) starting with 800 and ending with 898. Some of these muhallas, such as 820, 824, 826, 828, and 830, would be the primary focus of our offensive operations due to the amount of insurgent activity associated with them. Muhalla 824 was the worst by far. Of all the casualties our brigade sustained in East Rasheed, the majority came from this area.

Baghdad had an estimated population of 6.4 million people. Of that, 4 million were Shiites, 2 million were Sunni, 300,000 were Christians, and 100,000 belonged to other religious and ethnic groups. At least 40 percent of this mixed ethnic population resided in our AO, which contained a mixture of all sects and numerous tribal affiliations. The majority of tribes were somewhat peaceful and kept to themselves; however, our AO contained some of the most volatile tribes, who were most commonly associated with supporting and carrying out the insurgency. These included the Janabi, Dulaymi, Mashadani, Tikriti, Jabouri, Tamimi, Obeidi, Ithawi, and the Karagholli tribes. Typically, 90 percent of the insurgent attacks were affiliated with one of these tribes. Of these, the two most prominent or common perpetrators were the Sunni-based Jabouris and the Shiite-based Tamimis.

During my last tour in 2009–10, I often had dinner with leading sheiks of both these two tribes, Sheik Omar al-Jabouri (head of Jabouri tribe) and Sheik Mohammed Bakr al-Tamimi (head of the Tamimi tribe). There I was, sitting down having tea and kabobs with men whose hands were soiled with the blood of Americans and Iraqis. Those were truly uncomfortable situations, hard pills to swallow. By that point, the war had started to turn full circle: enemies were becoming allies. As the old adage states: "Keep your friends close and your enemies closer."

I certainly applied it in this case.

Based on the demographic and tribal makeup, it was a challenge to protect them from one another during the height of the sectarian violence that would occur on our watch in the coming weeks and months ahead.

Another key factor comprising our AO was the fact that there were more than 330 mosques, the majority of which were Sunni. Charting and plotting every mosque location was a critical task assigned to each land-owning subordinate battalion. In addition, subordinate units were tasked with monitoring the daily messaging using their assigned translators. Mosques were the vital communications link to all citizens in Iraq. By design, mosques were where imams broadcasted their spiritual messages to the local populace using loud speakers for those who could not attend. At times the messages broadcasted were anti-American or anti-Iraq in nature. Based on the message delivered, a mosque was classified as friendly, neutral, or hostile. These records were maintained throughout the deployment and passed on from unit to unit.

We were limited in our options to deal with hostile mosques. Under cultural respect category as per the established ROE, mosques were off limits unless we were being shot at from one; under those extreme conditions, we could return fire and enter them if required, but only if Iraqi security forces were present since they were the ones who were allowed to physically enter the mosques. Both Sunni and Shiite insurgents recognized this fact and started using mosques as central meeting locations to plan their attacks and future operations. Moreover, a lot of illegal contraband such as explosives and weapons were stored inside mosques.

Enemy Situation

By the time I got to Iraq for my second tour, the insurgency was in full bloom. Baghdad was the central hub for insurgent activity. Iraq's capital city was home to the newly elected government of Iraq (GOI), which had become one of the enemy's strategic objectives. Although there were not enough enemy forces in terms of sheer numbers to topple the GOI, there were enough to wreak havoc against U.S., coalition, and Iraq security forces (ISF), and doing so would create a perception of chaos and instability.

The enemy as a whole was referred to as anti-Iraqi forces. This had not changed from when I last departed. However, the insurgent groups had multiplied, especially amongst the Shiite-based militias. Al-Qaeda in Iraq was still present in our AO and centrally operated out of the West Rasheed area with numerous direct attack, IED, and VBIED cells totaling approximately 200 to 250 enemy personnel. Their stated objective had not changed; it was to rid the Middle East of all Western influence and to return to the Islamic Caliphate. They attempted to achieve this objective by attacking U.S. personnel, ISF, other GOI targets, and any of the population that supported us to create an environment of instability and further undermine the legitimacy of the GOI. The majority of their attacks were conducted against U.S. forces and ISF in the form of direct-fire ambushes and IED attacks along the major routes that ran through the AO. U.S. military convoys were easy targets for them.

The roads in and around Baghdad were packed with military supply convoys that operated all hours of the day. These convoys were prone to attack because they did not have the heavily armored vehicles such as M1 Tanks, BFVs, or Stryker vehicles within their formation or as escorts. These convoys are often referred to as "soft skin" targets. Rarely would the enemy attack and challenge a combat patrol using direct fire; when they did, the outcome was not favorable for them. Instead, they would attack with IEDs and in most cases were able to inflict severe damage, especially along routes Irish and Jackson. Later on in the year, they started targeting the Shiite population with suicide car bombs and other direct attacks on the population based on their perceived support of us and favoritism they received by being the ruling majority based on 2005 election results.

As for the Shiite-based enemy, these were mainly small, organized militias originally formed to protect the Shia population, religious sites, and other political interests against Sunni aggression and incursion. According to CPA Order 91, a militia is defined as a military or paramilitary force that is not part of the regular ISF. During his tenure as prime minister, Ayad Allawi negotiated with the nine major militias in Iraq, all of which agreed to disband or integrate into the ISF. Allawi later stated that all armed forces not under state control were to be considered illegal. Nonetheless, militias in their current state continue to play a major role in the insurgency and politics in Iraq. The persistence of militias within Iraq is fueled by the deeply rooted insecurity that each of the main ethnic and religious groups in the nation feel.

Compounding the situation, militias are composed mostly of civilians, all of whom have the ability to assemble—or disappear—on short notice. Early on, postinvastion, these militias were not a threat to us. However, in late 2004, they turned their attention toward attacking U.S. and coalition forces once they figured out that we were an occupying force rather than simply a liberating force. Our own actions, such as the Abu Ghraib prison abuse scandal, contributed to the aggression against us.

Five prominent militias or splinter groups were in our AO: Jaysh al-Madi (JAM), Wolf Brigade, Hizb al-Dawa, Khadamiyah Militia, and the Iranian-backed Badr Corps. Each of these Shiite-based factions had a specific mission and charter. The most prominent and dangerous of these groups was the JAM, the official armed wing of the outspoken cleric Muqtada al-Sadr. This militia's sole charter is to integrate themselves into the Iraqi government in attempts to infiltrate its ranks and ultimately seize control of the government. It is estimated that the total militia strength in our AO consisted of approximately 500 personnel. Aside from al-Qaeda and the Shiite militias, there were criminal groups totaling approximately 200 members who operated in our AO simply to take advantage of and capitalize on large amounts of money to be had by selling military weapons and other illegal contraband on the black market. These groups presented quite a problem for us to negotiate and counter.

Not only did the threat groups expand, their tactics evolved and became more advanced. This advancement resulted in greater lethality on the battlefield. IEDs remained the chief threat and killer of U.S. and coalition troops. However, the insurgents were smarter in how they set up and emplaced them. In 2003–04, they would simply pack an empty mortar round or an artillery shell with explosives and then emplace it in the middle of the road or on the shoulder and run an electrical wire to it from a hide site. When a U.S. convoy approached, they would detonate the device using a battery or some other electrical firing device. Upon detonation, they would flee the area. Nowadays, the enemy links together several artillery shells, known as "daisy chaining." Prior to emplacing them, they packed the shells with explosives, nails, steel ball bearings, and other metal objects to increase the blast radius of shrapnel. This allows for a larger kill zone and increases the probability of wounding or killing someone.

Today, instead of wire, the enemy uses cell phones wired to the IEDs. In order to detonate, they just have to call the number on the phone, and when it rings, an electrical charge sets off the IED. They even use infrared motion detectors like those found in home security systems as detonation devices. These devices are set in place at the ambush site and are armed remotely prior to a convoy approaching the kill zone. Once the lead vehicle breaks the infrared beam, the IED detonates. It seems pretty simple to construct, but it is not. In a lot of cases, we would find insurgents who had blown themselves up in the process of either making or emplacing the device. The enemy went so far as to emplace IEDs inside animal carcasses, tree trunks, and piles of trash, and even mounted them to the tops of bridges in order to conceal them from detection.

The enemy also continued to use VBIEDs to target large crowds and key government or military buildings. These bombs were the most lethal and, depending on the amount of explosives packed inside of a car or truck and where they were detonated, could topple buildings. Most often, they were detonated in crowded market places, resulting in hundreds wounded or killed. On occasion, we were successful at stopping these if and when we had received intelligence as to where they would strike.

The most technological advancement we saw being implemented was the production and employment of an IED known as the explosively formed projectile (EFP). These are the most lethal IEDs out there. They were introduced and used by Shiite militias with what is believed to be a weapon produced and backed by Iran. The technology for producing these deadly bombs has since been passed on to other enemy groups and can no longer be tied strictly to Shiites. The round itself is a shape charge that when produced is nothing more than a 4- to 6-inch copper disc placed in what looks like a paint can with explosive packed in behind it. The device is ignited by various means that when detonated forms a lethal shape charge that travels at an enormous speed toward its target with such velocity that it can cut through 4 to 6 inches of armor. These weapons are detonated using the types of detonators found on other IEDs, including cell phones, washing machine timers, infrared motion detectors, and pressure switches. As with IEDs, the enemy emplaces multiple EFPs, sometimes those that are dual or triple arrayed. A direct hit from one of these is usually catastrophic. This round is by far the most lethal weapon the enemy has at its disposal, and it is killing soldiers at an alarming rate. Soldiers traveling the streets in and around Baghdad know it is only a matter of time before they encounter one. The question most often asked was when, not if, you'd be hit by an IED.

Aside from the advancements in IEDs, the enemy still used direct-fire weapons such as AK-47s, RPK machine guns, RPGs, snipers, mortars, and rockets. Typically, they would not attack a heavy-mounted combat patrol based on the fact that they were numerically inferior and lacked the firepower to stay in a sustained gunfight. At times when they choose to attack us, it did not end favorably for them. Based on the enemy advancement and increased lethality of these latest weapons, the U.S. military countered by rapidly producing and fielding the up-armored Humvee, known as the M1151. Meanwhile, research and development was taking place stateside to produce even better, more advanced combat vehicles that could withstand the effects of EFPs and other lethal IEDs. The main goal of these vehicles was to increase the survivability rate of soldiers and all occupants.

Research and development started in earnest in 2005, and by the summer of 2007, the first variants of the Mine Resistant Ambush Protection Vehicle (MRAP) were produced and shipped to Iraq and Afghanistan as they rolled off the production line. The Department of Defense's speedy development of the MRAP vehicle—two years from concept to mass deployment—was a remarkable feat and changed the way the Army operated in Iraq and Afghanistan. In comparison it took the Army ten years from concept to fielding the BFV. These vehicles were truly worth their weight in gold. The survivability rate of our soldiers increased drastically, reducing the casualty rate to 6 percent. By comparison, the M-1 Abrams main battle tank was said to have a casualty rate of 15 percent, and the uparmored Humvee, a 22 percent casualty rate.

I witnessed a couple of IED strikes and in one case an EFP attack against these vehicles during my last tour in 2009–10. Outside of a couple of bruises and a concussion, every soldier survived and walked away unscathed. If these same strikes had occurred against a Humvee instead of a MRAP, it is likely that significant casualties would have resulted. Other drawbacks due to the fast pace fielding is that soldiers have less time to train on the vehicles, whose height, size, and high center of gravity make them prone to rolling over: as of 2008 there had been twenty-four accidents in Iraq, and fewer than ten in Afghanistan; in some of these incidents soldiers have been killed. Regardless of these mishaps, the fielding of this vehicle is better than the alternative. A lot of soldiers have returned home today thankful they operated in them. The MRAP series of vehicles is hands down the most survivable platform operating on the battlefield today. Based on the overwhelming success of the vehicles in combat, the DOD has spent $26.8 billion on the MRAP program since fiscal year 2006.[2]

The Army made other breakthroughs in technology and equipped the force through a program known as the Rapid Fielding Initiative (RFI). This program started holistically in 2005 and was designed to equip soldiers headed to the fight with the latest and most advanced or improved force protection equipment available. Prior to deploying for this current tour, we received advanced body armor, improved ballistic eyewear, fire resistant gloves and uniforms, and a plethora of other gee-whiz gadgets. Clearly the Army listened and acted on the lessons learned from past deployments and spared no expense to ensure we had the best equipment out there—and rightfully so.

Friendly Situation

To accomplish the overall mission assigned to us, our brigade utilized the six subordinate battalions within our task organization and a Georgian battalion, which mainly provided internal security of historic sites within IZ. Our two land-owning battalions were the 8-10 Cavalry Squadron, commanded by Lieutenant Colonel Gian Gentile, assigned to West Rasheed, and the 2-506 Infantry Regiment, commanded by Lieutenant Colonel Greg Butts, assigned to East Rasheed. The 2-506 was not organic to the brigade; they were detached from the 4th Brigade, 101st Airborne Division assigned to us. Likewise, we detached 3-67 Armor Battalion and sent them over to 4/101.

The armor battalion was not a great fit in East Rasheed, in particular in the Dora area. This was a congested, built-up urban area with very narrow streets and alleys. It would have been tough for M1 Abrams tanks to negotiate and patrol the streets. Moreover, the battalion did not have the requisite number of dismounted soldiers assigned to it compared to that of an infantry battalion. East Rasheed required maximum numbers of dismounted soldiers on the ground to effectively patrol the streets.

1-12 Infantry Battalion, commanded by Lieutenant Colonel Rob Estes, was assigned the mission of securing the IZ. 1-12 IN was our best-trained and most aggressive battalion. Why we assigned them to the IZ mission as opposed to giving them an AO outside the wire puzzled me. In the beginning I did not agree with the choice, and Estes argued against it as well. If ever there was an aggressively led battalion that needed to be outside the wire executing counterinsurgency operations, it was 1-12 IN. In retrospect, after having spent three tours in Iraq, I finally saw the light.

First and foremost, I recognized the fact that we, the U.S. Military, were not going to kill our way out of Iraq, much like we did not kill our way out of Vietnam as some had hoped we would. This was not a "body count" mission. Securing the IZ was our priority mission; it was the center of gravity for all of Iraq being that it was headquarters for the GOI, Iraqi parliament, U.S. embassy, and Multi-National Force–Iraq (MNF–I). If we failed to secure it, then, ultimately, the entire Iraq mission could have failed. Any successful breach of the IZ or attack against the GOI would have been seen by all Iraqis as a complete failure. It would have been seen as an overwhelming success by the enemy, further fueling their cause. It also would have demonstrated to all Iraqis that if neither the GOI nor U.S. forces could protect themselves, then nor would they be able to protect Iraqi civilians. The U.S. military could not take that risk, so the best battalion was assigned to this highly visible strategic mission.

During our tenure, more than a dozen attempts were made to attack and breach the perimeter, all of which failed. The one attack we could not prevent was the daily indirect-fire attacks from rockets and mortars shot from northeast Baghdad. The one option we had would have been to return counterfire using our artillery assets, but this option was off the table because Sadr City, like all of Baghdad, was an urban area and the risk of collateral damage was too great. We attempted several nonlethal tactics and other measures, but no matter how hard we tried, we could not prevent these attacks from happening. The majority originated in Sadr City, a suburb located approximately 4 kilometers (about 2.5 miles) northeast of the IZ once known as Saddam City and named for the Imam Mohammed Sadr, an Iraqi religious leader killed by Saddam Hussein.

Many residents still call it Al Thawra, meaning "Revolution City." Sadr City is predominantly (99.9 percent) populated by Shiites. The district is one of the poorest in Baghdad. Homes are in despair, electrical services are intermittent, and parts of city are flooded with sewage from long-neglected pipes. The streets are littered with trash as residents dumped their refuse on the medians and in the pot-holed streets. I flew over Sadr City in a UH-60 Blackhawk Helicopter on numerous occasions and witnessed the despair and neglect. You could actually smell the stench from the air.

In early April 2004, U.S. and coalition troops fought several gun battles against members of JAM, who resided in Sadr City. However, U.S. forces were not permitted to enter the city and execute a full siege of it like the operations conducted in Fallujah and Samarra. Often requested by senior military leaders, this operation was prohibited by Iraqi Prime Minister al Maliki and the GOI based on intense pressure placed on them by the radical cleric Muqtada al-Sadr and the Shiite political base. As a result, rockets and mortars continued to rain down on the IZ without repercussion. The tragedy in all this is that innocent civilians and soldiers were either wounded or killed by these attacks, yet we could not go after those responsible.

This actually hit very close to home when a great friend of mine, Major Rich Casper, was severely wounded by a rocket attack on March 27, 2007. Casper had been personally requested by Petraeus to come over to Iraq and work as a special assistant on the MNF–I staff. The day that this incident happened, he was less than eight hours from departing theater after his yearlong tour was complete. Casper had his bags packed and was waiting for transportation that would take him from the IZ to Baghdad International Airport so he could fly out of the country. Prior to departing, he stopped by the gym located at Adnan Palace for a short workout. While running on the treadmill, several explosions rocked the building. It was a direct hit from several 107-mm Soviet-made Katyusha rockets. The rounds penetrated the building and exploded near Casper's location. He was caught in the blast radius of shrapnel and other flying debris, severely wounded by the intense blast, and knocked unconscious.

Soldiers and civilians rushed to his aid and quickly treated and evacuated him to the nearby Army hospital. When he awoke, he could not remember much of what had occurred. Casper was lucky to be alive, but two other Americans were not as fortunate. Someone was looking out for him that day. After Casper was stabilized in country, he was flown to Germany and further evacuated stateside to Brooke Army Medical Center, located at Fort Sam Houston, in San Antonio, Texas, where he would undergo years of intense testing and outpatient treatment.

Our three other subordinate battalions served more in a supporting role to accomplish the overall mission. 2-77th Field Artillery Battalion, commanded by Lieutenant Colonel Kurt Session, was assigned the dangerous mission of convoy security and escort for the U.S. State Department. They spent the majority of time outside the wire escorting critical U.S. government officials around the country as well as providing security for the distribution of U.S. and Iraqi currency. 4th Special Troops Battalion, commanded by Lieutenant Colonel Kevin Griffith, provided all the communications and intelligence systems for the brigade. They also established and ran our brigade detention facility and had responsibility for all the civil military operations and projects we planned and executed. Finally, 704th Support Battalion, commanded by Lieutenant Colonel Victor Harmon, provided all the logistics including fuel, water, ammunition, and maintenance to keep our vehicle fleet running. Outside of our organic task organization, we were partnered with the 5th Brigade, 6th Iraqi Army Division, with whom we shared the AO and executed partnered combined operations on a daily basis. The 5/6 IA was an aggressive unit despite being short on personnel and equipment. They were a fairly new Iraqi Army unit that had recently been constituted and employed on the streets of Baghdad. Truth be told, like all other Iraqi Army units, they lacked leadership and discipline.

Leadership in the 5/6th was mainly driven through the use of brute force by those in charge. The real issue at hand was that they were not respected or trusted by the local population based upon their actions when dealing with Iraqi civilians. They were disrespectful to them and were heavy-handed in their tactics, reliving the days of rule under Saddam. Moreover, their ranks were filled with corrupt officers and soldiers, top to bottom. Despite these challenges, we had come a long way from where we first began with the formation of the ICDC in 2003. At least we had the semblance of an Iraqi Army that we could partner with and execute combined operations. However, there was a lot of room for improvement before the desired end state was reached: an Iraqi Army fully trained and capable of assuming the lead and overall responsibility for security operations. We tried hard to reach this goal during this tour, but our attempts fell short due to the sectarian and other violence that erupted in theater. In reality, this transfer of authority would not occur for another three years until June 30, 2009, with the signing of the SOFA agreement. Again, I would have a front-row seat and witness this historic achievement and was fortunate to see it play out.

This was the current operational set for both enemy and friendly personnel. We would certainly be challenged in the weeks and months ahead. Other events that had taken place prior to our arrival had shaped the complexity of the environment we were fighting and impacted our mission drastically. Since my first tour, things had gone from bad to worse on all levels. At the strategic level, top brass and senior DOD officials struggled with containing the fallout and aftermath from the Abu Ghraib Prison abuse scandal.

As I departed theater in March 2004, this incident was still unfolding. The case erupted in April 2004, after articles describing the alleged abuse to include rape, sodomy, torture, and murder. Pictures were released showing U.S. soldiers appearing to abuse prisoners. These articles and pictures were made public during a CBS *60 Minutes* news report and later in an article published in *The New Yorker* magazine. An Army investigation was already underway when this story broke publicly. The DOD did everything it could to preempt and limit the collateral damage of the incident by requesting that the pictures and news segment be delayed by two weeks in order to allow for mitigation and damage control within the theater. CBS News complied and honored the request. Once the story broke, shock waves could be felt throughout the Middle East and other Muslim countries. The Muslim population was infuriated, especially the citizens of Iraq.

Insurgents took advantage of the situation and capitalized on the opportunity to use the negative propaganda to drive a wedge between the U.S. military and the population, playing on the theme of how the Western world was in Iraq as conquerors and did not respect Muslims and the faith of Islam, as evidenced by our actions at Abu Ghraib. Moreover, both Sunni and Shiite groups used this event as a tool to recruit and expand the numbers of fighters in their ranks. The effects of this incident were visible on the streets of Baghdad and elsewhere in the country as insurgent attacks increased drastically. From April 2004 to October 2005, insurgent attacks tripled; the U.S. death toll reached 2,000 soldiers killed since the invasion occurred. October 2005 was recorded as the fourth deadliest month since the invasion as ninety-two service members were killed in action. On the national level, Iraqi parliament members and other outspoken leaders such as Muqtada Al-Sadr immediately denounced the situation and called for the immediate punishment of all involved.

Once DOD concluded the investigation, seventeen soldiers and officers were relieved from duty, and eleven of those were charged with dereliction of duty, maltreatment of detainees, aggravated assault, and battery. Between May 2004 and March 2006, all eleven were convicted in courts martial, sentenced to military prison, and dishonorably discharged from the military. Most notably of the convictions was that of Specialist Charles Garner and his former fiancée, Specialist Lynndie England, who was seen in several of the released pictures. They were sentenced to ten years and three years in prison, respectively, in trials that ended on January 14, 2005, and September 26, 2005. The overall commanding officer of all Iraqi detention facilities, Brigadier General Janis Karpinski was reprimanded for dereliction of duty and was reduced to the rank of Colonel. Karpinski denied knowledge of the abuse, claiming that the interrogations were authorized by her superiors.

The issue that I have with this whole case is the fact the detainees who were being interrogated and in some cases abused were really of no intelligence value to us. In other words, these were common insurgents, often referred to as low-hanging fruit, who were captured on the street during attacks, raids or by some other means. In most cases, any significant intelligence they had to offer was already obtained by units at the point of capture during tactical interrogation and was acted upon immediately. This was certainly the case during my first tour: Upon capture or arrest, we would question detainees immediately and obtain whatever actionable intelligence we could. Once complete, the detainees would be processed and sent to Abu Ghraib for confinement and eventual prosecution by the Iraqi criminal court. There simply was no reason for the abuses and illicit interrogations to take place. Cleary there was a lack of leadership and oversight at the facility. Based on the investigation reports, it appeared that the soldiers assigned to the facility were bored and lacked discipline.

To this day, I am still unsure of what their motives were. Regardless, the incident had severe lasting second- and third-order effects at all levels of command. At the strategic level, it served counter to our overall strategy and message the United States was trying to convey to the Iraqi people. At the operational and tactical levels, it negated a commander's ability to conduct tactical interrogations upon capture.

The result was that actionable intelligence could no longer be obtained on site, thus causing delays or altogether negating follow-on operations to kill or capture insurgents. The Abu Ghraib scandal was a senseless criminal act, an act that served counter not just to our overall strategy, but counter to American values and moral fiber. It would take years to recover from this. The real tragedy was the fact that because of the indiscipline and stupidity of a few soldiers and leaders, more soldiers and civilians lost their lives through increased insurgent attacks. Certainly the second- and third-order effects never crossed the minds of those who were involved in carrying out these heinous acts of indiscipline. I feel this collective group got off easy.

The other challenge that faced us was the dealing with the fallout and aftermath from the national elections that had occurred on December 15, 2005. Iraqis went to the polls to elect 275 members who would form the new Iraqi parliament. This was the first democratic, national election ever conducted in Iraq. Voter turnout was high. By all accounts it was estimated that 76 percent of the 19 million registered voters participated. In official results released by the Independent Electoral Commission of Iraq, the United Iraqi Alliance, the Shiite Muslim's most powerful party, won in a landslide, receiving more than 5 million votes (41 percent) earning them 128 of the 275 seats. In a distant second place was the Democratic Patriotic Alliance of Kurdistan receiving more than 2.6 million votes (21 percent), giving them 53 seats. The Sunnis' main party, the Iraqi Accord Front, placed third receiving 1.8 million votes (15 percent), giving them just 44 seats. The remaining 50 seats were scattered across nine other splinter alliances.

The results of the election outraged the Sunni population, which had been the rulers of Iraq until the invasion in 2003. Because they were no longer in charge and were truly the minority party, they went on the offensive. Sunni-based insurgent groups such as al-Qaeda and other affiliates saw this as a window of opportunity to exploit the situation, creating even more chaos in order to destabilize the country and undermine the government. Sunni insurgents executed a series of deadly attacks against Shiites and U.S. and coalition forces. The most serious of these attacks occurred three weeks after the elections had ended.

On January 6, 2006, a series of car bombs and suicide vest attacks occurred in the cities of Ramadi, Baghdad, and Karbala. Altogether, approximately 140 people were killed that day, including five U.S.

soldiers. The attack in Karbala, the deadliest of the attacks, was perpetrated by an insurgent wearing a suicide vest packed with explosives. According to eyewitnesses, the bomber detonated himself 30 yards from the Imam Hussein shrine. Many of the victims were Shiite pilgrims who had gathered outside the Zainabiya gate to the shrine waiting to be let in. Approximately 54 were killed and more than 143 wounded. Most Iraqi citizens and police blamed Abu Musab Zarqawi for the attacks.

Over the course of the next year, the situation in Iraq would worsen on all fronts. The attacks on January 6, 2006, were merely the tipping point that served as the match that ignited sectarian violence throughout the country—violence so widespread, severe, and grotesque it pushed Iraq to the brink of all-out civil war. Whether a self-inflicted wound or as a matter of democracy taking its natural course, this was the hand we were dealt.

Our brigade had drafted a solid campaign plan to achieve the desired end state: neutralize anti-Iraqi forces in AO Cobra. ISF was to assume the lead in counterinsurgency operations in order to allow for the unhindered development of the GOI and set conditions for self-reliance.

Whereas during my first tour in 2003–04 we had no such plan, we now at least had turned the corner on this front, as far as having a comprehensive plan that included milestones and metrics used to measure progress. Although our campaign plan was overly optimistic and ambitious given the current conditions, it did serve as a roadmap for keeping us on track. Our campaign plan was modeled after our higher headquarters two levels up. Our immediate headquarters plan consisted of four lines of operation (LOOs): security, transition, governance and economics, and communication. Our plan took these four and combined them into three manageable LOOs. The first was the security LOO that governed all counterinsurgency/offensive and internal defense operations. The second was the transition LOO, which focused on all civil military operations, including local and national governance, economics, and essential services. The third and final LOO was communication. This LOO focused on operational and strategic messaging with the goal of having the population perceive that the ISF could provide security and maintain the rule of law. Every operation we conducted, whether it was lethal (offensive) or nonlethal (civil military operations), always had an information operations component associated with it.

Every message released always placed an Iraqi face on the operation so they would receive the credit in the eyes of Iraqis. A work group managed each of these three LOOs, with a charter to plan, execute, and monitor all happenings within the LOO and update and refine as required. The security LOO was our main effort and was supervised by S-3 Maj. Rich Morales. In addition to running TOC operations and logistics, I supervised the transition and communication LOO, which was our secondary effort. Assisting me was our civil affairs officer, Major Jose Acosta, and our public affairs officer, Major Mark Cheadle. Both of these staff officers were subject-matter experts in their field and were invaluable members to our nonlethal team.

As the old Army adage states, "no plan survives first contact," and that couldn't have been more true in this case. As hard as we worked to obtain our goals in each LOO, the enemy was not briefed on our plan and therefore was uncooperative. Based on the persistent violence, all of our time, energy, and resources were consumed and dedicated to the security LOO. Even if conditions had been permissive, we still lacked the subject-matter expertise, such as the provincial reconstruction teams (PRTs), to fully exploit and advance along the other two LOOs, particularly in the area of economics and essential services.

We simply did not have on hand the civilian experts who possessed the requisite training and experience to draft a plan to improve economic conditions in our AO. PRTs were not fielded and assigned to brigades until summer 2006. The one thing we did possess, much like during my previous tour, was money. We had a lot of money at our disposal, and we used it. Short on knowledge and experience, we simply did what we thought was right and infused the area with a lot of new construction projects, such as market renovation.

While this provided short-term employment for locals, it did nothing to boost the local economy. The crux of the challenge was security. Once these old market areas were renovated, we did not factor in how to properly secure and protect them. Days later, a VBIED destroyed the entire place. Not to be deterred, we rebuilt the market, surrounded it with concrete barriers, and gave the mission to the ISF to guard. But this was strictly a short-term, shot-in-the-arm project that did nothing to impact long-term economic growth.

As January came to a close, we were still getting acquainted with our AO. Security in the IZ remained steady without incident, even as the Iraqi parliament was attempting to seat its newly elected officials. If ever there was a right time for insurgents to attack, it was then. A direct mortar or rocket strike on the parliament building could have been devastating and really would have sent the country over the edge.

As we entered February 2006, insurgent attacks carried out by al-Qaeda or JAM remained steady. While the majority of these attacks were concentrated against us, we continued to monitor and see an increase in sectarian-related deaths. Each passing day and week saw an increase in the number of Iraqis being killed at the hands of so-called Sunni or Shiite "death squads." The majority of these sectarian-related killings occurred in our AO, particularly in East Rasheed and West Rasheed, but were widespread throughout the country. The challenge was that we did not have the required troop strength to be everywhere at once. This was evident to all levels, even to embedded reporters. An Associated Press article on January 24, 2006, referred to our operations in Iraq as the "thin green line." In addition, the ISF, both the Iraqi Army and police, were inept and did little to assist us in preventing these attacks. First and foremost, they were very immature, and they lacked the training and resources required to counter these attacks. The corruption in their ranks often led to them turning a blind eye when death squads came calling in the night.

The ISF were supposed to assume the lead for all security and counterinsurgency operations, and we were to be there strictly in a supporting role or as a combat enabler. Turns out this was a gross overestimation of their capabilities. The development and growth of the ISF was not keeping pace with the morphing conditions on the battlefield. We were still three to four years away from having them assuming the lead with any confidence. Based on these factors and continued spikes in violence, both military and sectarian, our mission evolved and, once again, we took center stage and assumed the lead for security and counterinsurgency operations. At the strategic level, this was an obvious setback based on the timeline and milestones established. Conditions would continue to deteriorate. Inevitably this would lead to the "surge" of 2006–07. Even at this point, top administration leaders in Washington, D.C., were still denying the magnitude of the problem in Iraq and the commitment it would require to see it through. On February 2, 2006, Secretary of Defense Donald Rumsfeld was asked by a reporter from the *Washington Times* during the daily press briefing at the Pentagon "Is Iraq going to be a long war?".

Mr. Rumsfeld answered, "No, I don't believe it is."

It was even more evident then that he was out of touch with reality on the ground, and everyone in the Pentagon and in theater knew it.

On February 22, 2006, reality hit home not just to those fighting in Iraq, but to leaders in Washington, D.C., and others around the world as to how dire the situation in Iraq had become. I was awakened that morning by a loud knock on the door of my room. One of the night shift radio operators told me to come to the TOC quickly as there had been a major insurgent attack on a mosque in Samarra. As I cleared my head, knowing I had patrolled the streets of Samarra over two years ago, my first reaction was "No way. It could not have happened."

When I walked into the TOC, there it was, front and center, being broadcasted on CNN on the overhead television screen. It was true: The gilded dome of one of Shiite Islam's holiest shrines, known as the "Golden Dome Mosque," was smouldering. On the scene in Sadr City, thousands of young Shiite men gathered clutching pistols, AK-47s, grenade launchers, and other weapons outside of Muqtada al-Sadr's main headquarters.

Armed demonstrations were breaking out all over Iraq in predominantly Shiite cities, including Karbala, Najaf, and Basra. Though there were no reported casualties, the bombing was the most destructive attack on a major religious shrine since the U.S.-led invasion. Iraqi leaders, specifically al-Sadr, stated that the sole purpose of this attack was to draw Sunnis and Shiites into war.

"This is as 9/11 in the United States," said Adel Abdul Mahdi, a Shiite and one of Iraq's two vice presidents.[3]

Shiite leaders, including the most influential Shiite religious leader, Grand Ayatollah Ali al-Sistani, called on Shiites to take to the streets, but in a peaceful manner. Other Shiite leaders, including Iraqi Prime Minister Ibrahim al-Jafari, denounced the attacks, blaming them on Abu Musab al-Zarqawi's al-Qaeda in Iraq. Elsewhere, Sunni political leaders said retaliatory attacks hit more than twenty Sunni mosques across Iraq with gunfire, bombs, and arson. Later, President Bush released a statement saying that "Violence will only contribute to what the terrorists sought to achieve by this act … I ask all Iraqis to exercise restraint in the wake of this tragedy."[4]

The investigation into the attack revealed that it was, in fact, the work of al-Qaeda operatives who had infiltrated the ranks of ISF and planted bombs inside the mosque the evening prior. Days later, in Sadr City, representatives of Sadr called for restraint and sought to deflect blame from Iraq's Sunnis. At a rally in Sadr City, a Shiite imam of Sadr, Abdul Zara Saidy, shouted to the masses using a bullhorn, blaming the mosque attack as work of the "occupiers" or Americans and "Zionists." In, Iran, Shiite leaders echoed the accusations.[5]

This single attack had far-reaching second- and third-order effects throughout Iraq, further complicating an already-dire situation. It was inevitable that Shiites and Sunnis would battle each other, based on the years of Shiite oppression while under the rule of Saddam and the Ba'ath Party. The bombing of the Golden Dome Mosque was the last straw. For all intents and purposes, civil war had unofficially broken out, and we were smack-dab in the middle of it.

Over the next few months, we witnessed a dramatic rise in sectarian violence throughout our AO and elsewhere in Iraq. From March through August 2006, more than 500 corpses were discovered in AO Cobra. Sunni and Shiites alike were being killed at an alarming rate. The majority of these bodies were found in a neighborhood in East Rasheed known as Dora. 2-506 Infantry Battalion had responsibility for this area and was partnered with the national police and Iraqi police. These units were predominantly made up of Shiite men and were heavily infiltrated by members of Shiite militias.

Therein was the problem. Dora was predominantly a Sunni neighborhood being patrolled by Shiites from the Iraqi and national police units. This was a recipe for disaster. It was easy for Shiite death squads to gain access into the neighborhood and carry out sectarian attacks. According to Lieutenant Colonel Greg Butts, commander of 2-506 IN, the local Sunni population would not accept the national or Iraqi police and viewed them as nothing more than an extension of the militia. Sunni residents voiced their concerns and distrust over the police assigned to the area, only to later end up dead. It was a no-win situation for them.

Sunni death squads would conduct reprisal attacks in West Rasheed and other Shiite dominated areas. The majority of these sectarian attacks would occur at night, and the corpses would be hauled to random locations and dumped in alleys or on street corners. In some cases, multiple bodies would be discovered. Every morning when our brigade commander and staff would assemble for the battle update brief, the first thing reported to him was how many bodies had been discovered that morning. Moreover, when the daily body count was briefed in the evening to our division commander, Major General James D. Thurman would often come unglued and in a very direct way tell us to eliminate this problem. It was evident that Thurman was being pressured from superiors to make this problem stop. Simply put, there was little we could do to prevent it. We tried at times to concentrate forces in a particularly volatile area, only to see the bodies killed and dropped off blocks away in areas where there was no U.S. presence. Bottom line: we did not have the manpower to be everywhere at once.

This goes back to the situation in 2003–04. It was the "whack-a-mole" strategy all over again. The Iraqi Army and both the national and Iraqi police continued to be of little value. If anything, they were condoning the attacks, and only when closely supervised by U.S. forces would they act with authority and intervene. The problem was getting out of hand. Something drastic needed to be done.

During this period of sectarianism, it became apparent that victims were being tortured. The bodies we found were totally mutilated and unrecognizable. It was ever apparent that the victims had been tortured prior to being killed and dumped in random neighborhoods. Many victims had their hands and feet bound by a rope, and their kneecaps and skulls had been drilled completely through by a large 2-inch drill bit. Some victims' heads had been severed. It was morbid and grotesque, to say the least.

The discovery of these victims became commonplace. Along with the discovery of mutilated bodies came the discovery of the torture chambers where these morbid acts were carried out. Eventually these killings came to be known as extra-judicial killings or simply "EJKs." These images are forever embedded in my mind, and nothing that I read in newspapers or witness on television will top this. If anything, I became numb to it altogether. The problem for me was that I could not let it go because I was reminded of it all over again during my third tour in 2009 when I sat down and had dinner with Iraqi sheiks who were responsible and played a major role in these sectarian killings and attacks against us.

While sectarian killings increased, so too did the attacks against U.S. forces. What led to the spike in attacks against us was a report released in April 2006 by a Pentagon-commissioned team. The team could find no evidence that Iraq possessed weapons of mass destruction.[6]

This finding exacerbated the problem and further fueled the notion that the United States was in Iraq as occupiers seeking to conquer Muslims. Although this was not the case, the insurgents did a great job of exploiting the report in the media as though it was true.

Some good news, though, finally came on June 8, 2006. In an air raid carried out by joint special operations forces and U.S. Air Force bombers, Abu Musab al-Zarqawi, the infamous leader of al-Qaeda in Iraq, was killed near Baqubah. A tip was received through human intelligence channels and was acted on by joint special operations forces. The team scouted the safe house believed to house Zarqawi, members of his family, and his spiritual advisor. Upon confirmation that he was there, an Air Force-guided bomb landed within minutes on his house, killing all inside. Upon investigation of the house, it was determined that, in fact, Zarqawi had been killed. This news spread like wildfire throughout Iraq and the Middle East. There was little time to relax and enjoy the accomplishment, though, as in the days following the attack al-Qaeda stepped up their retaliatory attacks against us and the number of U.S. troops killed in Iraq surpassed 2,500.[7]

Another growing concern and driver of instability the GOI and United States had to deal with as a result of the violence was the growing number of Iraqi citizens being displaced, known officially as Iraqi displaced persons or simply "IDPs." Neighborhoods throughout Baghdad and elsewhere were being cleansed. Sunnis and Shiites were forcing families to depart the area and move out or else face the wrath of death squads. In October 2006, it was estimated by the Office of the United Nations High Commission for Refugees (UNHCR) and the Iraqi government that more than 365,000 Iraqis had been displaced since the bombing of the al-Askari Mosque in Samarra.[8] That number has grown significantly from February 2006 through December 2007.

In 2007, UNHCR estimated that nearly 5 million Iraqis were displaced. The majority of these refugees fled to neighboring countries, including Syria and Jordan. Another 500,000 could not afford to move and lived as squatters in slum areas with no assistance or legal rights to the properties they occupied.[9] I would get an up close and personal view of this dire situation during my third tour in 2009 as I served as a member of U.S. State Department IDP Board. As a member of this board, I visited more than a dozen IDP squatter camps in our AO and worked with the State Department and Iraqi Government Ministry of Displacement/Migration to figure out solutions to help IDPs move back to their original homes.

Operation Together Forward

Amid all the violence and pressure to stop the sectarian killings, 4th ID or MND–B in cooperation with the GOI launched a new offensive operation focused in East Rasheed. Operation Together Forward, known in Arabic as Amaliya Ma'an ila Al-Aman, was set in motion in an attempt to significantly reduce the violence in Baghdad. The plan was announced publicly on June 14, 2006, by Prime Minister Nuri al-Maliki, and was intended to increase security conditions in Baghdad by instituting major new measures. The operation was to be led and executed by the ISF with coalition support. About 75,000 Iraqi and coalition troops would participate on the streets of Baghdad. The plan called for an immediate curfew to be put in place from 2100 to 0600 hours. Increased patrols and checkpoints were added to deter further sectarian aggression. Finally, a weapons policy was put in place that restricted Iraqi civilians from carrying weapons on the streets, and each household could only possess one weapon for self-defense. Simultaneously, U.S. and Iraqi Army troops executed continuous raids targeting known terrorist cells and cell leaders. While the plan was highly touted and publicized at the time, it failed to meet the end state of increased security and reduce violence. On the contrary, the attacks heading into August spiked significantly.

The issue was the fact that the ISF remained inept and units were severely undermanned. Prior to the operation being executed, it was planned for six Iraqi Army battalions to participate. As the operation commenced, only two of them showed up. Moreover, our brigade did not have the manpower to maintain a 24/7 presence. Our troops soon became exhausted. It was summer in Iraq with daytime temperatures soaring beyond 95 degrees Fahrenheit. These soldiers executed cordon and search operations in Dora and in Risala, going house to house, block by block, neighborhood to neighborhood. In a day's time, more than 4,000 houses had been searched—but there were more than a million homes or dwellings in these focused areas to search. These intense and exhausting operations were simply not sustainable. Moreover, the insurgents were usually tipped off by complicit members of the ISF ranks and would simply flee the area. Again, we were executing the "whack-a-mole" strategy without any tangible results.

Another issue that led to the failure of this operation was the implementation of the GOI weapons policy. We were removing weapons from the wrong hands; the enemy had fled the area. It was only a matter of time before we would depart the area and move to search another. When we did, the insurgents would return and execute further attacks. Innocent Iraqis could not defend themselves. This policy indirectly or directly led to the loss of innocent lives. Bottom line: the operation as implemented was not sustainable because we could not secure the neighborhoods after we cleared them.

August 2006 was by far the worst month in Iraq since 2003. It was the deadliest month for Iraqi civilians, with 3,438 killed at the height of sectarian violence. Moreover, 1,666 bombs had exploded in July 2006, the highest monthly total of the war. Senior military leaders finally acknowledged that Iraq was on the brink of civil war. On August 7, 2006, the top U.S. commander in Iraq, General George Casey, said that civil war in Iraq is "certainly possible," calling it "the most significant threat right now" in the country.[10]

Iraq was in total chaos. Sectarian violence was so widespread and frequent that the morgues could not keep up with the influx of bodies arriving on a daily basis. In Baghdad, the central morgue revised the August death toll upward of 300 percent.[11] As we rolled into September, the number of Iraqi civilian deaths continued to climb. An Associated Press report cited that Iraq had reached an unprecedented level of civilian deaths. More than 6,559 violent deaths had occurred since the bombing of the Golden Dome Mosque in February 2006. Researchers also noted a rise in "honor killings" of women by sectarian militias and death squads. The White House reaction to this violence was described by President Bush as "just a comma" in history.

Operation Together Forward II

As we entered September 2006, military planners went back to the drawing boards and published a revised plan for combating the violence and increasing security. The plan was known as Operation Together Forward II. This time around, several adjustments were made to the plan based on lessons learned from the previous failed operation. Under Operation Together Forward II, Iraqi and coalition troops planned to move neighborhood by neighborhood, using the "Clear, Hold, and Build" strategy for tactical counterinsurgency operations. Under this approach, we would move into neighborhoods along with ISF forces, methodically clearing the area of insurgent cells and cell leaders. After clearing the area, we would hold and secure areas using designated U.S. and ISF troops, as opposed to earlier efforts during which we cleared them only to allow insurgents to return as we transitioned to another area. Once an area was secured, we would commence with the building phase by injecting a series of projects designed to improve essential services and overall infrastructure, such as renovating local marketplaces that had been destroyed by insurgent VBIED attacks. Whereas we did not have enough troops the first time, Casey extended the tour by three months of the 172nd Stryker Brigade Combat Team.

The 172nd Stryker Brigade Combat Team was in the middle of redeploying back to its home base in Alaska. The unit had just completed a tough twelve-month tour in northern Iraq, mainly in the volatile city of Mosul. Lieutenant Colonel John Norris commanded 4-23 IN, "Tomahawks," a subordinate battalion assigned to the 172nd Brigade Combat Team. Norris actually had troops who had already returned home to their loved ones, only to have to break the bad news and recall them back to Iraq for operations in Baghdad.[12]

By design, Operation Together Forward II was clearly a better approach than the previous operation, but it was not without flaws. In September 2006, our brigade took to the streets of Dora and Risala. My role in this operation was to supervise TOC operations and facilitate command and control of the operation and reporting to our higher command. In addition, I planned and facilitated the nonlethal aspects of this operation, including the strategic messaging and public affairs news releases. To assist us with execution, MND–B assigned us two additional battalions: 2-1 IN, a Stryker battalion from 172nd Stryker Brigade, and 2-6 IN, a mechanized infantry battalion assigned to 1st Armor division based out of Germany, which had just arrived in theater. We deployed more than 2,000 U.S. soldiers and more than 5,000 ISF forces throughout East Rasheed and West Rasheed. The majority of these forces were concentrated in the Dora neighborhood of East Rasheed. Clearing operations commenced on September 1, 2006, and lasted through the end of November 2006. Soldiers executed the operation flawlessly, searching homes and buildings they had entered weeks earlier. Weather conditions were even worse this time around, with temperatures soaring beyond 100 degrees Fahrenheit. When combined with the heavy load soldiers carried, clearing operations slowed to a snail's pace. Adding to the stress and rigor during execution was the fact that our higher command placed greater emphasis on the pace of clearing operations rather than on holding and rebuilding cleared neighborhoods. It was a rush to failure.

By October 1, 2006, Dora had been completely cleared for the second time in less than two months, with the same negligible results as the previous operations. Once again, the enemy had been tipped off and fled the area. The clearing of these areas was easy. The challenge was that we still did not have the requisite number of troops—even with the two additional battalions—to hold and secure these areas to allow for the building phase to commence. ISF continued to be of little value. Just as during Operation Together Forward, they remained inept and were incapable of securing areas, even with our assistance. We were back to square one. Operation Together Forward II netted the same result as the previous operation. Bottom line: it failed to curb the growing violence in Baghdad.

Because we could not properly secure areas and hold the ground, insurgents were able to reinfiltrate these neighborhoods and wreak havoc on civilians. The Iraqi Study Group report released in December 2006 documented the failures of Operation Together Forward II:

> "The results of Operation Together Forward II are disheartening. Violence in Baghdad already at high levels jumped more than 43% between the summer and October 2006. U.S. forces continue to suffer high casualties. Perpetrators of violence leave neighborhoods in advance of security sweeps, only to filter back later. Iraqi Police have been unable or unwilling to stop such infiltration and continuing violence."[13]

Officially, October 2006 went on record as the highest monthly level for U.S. wounded in action or killed. A total of 100 Americans were killed, up by 23 from the 77 killed in September. By the beginning of November 2006, Operation Together Forward II was abandoned. It was during this time that our brigade redeployed back to Fort Hood. I was surprised that we were given the approval to redeploy. Based on the dire situation at the time and the previous recall of units, it was inevitable that we would be extended. We began the transition out starting on October 15, 2006. We were replaced by 2nd Brigade, 1st Cavalry Division, "Blackjacks," our sister brigade, also based out of Fort Hood. The transition went without a hitch, and they assumed the reigns of the former Cobra AO. It would be a defining period for them and all the other units arriving in theater.

Our year was complete with little to show as far as milestones achieved in Iraq. The security situation in Baghdad had deteriorated so badly that it seemed the country could implode at any moment. Despite this, our soldiers fought hard with bravery and honor. Along the way we lost several soldiers and sustained more than seventy-five wounded in action. A lot of time, sacrifice, and bloodshed went into this tour in an effort to curb the violence and set the conditions for the transfer of authority for security to the ISF and GOI. However, we were still years away from turning the corner; there was still a lot of work to be done. Ultimately it would be up to the people of Iraq to decide their fate. They could either step forward to take a stand against the ethnic cleansing and associated violence or sit on the sidelines and watch as their loved ones and nation perished.

I left Iraq en route to Kuwait to supervise deployment operations with a bit of satisfaction. On November 5, 2006, Saddam was found guilty by the Iraqi High Tribunal Court of crimes against humanity and sentenced to death by hanging. I wondered whether this could be the event that provided Iraqis closure on decades of brutality and gave them hope for a better future or whether it would have the opposite effect and simply fuel sectarian tensions to the point where Sunnis and Shiites completely destroyed one another. The United States was partly to blame for this mess, and it was ours to fix. The only hope we had remaining was for a surge of troops to right the ship. Somehow as I departed, I knew I would be back to see it unfold.

CHAPTER 7
THE SURGE
November 2006–June 2009

❝ The gates of freedom remain open today because of our fallen comrades: noble and gallant warriors who gave everything so others can enjoy life, liberty, and happiness. We will honor their memory and remain dedicated to ensuring their sacrifices are never forgotten. ❞

Lt. Gen. Raymond Odierno, Baghdad, Iraq, 2008

I returned home to Fort Hood on November 15, 2006. Just like before, we were treated to a hero's welcome. Upon arrival at Killeen Regional Airport, we executed the same drill as at the end of my first deployment. Soldiers from the rear detachment were on hand to in-process us and sign for and receive sensitive items, including M-4 carbine rifles, night observation devices, and any classified material we had returned with. Several soldiers once again kissed the ground as they stepped onto the tarmac.

It was great to be back home in the good ol' U.S.A. Even more exciting was the thought of uniting with my family in less than an hour. Once again, we had to make a twenty-minute trip from the airfield hangar over to the base gymnasium where families and loved ones waited anxiously for our arrival. The homecoming ceremony was similar to the last one: emotional, overwhelming, and surreal.

Upon return to the base after a four-day pass, we executed reintegration training. This time around, it was better planned and more thorough, covering an even broader range of topics including PTSD, traumatic brain injuries, and suicide prevention. This training lasted ten days and, once complete, we departed for thirty days of block leave. I traveled to Mesquite, Texas, and was met by my soon-to-be new wife and children, who made the 800-mile trek from Colorado Springs, Colorado. I had yet to see them since I returned and anxiously awaited their arrival. While I was deployed, my fiancée was reassigned to Division West and had moved to Fort Carson, Colorado. During that period, she was able to spend quality time with my children and developed a great relationship with them. It could not have worked out better for us.

During leave, which fell over Christmas, I received some great news from the front lines of Iraq. As I turned on the morning news during breakfast on December 28, a special breaking news report came on Fox News live from Baghdad: Saddam Hussein had just been executed by hanging. The execution came on the eve of the Sunni Muslim celebration of Eid al-Adha. I was truly elated, as were millions of others that we had finally rid the world of this evil tyrant.

The remaining time spent on block leave afforded the opportunity during moments of solitude to reflect on the past twelve months spent in Baghdad. Granted, our brigade did not reach all the milestones that we had originally planned. If anything, the campaign plan we had drafted was far too ambitious and unrealistic given the environment we found ourselves fighting in. The security conditions in Iraq changed—they deteriorated in our case—but we stayed the course and did not scale back our goals and expectations.

This was happening on all levels of command, starting at the top with Multi-National Force–Iraq (MNF–I), Multi-National Corps–Iraq (MNC–I), and Multi-National Division–Baghdad (MND–B), all the way down to our brigade. Essentially, we remained stubborn and kept trying to drive the square peg (U.S. strategy) into a round hole (Iraq insurgency and sectarian strife). U.S. strategy was not working and did not fit the environment in Iraq at the time. The change in strategy we made in August 2006 to the clear-hold-build-methodology was great—in theory. However, it was flawed in its application and doomed for failure before the first house in Baghdad was cleared by U.S. forces and ISF.

The main reason our strategy was not working was the lack of U.S. soldiers available on the ground to properly implement the intended effects. The activities of death squads and Shiite militias helped sustain the never-ending cycle of violence in Baghdad and elsewhere. Their continued growth and ability to conduct ethnic cleansing stemmed from an absence of security. Exacerbating the problem was the displacement of hundreds of thousands of local Iraqis who were forced out of their homes. We were not resourced to be successful. Clearing areas was the easy part. But after clearing them, we could not hold them to allow the building phase to begin. Security was the lynchpin, and it hinged on securing the population. If we could not do that, there would be no further progress at any level.

Executing this new strategy was contingent on the ISF being in charge and assuming the lead for security operations once the areas had been cleared of insurgents and transitioned over to ISF control. Doing so allowed us to move on and execute clearing operations in other parts of the city.

It briefs well on a PowerPoint slide, but in reality this was a bridge too far. Our expectations of the ISF's abilities missed the mark. They were inept, untrained, corrupt, and too ill equipped to handle the responsibility of securing the population.. Moreover, their ranks were filled with operatives, either Shiite militia members or al-Qaeda operatives who actually facilitated or perpetrated the sectarian violence in Baghdad and elsewhere throughout the country. As a result, we were conceding ground we had just won. Up to that point in late 2006, we had cleared Dora, Risala, Samarra, Fallujah, and Ramadi as many as three or four times, only to concede it to insurgents. It was a recipe for disaster.

We had little valuable help from the ISF, and the GOI was of no value as they were in no position to effectively govern. Coinciding with these operations, the death toll of U.S. service members and Iraqi civilians continued to climb at an alarming rate. In November 2006 alone, more than 2,500 Iraqis lost their lives as a result of the ethno-sectarian violence. In December 2006, that benchmark was surpassed.[1]

Taking this one step further, had we been able to secure these areas, another challenge would have presented itself during the building phase. We outright lacked the resident knowledge and expertise of U.S. Department of State personnel, such as those who constituted the Provincial Reconstruction Teams, to properly plan and facilitate long-term, sustainable projects. It is true that we could and did introduce short-term projects such as local market renovations that provided an immediate shot in the arm into the local economy. However, it was strictly short term and did not provide for long-term economic and job growth.

Although we built these markets, we could not protect them. The majority were destroyed by suicide bombers. It was hard to watch, having been there on two previous occasions and knowing that the sacrifice paid by our brave soldiers could all be for naught. Bottom line: Iraq was on the verge of collapse, and we were staring at complete mission failure if something did not change drastically in the waning months of 2006.

On January 10, 2007, President Bush addressed the nation on television, announcing the approval of "surge" forces. President Bush ordered the immediate deployment of more than 20,000 additional troops. This troop increase amounted to five additional combat brigades, and the majority of these units were committed to Baghdad. Furthermore, to ensure we had the combat power required to execute the mission, the tours of Army and Marine units already in Iraq were extended. The surge had been developed under the working title "The New Way Forward" and was built upon six fundamental elements:

1. Let the Iraqis lead;
2. Help Iraqis protect the population;
3. Isolate extremists;
4. Create space for political progress;
5. Diversify political and economic efforts; and
6. Situate the strategy in a regional approach.

During his address, President Bush described the overall objective as establishing a "unified, democratic federal Iraq that can govern itself, defend itself, and sustain itself, and is an ally in the War on Terror."

The basic premise of the strategy was what was previously attempted during Operation Together Forward II to no avail. President Bush stated that the U.S. military would "help the Iraqis clear and secure neighborhoods, to help them protect the local population, and to help ensure that Iraqi Forces left behind are capable of providing the security."

As I listened to this address, I could tell that it was "clear, hold, build" all over again, except this time round assets and resources were being sent over to ensure we could accomplish it. The President concluded by saying that the surge would provide the "time and conditions conducive to reconciliation among political and ethnic factions."[2]

This announcement had an immediate impact on morale for our troops currently serving in Iraq and for those deploying as part of the surge forces. If anything, it provided renewed optimism for leaders prosecuting the campaign. More importantly it sent the message to all soldiers, their families, and loved ones that we as a nation were committed to seeing this thing through and would not let the sacrifice of our brave soldiers past and present be in vain.

The surge decision made by President Bush did not come easy. Numerous advocates and organizations inside and outside of Washington opposed it and spoke out against the surge. Even top commanders in Iraq opposed it. On January 2, 2007, Casey warned against troop escalation. In a *New York Times* article, he was quoted as saying "It's always been my view that a heavy handed and sustained American military presence was not going to solve the problems in Iraq over the long term."[3]

The greatest hurdle to overcome was the opposition posed by the Democratic Party. During the 2006 general election, the president and Republicans alike suffered a heavy blow and lost control of Congress. The news media viewed this defeat as Americans punishing President Bush and the Republican Party over ethics scandals and for the failing conditions of the war in Iraq. The strongest opposition and most outspoken in Congress was newly elected House Speaker Nancy Pelosi. During her final days of campaigning in 2006, she stated: "This election is about Iraq. If indeed it turns out the way that people expect it to turn out, the American people will have spoken, and they will have rejected the course of action the President is on."[4]

Upon assuming her position as Speaker of the House, on November 17, Pelosi wrote an article titled "Bringing the War to an End Is My Highest Priority As Speaker" published in the *Huffington Post* on January 17, 2007. A month before, on December 11, 2006, President Bush held a private meeting at the White House with a select group of Iraqi experts, including retired four-star generals Wayne A, Downing, Barry McCaffery, and John Keane, along with academia's Stephen Biddle and Eliot Cohen, who had studied counterinsurgency campaigns.

The meeting focused on the review and analysis of the newly released Iraqi Study Group Report. The group disagreed on the key issue of whether to send more troops to Iraq. Keane argued that several thousand additional soldiers could be used to improve security in Baghdad, but others expressed doubt about the proposal. Collectively, the group suggested that the President replace personnel in his national security team.

Two days later, on December 13, President Bush and Vice President Dick Cheney met with members of the Joint Chiefs of Staff (JCS) to discuss different military options for Iraq. While "no dramatic proposals" were put forward, a "pragmatic assessment of what can and cannot be done by the military" was offered.[5]

They did not favor adding significant numbers of troops to Iraq but saw "strengthening the Iraqi Army as pivotal to achieving some degree of stability." JCS pressed for "greater effort on economic reconstruction and political reconciliation." They said there was "no purely military solution for Iraq" and "without major progress on the political front and economic fronts, the U.S. intervention is simply buying time." They also urged "that any new strategy be sensitive to regional context, particularly the impact of political or military decisions." They also feared that throwing too much support to the Shiite majority might lead Sunni nations in the region to step up support of Sunni insurgents, and that a crackdown on Iraq's largest Shiite militia, the Mahdi army, might instigate more interference by Iran.[6]

While all these points and concerns were valid, there was no time for further political bickering. Something needed to be done immediately to get the security situation on the ground stabilized. What mattered most to soldiers on the front lines carrying out this strategy was to get reinforcements over as soon as possible—or else we risked losing Iraq forever, and everything we had fought for and sacrificed would be for naught.

President Bush knew what was at stake. Speaking to reporters after concluding his meeting with the JCS, President Bush said, "Our military cannot do this job alone. Our military needs a political strategy that is effective." He also stressed his ongoing commitment to securing Iraq, saying "If we lose our nerve, if we're not steadfast in our determination to help the Iraqi government succeed, we will be handing Iraq over to an enemy that would do us harm." When pressed for when he would announce his new way forward, he said he would not be "rushed into a decision and was still reviewing his options."[7]

The announcement was originally planned for late December 2006; however, it was delayed as President Bush wanted more time to gather information. According to reports by CNN, administration officials stated that the President was "not satisfied" with the information he was getting and "is asking people to get him more information on various options in Iraq."[8] First and foremost, he did not like the proposal by the Iraqi Study Group of a phased withdrawal of U.S. troops and further engagement of Iraq's neighbors.

Finally on January 5, 2007, the American Enterprise Institute, a conservative think tank led by Frederick Kagan and retired General Jack Keane, published a report titled "Choosing Victory: A Plan for Success in Iraq." This report called for a change in strategy to focus on "clearing and holding" neighborhoods and securing the population, a troop increase of seven Army maneuver brigades and Marine regiments, and a renewed emphasis on reconstruction, economic development, and job creation. Included in this document were reports from Senators John McCain and Joseph Lieberman.[9]

As the report was being drafted, it was presented behind the scenes by Kagan and Keane to President Bush, Vice President Cheney, and other top administration officials on December 11, 2006. AEI published its final report to the media on January 5, 2007, under the title "Iraq: A Turning Point." Included with it were the reports of Senators McCain and Lieberman. Five days later, on January 10, 2007, President Bush announced the new strategy for Iraq titled "New Way Forward." Within his report were echoes from the report released by Kagan, who for all intents and purposes, was known in inner circles as the prime mover of the surge option.

This new strategy outlined by President Bush was nothing new to the soldiers and leaders on the ground in Iraq. This was the same plan we had already attempted in theater months earlier during Operation Together Forward II. The only major change was that it came with the additional troops and resources to properly execute it. If anything, it was "clear, hold, build" on steroids. The best things about it were that it got Congressional and American public support and it came with a lot of resources, namely the troop surge. Moreover, it served as a vote of confidence and reassurance to all the men and women fighting on the front lines in Iraq, a signal that the nation was committed to seeing this war through, that true victory was the only acceptable outcome. This vote of confidence went a long way for our brave soldiers executing operations on the ground.

One of the immediate drawbacks to the plan, however, was the fact that the 20,000 additional troops being deployed to Iraq would not have the advance armor protected vehicles that most units had been outfitted with. According to an article published by the *Baltimore Sun*, "The thousands of troops that President Bush is expected to order to Iraq will join the fight largely without the protection of the latest armored vehicles that withstand bomb blasts far better than Humvees in wide use, military officers said."[10]

The problem was not the fault of the Bush administration, but rather a timing issue with industry. These advanced vehicles were being produced as quickly as possible, but production could not keep pace with the newly announced troop increase. I commend the military industrial complex for their efforts; they produced and fielded these vehicles as fast as if not faster than humanly possible.

One of the key underlying factors in getting this plan approved was the replacement of Secretary of Defense Donald Rumsfeld with Robert Gates. It was widely known in the inner circles of the Pentagon that Rumsfeld was an obstacle to progress and was not a strong advocate of this new approach. While I commend him for his years of public service and contributions in the defense of our great nation, it was truly time for him to move on.

Another driving factor that ultimately led to the surge was the capture of some midlevel al-Qaeda leaders just north of Baghdad. According to an article written by Odierno, who had returned to Iraq as the MNC–I Commander:

"On December 19, 2006, we captured some mid-level al-Qaeda leaders just north of Baghdad. Upon them was a map that clearly depicted al-Qaeda's strategy for the total and unyielding dominance of Baghdad, betting that control of Iraq's capital and its millions of citizens would give them free rein to export their twisted ideology and terror."[11]

The surge could not have come at a better time. From January to June 2007, surge forces gradually deployed into theater. In December 2006, thirteen battalions were stationed throughout Baghdad and the surrounding areas. At the height of the surge in summer of 2007, this increased to twenty-five battalions.

-As surge forces arrived, offensive operations began immediately. However, there was a change in mindset this time around. The priority shifted to protecting the population where the citizens of Iraq lived and worked and where their children played and went to school. In order to protect the population, we established new tactics, techniques, and procedures. No longer were troops able to commute to work. In other words, they would not live on the friendly confines of large FOBs such as Victory Base Complex or LSA Anaconda. As a result, orders were given from MNC–I for units to move off the large bases and live amongst the people. Based on that guidance, units began establishing combat outposts (COPs) and joint security stations (JSSs) throughout Baghdad and in towns all over Iraq. Additional measures were taken to protect the population, including the emplacement of checkpoints and hundreds of thousands of concrete barriers (T-walls) around neighborhoods and markets.

Also included this time around were the added troops, both U.S. forces and ISF, to guard these areas 24/7. No longer could insurgents have free access into these areas. Another change that came about was our approach to insurgent targeting. The new strategy called for a balance in targeting. In previous years, the GOI would protect Shiite militia members from being targeted. As part of the New Way Forward, the GOI bought in and agreed to its parameters. All the cards were on the table. If you were a Sunni, Shiite, Kurd, Christian, or a foreign-based insurgent, then you were targeted, regardless of sect or affiliation.

Another measure taken was a renewed emphasis on forging a partnership with ISF. This major area needed attention if the new plan was to succeed. Most notably was the purging of their ranks of all insurgent infiltrators. This daunting task fell on the GOI, specifically the ministries of defense and interior, to resolve. As for U.S. assistance, we drafted and implemented new plans to improve their capacity and integration of their forces into our military efforts. With this came training programs established by Multi-National Security Transition Command–Iraq (MNSTC–I). The military also added military transition teams and police transition teams, whose sole mission was to train and advise Iraqi Army and police forces on operations.

We actually attempted this concept during my second tour in 2005. The issue at the time was that brigade-level units were charged to build and field these teams out of their own personnel pool. There was no formal training program for them as to how to properly integrate and serve in the capacity of trainers, advisors, and mentors to their partnered units. However, with the new strategy came a sweeping change in how we trained and fielded these transition teams. The Army actually developed a formal training program located at Fort Riley, Kansas.

Highly skilled, experienced noncommissioned and commissioned officers in the rank of staff sergeant up to colonel were selected by the Army's human resource command (HRC) and placed on orders to serve as a member of these teams. A team consisted of ten to fifteen soldiers, depending on what level they were assigned to, from Iraqi battalion all the way up to senior Iraqi commands. These teams were made of soldiers whose Army skill sets included experience in operations, intelligence, and logistics. Once a team was filled out, the entire team would report to Fort Riley and undergo an intense four-week training that focused on leadership, marksmanship, first aid, tactics, the military decision-making process (MDMP), cultural and language training, and how to serve as an Iraqi trainer and advisor.

This formalized training regiment was long overdue, but once implemented was worth its weight in gold and paid huge dividends in building capacity for the ISF. If anything, the Army reviewed the lessons learned from the Vietnam War, specifically the lack of formal training for the Military Assistance Command–Vietnam advisors. This time they got it right. This program was truly one of the best initiatives by the Army that helped us turn the corner in Iraq. This program was so important to the Army and our missions in Iraq and Afghanistan that it became the Army's number one priority for manning from 2007 to the present.

The final measure taken was the addition of embedded Provincial Reconstruction Teams (ePRTs). ePRTs were small, typically fifteen to twenty-five people, and consisted of State Department-led units inserted into U.S. combat brigades. Their sole charter was to support counterinsurgency operations by helping local Iraq communities pursue reconciliation, foster economic development, and improve public services to mitigate sources of instability. These teams were first attempted in Iraq in 2005 but were underresourced. Initial teams consisted of four members each: a State Department Foreign Service officer (FSO) as the team leader, a military or civilian appointed deputy team leader, a U.S. Agency for International Development (USAID) officer, and an interpreter.

The military is partly to blame for the initial challenges in integrating these teams early on. Bottom line: back then we did not know how to properly integrate them, and we lacked any such plan for properly employing them.

Our operations were solely focused on killing insurgents and getting the security situation under control through lethal means. Basically the Army did not completely buy into the concept. On the contrary, the Department of State was not forthcoming with how it intended to lay out how they could best enable operations and be an asset to us, better known as a "combat multiplier." The whole notion for implementing an ePRT was "discovery learning" at best. If asked back in 2005 during my second tour what an ePRT was, I would have to say that I had never heard of it and certainly had no idea how to gainfully employ it. Personally, I never saw these guys, if they were around then.

In 2007, that all changed with the implementation of the new strategy. The ePRT mission evolved and they became integrated into daily combat operations. As a result, the teams grew in size. Likewise our train-up prior to deploying included education on the capabilities and implementation of these teams. Moreover the State Department actually deployed ePRTs to participate in a unit's MRX at one of the three major combat training centers. This was simply another step in helping to turn the corner in Iraq. Moreover, I became intimately familiar with ePRT activities. During my third tour in 2009–10, I would actually supervise an ePRT and coordinate all the nonlethal activities for our brigade. Having served in this capacity, I gained a new appreciation of their effectiveness and can testify as to how invaluable they were to overall mission accomplishment.

During the height of the surge, ePRTs consisted of anywhere from twenty to twenty-eight members, including a FSO team leader, a military deputy team leader, USAID officer, a U.S. Department of Agriculture (USDA) officer, a governance officer, economics officer, four to five interpreters, and several other subject-matter experts, depending on the area employed. During major combat operations, these teams provided important support to military counterinsurgency efforts at the local, provincial, and national levels. Their greatest contributions were the assistance provided to local government officials to help them prepare for self-reliance and the development of long-term, sustainable projects that led to local job growth, which kept would-be civilians from joining the ranks of insurgents or militias.

Beginning in early February 2007, as surge troops started showing up in theater, MNC–I had to determine where best to employ them in and around Baghdad and in the volatile Sunni-dominated Anbar province in the western deserts of Iraq. It also meant sequencing them in such a manner that they would have the greatest impact. The majority of these forces were deployed in Baghdad proper and the surrounding areas. From February 2007 until July 2007, a total of twelve additional battalions were employed on the ground in Baghdad and in Anbar, bringing a total of twenty-five battalions operating in these contested areas. Offensive operations commenced immediately beginning with Operation Phantom Thunder, as coalition and ISF forces aggressively targeted and attacked the enemy in places that had long been sanctuaries of al-Qaeda, including Samarra, Baqubah, Fallujah, and Ramadi. Some of the heaviest fighting took place in Baqubah, the location where al-Qaeda leader al-Zarqawi was killed. According to embedded reporter Mike Gilbert of the *News Tribune*:

> *"The 3rd Stryker Brigade Combat Team of the 2nd Infantry Division (3/2) appears to be shouldering the brunt of the combat. The soldiers from the 3/2 'killed 24-36 enemy fighters and detained nine ...'*
>
> *They found and destroyed 16 other roadside bombs, four houses that had been rigged to explode, and two car bombs. They found two safe houses, destroyed what he described as a mobile weapons cache, and captured two other weapons caches, including 'a significant IED cache.'"*[12]

Another volatile area that saw a lot of intense fighting was in the Dora neighborhood of East Rasheed, my former AO, located in southeast Baghdad. Major Steve Phillips, a good friend of mine, was serving as a rifle company commander with 2-3 IN and was sent into Dora as part of the surge in June 2007. His battalion had been chopped from its parent brigade, 3-2 SBCT, and reassigned to reinforce operations in Baghdad. According to Phillips, "Within the first eighteen hours of occupying this area, our battalion lost six Stryker vehicles that were catastrophically destroyed and sustained fifty-four causalities."

Similar offensive operations as 3-2 SBCT had conducted were taking place all over Iraq, with similar results. As the enemy was attacked and either killed, captured, or driven out of these areas, immediate presence was established by units establishing COPs and JSSs. At the height of the surge, U.S. forces had established more than five hundred COPs or JSSs throughout Iraq. This was a monumental accomplishment. The significance of establishing these outlying security stations was intended to send a strong message to the local population that we were there to stay in order to protect them and that we would not allow insurgents to return. It also demonstrated to insurgent groups that these towns and villages would no longer be sanctuaries for them. Simultaneously, we were targeting Shiite militias that were responsible for sectarian-motivated killings, displacing Sunni families, and intimidating the local populace. No faction was off limits.

According to Odierno: "Given the additional troops, the coalition employed them to protect the population. This commitment to the people of Iraq made a difference both directly and indirectly."[13] As Operation Phantom Thunder concluded, MNC–I launched Operation Phantom Strike in other key locations designed to keep insurgents off balance.

Implementation of New Counterinsurgency Doctrine, *FM 3-24, COIN*

On February 10, 2007, Petraeus took command of MNF–I from Casey. Casey's new assignment as the chief of staff of the Army took him out of the country in which he had served for the previous thirty-one months and away from the deteriorating conditions that Iraq found itself in.

The change of command authority wasn't the only change that occurred with the arrival of Petraeus. The way in which U.S. forces in Iraq approached counterinsurgency operations changed, too. Petraeus brought with him the Army's shiny new field manual, *FM 3-24, Counterinsurgency*, and rapidly began implementing throughout the country the doctrine that he was instrumental in developing. The new doctrine's test bed was to be the capital city of Baghdad, and Petraeus immediately set to work. Prior to this, Petraeus served as the commander of the U.S. Army Combined Arms Center, located at Fort Leavenworth, Kansas. While there from October 2005 to February 2007, he recognized that our efforts were not unified and were failing. Furthermore, he recognized the need for a doctrinal manual that outlined the principles and guidelines for counterinsurgency operations.

It had been twenty years since the Army published a field manual devoted exclusively to counterinsurgency operations. Moreover, it had been twenty-five years since the Marine Corps had one. With that understanding, Petraeus organized a joint team of experts, military and civilian alike, including Lieutenant Colonel John A. Nagl, Dr. David Kilcullen, and retired Lieutenant Colonel Conrad Crane. Also influential in the drafting of this document was the book *Counter Insurgency Warfare: Theory and Practice*[14] by David Galula, a French military officer who drew many valuable lessons from his service in France's unsuccessful campaign against Algerian insurgents.[15]

FM 3-24 was officially published in December 2006. Both the U.S. Army and Marine Corps published the new manual, though under different names. However, it had yet to be fully digested and put into application by units in the field. The new COIN manual placed a premium on protecting the population; as defined by *FM 3-24*, it is the center of gravity for successful execution of counterinsurgency operations. Likewise, the manual stressed the important role of nonlethal activities and the decisive role that governmental and nongovernmental agencies play in achieving overall success.

In Chapter 3, "Intelligence," the field manual showed an understanding that, while firepower is the determinant of success in conventional warfare, the key to victory in counterinsurgency is intelligence on the location and identity of the insurgent enemy derived from a supportive population; one of the principles of counterinsurgency is that intelligence drives operations. The field manual also introduced new doctrinal constructs for drafting a cohesive campaign plan and logical lines of operations. The manual ends with several appendices; the most important and useful of them is "Appendix A: A Guide for Action." This appendix was influenced by the writings and teachings of counterinsurgency expert Dr. David Kilcullen. It includes tips and guidelines for sergeants and young officers called upon to execute the precepts of counterinsurgency on the streets of Baghdad or the remote mountainous villages in Afghanistan.

After reading this manual cover to cover, it struck me that during my two previous tours, we already had been using and executing a lot of the tactics and principles cited in it, though more out of our own initiative as opposed to any formalized training or experience in COIN. For instance, during my first tour in Balad, we took it upon ourselves to recruit and train an Iraqi police force that was able to enforce the rule of law at the local level. We denied sanctuary to insurgents (granted, through the maximum use of force). At the time, absent of a

COIN doctrine, that is what we were trained to do, and we did it well. Moreover, this technique worked this best given that what Iraqis knew and respected most was authority. In 2003–04, we were the authority, and we did our best to quell any and all violence. That approach obviously backfired on us.

Aside from killing insurgents, we planned and executed other nonlethal activities to complement our offensive operations. Most notably, we organized local city councils and held the first free democratic local elections ever in Iraq. We were truly ahead of our time.

During my second tour in Baghdad, we executed similar operations. However, this time around, we drafted a comprehensive campaign plan with logical supporting lines of effort that guided us and helped us stay on track with what we were trying to achieve. Each previous rotation had a flavor of COIN contained within it, though nothing was codified. The one fatal mistake we and all other units made prior to 2006 was that we did not put a premium on protecting the population. All of our actions served counter to this and actually alienated the population. We finally figured it out in 2006 with the execution of Operation Together Forward II. The clear, hold, build approach was genius by design. The issue then was that we simply did not have the combat power or governmental resources to adequately protect the population and to isolate them from insurgents. The ISF forces were incapable of doing it on their own, hence the surge.

FM 3-24 was truly evolutionary and perhaps the most anticipated doctrinal manual ever published in the history of the U.S. Army. Its impact on both planning and execution were felt immediately on the streets of Baghdad. The greatest contributions were that it provided the Army with a codified doctrine and created a unity of effort. It was institutionalized and was being taught in schools and home station training programs, starting with basic and advanced individual training programs for preentry soldiers, in noncommissioned and commissioned officer courses, and at our three national training centers. Nagl stated its contributions the most succinctly when he said:

> "The most important contribution of this manual is likely to be its role as a catalyst in the process of making the Army and Marine Corps more effective learning organizations that are better able to adapt to the rapidly changing nature of modern counterinsurgency campaigns."[16]

FM 3-24 was officially implemented in Iraq in February 2007. I was at Fort Hood at the time and had just received official notification that I was going to be an infantry battalion commander. I was slated to take command in June 2007 of 1st Battalion (Airborne), 509th Parachute Infantry Regiment located at Fort Polk. It had been a long time coming; at that point, I would have taken a weather station in Antarctica if it meant commanding troops again.

Upon hearing the news, I began the process of transitioning from my unit at Fort Hood. Prior to assuming command, the Army directs that all incoming commanders attend the precommand course at Fort Leavenworth. The course is three weeks long and is designed to bring commanders up to date on the current status of the Army, including any new or current doctrinal changes and any policy or regulation amendments. Within the curriculum is an opportunity to hear several current or former battalion and brigade commanders address lessons learned from both Iraq and Afghanistan. During the course, officers are organized into small groups and assigned both military and civilian instructors. The military instructors are all combat veterans who, in most instances, had just returned from either Iraq or Afghanistan.

After the course concluded, I returned to Texas, where I married my beautiful new bride Wendy Scott. A short time later, it was time to report to Fort Polk. I was fortunate to have Lieutenant Colonel John Norris as my instructor. Norris, whom I had met briefly in Baghdad months earlier, was by far the best instructor of the bunch. I was impressed with his knowledge and professionalism and how he approached the course curriculum. I gathered quickly that he was one of our Army's best and most talented senior leaders and destined for brigade command and beyond. At that point, I had no clue that I would have the honor to serve with him in the not-too-distant future.

Upon arrival at Fort Polk, I started my transition with the current and outgoing commander of 1-509th, Lieutenant Colonel John King. The transition lasted approximately three weeks. It was by far the best and most thorough transition I had ever had. King and his wife gave me the warmest reception possible and made the transition go as smoothly as one could hope for. It is never easy giving up the mantle of command. This was certainly the case for me anytime I had to relinquish command of a unit.

The day of the Change of Command approached quickly, and on June 19, we executed the Change of Command Ceremony. The day was blessed with heat in excess of 90 degrees Fahrenheit, and the humidity was even worse. In attendance were Brigadier General Dan Bolger, Commanding General of Fort Polk and Joint Readiness Training Center; Colonel Kevin Owens, Commander of the JRTC Operations Group; Command Sergeants Major Roy Malloy and Robert Gallagher; former Sergeant Major of the Army; and retired Sergeant Major of the Army Julius W. Gates. In addition were several fellow commanders, and family and friends of 1-509th "Geronimo" Battalion.

The ceremony included the traditional inspection of the troops by both King and me. Then we centered on the battalion colors and passed them around, starting with King and ending up with me and back to the battalion CSM. This passing of the colors is a time-honored tradition that symbolizes passing of authority and the mantle of leadership from one commander to the next. After that, we returned to our posts and addressed the audience with our prepared change-of-command speeches. First, the presiding officer, Col. Owens, gave his speech, followed by King. In all cases, the outgoing commander gives the longest speech as they reflect back on the past two years of command.

When he concluded, I stepped up to the podium and thanked Brig. Gen. Bolger and Owens for the opportunity to command. I thanked my parents, wife, and children for always being there and supporting me as I pursued my military goals. It was a flawless ceremony, professionally executed, in keeping with the highest standards of the Army. The mantle of leadership was now mine, and I was truly honored and humbled to have the opportunity to lead these great men and Paratroopers of 1-509th, "Geronimo."

This command tour meant that I would be grounded for two years and would not deploy based on my unit's current mission. As a result, I did not see action in Iraq during the surge period. At first I was somewhat heartbroken over the notion that I would not deploy a battalion to combat. Every quality infantry officer I know who is dedicated to the profession aspires to lead troops into combat during wartime. But I quickly got over that and was honored to be leading the battalion I was chosen by the Army to lead. While the mission assigned to us was not as dangerous as leading troops in combat, it was just as important, if not more important: It would fall upon us to train the units and soldiers headed over to fight. How well we executed this training would impact lives saved and missions accomplished for those units.

The other advantage to commanding Geronimo was the fact that I was an independent battalion and did not belong to a parent brigade headquarters. I answered to an immediate supervisor, known as the commander of operations groups (COG). Owens was the COG at the time. He had previously relinquished command of the 173rd Airborne Brigade Combat Team based in Vicenza, Italy, where he deployed and fought with them in Afghanistan. To this day, he is one of the finest and most talented officers I know. He is no nonsense, straight shooter, and tells it like it is. I have the utmost respect for Owens, and it was an honor to serve with him. During my initial in-brief with him, he provided clear guidance and intent for the execution of our mission supporting the rotations as the OPFOR. As for all other training and administrative matters, I was given wide range of options and open fields of fire to command how I saw fit. I certainly took advantage of the liberty.

1-509th Geronimo is one of three distinct and unique units in the Army. Unique because they currently serve as the OPFOR at one of our three "Dirt" Combat Training Centers: National Training Center, Fort Irwin, California; Joint Readiness Training Center (JRTC), Fort Polk, Louisiana; and Joint Multi-National Readiness Center, Hohenfels, Federal Republic of Germany. These world-class training centers are the Army's premier large-scale training facilities and provide force-on-force combat simulation to infantry brigade task forces and digitally supported combat simulations above brigade level.

The mission of the OPFOR is to portray a realistic enemy using enemy equipment, order of battle, tactics, and equipment. It is by far the best and most realistic training a unit receives prior to deploying to the war zone. At JRTC, our mission focused mainly on training light/airborne or special operations forces. On an annual basis, we would execute ten rotations, each lasting a month from start to finish. Each of these rotations included a five-day force-on-force portion. The JRTC training scenario is based on an organization's mission essential tasks list, which is the core competencies that they must be trained in and proficient at before deploying. The exercise scenarios replicate many of the unique situations and challenges a unit may face in combat, including host national officials and citizens, host nation security forces, insurgents, media coverage, and governmental and nongovernment organizations.

When I took command of Geronimo, the immediate priority and mission was to train surge brigades that had been mobilized for immediate deployment to Iraq. It took me about three rotations to really grasp the OPFOR mission and assess how we were doing to achieve the desired end state, providing deploying units with the most realistic, stressful, and challenging training as possible. I soon realized that the current portrayal or replication of the enemy in Iraq was flawed. JRTC by design is the last major training event a brigade task force will conduct prior to deploying overseas. It is the culminating event and should be as realistic as the real-time, current conditions found in theater. Granted, there is lag time as conditions in Iraq or Afghanistan changed on a weekly basis. Based on the scenario we were executing, it was one to two years behind current operations in Iraq. Too much emphasis was placed on attacking the rotational unit and inflicting as many casualties as possible using tactics that were not consistent with what the insurgents were doing in present-day Iraq.

Aside from having the enemy scenario wrong, there was no real portrayal of host nation security forces. As part of the scenario design, I tasked a small handful of soldiers with performing and serving in the role as host nation security forces, in this case the ISF. The issue was that there were only a handful of people (no more than thirty or so) to cover a 4,000-man brigade task force. It simply was not working. In Iraq, the ISF had a strength of more than 500,000, including Iraqi Army soldiers, Iraqi police, and national police. Furthermore, with the implementation of COIN doctrine, a greater emphasis was placed on the ISF being in the lead conducting combined operations with U.S. forces in a supporting role.

Back at JRTC, we had it wrong. Rotational units were executing all operations as if the ISF were not there. The ISF forces that a battalion had may have been a squad size (eight to ten soldiers) at best, and they simply followed in trail behind them and were really not integrated into their operations. They were definitely not in the lead. Essentially we (JRTC Operations Group) were collectively behind the times on the operations side of the house and in our enemy set or replication. We were not giving the deploying unit an accurate portrayal of conditions or operations in theater. Bottom line: our scenario was based on 2004–05 conditions.

The results of this had second- and third-order effects on operations in theater. The greatest impact was felt at the squad level, exactly where we did not want it and could not afford for it to be. Soldiers and leaders would depart JRTC with the wrong mindset going into Iraq, especially our junior soldiers. For instance, at JRTC, rotational units' soldiers were constantly being attacked by insurgent forces, even in the towns and villages that were known to be supportive of U.S. efforts. This was happening day after day during the force-on-force portion. As a result, soldiers departed JRTC with the mindset that this was exactly the way it was in Iraq.

Once they arrived in Iraq, they were more apprehensive and of the mindset that everyone, including the local population, was out to get them. Based on that belief, soldiers were prone to shoot first and ask questions later when, instead, they needed to use discretion and see how the situation developed before acting with lethal measures. This misconception led to further alienation of the population. The fight in Iraq was won or lost at the squad and platoon levels. These were the elements on the ground that were executing daily combat operations and were in constant view and contact with the local population. Any misstep or incident could have strategic consequences. In several cases, such incidents left a mess for senior level leadership to clear up.

The best known and most publicized of these incidents occurred on September 16, 2007, in Baghdad involving U.S. contractors, not soldiers. According to eyewitness reports, Blackwater military contractors allegedly shot and killed seventeen innocent Iraqi civilians in Nisour Square. The fatalities occurred while a Blackwater Personal Security Detachment was clearing the way for a convoy of U.S. State Department vehicles en route to a meeting in western Baghdad with USAID officials.[17]

Both a Federal Bureau of Investigation and military investigation concluded that Blackwater guards opened fire without provocation. The investigation also determined that at least fourteen of the shootings were unjustified and violated deadly-force rules.[18]

I use this case as an illustration not to prove innocence or guilt, but rather to show that if training at home stations does not address the need to protect the population at all costs no matter who's involved, then we are setting soldiers up for failure and incidents like this one, with lasting strategic consequences that serve counter to what we are trying to achieve in Iraq. This incident drew a lot of scrutiny inside and outside of Iraq, especially since all charges against the contractors involved were dropped. Even after this incident occurred, we were still training units to be aggressive and lethal in the application of force versus being discriminate and measuring the response in order to limit collateral damage, as outlined in *FM 3-24*.

More evidence supporting this claim was provided by my new wife based upon responses given to her during one-on-one interviews. Captain Wendy Wright took command of a reserve military history detachment in 2007 based out of New Orleans, Louisiana, and was mobilized and deployed to Iraq from August 2008 to July 2009. Upon arrival in Iraq, she was assigned as the division historian for Multi-National Division–North based out of Camp Speicher in Tikrit, Iraq. It was her mission to go out into the field and interview soldiers and leaders in order to capture their stories and lessons learned for eventual collation by the Center for Military History. A lot of these units were deployed to theater as part of the surge force package.

Wright stated that a common theme she heard during her interviews was that units had trained and prepared for the current deployment like they had experienced during their last, and that this time around, conditions had totally changed and were nothing like their last deployment.

In other cases, soldiers were shooting at cars occupied by innocent civilians, oftentimes wounding or killing them because they were traveling too close to the convoy they were riding in due to the fact the soldiers felt threatened as if the vehicle were a car bomb or some other target. A lot of these engagements were executed in accordance with the ROE, but the accidental shootings still served counter to what we were trying to achieve. Something had to change or we would continue to reinforce failure and further alienate the population.

With the implementation of the new COIN doctrine in February 2007, the senior leadership at JRTC and operations group conducted a review and assessment of the overall scenario and made the determination that our current scenario was in fact dated and needed to be adjusted. Another major factor that influenced this change was the feedback we received from forward deploying units. One of the best initiatives established by operations group was in fact this reach back program. This program was designed for deployed unit commanders to share feedback and lessons learned from the front lines with us at JRTC so we could keep pace with conditions, best practices, and changes in theater. Of the feedback received, the majority of commanders stated that the training they had previously received at JRTC was nothing like the current conditions they were facing in Iraq. With that feedback and the results of the review, Brigadier General James C. Yarbrough gave guidance to the operations group commander to reassess our scenario and change it to better replicate current conditions.

With that guidance, operations group executed a complete overhaul of the current scenario. Work had already begun within my battalion, as I had anticipated that this change was coming based on observations during earlier rotations. To address the host nation security forces issue, I gathered my staff, namely my executive officer, Major Mark Landis, and other officers, including intelligence, operations, and logistics officers, and provided them with specific guidance. I then had them work up a couple of courses of action that would allow the battalion to field two companies' worth of host nation security forces and a company to maintain our insurgent threat groups. Since we would be increasing the host nation security forces' footprint, far fewer enemy insurgents would be on the battlefield. As such, it meant that this group would have to be smarter and more deliberate in their planning and execution of attacks.

To ensure we were creating the right enemy signature, I sent a handful of key leaders and soldiers, including CSM Doug Maddi and myself, to "Mirror Image," a week-long course hosted by ex-CIA agents and other counterterrorism experts. The course is designed to indoctrinate you to act, think, eat, sleep, and pray like a radical Islamic terrorist. Upon arrival, students are stripped of all creature comforts and necessities, including cell phones and civilian clothing. These items are replaced with a dishdasha (commonly known in slang to soldiers as a "man dress"), a Koran, and a prayer rug. Next, students are assigned fictitious Arabic names and divided into insurgent cells consisting of eight to ten members. The training environment took place in a remote area in the northern hills of North Carolina.

The area is a replicated terrorist training camp. Each day students role-playing as would-be terrorists attend morning and evening prayer sessions focused on studying the Koran and reciting the Islamic prayer salutation. After morning prayer was completed, we would receive blocks of instructions on past terrorist actions focusing on the planning and execution of these attacks. Most notably of the attacks studied were the 1973 kidnappings and murder of Israeli athletes during the Olympic Games held in Munich, Germany. We dissected these events to examine the critical factors that enabled these attacks to be successful. In the afternoon sessions, we would plan and execute simulated attacks such as emplacing IEDs and performing assassinations, kidnappings, and ambushes. For breakfast and lunch, we feasted on pita bread and hummus. Then in the evening we were treated to a hot meal in a nearby dining facility. The course was by far the best training I had received to date regarding how our enemy thinks and fights and what motivates them.

Once complete, we returned to Fort Polk and used the experience to design our own formalized terrorist training program to teach new soldiers to be better OPFOR soldiers, i.e., "terrorists" when assigned the specific mission. This training paid huge dividends to deploying units as our replication of the enemy during rotations was more advanced and realistic, and as close to current conditions in Iraq as possible.

Once we had the redesign about right, we briefed and had our plan approved by Colonel Jon Lehr, who had recently replaced Owens as the commander of operations group. While I worked the revamping of the OPFOR and host nation security forces, operations group and the plans division overhauled the baseline scenario. Greater emphasis was placed on rotational units serving in a supporting role to host nation support forces. Civil military operations played a greater role, and ePRTs provided by the State Department participated in the rotation. To add to battlefield realism or atmospheric enhancements, each mock village or town got a makeover to better resemble towns and villages in Iraq or Afghanistan, including the addition of mosques, Arabic street signs, and even live animals such as goats and chickens. In addition, more local civilians were hired as role players to better replicate civilians on the battlefield.

Operations group established several situational training exercises lanes that units would execute prior to the five-day force-on-force portion. These lanes included dealing with insurgent snipers, suicide bombers, and sectarian violence, controlling angry crowds, performing civil military operations, and undertaking key leader engagements. All of these lanes included media on the battlefield, civilians, and host nation security forces integrated as part of the scenario. This cutting-edge training prepared them for situations they would face during the force-on-force and, more importantly, for likely situations they would encounter in Iraq. No longer would deploying units focus on strictly maneuver and offensive operations; they also would be challenged and faced with situations like calming angry crowds and negotiating with or befriending tribal leaders who spoke no English.

Another notable change occurred amongst unit evaluators. No longer were they simply a third set of eyes that provided the unit a critique. They transitioned to the role of OC/T and took on the role of coaches, trainers, and mentors. From start to finish, they provided the unit leadership and soldiers with advice, training, and mentorship based on lessons they had learned themselves and from current best practices shared by units in theater. OC/Ts were the Army's catalyst for making COIN a reality. The greatest addition made was the hiring of former Iraqi military officers who had since departed Iraq and took up residence in the United States. These former officers served as the commanders of the host nation security forces that my battalion provided.

This change provided my first introduction to Mohammed al-Samare, known as "Hawk," a former Iraq Army battalion commander who departed Iraq in 2006 during the height of sectarian violence. Al-Samare was my direct counterpart and served as the overall commander of the ISF. I served as his deputy to ensure we stayed on our rotational objectives. Over the course of the next five rotations, we developed a lasting friendship that endures to this day. Also to ensure realism, other Iraqi nationals were hired to serve as translators and were provided to all units, from brigade level down to company level, while others portrayed imams and sheiks in the mock villages. These changes had a lasting effect on deploying units and enhanced their overall mission accomplishment. Altogether these sweeping changes took approximately ninety days to implement.

JRTC officially introduced the new scenario in November 2008, starting with the 56th Stryker Brigade Combat Team Pennsylvania Army National Guard rotation. The 56th SBCT, led by Colonel Marc Ferraro, is the Army's first and only Reserve/National Guard Stryker Brigade. During their rotation, they were exposed to the new scenario and performed well. As a matter of fact, they were one of the best units I had witnessed to date in terms of discipline, SOPs, staff planning processes, targeting, and willingness to absorb the training to better enhance their mission in Iraq. A truly remarkable outfit! During their deployment to Iraq, they were assigned to MND–B and covered the volatile area of Taji, located approximately 15 kilometers (9.3 miles) north of Baghdad. According to all accounts from senior military leaders, the unit performed well as they had previously at JRTC.

I ran into Ferraro in passing in Iraq in September 2009 as they were departing and asked him how JRTC had prepared them. His reply was "It could not have been any better. It was as close to current conditions in Iraq as possible." I shook his hand and commended him for a job well done, and wished him and his unit well in their future endeavors. Ending with their rotation in December 2008, I would execute ten more. Each subsequent rotation was better than the previous one as units had absorbed and trained on the new COIN doctrine prior to showing up.

The deployment of these brigades as part of the surge forces, coupled with the COIN training received at JRTC and elsewhere at home station, had an immediate impact on operations in Iraq. First and most significant was that overall attack trends in the restive Anbar Province and Baghdad decreased dramatically. By November 2007, enemy attacks had dropped to their lowest level since 2004–05. According to military records, there were thirty attacks in Anbar Province during the last week in October 2007. A year prior, there had been more than three hundred. In Baghdad, attacks decreased by nearly 60 percent. Sectarian violence also was reduced. In 2006, civilian deaths throughout Iraq reached more than 3,000 in the month of December. Based on the deployment and integration of surge forces, death totals declined by 70 percent. In the Baghdad security districts specifically, ethno-sectarian attacks and deaths decreased by 90 percent over the course of 2007.[19] U.S.- and ISF-partnered offensive operations were taking a toll on insurgent forces—with the desired effects. Insurgents affiliated with both al-Qaeda and with Shiite militias were being killed or detained at an astonishing rate, so much so that Muqtada al-Sadr called for and enacted a ceasefire amongst his militia members. Of those who survived, many were forced out and away from Baghdad and the surrounding areas.

It was clear that the surge was having a positive impact. The surge was also responsible for enhancing ISF capacity. More U.S. brigades and battalions led to more partnered units for the Iraqi Army and police forces. According to Odierno in March 2008, while serving as MNC–I Commander, "When it comes to developing the ISF, there is simply no substitute for partnership." Partnership allowed Iraqi Army and police forces to see firsthand what right looks like when it comes to tactical operations and pursuing the enemy.

The commitment of surge forces and the dedication to protecting the population led to another initiative known as the Sunni Awakening, or "Sahwa Movement." The movement started in Anbar Province in

2006 prior to the actual surge. At the time, it was given little notoriety until surge forces showed up in 2007. From then, the movement quickly spread throughout the country, particularly in Baghdad.

The Sahwa Movement was a grassroots initiative implemented by Sunnis, some of which were former insurgents who were fed up with the violence and atrocities being committed by al-Qaeda and Shiite militias and turned against them. They made a decision to reject al-Qaeda and extremism. Based on this, commanders in the field seized the opportunity and hired them to assist the Iraqi police and Army in providing security in areas where police and army presence was inadequate.

At first, U.S. commanders were reluctant to negotiate with Sunnis, who had long been our adversary. But there really was no other alternative. The initial movement was known as the Concerned Local Citizens. Over time it evolved and became the Sons of Iraq. For all intents and purposes, this was an armed community watch group employed by the United States and GOI to protect their local population. When the program first began, members were paid roughly $300 a month. The program kept military-aged Sunni males from joining the ranks of al-Qaeda by providing them a job and a source of income. It also employed former insurgents who defected from al-Qaeda. Along with the income came a promise that they would no longer attack U.S. forces or ISF. Based on the success of these local groups, the program spread like wildfire throughout towns in Iraq including Baquba, Samarra, Fallujah, Taji, and Balad. According to Odierno:

"The impact of the Sons of Iraq went beyond security and paved the way for improvements in basic services, economic progress, and local governance ... Additionally, there is a second-order effect in that every dollar paid to the Sons of Iraq gets spent at least two additional times as they provide for their families and then local markets buy wholesale goods to stock their stands. In places where we have employed the Sons of Iraq, we average a ten-fold increase in the markets, for example going from 40 to 400 stands. Finally, the Sons of Iraq are now branching out across Iraq and increasingly include Shia groups and, in some cases mixed sects."[20]

As security conditions improved across Iraq, the surge helped set the conditions for improvements in governance and economic development through the integration of ePRTs. Based on previous levels of violence, ePRTs could not access troubled areas such as Abu Ghraib and Nasir

Wasalam to the west of Baghdad. These areas were now safe for the teams to implement new projects and assist local leaders with establishing city councils and other governance programs. One of the major economic initiatives was the overhaul and reemergence of the farm industry. ePRTs added experts from the USDA to their teams. These teams went out into farming regions like those found in Taji and Abu Ghraib and taught local farmers advanced techniques of "green house" farming designed to conserve water and enhance crop production. This program quickly spread throughout most of Iraq, and ever since farming and crop production reemerged as a major source of income to Iraqi families.

While the surge was in full swing, things on the political front at home were not going as well. First, President Bush's approval rating dipped to an all-time low of 28 percent, according to a Gallup poll.[21] Lawmakers and other retired military leaders publicly criticized the administration's plan. On October 12, 2007, retired Lt. Gen. Ricardo Sanchez, in one of his first public speeches since leaving the Army, blamed the Bush administration for a "catastrophically flawed, unrealistically optimistic war plan" and denounced the current surge strategy as a "desperate" move that would not achieve long-term stability.[21]

This speech came on the heels of Petraeus's September 10, 2007, testimony before Congress during which he reported progress under the surge strategy and warned against a premature troop withdrawal. As this political bickering wore on, it was clearly having an effect on troop morale in Iraq. Soldiers would discuss these issues over dinner, noting that they felt as though their fellow Americans couldn't stomach the violence in Iraq, fearing that the country had lost its will, as had happened during the Vietnam War. Many felt as though much of the country wanted the military to leave Iraq before the mission was complete.

To make matters worse, on November 6, 2007, six American soldiers were killed in three separate attacks, taking the number of deaths to date that year to 852. The toll made 2007 the deadliest year of the war for U.S. troops.[22] Despite the rhetoric and political pressure to withdraw, President Bush and the administration stayed the course by placing trust and confidence in the senior military leadership and soldiers on the ground in Iraq and were able to persevere.

On July 22, 2008, the last five surge combat brigades left Iraq, leaving approximately 147,000 American soldiers remaining in the country.[23] Through many trials and tribulations, both in Iraq and at home in the

United States, the surge had ultimately achieved its desired end states: ending the current cycle of sectarian violence, setting the conditions for the ISF to emerge as the dominant security force, and facilitating the protection and security of the population centers. The majority of insurgents and extremists had been killed, captured, or driven out of Baghdad and the surrounding areas. The overall security situation was more stable than it ever had been, while attacks and casualties reached an all-time low. Iraqi citizens were taking to the streets and shopping at local marketplaces such as those found along the famed Haifa Street in downtown Baghdad. Iraqi children were back in school and able to play soccer outside without fear of being kidnapped or killed. An even better illustration of how security conditions had improved were the numerous pictures shown on the news of Petraeus walking the streets of Baghdad without body armor, helmet, or weapon. Odierno summed up this period the best:

"For the government of Iraq, the surge has provided a window of opportunity. This window will not remain open forever. To capitalize on the reduction of violence in 2007, Iraqi leaders must make deliberate choices to secure lasting strategic gains through reconciliation and political progress. The set of choices and their collective effect will be decisive, I think."[24]

For U.S. forces starting in July 2008, operations would focus on sustaining the security gains while improving Iraqis' lives and building capacity in the government and continued capacity in the ranks of the Iraqi Army and police forces. Somewhere in the back of my mind, I knew I would return to Iraq to see it play out.

Surge Versus COIN

There is a great debate amongst military leaders, strategists, and pundits who argue about whether it was the surge or the implementation of the new COIN doctrine that led to success in Iraq from 2007 to 2009 and set the conditions for irreversible momentum. Some would argue that COIN was the tipping point that allowed us to turn the corner in Iraq. I believe it was the surge of troops.

In late 2006, Iraq was on the verge of total collapse, the security situation was tenuous at best, and violence had spiraled out of control. A philosophical and strategic paradigm shift was not going to profoundly alter daily events on the ground in Iraq. Control of the ground, securing the population from attack, and nation building is the end state that the U.S. required. The immediate concern was security and reduction of sectarian violence to allow for bottom-up reconciliation. The only way to address security and reduce the violence was to increase U.S. troop presence, as the ISF was immature and incapable at the time. Without a relatively secure and stable environment, there would be no implementation of COIN. The only way we were going to get the security issues under control was by troop presence. If COIN had been introduced without the surge of troops to implement it, then it would have failed, much like Operations Together Forward I and II did.

Those operations were built around the principles of "clear, hold, and build," cited in *FM 3-24*. The reason they failed was due to a lack of troops to properly carry them out to completion. A lot of the tactics and principles cited in *FM 3-24* were nothing new to the Army. Soldiers and leaders had and were executing COIN before it was formally introduced, institutionalized, and trained. The new doctrine was a masterful document that took everything available on counterinsurgency and codified it into a central thesis that provided the Army and sister services a model to fight from, thus creating a unity of effort in Iraq and Afghanistan. The COIN doctrine allowed commanders and soldiers to plan, train, and execute from a set standard, and not from having to rely upon discovery learning.

Given the current fight and its enduring nature, *FM 3-24* could not have been timed any better. Moreover, the institutionalization of the doctrine played a major role in educating soldiers and leaders to be better practitioners that led to mission success. The overarching question was not whether COIN needed to be implemented in Iraq, but rather how to achieve conditions on the ground that would allow COIN to be effective and successful. The battlefield needed to be stabilized, and the surge was the tactical and strategic tool of choice.

As I entered my second and last year of command, surge rotations ended, and we continued with a steady diet of regularly scheduled rotations for units deploying to Iraq and Afghanistan. For a couple of months starting in July 2008, my battalion got a reprieve: no training rotations were scheduled. This gave me an opportunity to train leaders and soldiers on other tasks. Beyond the OPFOR, the battalion had a go-to-war mission to train on, just like all other infantry battalions.

The reason behind this was that during a worst-case scenario we could be called upon to deploy; therefore we had to be proficient at wartime tasks. I was able to draft a challenging and rigorous training plan to achieve proficiency in core infantry tasks.

Unlike most deploying units, I was not tied to COIN-centric training. I had the luxury to train across the full spectrum of operations, including low-intensity conflicts, COIN, and high-intensity conflicts or major conventional warfare. All of my leaders got first-hand experience with COIN simply because they executed it once a month and because they also got to observe units executing the training we supported. Based on that, I chose to focus our training on high-intensity or conventional offensive operations. Because it was an airborne unit, we also trained on forced entry operations such as airfield seizures. What was most rewarding was the fact that I got to teach young platoon leaders and junior company commanders how to properly plan, execute, and assess training, a process better known as training management. I executed this through a series of officer professional development sessions, tactical exercises without troops, terrain walks, fire coordination exercises, and "Omega Platoon" live-fire exercises.

Omega Platoon live-fire exercises involve all the officers in the battalion, organized into an infantry platoon structure. Platoon leaders and other junior officers serve as team leaders and riflemen, company commanders serve as the squad leaders, and I served as the platoon leader. This concept was started by the 75th Ranger Regiment. I adopted it from a former battalion commander of mine from the 82nd Airborne Division, Colonel Roy "Chuck" Waggoner (Ret.), who had served as a company commander with 2nd Battalion, 75th Ranger Regiment. By far he was the most influential officer in my career, who taught me everything there was to know about training infantry platoons. Before the live-fire exercise was executed, we planned the scenario in order to teach live-fire planning and synchronization principles, resourcing and logistical support, and the individual and collective task crosswalk to ensure we covered all the requirements.

The whole exercise from planning to execution served as a "train the trainer" program. My purpose for doing this was to show young platoon leaders how to properly plan, resource, execute, and assess training the right way. This is a dying art in the Army today. Prior to the September 11, 2001, attacks, the Army was proficient at conducting live-fire exercises. We trained it all the time and culminated with company-level nighttime live fires using night observation devices.

That was standard operating procedure. I wanted to ensure that the next breed of senior leaders in the Army, NCOs and officers alike, were well rounded and not simply just COIN-centric experts, as the campaigns in Iraq and Afghanistan would eventually end and we would refocus training across the full spectrum of operations. I wanted them to have a head start.

Overall, command was a great experience and by far the most rewarding time of my career. I was blessed to be surrounded by talented soldiers, NCOs, and officers whose value and contributions in training deploying units for success in combat were immeasurable. The day was nearing when I would relinquish command to Lieutenant Colonel Anthony "Tony" Judge. Two years had flown by fast from when I first donned insurgent garb and took on multiple roles as a battalion commander and insurgent leader fighting against training units.

In May 2009, I was reassigned to the 4-2 SBCT, "Raiders," at Fort Lewis, Washington, where I would reunite with Colonel John Norris to serve as his deputy commanding officer (DCO). Previously, in March 2009, 4-2 SBCT received news from the Army that they were being accelerated by ten months and would deploy to Iraq in September 2009. Based on that, they were scheduled for their MRX at Fort Polk in June 2009. The timing of their rotation could not have worked out better for me. I was a month out from changing command and was in position to participate with them in their rotation. By participating, I was allowed to get to know the brigade staff and other key leaders in the unit and witness firsthand how they planned and executed operations. Essentially this was my transition period to the DCO position as the next time I linked up with the unit would be in Iraq in September 2009.

4-2 SBCT had a great rotation; they were light years ahead of most units considering that they had been accelerated in the deployment timeline. I actually integrated with them as the DCO all the while controlling and supervising the ISF and OPFOR against them. Norris was able to validate his campaign plan known as the "Partnership Strategy," which I had an integral role in developing a month earlier. The brigade met all other associated training objectives established during the rotation. I was excited to be a part of the Raider Team and could not wait to deploy with them in the coming months and see this strategy play out.

CHAPTER 8
"WAHID" IRAQ
June 2009–March 2010

   " There are a lot of expectations out there on behalf of the population. They
think they should be the Japan of the Middle East, and they ought to be. **"**
General David Petraeus

My command officially ended with a cold Gatorade shower planned
and executed by my headquarters and headquarters company
commander, Captain Guy Girouard. That was the first of its kind I had
ever seen at a change of command. Nonetheless, I felt extremely
proud that day for what the battalion and I were able to accomplish
during the past two years. Even better for me was that I would get a
firsthand look at how the COIN training units received at JRTC was
paying off in theater in the coming months. I really did not have a lot
of time to reminisce about the past as I was on a tight timeline to get

to Fort Lewis, Washington, and focus on the impending deployment to Iraq with 4-2 Stryker Brigade Combat Team (4-2 SBCT). I was thrilled for the opportunity to get back to the fight. It is tough to keep infantrymen away from the battlefield. Somehow we always vector or run to the sounds of the guns.

Unfortunately, my wife Wendy was still serving in Iraq and would not return home until mid-July 2009. To make matters worse, upon her return we could spend only about three or four weeks together before I returned to Iraq. In the five years we had known each other, including two years of marriage, we had physically been together for eight months. We knew going into our marriage there would be time apart, but we did not think it would be this bad. Regardless, when you sign up and take the oath and choose to live this lifestyle, lengthy separation is often the result.

I signed into Fort Lewis on August 22 and began preparing for deployment. The biggest and most time-consuming hurdle was to complete the predeployment tasks at the soldier readiness processing (SRP) site. All soldiers prior to deployment must process through the site before being validated for deployment. The SRP tasks include medical screening, vaccinations, eye exams, hearing tests, and ensuring legal matters such as wills and powers of attorney are covered. This process can be frustrating at times, but it's necessary to ensure soldiers are prepared for deployment and that their families are taken care of while they are away. Being that I was days from deployment, the process was expedited to just two days. Following SRP, I visited the Central Issue Facility and drew all the new equipment required for the fight. The most significant piece of equipment I signed for was some new and improved body armor that was lighter and stronger than previous versions. The Army spared no expense to ensure all soldiers were equipped with the newest and most advanced equipment available.

The brigade cased its colors on August 25 at Fort Lewis, and soon after the completion of the ceremony, units began departing for Iraq. During the next two weeks, a steady flow of troops said their farewells to loved ones. Once I completed all the prerequisites, I linked up with the brigade commander, Colonel John Norris, and reviewed the final plan and any last-minute changes in theater. Norris and Command Sergeant Major Jeff Huggins were departing for Kuwait the next day; I would trail them by ten days. During my last few days at Fort Lewis, I tried to maximize time with my family.

During the eight months preceding our arrival in theater, several changes had taken place in how the 4-2 SBCT approached planning and executing security operations. The first change was at the strategic level leadership. On September 16, 2008, Odierno officially took over as MNF–I commander, succeeding Petraeus, who took over as commander of CENTCOM. This change was widely anticipated and a logical progression. For the troops on the ground, it meant that we would have continuity at the top level since Odierno had orchestrated and commanded the execution of the surge operations. In his first brief comments as commander of MNF–I, Odierno said, "We must realize that these gains are fragile and reversible, and our work here is far from done."

On the political front, Christopher Hill replaced Ryan Crocker as the U.S. Ambassador to Iraq and would partner directly with Odierno in the coming months to continue in our efforts to build capacity amongst the GOI and ISF. Again this change was anticipated in theater based on the recent election of President Barack Obama and the appointment of Secretary of State Hillary Clinton and their desire to appoint a representative to carry out the new administration's foreign diplomacy agenda in Iraq. Ambassador Hill's lack of Middle East experience made him a controversial choice for the position. It would be his sole charter to oversee a crucial moment for the nascent democracy following the provincial elections. Also, it would fall on his shoulders to broker a deal on the formation of a new government with the upcoming 2010 Iraqi national elections. For troops on the ground, this move really did not impact our operations or what we were trying to achieve. We knew going into this period of unchartered waters that our mission orders would come directly from Odierno and would be nested with what was trying to be achieved at the strategic level. It was business as usual.

The most significant change was the security agreement signed by the Iraqi and U.S. governments on November 17, 2008, during an official ceremony in Baghdad. The agreement is more commonly known as the Iraq Status of Forces Agreement (SOFA). We have several of these in foreign countries where we have a permanent troop presence, including Germany and South Korea. This historical agreement listed several stipulations we had to abide by. The first and most prevalent was that all U.S. forces had to withdraw from Iraqi cities by June 30, 2009, particularly Baghdad. Second, U.S. forces could no longer execute unilateral operations. All operations must be partnered operations between U.S. forces and ISF. Third was the requirement for all U.S. forces to be completely out of Iraq by December 31, 2011.

The agreement also required criminal charges for holding prisoners more than twenty-four hours during which time they had to either be charged or released and required a warrant to be issued to search homes and buildings not related to combat. Finally, it stated that U.S. contractors working for U.S. forces would be subject to Iraqi criminal law, while contractors working for the U.S. State Department and other U.S. agencies would retain immunity. With the signing of the document went complete sovereignty and control to the GOI (see Appendix G).

One thing was certain: the U.S. military was no longer in the lead. The ISF had taken over complete responsibility for security operations, and we were strictly in a supporting role. This monumental change and accomplishment was made possible because of the security gains achieved by surge forces and the implementation of the new COIN strategy. Equally if not more important was the contributions by the Sons of Iraq program. Due to their efforts, daily attacks against U.S. forces and ISF were at an all-time low; however, attacks against the population were still prevalent, particularly in the form of suicide vests or massive car bombs in congested areas or against government ministries. It was nearly impossible to predict where and when these bombings would take place.

SOFA did contain a grey area subject to interpretation that provided commanders some flexibility or freedom of maneuver. Article Four, for example, stipulates that U.S. forces could take all measures possible to ensure force protections of U.S. soldiers, equipment, and infrastructure such as bases and the routes traveled throughout Iraq. Translated to tactical vernacular, this meant that we could continue to execute route clearance and counter-IED patrols along major routes traveled by our forces. Also, we could execute countermortar and counterrocket patrols to protect bases from the threat of indirect fire.

What we discovered early on was that the agreement had a paralyzing effect on units throughout Iraq, especially those operating in and around Baghdad. Norris and I sensed that units took the literal translation of the agreement and immediately retrograded to their FOBs and outlying bases, essentially suspending active security operations altogether. In August 2009, there was noticeably very little presence of U.S. forces outside the wire. There was not a true sense of partnership with the ISF, nor were many combined operations being conducted. Depending on where you traveled in theater, you would find commands and units doing different things; there was no consistency. For instance in Diyala province, an area assigned to Multi-National Division–North, units had completely withdrawn to their FOBs and remained static until requested by Iraqis to provide support for host nation forces. On the surface, it appeared that units were a "911" force (i.e. an emergency force, standing by postured and ready to go just waiting on the call) and were not pursuing an active partnership with ISF. The immediate issue with this was that U.S. forces were losing access, situational awareness, and understanding of their assigned AOs.

Partnership: By, With, and Through Iraqi Security Forces

Sensing this was the wrong intent of the SOFA agreement, Norris and our brigade staff reviewed SOFA and did not find it written anywhere in the document that we could not actively partner with ISF units. Prior to arriving in theater, Norris and I sketched out a plan to address how to pursue partnerships with the Iraqi Army, police, national police, Sons of Iraq, GOI, and the population itself to ensure a unity of effort was established to allow the brigade to be successful in creating sustainable security and stability and to improve ISF capability and capacity. If this strategy were successful in implementation, it would lead to initiation of irreversible momentum that would allow us to begin to responsibly drawdown U.S. forces in Iraq. The key factor in designing this strategy was to draft something simple that could easily be conveyed to all subordinate commanders, units, and soldiers assigned to the brigade. The brigade strategy for this deployment is captured in what we called the Unity of Effort or "Rope Strategy."

This strategy served as enduring guidance to all subordinate units that only through a unity of effort would the brigade be successful in creating sustainable security and stability and improving ISF capacity and capabilities. All operations, both lethal and nonlethal, took this strategy into account. In his address to the brigade during our deployment ceremony in August 2009 at Fort Lewis, Norris stated that:

"The brigade will work to build partnerships with the Iraqi Security Forces and local governance in order to provide security for the people. As we achieve some success and the overall violence drops, together we can improve the daily life of Iraqi citizens."

This message was the general theme and party line anytime our strategy was discussed to superior officers, Iraqi officials, and other key Iraqi citizens. Moreover, we had small, weather- and tear-proof 3x5 cards printed of the Rope Strategy and distributed them to more than 4,500 soldiers working under the brigade's control. Each soldier was required to keep it on his person while deployed and use it as a reference when required. We actually took it one step further and had these cards translated and printed in Arabic so we could provide them to Iraqi counterparts and other key Iraqi leaders. After all, this was the targeted group that ultimately would be the executor on the ground to carry out this strategy and make it work. We were simply arming them with a way to success.

The final piece was ensuring that every soldier knew how to be successful during the deployment as far as individual actions and standard of conduct in support of the overarching strategy. To express this strategy, Norris, Huggins, and other key leaders designed what is referred to as the "DEPART" card. This card gave all soldiers assigned to the Raider Brigade standing guidance to consider while planning and executing missions, interacting with the ISF and the Iraqi people, and conducting key leader engagements with local leaders. Following this guidance would allow for all soldiers to build rapport and an enduring partnership with their Iraqi counterparts, set the example for a professional army, and be respectful of the Iraqi government, security force, and people's sovereignty.

The premise behind this, much like it was for the Rope Strategy, was to provide all Raider Brigade soldiers a set of simple principles they could easily remember in order to help shape conditions for irreversible momentum, enabling us to depart Iraq successfully, knowing we accomplished our mission with dignity and respect and leaving behind a sovereign, stable, and self-reliant Iraq. This graphic illustration was printed on the reverse side of the Rope Strategy card, leaving no excuse for soldiers not to understand the big picture and where they fit in regarding achieving the commander's overall intent.

These two documents were well received by all we came into contact with, most importantly our Iraqi counterparts and the Iraqi people. Prior to issuing these, Norris and Huggins personally briefed all soldiers and leaders that we could no longer be "prisoners of our pasts." If we reverted to previous tours and operated the way we had in prior deployments, then we would be doomed to fail. This message resonated amongst us all and was the driving force behind the success we would enjoy during the next year.

I said goodbye to my family on September 12, 2009, and started the long journey back to the desert, perhaps for the final time. This particular goodbye, while somewhat routine, turned out to be the hardest of all. I was excited for the return trip, knowing our strategy going in was sound and if adhered to would leave a lasting legacy for our brigade. But more importantly, it would leave Iraqis with conditions and hope for a better future. The mission and tasks to be accomplished were daunting, but I was optimistic and up for the challenge. I finally arrived in Kuwait on September 14 after a grueling twenty-two-hour flight. My first stop was to Camp Arifjan before transiting to the staging camp located at Camp Buehring.

As I arrived at Camp Arifjan, I noticed how the base had changed over the past two years. It was much bigger, densely populated, and more advanced. It seemed that a lot of money had been invested for infrastructure development. There were permanent office buildings, large motor pools, maintenance facilities, supply warehouses, and four-story barracks for the soldiers assigned there. Even more shocking was an Olympic-size swimming pool, running track, and well-equipped gymnasium. Our military had built a fortress that would serve as an enduring staging base for operations conducted in the Middle East for the foreseeable future, even after the mission ended in Iraq.

After checking in with members of the brigade staff, I departed for Camp Buehring. Upon arrival there I noticed that the camp still looked the same as it had in previous years. I met up with the officer in charge, Lieutenant Colonel Michelle "Miki" McCassey, to receive an update on deployment operations and any changes that may have occurred. Deployment operations were running smoothly with no issues. Also, ships carrying Strykers and other equipment had arrived and were in the process of being downloaded at the port facility. Subordinate units were already training on the required tasks, including individual weapons zero, artillery gunnery, IED recognition, vehicle roll-over drills, and limited driver's training. Things were progressing well as we neared movement into Iraq. I was scheduled to be in Kuwait for approximately ten days, but that was interrupted the next day when I received a phone call from Norris telling me that he wanted his battalion commanders and me in Iraq much earlier than planned. The commanders and I accelerated our training, and what should have taken ten days was completed in three. On September 18, I departed for Baghdad on a C-17 cargo jet.

The theater had matured to a point where everyone had cable television provided by the American Forces Network, cell phones with international SIM cards, wireless Internet, and all kinds of other high-tech devices. All these outlets offer soldiers a way to stay in touch with family and loved ones on a near real-time basis. However, the military does govern and regulate use and what can and cannot be sent or looked at.

War has changed. Gone are the days during World War II, Korea, and even as recently as Vietnam when a soldier would handwrite a letter and send it home and it took months to get there, sometimes never showing up at all. If and when it did, the news was old and no longer relevant. These days, communication is real time. Any given soldier or journalist could narrate a play-by-play action of a firefight which could be recorded and broadcasted on YouTube or news outlets within hours. That was unheard of twenty years ago.

The plane landed at Baghdad International Airport, and as the ramp dropped, we could feel the blistering heat as if we had nose-dived into a burning furnace. An awful smell of exhaust from the aircraft combined with the stench of burning refuse was unbearable.

The climate and landscape had not changed in Baghdad, but operations outside the wire certainly had. One thing that had not changed was that Iraq, while more stable, was still a very dangerous place. The enemy still loomed large but was smaller in number, lacking organization and leadership. Surge operations had a major role in reducing the enemy's overall capabilities. The most persistent threat faced by the ISF and our soldiers operating outside the wire remained IEDs, particularly lethal Explosively Formed Penetrators. Equally threatening were suicide bombers and car bombs.

These high-casualty-producing weapons were mainly used to target large crowds of Iraqis and various government ministries. They were the weapons of choice for al-Qaeda and used solely for the purpose of creating massive death and destruction in order to undermine the legitimacy of the GOI and ISF and destabilize recent security gains. The other threat that still persisted was the mortars and rockets being fired at our bases. FOBs had become even more lucrative targets as U.S. troops had pulled troops out of cities and consolidated them on these bases. The population of the bases increased, providing an even larger signature for insurgents to target. Within two days of arriving at Victory Base Complex (VBC), I awoke to rocket fire that killed a soldier sleeping in his trailer and wounded several others.

One thing that made a difference was the antimortar/rocket defense warning system that had been established on the base. This system provided early warning for any indirect-fire attack. Sirens were broadcasted across the base using loud speakers. Another advanced system established in conjunction with this one actually allowed the incoming round to be tracked and engaged with direct fire before it landed. Indirectly these systems saved a countless number of lives by allowing soldiers and civilians alike to seek cover and protection from incoming fire or by destroying inbound enemy projectiles before they impacted. Of course, this was not a completely fail-safe system. It was subject to error, and in a lot of cases it failed. Nevertheless, it was the best system we had. Based on the expensive nature and resources required to install and operate them, they were only established at large FOBs such as Victory Base and LSA Anaconda. Our smaller FOBs, COPs, and JSSs did not get this kind of active coverage.

The threat of direct-fire attack or an ambush by insurgents was not as prevalent as in years past. The enemy was smaller in numbers and could ill afford to lose more insurgents from their ranks. In typical direct-fire contacts initiated by insurgents, they usually came up on the short end and suffered a high rate of casualties. Direct-fire fights were clearly not their strong suit.

The enemy threat groups remained the same. We were still opposed by Sunni-based al-Qaeda groups and numerous Shiite militias such as JAM. On the surface, it appeared that the Shiite militias were moving more toward a political agenda and jockeying for position for the upcoming national parliamentary elections. Meanwhile, al-Qaeda groups focused the majority of their efforts on conducting massive bombings against the population and other high-value government targets. Overall violence and attacks had decreased, allowing us to focus on capacity building with our ISF partners, local councils, and the Iraqi population. In all actuality, this period in Iraq would be defined more by partnerships established and relationships built and less on the number of combat operations conducted to kill or capture insurgents. As the weeks and months passed, the ISF would mature right before our eyes.

Once I got my feet under me, the official relief in place/transfer of authority (RIP/TOA) process began in earnest. The unit we were replacing was 2nd Brigade, 1st Infantry Division based out of Fort Riley, Kansas. To date I had been involved in four such events, either coming or going. However, this one was different. It was not a traditional RIP/TOA. Typically, during a standard RIP/TOA process, an entire unit deploys into theater along with brigade headquarters, and everyone starts the process together. RIP/TOA operations run parallel at all levels. On this occasion, brigade headquarters deployed into theater first and executed the RIP/TOA without subordinate battalions. As this was going on, 2-1 ID had already executed RIP/TOA operations internally and had released their units to redeploy stateside. 2-8 Cavalry Squadron from 1st Cavalry Division was cross-attached to 2-1 ID prior to our arrival in theater. It was directed by Major General Dan Bolger that 2-8 Cav would remain in theater and take responsibility for the entire 2-1 ID area of operations partnering with the 6th Iraqi Army Division units assigned to these areas until relieved by our brigade.

In other words, a battalion-size unit was holding onto ground that once was held by a brigade-size element. They did this by assigning a subordinate company to take over the area once held by a battalion. They would remain in place until relieved by one of our battalions. This was a risk that Bolger, Multi-National Division–Baghdad (MND–B) commander, and Odierno, Multi-National Command–Iraq commander, had assumed. At the time it did not make sense to our staff or me, but we soon realized that theater conditions had changed for the better.

The threat was not as great, and even more promising was the fact that the ISF had matured to a point that they were capable of providing the bulk of security. Once we completed the two-week transition with the 2-1 brigade staff, we pulled our subordinate battalions up from Kuwait one at time and executed the process with their respective U.S. company and Iraqi Army counterparts. The transition went as smoothly as could be expected. Our subordinate battalions executed the RSR/LSR and gained familiarity of their assigned areas. More importantly, they were introduced to their respective Iraqi Army counterpart and immediately began forging the relationship. The success of this nonstandard RIP/TOA was that there was no degradation of security in the area. ISF were able to hold the line. There were no large-scale attacks conducted by insurgents. On occasion, an IED attack would occur, but nothing too drastic for us to overcome. If anything, the success demonstrated where the military was at during this point in the fight and served as a metric that we were truly nearing the time to depart.

As we continued the RIP/TOA process, I linked up with my deputy commanding officer (DCO) counterpart from 2-1 ID, Lieutenant Colonel Chris Beckert. Beckert was a great officer, whom I had met in 1988 at Fort Benning, Georgia, and not seen since. He made me feel welcome, and we got after the transition and battle handoff. For the most part, the transition was easy, as our duties and responsibilities matched. Depending on the brigade, DCOs are used in different ways at the commander's discretion. In this case, I would be responsible for supervising and managing all nonlethal operations for the entire brigade the same as Beckert had during the past year. For a solid week, it was death by PowerPoint as we reviewed more than 10,000 slides that covered all the nonlethal and other civil military operations completed to date. Also included were projects that had just been started or were in the process of being executed. In addition, I was introduced to the ePRT team that would be staying on board and continuing to execute operations throughout our deployment. The best part of the transition were the days we traveled outside the wire to get a first-hand look at the projects they had completed and ones in the building phase as it would be our job to monitor and see these through to completion.

On one particular trip, we stopped off at the main marketplace in Abu Ghraib. We walked approximately 2 kilometers as Beckert oriented me to projects and initiatives they had previously completed. My first impression of the market area was that it was a shit hole. Tons of trash and other refuse in the street appeared to have been left there for years. As we walked along the market front, we saw numerous pools of goat's blood from recent slaughters by local butchers. The stench was so bad it was enough to make you puke.

The other thing that stood out was the fact that Iraq had truly changed for the better. A year ago it was highly unlikely that you could have walked the same street without getting shot at by a sniper or even hit by an IED hidden in a random trash pile. Also, you could tell who the new guys in town were and who was on the way out. The soldiers of 2-1 ID were more relaxed in their posture and stance, while my security detachment was on guard. As we walked down the street, my squad would move ahead and execute a quick search of stores, street corners, and alleys. They would not allow any local civilians to get within 25 meters of us. These soldiers were executing as they had been trained, which was in contrast to the soldiers from 2-1 ID, who were more casual in their approach. It just goes to show how a year in theater wears on you to the point where you let your guard down because you have been run ragged and on the edge for so long. When it gets to this point, soldiers are the most vulnerable. As leaders, we have to impress upon our soldiers to always treat the last day in theater like the first: Never assume anything and never let your guard down.

We continued our tour outside the wire for at least a week. I was fortunate to see the majority of our area of operations and all the nonlethal initiatives that had been completed or were ongoing. I was introduced to all the key Iraqi civic leaders and numerous influential sheiks who resided or worked in our area. The one that stands out the most was my first introduction to Sheik Hussein al-Tamimi. Al-Tamimi was a Shiite who resided in Abu Ghraib, a predominantly Sunni town, and was selected by his peers and fellow sheiks to serve as the head of the Abu Ghraib Sheik Support Council. This council was comprised of influential sheiks from the surrounding Qadaa (similar to a county in the States). Its charter was to represent and take care of the daily issues for their fellow citizens and tribesmen. The council met once a week with the mayor, city officials, Qadaa managers, and other public officials in order to discuss issues such as basic utilities, security concerns, economics, and other concerns that affected their daily lives. Their focus was on security and stemming trends in violence. After discussing the security issues amongst themselves, al-Tamimi would engage the Iraqi Army division commander or the local Iraqi police chief to resolve any issues. During the transition, Beckert introduced me to all of them in an open forum.

After the meeting concluded, I shook each of their hands. As I was introduced to al-Tamimi, I extended my hand and, in my best Arabic combined with a slow southern drawl, said, *"Salam Malekum, Ishmay Mukadum Wright"* ("Hello, my name is Lieutenant Colonel Wright"). He replied with his name, and I lost him from there. The rest of the conversation was translated through my interpreter, Johnny Albazi, an Iraqi national from Surprise, Arizona. He told me he was looking forward to working with our brigade and me and hoped that we could make Abu Ghraib a better place. I told him we would do our best and that I, too, looked forward to working with him and his fellow sheiks and councilmen. We forged a great working relationship in the months ahead and an even better friendship over the year-long deployment.

This council ultimately became my main focus and priority as the Abu Ghraib Qadaa was our brigade's main effort and focus for security and civil capacity operations. Over the remaining days of our transition, Beckert would introduce me to several national Iraqi government officials, and we attended council meetings in Taji, Baghdad, Kadimiyah, and Nasir Wa Salaam.

By the time the ten-day transition ended, I had a pretty good grasp on who was who in our AO and where to go if I needed help. At that very moment, I knew my days of door kicking and being the steely-eyed killer on the battlefield had ended. No longer was I planning raids, air assaults, and other offensive operations. Rather, I was somewhat of a de facto mayor during an election year. Oftentimes, I was referred to by the locals as the "Grand Sheik" of Abu Ghraib. My life was now dedicated to going out into the community, meeting and listening to the people, shaking hands, posing for pictures, and hugging little Iraqi babies. The pendulum had swung from one extreme to the other.

As I was conducting my transition with my counterpart, similar events were happening at all levels of command. Norris had decided early on that I would manage nonlethal and civil operations. With that included all the nonlethal key leader engagements. Meanwhile, Norris focused on all things lethal or, in this case, security operations, which meant that he would work directly with the 6th Iraqi Army Division Commander, local and federal police, and related security forces. His charter was to establish and forge an enduring partnership with the ISF in our area and apply combat and all other available resources that they required to enhance their operations. A secondary effort was to train and mentor them at all levels of command, from company to division, as requested or where required in order to strengthen and build lasting capacity. In turn this would allow them to unilaterally assume total control of security operations as we transitioned out of theater. Even though SOFA made it official that they were in charge, they still required and wanted U.S. military assistance. During the RIP/TOA process, Norris and subordinate battalion commanders worked tirelessly, traveling around the area of operations meeting their Iraqi military counterparts to lay the groundwork for a strong and enduring partnership. ISF and especially the Iraqi Army were overjoyed that we wanted to pursue an active partnership and not strictly be a 911 force as other units had chosen to be.

On September 28, 2009, the RIP/TOA was complete, and we executed the transfer of authority between us and 2-1 ID. In an instant, the AO and all challenges and responsibilities that went along with it were ours. With the implementation of our new COIN doctrine came several changes in military terminology. What once was an AO had been changed, and was now referred to as the operational environment (OE). Upon assuming the OE, our official mission given to us by 1st Cavalry Division Commander Bolger, who was serving as the commander of MND–B, was as follows:

> *Brigade Mission:*
>
> *4-2 SBCT conduct Full Spectrum Operations by, with, and through ISF until 30 July 2010 to secure the population, neutralize enemy networks, and support civil capacity development in Baghdad and Northwest Belt in order to enable ISF to sustain security, enable GOI to continue political and economic growth, and allow U.S. Forces transition to stability operations.*

Raider OE: Terrain and Population

Our OE mainly covered the northwest belt of Baghdad, including the majority of downtown Baghdad and all cities to the north and west, including the volatile areas of Abu Ghraib, Nasir Wa Salaam, Zaidon, Taji, Tarmiya, Mushada, and Abayachi. From north to south, it covered more than 97 miles. When added together, it covered more than 650 square miles. (In comparison, the metro Seattle area is only 142 square miles.) The OE was densely populated with more than 5 million inhabitants, a population greater than that of Los Angeles. Of these inhabitants, at least 60 percent were Sunni; the remainder were a mixture of Shiites, Christians, and others.

To cover all this terrain, five subordinate maneuver battalions were assigned to the brigade, which partnered with a respective Iraqi Army unit that, in some cases, overlapped the sectors assigned to the subordinate battalions. This simply meant an Iraqi Army brigade commander might have had two of our units to partner with. In the southwest covering the area known as Zaidon was 2-1 Cavalry Squadron, "Blackhawk," commanded by Lieutenant Colonel Rick

Heyward. Directly to his north located in Nasir Wa Salaam was 4-9 Infantry Battalion, "Manchus," commanded by Lieutenant Colonel Mark Beiger. Center in our OE covering all of Abu Ghraib Qada was 1-38 Infantry Battalion, "Rock," commanded by Lieutenant Colonel John Leffers. In the far north/northeast covering Taji and Tarmiyah was 2-23 Infantry Battalion, "Tomahawk," commanded by Lieutenant Colonel Mike Lawrence. Finally, in the northwest portion of Baghdad proper, covering the districts of Kadimiyah, Muthana, and Mansour, was 2-12 Field Artillery Battalion, "Viking," commanded by Lieutenant Colonel Kevin Murphy and later by Lieutenant Colonel Terry Braley.

The remaining battalion, 702 Brigade Support Battalion, "Forge," provided all logistics to the brigade and was commanded by Lieutenant Colonel Gary Martin. Forge was based at Camp Victory along with the brigade headquarters located at Baghdad International Airport. In December 2009, our OE set expanded as U.S. brigades began to off ramp and depart theater as part of the responsible drawdown. When this occurred, we sent 2-1 Cavalry Squadron north to Camp Taji, and they took over responsibility for the Tarmiyah area while 4-9 IN absorbed their OE in Zaidon.

In assigning these areas, we did the best we could to match our battalions with the respective Iraqi Army unit or police force that covered the same area. Under the current partnership model, U.S. brigades were matched with an Iraqi Army division while our battalions were matched with Iraqi Army brigades from the same division. Our OE was predominantly covered by the 6th Iraqi Army Division, commanded by Karem, who was later replaced by Ahmed in November 2009.

This change in leadership could not have been timelier. Karem was corrupt beyond imagination, consistently charged by members of the Sheik Support Council with taking bribes from Shiite leaders and mistreating Sunnis. He marched to the beat of his own drum, did not fully embrace the partnership we were trying to form, and would call only when he was in a bind. Because of his reluctance to use our brigade as an asset, his division suffered. Once he was replaced by Ahmed, the division instantly got a face lift. Morale amongst the soldiers improved drastically, and the partnership flourished, as did their tactical success.

Norris and the brigade staff partnered directly with the 6th Division and their respective staff counterparts. At the time, the 6th Iraqi Army

Division was headquartered out of FOB Constitution located on the north side of Victory Base Complex. We also partnered with local and federal police units in certain locations within our AO.

For our subordinates units, 4-9 IN, "Manchus," based out of JSS Nassir Wa Salaam was partnered with 24th Iraqi Brigade of the 6th Iraqi Army Division commanded by Col. Rahim. 2-1 Cavalry "Blackhawk" shared this partnership with Manchus. 1-38 IN, "Rock" based out of Victory Base Complex covering Abu Ghraib had two different partnerships, including 24th IA Brigade and the Abu Ghraib Iraqi Police. 2-12 FA "Vikings" also based out of Victory Base Complex covering the western portion of Baghdad was partnered with 54th Brigade, 6th Iraqi Army Division commanded by Col. Ali, who was based out of Muthana Air Base. 2-23 IN "Tomahawks" based out of FOB Justice and partnered with 22nd Brigade, 6th Iraqi Army Division commanded by Col. Mahdi. When we expanded the OE in December 2009, 2-12 FA moved from Victory Base to FOB Justice and took over partnerships with both 54th and 22nd brigades. Simultaneously, 2-1CAV and 2-23 IN moved to Camp Taji and formed new partnerships with IA brigades assigned to the 9th Iraqi Army Division (36th and 37th brigades, respectively). Assisting us in our partnership, each Iraqi Army brigade and division had an Army military transition team (MiTT) assigned to it.

The MiTTs had come a long way from when they were first introduced in 2006. First, they were better trained and equipped to handle the duties and responsibilities as mentors, trainers, and advisors for the Iraqi Army. They were hand-selected by the Army for the assignment, and they had all trained together prior to deploying into theater. In years past, they were ad hoc teams without any formal training. Likewise, each Iraqi police and federal police had police transition teams (PTTs) assigned to perform similarly as MiTTs. These teams were true combat enablers and played an integral role in training and building capacity within the ISF. Simply put, they were worth their weight in gold.

While these partnerships continued to evolve and strengthen over time, sudden, no-notice leadership changes occurred at all levels of command. In the Iraqi Army, no one's job was safe. Soldiers could be replaced in the blink of an eye. Regardless, we stayed consistent with our mission no matter who was in charge.

During this year-long journey, talented, capable staff, including Battalion Executive Officer Major Dave Voorhies and Brigade Operations

Lt. Col. Darron Wright's personal security detachment execute precombat checks for a pending civil military operation, February 2010.

Pictured left to right: Lt. Col. Darron L. Wright, Lt. Col. Mark Beiger, Johnny Albazid, and Sheik Husayn al-Tamimi. Soldiers and leaders of 4-2 SBCT look on and listen attentively during the Abu Ghraib Shieks Support Council Meeting.

Col. John Norris shares a laugh with an Iraqi Federal Police Officer during combined security operations in Baghdad, June 2010.

Iraqi Army Commandos from the 6th Iraqi Army Division demonstrate their offensive capabilities during a show hosted by Maj. Gen. Ahmed, 6th Iraqi Army Division Commander, July 2010.

A U.S. Soldier and Iraqi Army Soldier display their skills in combatives. The show was part of a special event hosted by Maj. Gen. Ahmed, 6th Iraqi army Division Commander, July 2010.

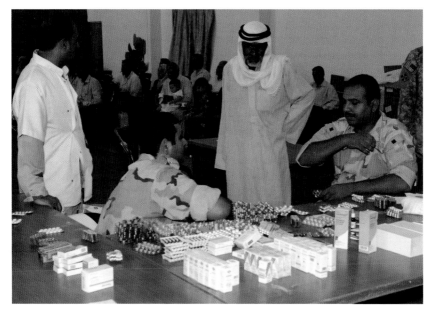

A local Iraqi citizen looks on as Iraqi physicians discuss treatment options during a combined medical assistance operation hosted by Iraqi Army and soldiers from 4th Stryker Brigade, 2nd Infantry Division, May 2010.

Lt. Col. Darron L. Wright and his interpreter Johnny Albazid engage local civilian leaders during a key leader engagement at the Abu Ghraib Agriculture College, June 2010.

Pictured left to right: military interpreters Amro Shadi, Johnny Albazid, Lt. Col. Darron L. Wright, and Maj. Kevin James pause for a photo outside the Mansour District Council Office located in downtown Baghdad, January 2010.

Pictured left to right: Sgt. Maj. Brian Hollis, Lt. Col. Darron L. Wright, Command Sgt. Maj. Jeff Huggins, Col. John Norris, Maj. Dave Voorhies, and Maj. Tony New outside their headquarters building located at Victory Base Complex, Baghdad, Iraq, July 2010.

A local Iraqi child gives a high five to a soldier from 4th Battalion, 9th Infantry Regiment during combined security operations in northwest Baghdad. February 2010.

Iraq Army commanders observe weapons confiscated by soldiers from 6th Iraqi Army Division during security operations in northwest Baghdad. July 2010.

Pictured left to right: Farouk, Lt. Col. Darron L. Wright, and Col. Rahim, Commander, 24th Iraqi Army Brigade, 6th Iraqi Army Division. Leaders walk and discuss partnership during an event hosted by Maj. Gen. Ahmed, 6th Iraqi Army Division Commander, July 2010.

Lt. Col. Darron L. Wright and Military Police soldiers who make up his personal security detachment pose for a historic photo at the Iraq/Kuwait border. These soldiers were members of the last official combat brigade in Iraq and made the historic last patrol out of theater. August 16, 2010.

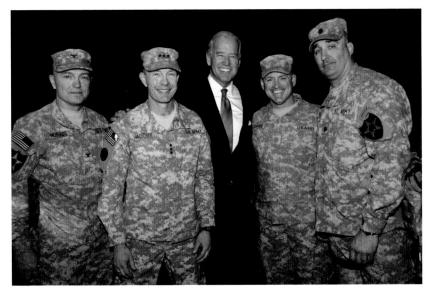

Pictured left to right: Col. John Norris, Lt. Gen. Charles Jacoby, U.S. Vice President Joe Biden, Maj. Dave Voorhies, and Lt. Col. Darron L. Wright share a photo op with the vice president during one of his visits to Baghdad.

Lt. Col. Darron L. Wright lites up a cigar in celebration after crossing the border out of Iraq into Kuwait. Wright was a member of 4-2 SBCT and led the briagde on the historic road march out of Iraq into Kuwait. August 16, 2010. (*Associated Press*)

A local Iraqi citizen, shown here outside of a Baghdad polling station, displays his excitement about and official declaration that he voted as represented by his purple finger.

Commanders and command sergeant majors from 4th Stryker Briagde, 2nd Infantry Division, commemorate the Last Patrol with Gen. Odierno and Col. John Norris, pictured in the center, August 2010.

Lt. Col. Darron L. Wright and Mohamed Al Samarae at Fort Polk, Louisiana (JRTC)

LEFT: Darron and Wendy together at Fort Polk, Louisiana.

BELOW: The Wright's celebrate the promotion of Darron to COL, May 2011, from left to right, Chloe, Darron, Wendy, Kyle and Dillon.

Officer Major Jarett Broemmel, did an excellent job at designing a campaign plan that complemented the unity of effort strategy. In the beginning of our tour, we had three primary lines of effort: partnership, security, and civil capacity. As conditions in theater changed, these were refined. Every operation we conducted, whether lethal or not, was planned and executed by, with, and through the ISF, local government officials, tribal sheiks, and, in some cases, the GOI.

Our main effort or decisive operation was the partnership with ISF. According to Norris, "partnership is the ability to create access to our Iraqi brethren." It was important for us to have access. Whether it was by executing combined security patrols with ISF or planning and executing combined offensive operations to interactions with tribal or government leadership, access would lead to situational awareness which eventually enhances force protection—both theirs and ours. The only way we were getting access was by establishing an active partnership. The main objective behind the partnership was to allow us a window of opportunity to focus all of the brigade's resources and assets on building long-term capacity within the ISF formations, thus allowing them to fully take control of security operations as we departed. Our partnership model was founded on three principles: presence, persistence, and patience.

We forged our partnership through six fundamental initiatives: leading by example, establishing joint operations centers (JOCs), combined training with the Iraqi Army and Iraqi police, stabilizing the Sons of Iraq, integrating the police, and planning and executing combined offensive operations. While all of these initiatives were important, two stood out as the underpinnings to our successes.

First was the establishment of JOCs, later called combined tactical operations centers (C-TOCs), to be more doctrinally correct. Our goal was to mirror operation centers much like the ones we used to track, synchronize, and command and control the daily fight. In establishing these nodes, we integrated both Iraqi Army and police officers whose skill set and experience covered operations, intelligence, logistics, and communications. Through a C-TOC there was a combined, integrated, and synchronized effort at synergizing security within the OE. All security forces are alerted, informed, integrated, synchronized, and launched to respond to the given threat at hand. U.S. forces and ISF battle command became one in this regard. The first C-TOC established was the 6th Iraqi Army command post located at FOB Constitution.

Once established, the C-TOC allowed our ISF partners to understand the situation, visualize a plan, and direct appropriate forces and other enablers to the scene according to the situation. For instance, on one occasion in October 2009, twin suicide car bombs exploded in downtown Baghdad near the Ministry of Interior, causing significant casualties and damage to the area. Within minutes, ISF commanders on the ground were calling in reports to the division C-TOC. Ahmed dispatched Iraqi Army forces to establish a cordon, and he also was able to coordinate the federal police so they could take charge of the actual incident site.

This type of communication and cooperation was unheard of two years earlier. The two groups operated independently of one another without rhyme or reason. Oftentimes, they would both show up at a scene unannounced, resulting in one side engaging the other with direct fire simply because there was no prior coordination. The ISF leadership simply did not have the capability or know-how to properly coordinate and synchronize assets to respond to these and other similar incidents. In order to achieve this unity of effort, we had to break down cultural and political barriers that enabled the Iraqi Army and police forces to share intelligence and coordinate integrated operations.

The C-TOCs we established changed all that. Based on the initial success and proven utility, the facility quickly became popular amongst senior leaders in the Iraqi Army, so much so that the senior Iraqi Army commander ordered division commanders from all over Iraq to visit the facility to see its operations in person. He wanted them to mirror the operation the 6th IA and our brigade had started. Soon after that, the concept spread like wildfire, and C-TOCs were being established daily, using our template as the model. Moreover, as we continued to integrate the Iraqi and federal police into the facility and introduced new and advanced digital systems, the C-TOC grew in size and needed to be expanded. Based on that, we spent more than $1 million to construct a new facility. I gave the opening remarks at the grand opening ceremony attended by the Iraqi minister of defense, Baghdad operations commander, and several hundred other Iraqi and U.S. senior Army leaders.

During the course of our deployment from September 2009 through August 2010, we were able to establish these combined forces' command and control nodes, down to each of the six brigade-level headquarters locations. This was truly revolutionary for the Iraqi

Army and Police forces. To further enhance operations at the tactical level, Ahmed and his brigade commanders took it one step further and implemented the same structure down to the battalion and in some cases the company level, depending on where they were located. These command posts truly exercised battle command and are the nucleus of partnered and combined operations.

All reports, significant activities, enemy intelligence, and informant tips from the field generated by the Iraqi Army soldiers or police officers are sent for collation at their respective C-TOCs. From there, ISF commanders could analyze the information and direct forces accordingly. They also could request immediate support from U.S. forces or support of our enablers, such as attack aviation, unmanned aerial vehicles (UAVs) for surveillance, artillery support, and even bomb-sniffing dogs if needed. The capabilities of the C-TOCs were limitless.

Ultimately, the C-TOCs would get their greatest test and validation during the national parliamentary elections conducted in March 2010. How they fared in synchronizing the overall security plan would determine the success or failure of the elections and go a long way in establishing credibility and legitimacy with the Iraqi population. The most important take-away for us was that we left the ISF with a system and framework for success for when we eventually departed.

The second initiative most vital to our success was the advanced individual and collective unit training we conducted with the ISF. The majority of this training was accomplished by our MiTTs, supported by the subordinate battalion, which was partnered with the particular brigade. This training covered three areas: individual soldier, or "Jundi," level, unit or collective level, and battalion through division staff-level training. For the individual level, Jundis were taught advanced marksmanship, basic first aid and combat lifesaving measures, proper traffic control and search techniques, and a host of other classes, all designed to make them professional soldiers. For unit- or collective-level training, we started at the team and squad levels, training them on several battle drills including how to enter and clear a room and building and how to react to enemy contact including sniper fire, IEDs, and ambushes. This training culminated with a live-fire exercise at the platoon level.

It was truly amazing to watch these Iraqi soldiers in action, to see how far they had come from when we first started in 2003 with the forming of the ICDC. That is not to say that they were perfect by any means. They still had challenges and barriers to overcome, such as equipment shortages, lack of a functioning maintenance program, and corruption in their ranks. However, during operations on the streets of Iraq, they looked like and acted like a professional force. The population also noticed the change, so much so that they were more apt to trust and share intelligence with them. Eventually each of the C-TOCs in our area had to install multiple phone lines because they could not keep up with the influx of tips they were receiving. This simple metric spoke volumes about their performance and effectiveness.

Another effective program we trained them on was sensitive site exploitation. These crime scene investigation techniques allow ISF soldiers to preserve crime scenes in order to collect evidence that could lead to arrest and prosecution. What we discovered when the ISF took charge of security operations was that they did not have a system in place that allowed for or facilitated crime scene exploitation. For example, during a suicide car bomb attack on the Ministry of Interior in September 2009, the ISF, namely the national police, were the first responders along with fire department assets. Upon arriving at the scene, they began cleanup of the site, removing all debris and damage in the area, sterilizing the site as if nothing had occurred. The impact of this was that they removed potentially valuable intelligence from the site, such as a trigger device or other material that could provide clues and evidence as to who was responsible. There was simply no exploitation of the site to discover if any intelligence or evidence existed.

Based on that discovery, we trained Iraqi Army and police forces on how to properly secure and investigate crime scenes. This training took several months, but in the end it paid huge dividends. Case in point, during the December 2009 car bomb attacks, the federal police, who were the first responders, immediately secured the area using crime scene tape. Investigators wore rubber gloves while they placed sensitive debris or evidence in plastic bags and properly tagged them. Based on the success of this training, Ahmed and police commanders formed small crime scene investigation teams whose jobs were to deploy to attack sites and execute exploitation. These teams collectively formed the Exploitation Task Force and were often referred to as "CSI Baghdad" after the popular television shows. It was amazing to witness them in action. They had truly come a long way and were slowly becoming experts at site exploitation. In several cases, the evidence they collected led to insurgent arrest and prosecution.

At the staff level, we focused our efforts on teaching respective staff counterparts about battle command and how they fit into the overall operation. Regardless of whether they were communications specialists or logisticians, each had an important role. The greatest illustration of this training was in the area of intelligence sharing and targeting. Our brigade intelligence officer, S-2, Major Sam Fiol, did an outstanding job of training and working with the 6th IA Division G-2, Col. Hamza and his subordinate intelligence soldiers. Sam was by far one of the best military intelligence officers with whom I have ever served. The majority of his waking hours were spent at the 6th IA headquarters working with Hamza and teaching him and his subordinates all about insurgent targeting and how to develop human intelligence sources. He developed such a strong working relationship and friendship with Hamza and his subordinates that they actually invited us to numerous cookouts and soccer games.

These individual partnerships went a long way in facilitating our brigade's and subordinate units' access. Just with the relationship Fiol had established, Norris went the extra mile to build and nurture a similar relationship with Ahmed, the 6th IA Division commander. Once Ahmed came on board, the partnership flourished. Immediate admiration and respect was gained between Ahmed and Norris. They both wanted the same thing: an Iraqi Army that was trained and capable of defeating any insurgent force and able to provide security for a free and stable Iraq.

Ahmed was wise beyond his years; he recognized and knew that we were an asset and that, if properly managed, we could provide him the leadership and means necessary to achieve his goals. Norris and his interpreter Farouk spent countless hours, often late at night, in Ahmed's office sipping on Turkish tea that tasted like burnt turpentine while listening and entertaining his great and sometimes wild ideas on how to defeat the enemy and how to train his division to be one of the best in the Iraqi Army. Other times were spent together outside the wire on patrol or conducting battlefield circulation calling on their subordinate units. Ahmed could be trusted with any information and valuable intelligence gathered by various sources. When called on, he would act without hesitation or reservation.

In one case specifically, I was the acting commander while Norris had departed theater for two weeks of midtour leave. While he was away, we encountered a spike in IED activity that was targeting U.S.

supply convoys along Route Tampa in our southern OE. Some of these attacks seriously wounded or killed U.S. soldiers. Our challenge was that we could never catch the insurgent cell in the act, no matter what we tried. One night we caught a break and were able to collect information about some of the names of those involved. Once I confirmed this information, Fiol and I visited Ahmed at his office and laid it all out for him. After the briefing, he said he would take care of it. The next night, I got a call to come over to his headquarters. I raced over there to find that he already had detained the individuals in question. He had taken his own personal security detachment on a nighttime raid and rounded them up. That moment built trust and validated that our partnership model was achieving what we had envisioned. Ahmed is by far the exception and not the rule. He is one of two Iraqi military officers that I would trust with my life; the other is my good friend Mohammed al-Samare, better known as "Hawk."

These relationships were occurring at all levels of command, and every single one of them was integral to the overall accomplishment of the mission. Our partnership strategy was nothing new. The same model we used was similar to the exit strategy known as "Vietnamization" implemented by President Nixon during the Vietnam War.

Following the Tet Offensive in 1968, the Nixon administration sought to expand, equip, and train the South Vietnamese Army, enabling them to take a lead role and the responsibility for fighting the war. This would allow U.S. forces to gradually draw down. While the concept was theoretically the same as what we were doing in Iraq, it worked in our case because of the willingness to establish meaningful relationships.

This successful partnership would not have been possible if not for the efforts of our great soldiers. They are the true unsung heroes who worked tirelessly in some of the most austere conditions; young privates, specialists, corporals, and sergeants who took the Iraqi Jundis under their wings and trained them to be better marksmen, taught them advance combat lifesaving techniques, and showed them how a professional soldier really looks and acts. Without their initiative, dedication, and sacrifice, this partnership certainly would have failed. We were simply the leaders in charge, providing them the orders and guidance to execute. So any credit earned is solely theirs.

Our shaping operation or secondary line of effort was focused on security operations. This line of effort included all offensive operations conducted either unilaterally by ISF or combined operations supported by U.S. forces to disrupt and prevent insurgent attacks against the population, ISF, GOI, and U.S. forces. As mentioned previously, SOFA allowed us to execute operations designed to protect our force from insurgent attacks. These operations fell into two categories: counter-IED or route-clearance operations and counter-rocket/mortar denial operations.

During the first four months following our arrival in theater, counter-IED and route-clearance patrols were conducted unilaterally. As time went on, we trained and integrated Iraq Army engineers and infantry units into these complex operations. As we departed in August 2010, ISF had taken possession of these operations and were conducting them independent of U.S. forces. This was yet another metric demonstrating how far they had progressed and further validated that we were nearing the right time for departure.

All other associated offensive operations, such as raids or cordon and search missions to capture high-value targets, were combined operations at the request of partnered units. In addition, we worked behind the scenes to gather solid, credible evidence to prosecute insurgents who had been detained and were in U.S. custody. It was mandated by the GOI that if we did not prosecute these detainees in the Iraqi criminal court, we would have to release them back into society. This was an urgent mission that required due diligence and undivided attention. So we established a prosecution task force whose mission was to review all files known as "Red Cases" and see where there were gaps or lack of evidence required to prosecute.

When gaps were identified, units operating in the area where the detainees were arrested would seek out eyewitnesses and other associates to obtain sworn statements and any other evidence that would support a stronger case. This task force was headed by the brigade staff Judge Advocate team led by Major Eric Stafford, Captain John Olson, and Staff Sergeant Philip Neal. This legal team did a phenomenal job at ensuring that hardcore insurgents were prosecuted and put behind bars. According to Olson: "When we first assumed responsibility for the OE, we were given several boxes containing over 800 Red Cases. Of that, our Prosecution Task Force was able to successfully prosecute 95 percent and transfer them to ISF for long-term detention."

Two offensive operations conducted during our deployment exemplify how far the ISF had progressed since their inception in 2003. The first operation occurred early on during our deployment.

In October 2009, we received a tip from a local Iraqi citizen who reported that a suicide truck bomb was being constructed in a neighborhood close to our base. Based on this information, we gathered our planning staff, including our operations officer, Major Jarett Broemmel, and Fiol, and conducted a link-up with the 6th IA Division Staff. Together we analyzed the information and formulated courses of action to seize the truck bomb and detain the insurgents responsible for manufacturing it. Once the intelligence was verified and the course of action was complete, the IA Division Commander notified Colonel Rahim, 24th IA Brigade Commander, and issued him an operations order to execute the raid to seize the target.

Rahim requested support from his partnered battalion, 4-9 IN. He requested them to establish the outer security cordon while his battalion would execute the raid on the target house that contained the potential truck bomb. Within four to six hours, the house was cordoned off, and the Iraqi Army executed the raid on the target house. The intelligence received was in fact credible, and the raid netted three insurgents who were part of a terrorist cell operating in the area. They also seized a midsize bus that had been gutted and was being converted into a large truck bomb disguised as a local passenger bus. Had the Iraqi Army not acted quickly, the bomb could have resulted in death and destruction in the thousands depending on the potential target. This served as a demonstration of what mutual cooperation and partnership could lead to, and it reinforced the capability and progress the ISF had made.

We would execute numerous combined missions similar to this during the year. As each operation occurred, it became more and more evident that the ISF possessed the capacity and capability to function unilaterally. The most significant operation to cement this fact occurred on April 19, 2010, when ISF commandos and intelligence agents supported by U.S. assets executed a raid near Lake Tharthar and killed the top two leading al-Qaeda figures in Iraq: Abu Omar al-Baghdadi and Abu Ayyub al-Masri. Later that day, we watched as Iraqi Prime Minister Nuri al-Maliki confirmed on state television that the two al-Qaeda leaders had in fact been killed. To prove his point, he displayed pictures of both men before and after their deaths. The raid itself was pretty simple in execution. The story leading up to it and how it developed is the most intriguing.

Col. Ali, commander of the 54th IA Brigade and one of our partnered units, had acted on intelligence obtained from his human source network. Based on credible information, he executed a raid on a suspected al-Qaeda safehouse near his OE and detained several al-Qaeda insurgents. After conducting a detailed search of the premises, he discovered several documents, including al-Qaeda's master strategy document for Iraq. This discovery and the compromise of such valuable information led to the subsequent raid and killing of the two top al-Qaeda leaders.

The discovery of this intelligence and the subsequent raid could not have been more timely as al-Qaeda had plotted to carry out some significant attacks against GOI and U.S. military targets. From start to finish, this was an incredible accomplishment by the ISF and the GOI. This event clearly illustrated that the ISF had truly evolved into a capable force, were up to task, and possessed the capacity to function in all facets of security operations including intelligence collection, analysis, planning, and execution of high-profile operations.

From April 2010 until our departure in August 2010, the ISF continued to execute security operations with confidence and precision. It was noticeable on the streets in northwest Baghdad that this was a professional force that could provide for the security of its people and defense of its nation. If somehow they could eliminate the corruption in their ranks, they would rival any Middle Eastern army. Major Steve Phillips was assigned as the operations officer for 4-9 IN during this deployment. He had served in Iraq during the surge period, planning and conducting combined operations with ISF. Based on his past experience with them, he noticed a marked improvement this time around. He described his experience with 24th Brigade, 6th Iraqi Division:

"My experiences with the 24/6 IA BDE in 2009–10, while always challenging, showed a marked increase in capability of Security Forces in Baghdad Province since I last left them in September 2007. They had a strong NCO and junior officer corps, and they were very keen to ensure that they kept the populace as a foremost concern in their daily duties and actions.

The three most notable improvements in ISF's performance during The Surge to the 2009-10 timeframe were:

1. They knew that they were in the lead, for real, in 2009. The Security Agreement, signed by both Iraq and the U.S. in JUN09, was not a token piece of diplomacy for the ISF. They knew that they were finally the ones that had the onus of securing their people, and their own country. They took pride in that fact, and that US Forces were now truly a supporting effort.

2. Equipping. In 2009–10, ISF uniforms, equipment, and combat systems were far more present and pronounced than during The Surge. They had concerns for maintenance, their supply channels (while still horribly corrupt) were coming online, and their confidence in their Army's ability to fund the necessary resources was becoming apparent.

3. An understanding that information operations were critical to their success. The ISF became aware that they could fight their enemies on more than just the streets of Iraq. They could fight them through the media, and they used this to their advantage. They embraced Iraqi and international media, and they planned them into their operations."

It was clear to me that the ISF had made several marked improvements and were growing in capacity as each day and week passed. My experience with the ISF is broader than that of Phillips. I was fortunate enough to witness their transformation from inception in 2003 through the transfer of security operations to ISF in 2010. I can honestly say without hesitation that the ISF had truly come full circle.

Our third line of effort, known as our sustaining operation, was civil capacity. This effort rested on my shoulders and the great team of soldiers, leaders, and civilians I was surrounded with and fortunate enough to have had the opportunity to lead. Our main objectives were to improve the overall quality of life for Iraqi citizens through projects focused on improving essential services and local security. Next was to promote economic development and positive job growth through projects, technical programs, and other initiatives. Finally, it was to enhance the legitimacy of the GOI and ISF as well as the tribal sheiks by integrating them into our civil capacity operations. Every civil capacity operation or project started that was seen by the public as being initiated by GOI, ISF, or local organizations would go a long way in earning the population's faith and trust, ultimately leading to popular support versus supporting the illegitimate insurgency.

When I was first assigned this mission, it seemed like an unachievable task. It was daunting to say the least. But I had the luxury of working with some of the best and brightest minds and talent in the business. My team included Major Pat Hemmer, who was our overall project manager. It was his job to draft and submit projects to our higher command for approval and oversee the disbursement of millions of dollars from a program known as the Commander's Emergency Response Program (CERP). CERP funds came from a large pot of money allocated to commanders for use in their OEs to shape or improve conditions for the population and to improve local security through short- or long-term projects. In the past, the Army had issues with soldiers abusing these funds and actually prosecuted several for embezzlement. Since that time, the Army tightened up its procedures and the process became very stringent.

Hemmer and his team, including Captain Talgin Cannon, accounted for every U.S. tax dollar spent and ensured the money was put to good use for the benefit of Iraqis. Major Kevin James, our information operations officer, supervised all strategic, operational, and tactical messaging used to garner support for the GOI and ISF. He also designed a key leader engagement strategy to ensure that we stayed on message and theme when meeting with ISF, GOI, sheiks, and other influential leaders. James was my battle buddy and accompanied me on virtually every mission and key leader engagement that I conducted. There was never a dull moment when he was around. I am forever indebted to him for his sound advice and keeping me straight when I started to leave the script while discussing important topics with a sheik or GOI official.

Another important member and nucleus of our team was Captain Gabi Niess. Niess, a Medical Corps Service Officer by trade, was pulled away from those duties about two months into the deployment and made the brigade's nonlethal planner. She is truly a rare talent that does not come along too often in our ranks.

The challenge that led to this was the fact that our civil capacity plan was all over the map and was not succinct. We were running a hundred miles per hour, but nothing was captured or codified on paper. Recognizing Niess's talents and potential, I gave her several stacks of paper and specified guidance and told her to turn it into a coherent plan that was easy to understand and one that soldiers and civilians, such as our ePRT, could execute off of. Within a couple of weeks a plan was drafted and the rest is history.

In addition to keeping us on task, Niess worked and implemented several medical initiatives that benefited the Iraqi medical community. Most notably, she developed a joint medical seminar known as Operation Medical Alliance by coordinating with the Iraq Ministry of Health whereby we brought U.S. doctors and other medical practitioners from our base hospital and escorted them to local Iraqi hospitals in our OE and provided medical training to Iraqi doctors on the latest treatment and advance surgical techniques. These seminars were conducted on a monthly basis and helped build capacity in the

Iraq medical field. The other benefit was that it exposed our doctors and medical professionals to conditions outside the wire, something they rarely ever got to see and experience. This program was the first of its kind initiated in Iraq and truly put our brigade on the map in the civil capacity realm.

Another initiative Niess planned and implemented was the wheelchair program. Each month, we would execute a combined medical outreach program somewhere in our OE that would pair Iraqi and U.S. doctors to conduct medical screenings and limited treatment for local civilians. We coordinated and advertised this program through the ISF and tribal sheiks. It was important that the ISF and sheiks got the credit in the eyes of the public. Moreover, Iraqi doctors were the ones providing the majority of the hands-on screening and treatment, while our doctors provided over-the-shoulder advice and mentorship. It was through this program that we started providing wheelchairs to disabled children. Early on there was limited participation by the local population. After the first two iterations, we added humanitarian assistance relief and started providing donated clothes, shoes, school supplies, soccer balls, and other items. This attracted a lot of citizens. The program instantly grew in size and popularity, so much so that we had to move it to a larger facility. We also gave it a new name: Operation No Iraqi Child Left Behind.

The other asset I had at my disposal to assist us in nation-building efforts and the reconstruction of Iraq was our resident ePRT. Our ePRT was led by Mark Powell and consisted of more than twenty members with various skill sets and operational experience. Included in this group were key members including USAID representative Christine Scheckler and governance expert Gary Anderson. Others included an agriculture expert, a rule of law administrator, a building engineer, and several local national interpreters. This quality team was an invaluable asset to our brigade, and their contributions to our success were immeasurable.

The stand out on this team was Scheckler. For example, Scheckler worked closely with and coordinated support with all the sanctioned U.S. government agencies, such as Office of Foreign Disaster Assistance and all the other nongovernment agencies such as Amnesty International that littered the OE and were executing projects that were not synchronized with our efforts. She was able to establish communications with these agencies and nest their operations with ours, creating a unity of effort in regard to civil capacity operations.

Scheckler drafted and implemented several programs that focused on human rights and were mainly centered on the rights of Iraqi women. She also established a month-long technical skills program that taught Iraqi women how to sew. Many of these women were widows whose husbands had been casualties of the war in some fashion. At the end of the training, every student received a brand-new sewing machine that was theirs free of charge. This program taught the women a valuable trade that enabled them to make clothes and other items for their children, and a few even opened their own businesses.

Scheckler also was instrumental in assisting with efforts to resettle Iraqi displaced persons (IDPs). She and I served on the U.S. Department of State IDP Working Group that met at the U.S. embassy every two weeks. She traveled with Lieutenant Caitlin Conley, my personal security detachment platoon leader, and visited several IDP camps in our OE to gain an understanding of the conditions and challenges faced by these people.

During one particular trip, the patrol they were being escorted by came under attack and was hit by an IED that wounded a couple of our soldiers. One of the soldiers, Specialist Andrew Toppin, was seriously wounded from shrapnel that pierced his legs. Upon evacuation, doctors were unable to save his lower right leg and had to amputate it. That was one of two of the most serious injuries our brigade sustained during the deployment. The other was a young medic, Sergeant Ian Ralston from 2-23 IN, "Tomahawk," who was paralyzed from the neck down as the result of a grenade attack.

Following deployment, Toppin showed up at our redeployment ceremony and was moving around quite well with his prosthetic leg, so much so that he was participating and competing in different sporting events for wounded warriors. It is truly remarkable how far Army medicine has advanced regarding prosthesis.

To say that Scheckler as a civilian was brave is an understatement. On a daily basis, she spent hours outside the wire, disregarding the danger that lurked. She worked tirelessly engaging the populace and coordinating programs all designed to improve the quality of life for local Iraqis, namely the women who in a Muslim culture are often mistreated, neglected, and overlooked. Of all the civilians who worked for us, she spent the most time in harm's way. She made a true difference for our team.

The ePRT was value added and did a tremendous job in helping our OE utilize their subject-matter expertise and unique skill sets. Once we expanded our OE in December 2009, we picked up another ePRT based out of Camp Taji located in our northern OE. This team was light years ahead of our original team as far as their aggressiveness in getting out and really taking the nation-building task to heart. The new ePRT was led by Karen Malzhan, a long-time employee of the U.S. State Department. She is intelligent and led our organization better than anyone I had witnessed in action. Her team's greatest contribution was the implementation of greenhouse farming in the Taji and Tarmiyah regions. This program was planned and implemented by Tim Lowry, a representative from the U.S. Department of Agriculture. Lowry was the nucleus of her team.

So successful was the greenhouse program that I brought Lowry down to Abu Ghraib, where he assisted in bringing greenhouse farming to our southern OE. This program was so successful that it grew in scope and value. Based on its magnitude, we named the program as Operation Green Acres after the wildly popular American television series starring Eva Gabor and Eddie Albert. When we first started, fewer than two hundred greenhouses were scattered throughout our OE. By the time we departed, there were more than two thousand.

It was a start to reinvigorate what once was a growth industry prior to the invasion. The impacts were felt immediately on the streets of Baghdad and the surrounding belts. Iraqi farmers were able to produce worthy crops to bring and sell at the local markets, thus generating new income for their families.

On the national level, the Iraqi government was able to import less produce from neighboring countries, even further stimulating the Iraqi economy. It will be years before we truly know how beneficial this program was, but in the short term, we left farmers with hope— a hope for the return of a thriving industry.

Tied into this program were technical training programs, including veterinarian training we established at the Baghdad College of Agriculture. In addition to the farming initiatives, Malzhan worked closely with Dr. Nehad from the Ministry of Education, and together they were instrumental in constructing several primary and secondary schools in our northern OE. Over the course of the year-long deployment, our nonlethal team developed and implemented six enduring civil capacity missions, some of which have been addressed. Others included Operation Bull Market, Operation Goodwill, and Operation Raider Refuge.

Operation Bull Market

The combination of a targeted focus on the provision of essential services to populated market areas and the use of micro-grants to breathe life into small businesses resulted in a layered approach to building civil capacity. The intent was to make market areas more appealing to consumers and entrepreneurs by enhancing basic essential services and by fostering fair free-market competition between small businesses, all of which benefits the population and stimulates the local economy. Increased civil capacity and essential services helped promote GOI legitimacy and reduce it as a driver of instability.

Operation Goodwill

This program provided aid and relief to local Iraqi citizens for humanitarian purposes typically in response to humanitarian crises, saving lives, alleviating suffering, and helping to maintain human dignity. It served as an important tool that helped ensure those within the country suffering from the effects of displacement, sectarian violence, or the loss of essential services had additional time and space to establish the means with which to provide for their families. The cooperative efforts of other nations and donor countries will help provide time and resources to the people of Iraq who most need it.

Operation Raider Refuge

This program focused our efforts on opening up lines of communications at internally displaced person camps located throughout our OE. The presence of Stryker Brigade amongst the IDP camps has had a positive information operations spin from both the Iraqi and U.S. side of the situation. Our brigade facilitated communication and movement that had been stagnant for way too long between GOI and UNHCR in attempts to find a viable solution for the resettlement of IDPs to their original homes. The IDP is an enduring issue that was not fully resolved under our watch, but our activity in promoting facilitation of communication and our efforts in providing humanitarian assistance brought a positive impact to the OE and strengthened our overall partnership with GOI and ISF forces involved.

None of these civil capacity missions would have been possible without the support of great soldiers who provided the daily escort and security of our team members to include the ePRTs. To execute these missions I utilized the Military Police Platoon assigned to our brigade as my team nonlethal personal security detachment (PSD). This platoon was led by Lieutenant Caitlin Conley, who by far is one of the best young officers that I have ever served with and witnessed in action. So talented was Conley that following our redeployment she applied for and met the demanding training requirements and was one of the first female officers ever accepted into a distinct special operations unit where she currently serves today. My PSD was the largest of its kind operating on the battlefield. I had the largest personal fleet of combat vehicles in which to execute these missions including four Stryker vehiclesm eight MRAPs, and more than twelve Humvees.

The greatest thing about my crew was my driver, Private First Class Denisha Gilmore. She was the first female Stryker driver in combat. If ever there is a case to be made about women serving in a combat role, she, along with Conley, have already proved that females are capable and have a role on the front lines; they proved it time and time again.

On one particular key leader engagement I was dispatched with Bolger to visit the Iraqi vice president along with Emma Sky, who was serving as Odierno's political advisor. My purpose for the visit was to provide the vice president a brief on our investigation findings of a sectarian related killing that had taken place in Zaidon, whereby thirteen Sunni civilians had been massacred together by insurgents who were posing as Iraqi Army soldiers.

The vice president was upset and clearly thought the killings were conducted by Iraqi Army soldiers assigned to the 24th Brigade. However, based on our investigation, they were in fact insurgents who had dressed like Iraqi soldiers and were carrying out a revenge attack or settling an intertribal dispute. Lieutenant Caitlin Conley, on short notice, prepared all the notes and diagrams for me from the investigation, facilitating my brief to him. The meeting went as well as could be expected. I am uncertain whether I really convinced the vice president that it was not Iraqi Army soldiers, but based on the evidence I presented to him, he could not dispute the facts.

Conley's greatest contribution was her role in IDP resettlement operations. She personally took it upon herself to travel the entire OE, visiting all the IDP camps and mapping them out to include the demographic make-up, services on hand, and services required. She and her team conducted a complete census of more than twenty camps that were located in some of the most violent areas in and around Baghdad. Conley also planned and executed several VIP visits that included the Chairman of the Joint Chiefs of Staff, Admiral Mullen, and a host of Congressional delegates and Department of State leaders.

Raider 8 TAC on Patrol

Because we were so often outside the wire conducting operations, we encountered a few close calls whereby through sheer luck or divine intervention we eluded death. The one situation that stands out the most was a trip we were on to visit the Baghdad National Museum, located in the heart of downtown Baghdad. The purpose of this mission was to conduct a walkthrough of the facility to determine the scope of the damage to the building so we could draft a project to restore to its original state prior to the invasion. Since that time, the facility had been shut down. Also, the majority of ancient artifacts had been stolen during looting that ensued right after the Shock and Awe bombing phase. We executed the patrol on December 8, 2009, departing the east gate of Victory Base Complex at approximately 0930 hours. As we entered Baghdad at approximately 1000, we were less than a half mile away from the museum when all of the sudden our MRAP vehicle was shaken by two or three large explosions. The explosions were so enormous they could be felt inside of the MRAP.

There was a sense of panic due to the proximity of the blast, and we had not heard explosions since they had been this close to us. We had a couple of civilians with us, an anthropologist from the United States and her cameraman, who were there to record and provide subject-matter expertise on the project to preserve the facility. Immediately following the explosions, there was an intense barrage of gunfire in very close proximity to my vehicle. I looked out the window and saw national police officers and Iraqi Army jundis firing their AK-47s in the air. I knew then that we were not in contact; this was the customary battle drill often executed by the ISF known in Army circles as the Iraqi "death blossom." For whatever reason, anytime there is an explosion or gunfire, they immediately emptied all their magazines. I have never figured out to this day why they did it; we certainly did not train them that way. Maybe they did it as a deterrent so the enemy would stay away.

After that escapade, I made the decision to turn our patrol around and head back to the International Zone and drop off the civilians, who were panicking. This would allow them to get out of immediate danger. As we attempted to get inside the IZ through the Iraqi Army checkpoint, they had everything blocked and locked down and would not allow us to proceed, so we had to exit the area and return to Victory Base Complex and get them back there later. We returned to the base without incident. Come to find out, though, that there were five separate suicide car bomb attacks in Baghdad that resulted in the deaths of 127 people and injured more than 450. It was reported to have been the work of al-Qaeda. The one bomb in particular that was so close to us, detonated near the Iraqi Criminal Court, was on our direct route to the museum. We were less than 300 meters away, and if the traffic had not been so heavy, there possibly could have been an engagement with us right at the location of the bombing. The Good Lord was riding shotgun with us that day.

Throughout the entire deployment, my PSD performed superbly. The unsung heroes are the enlisted soldiers and NCOs such as Sergeant Torrez and Staff Sergeant Eltringham, who constantly stood guard in grueling temperatures providing security for hours while we conducted our business. After operations ended and we returned to base, they spent countless hours ensuring the vehicles were serviced, fueled up, and made ready for the next day's operations. Never once did these soldiers complain, even when the missions were not all that sexy.

By March 2010, our civil capacity campaign had exceeded the objectives established. We executed more than a hundred short- and long-term projects, spending more than $200 million. The purpose was to build long-term capacity in education, medical, and agriculture and to improve security and the overall quality of life for Iraqis. These projects achieved that, and Iraq is ten times better off today than in years past.

One of hundreds of key leader engagements that I conducted proves that point. On January 16, 2010, I was talking to Sheik Jabber, an influential Shiite from the Shulla area (a well-known safe haven for Shia militias) in northeast Baghdad. During the conversation, he was discussing the advancements Iraq had seen in the years since we first invaded. He specifically stated to me:

"We have come a long way in the past seven years. If you look around the area all throughout Iraq, every house has a satellite dish, a television, refrigerator, and every family has a vehicle or two. This was unheard of before 2003. Saddam did not allow the citizens outside the loyal Ba'athists to have television period, except for state run propaganda that was aired by the stations that Saddam owned."

"The majority of Iraqis are very fortunate and thankful for the sacrifice and efforts of the coalition forces and they do recognize that you are here to provide them freedom, democracy and a better quality of life."

Everyone has benefited, some more than others, from our efforts, both in the security realm and in the civil capacity arena, including providing for essential services such as potable running water, electricity, sewage, and trash collection. This is symbolic of how the war has come full circle.

In 2003, when I was first in Iraq, market areas and restaurants were desolate and abandoned. Violence was the norm, not the exception. Rarely would you find anyone on the streets in the daytime, let alone at night. When I returned in 2005, I could see the growth in these areas, but any potential gain was negated by the onslaught of sectarian violence.

Thanks to the surge in 2006–08, markets, shopping areas, playgrounds, and soccer fields are full of life. People walk the streets all hours day and night. Commerce is on the uptick. Overall security is stable, and violence is minimal, thanks to a capable ISF.

These were strong indicators that our time and mission in Iraq was near completion. One hurdle remained: the national parliamentary elections. If successfully executed without any major attacks or catastrophic events, the elections would close out the final chapter on Operation Iraqi Freedom and allow for transition to Operation New Dawn.

CHAPTER 9
BALLOTS OVER BULLETS

Iraqi 2010 National Elections, March–July 2010

ff We will embalm ourselves for burial and take our coffins with us to the polling stations. JJ

Jalal al-Din al-Sagheer, Iraqi Parliamentary candidate

As we entered the new year, things were progressing well both in the security realm and in our civil capacity efforts. Insurgent attacks remained relatively low but spiked on occasion. In addition to projects and other initiatives, our time was consumed preparing for the national parliamentary elections that would take place in March 2010.

At the strategic level, several commands changed in name only. Multi-National Force–Iraq (MNF–I) merged with Multi-National Corps–Iraq (MNC–I) and became known as United States Forces–Iraq (USF–I). This change officially took place on January 1, 2010, as all coalition partners withdrew from Iraq and we were the only ones remaining. It was the first step in executing the responsible drawdown of forces. The one thing that remained was the top leadership. Odierno was still in charge, but his overall staff was smaller and not as robust. The MNC–I Commander, Lieutenant General Charles H. Jacoby, Jr., transitioned to the deputy commander for USF–I. With this change at the top level, all Multi-National Division Commands such as Baghdad, North, and South changed their names to United States Division–Baghdad (USD–B), –North, and –South, respectively.

Also during this period, our brigade campaign plan evolved and we merged our partnership and security lines of effort together and categorized it as "support to ISF for security." All the while we retained our civil capacity line of effort focused on building agriculture capacity, essential services, economic growth, and job creation. Ultimately we would transition this line of effort and hand it off to our ePRT in April 2010, allowing us to focus on transition and eventual departure from theater. The strategic plan for Iraq called for ePRTs to remain in theater and take complete responsibility for all civil military operations under the direction and supervision by the U.S. State Department. The State Department would assume control of overall nation-building efforts and would remain in Iraq long after all U.S. troops had withdrawn.

In the meantime, we focused our attention and resources on training and mentoring the ISF, ensuring they were up to the task to provide security for a safe and successful election. This was a critical period in the history of this war, and how it turned out could determine success or failure of our entire mission in Iraq and all that had been invested in the past seven years. Our soldiers and leaders worked tirelessly at all levels of command preparing the ISF for this daunting task.

An election in the best of times is a sophisticated and complex undertaking, no matter where it's conducted. In a war zone in the Middle East emerging from what can only be described as controlled chaos, it is a remarkably complex task. Our immediate task was the preparation of the 6th Iraqi Army Division to support election operations in their OE.

In an effort to keep pace with and counter the security, civil capacity, and political gains that had been achieved during the last year, the enemy switched their attack focus and began to target high-level political and military figures. The weapon of choice was a silenced pistol and a new and rather crude form of an IED. These new IEDs were small bombs magnetically attached to the undercarriage of vehicles detonated using timer devices and remotes such as cell phones. Some IEDs were even more sophisticated and used mercury switches and pressure pads that were connected to driver seats or steering columns. These methods of attack had emerged as the number one killer on the battlefield. According to statistics captured by our brigade and our higher command, 108 of 252 attacks were conducted in our OE alone, resulting in more than 75 deaths since January 2009. These attacks were perpetrated by both Sunni and Shiite threat organizations as a means of intimidation for upcoming elections.

We learned that these car bomb attacks were mainly carried out by Sunni extremists, perhaps with some affiliation to al-Qaeda operatives, as indicated by the fact that the majority of attacks targeted Shiite military or GOI officials. On several occasions, the insurgents would use magnetic car bombs to target ISF checkpoints in order to convince the population that the ISF could not protect them. This was a tough problem to counter, but one that we had to get under control or else it could derail the elections and ultimately alter the recent security gains.

To mitigate the threat, we trained ISF on how to take active measures to prevent such attacks. We also trained other GOI officials on how to properly search their personal vehicles to recognize the telltale signs of magnetic car bombs. To further assist them in combating this threat, we printed trifold information pamphlets in Arabic and distributed them to GOI, ISF, and other key leaders that listed techniques for searching and reacting to these bombs. These pamphlets benefited several Iraqi leaders who were able to discover bomb devices before they ever entered their vehicles.

While these attacks primarily targeted Iraqis, our forces remained a viable target for enemy attacks. The greatest threat to our forces remained IEDs, specifically the EFP device. Attacks remained steady at approximately one a week, primarily targeting logistic patrols, which operated on the roads at night as mandated by SOFA. Indirect-fire attacks on our bases, both rockets and mortars, were still persistent but had tapered off to one or two events a week. It was our belief that the attacks decreased due to a shift by the various threat groups, who were turning their focus from U.S. forces to the ISF and GOI in order to shape the elections.

On the other hand, silenced pistol assassinations were a growing concern. These attacks had increased even more dramatically than the magnetic car bomb attacks. In Baghdad alone, there was a 700 percent increase from December 2009 to March 2010. Analysis showed that these attacks were linked to and committed by Shiite militias or other Shiite special groups, as the majority of these were carried out against Sunni ISF and GOI leaders. These groups are affiliated with the former JAM or Muqtada al-Sadr's militias that were prominent during the height of sectarian violence from 2005 to 2007.[1] The purpose of these assassinations was to expand the influence of the Shiite-dominated government. They were carried out in order to influence, shape, and hedge Shiite political party positioning in a lead up to the elections. By conducting these violent attacks, Shiites sought to dissuade Sunni citizens from voting by instilling fear in them, thus ensuring a Shiite victory in the upcoming elections. It took us several months, but we finally figured out that these killings were linked to "Shiite Expansionism," an unpublished strategy categorically denied by top Shiite leaders.

Upon hearing this, I became curious about whether this strategy actually existed. If anyone could attest to it, I knew who could. So I turned to my good friend, Sheik Hussein al-Tamimi, head of the Abu Ghraib Sheik Support Council. I called on him through my interpreter, Johnny Albazi, and arranged for a meeting at a discrete and secure location. On the day of the meeting, I asked him point blank if a strategy existed amongst his sect known as Shiite Expansionism. Without hesitation he replied that it did. "Just look around at what is taking place and you will see it," he said.

He described how the strategy was being implemented in Abu Ghraib, in our own back yard. He stated that "The current Iraqi Prime Minister and fellow Shiite, al Maliki, had personally placed Colonel Rahim, 24th Brigade Commander, a Shiite in charge of the Iraqi Army Brigade that controls all of Abu Ghraib, which is made up of over 80 percent Sunnis." The reason, he continued, is "to allow him [Rahim] and the GOI to keep the Sunnis in check and ensure they do not get out of hand or rise up."

We agreed that it was evident that Col. Rahim was assigned to Abu Ghraib to suppress the Sunnis and dissuade them from voting in the elections, thus ensuring a Shiite victory. Since our arrival, local citizens, sheiks, and others had made numerous allegations that Rahim and his troops had abused, disrespected, and flat out beat down Sunni sheiks and other local leaders who spoke out, hindered, or otherwise opposed the way his unit did business.

During several key engagements I had with Doctor al-Sammrai, the president of the Sunni Endowment and a prominent Sunni who lives on the compound that houses the Umma Qura Mosque (better known as the Mother of All Battles Mosques or MOAB), stated that he personally had several conflicts with Rahim and knew about his illicit behaviors from past experience. "Prior to being reassigned as the commander of the 24th Iraqi Brigade in Abu Ghraib area, Col. Rahim was in charge of the Mansour area, an area in downtown Baghdad located on the western side. While he was in charge of this area, he had stolen a large sum of money from my brother-in-law and also used heavy-handed tactics to control the population (mostly Sunni) to ensure they were suppressed," al-Sammrai said.

At this point I really did not need any further evidence to support the existence of this strategy. I trusted that the information I received was credible. Needless to say I continued the investigation because I wanted more concrete proof from other sources to validate the assertion.

After engaging Sheik Husayn, Conley and I reviewed the documents from the recent pistol assassinations. We began to investigate these attacks, which led us to other documents and events that supported the theory of Shiite Expansionism. What I discovered was astounding.

The Iraqi Army, which is supposed to be nonsectarian in its efforts to provide security and defense for the people, was by no means neutral. The Iraqi Army is top heavy with Shiite officers serving in its highest positions, allowing them to maintain control of GOI. Its goal was to never lose power and to rule the Sunnis as Saddam Hussein had in years past. Of the top fifty Iraqi generals, only five were Sunnis. Rarely was a Sunni officer in command of an Iraqi Army division, even if the majority of the assigned sector was populated by Sunnis.

In our OE, for example, the majority of the population was predominantly Sunni (about 80 percent, according to the Iraq Ministry of Displacement and Migration). Of the three brigades assigned to cover the area, all of the brigade commanders were Shiite, including Rahim. This is a small sampling, but it was a trend that existed throughout Iraq. The higher up in the Iraqi Army chain of command you went, you would find Shiite officers filling those top leadership positions.

As we neared the elections, this problem became even more apparent, so much so that Norris, Powell, and I were invited to a meeting at the request of Sheik Omar al-Jabouri, head sheik of the al-Jabouri tribe and a parliamentary candidate. Sheik Omar resided in the Mansour district of Baghdad and was living in the house once occupied by the Iraqi minister of defense under Saddam. He called us specifically to discuss issues regarding the allegations of abuse by the 6th Iraqi Army and other ISF units. His main concern was to ensure that the ISF would protect and treat Sunni citizens fairly and allow them access to vote by providing the same treatment that Shiites would have. Norris assured him that the 6th IA Division had a sound, succinct, and fair plan that we had assisted them with developing. He also assured him that he and our staff would be on hand at the 6th IA Division Combined Tactical Operations Center (CTOC) on election day, monitoring the events. Sheik Omar accepted the answer Norris provided and asked Norris to call him directly if there were any issues. Norris agreed and we returned to Victory Base.

I was convinced that the strategy did exist and that it was the Shiite led government's way of paying back the Sunnis for all the years they were oppressed under the rule of Saddam. Even further, though it would go unproven, somewhere tied into all this was influence and backing by the Iranian government, which had a strategic interest in shaping Iraq's future and had been muddling in their affairs since the invasion. Iran had dispatched secret intelligence officers to work with Shiite militias, and the Iranian government provided expertise and training to them on how to build IEDs and EFPs.

I submitted my findings to higher headquarters and several political officers at the U.S. embassy. I knew they could not immediately change the situation, but it was something to be aware of and monitor as the elections neared. Depending on how the elections turned out, they could use this case to influence the GOI. The true victims in this were the innocent Sunnis. The only option they really had to alleviate this practice or counter this strategy was to get out and vote, ensuring Sunni leaders were elected who could balance out the power and influence of the ruling Shiite majority. March would be the tell-all month.

In the meantime, in addition to targeted assassinations, the greatest threat to the population and GOI remained the high-profile attacks such as the massive suicide car bombings or suicide vest attacks that killed, wounded, and maimed hundreds. Attacks such as these could really derail the elections and shatter any and all security gains, depending on the target they struck. From December 2009 through early March 2010, more than twelve of these catastrophic attacks targeted GOI ministries and other government institutions, including several foreign embassies. These attacks were predominantly carried out by al-Qaeda with the purpose of inciting fear, creating chaos amongst the population, and undermining the legitimacy of the ISF and GOI. As we neared election day, attacks occurred more frequently. They were difficult to predict and hard to prevent, but they were a priority concern and challenge for the ISF.

As we entered March 2010, we were ten days from the elections. As mandated by the prime minister and GOI, election security was to be executed exclusively by the ISF. There was to be no U.S. military presence visible on the street that day at or near a polling site.

Nowhere, however, was it mandated that we could not assist the ISF in their security planning efforts. As a matter of fact, Ahmed requested our assistance. The partnership between us had matured to a point that the ISF valued our input and trusted that we would provide oversight and mentorship to ensure they had a sound security plan. Bottom line: their job was on the line, and their success would be determined by whether they could secure the area and allow the population to vote.

Norris was more than willing to provide assistance. Starting in February 2010, our brigade staff and subordinate battalions spent countless hours working side by side with their ISF partners refining their overall election day security plan. Moreover, we provided them with hundreds of thousands of concrete barriers and other material to secure designated polling sites. We also assisted them with where best to place checkpoints in and around the OE in order to block off critical avenues of approach to prevent suicide car bombs from breaching the perimeter.

To assist with mitigating this threat, the GOI published orders to the population that restricted any and all vehicle movement on election day. The only vehicles authorized were ISF and other designated GOI transportation vehicles, such as buses that would shuttle citizens to the polling sites. We also were taken up on our offer to the ISF to use our aerial assets such as unmanned aerial systems to provide observation over critical election day targets and major routes that would provide early warning of a suspected car bomb. Altogether the 6th IA Division had a sound and succinct plan. All election day security operations in our OE would be supervised and directed from the 6th IA Division combined CTOC.

Even though security operations in support of the elections were strictly to be ISF executed, my nonlethal team and ePRT would have a major supporting role. Weeks out from the elections, we were tasked by the State Department and USF–I to escort several U.N. electoral observers around to polling sites located throughout our OE. The observers were a disinterested party that would attest and validate that the elections were conducted in a fair and impartial manner without corruption or tampering. This meant that I would be out on the streets and have a front-row seat for this historical event. Some telling details of the elections are:

- Nearly 6,200 candidates running for 325 seats in the Council of Representatives
- 18.9 million registered voters
- 300,000 poll station workers
- 50,000+ polling stations spread over 9,000 polling centers
- 613 total international monitors (per IHEC) from 19 countries, plus Arab League, and OIC; 200,000+ Iraqi observers; UNAMI sending out poll watcher teams.

In addition, six major parties or coalitions consisting of 2,569 candidates were running for the majority vote. Of these groups, it was widely believed amongst the population that this was a two-party race between the State of Law (current Prime Minister Nouri al-Maliki) majority Shiite party and the Iraqiyya Party, a mixed party headed by Ayed Allawi. It was widely believed that Maliki and his party would win the majority vote, but there was speculation that if there was a large turn-out of Sunni voters, former Prime Minister Allawi and the Iraqiyya Party would earn the overwhelming majority vote.

In the first national elections, the Sunni population as a whole did not turn out to vote. Therefore they did not get the representation in the Council of Representatives that they would have liked, and they had little power to balance out the majority Shiite government. The reason voter turnout was low was that sectarian violence in 2005 discouraged a lot of Sunni voters from getting out and voting. According to several Sunni sheiks I met with, the lessons were learned from the past, and Sunnis became fed up with the inefficiency and sectarian bias of the Shiite-led GOI. As a result, they were looking to let their voices be heard. They would vote in order to shape the future of the GOI and ensure their interests were represented. Based on early polling of the population, it was widely forecasted that the turnout total would be approximately 60 to 65 percent of registered voters, compared to 50 percent during the national elections of 2005.

Blasts and Ballots: Election Day

The day had finally arrived: March 10, 2010. There was no more planning; now it was all about execution. All the U.S. military could do was to sit back and watch. Mission accomplished or mission failure rested in the hands of the ISF.

It was if we were at the World Series of Poker: Our chips were committed into the pot, and our hand was the capacity of the ISF we had built over the past few years and months. We were holding a pair of kings going heads-up at the final table against an enemy that was playing ace–queen suited. Our hand was made through years of hard fighting, sacrifice, and bloodshed, along with the partnership and training of the ISF. We were all in on this one.

In order for the enemy to win, they needed a lot of luck. Would our hand (the ISF security plan) withstand the pressure? Or would it fall victim to the hand that the enemy was playing? To hedge their bets, insurgents distributed leaflets throughout Iraq, mainly in Sunni neighborhoods, warning people not to vote and telling them they would be targeted if they did.[1]

"Blasts and Ballots" was the day's opening headline on Fox News. CNN led with "Elections in Iraq Marred by Violence." These headlines were all true to an extent but far from on-the-ground truth.

At 0700 hours, I was with my PSD element along with a United Nations Assistance Mission for Iraq (UNAMI) observer team that we were tasked to escort to allow them to monitor the elections, allowing them to get a first-hand account of just how the voting process was going. We arrived in the heart of Baghdad, the ground zero of the polling places: the Mansour District. This area was the former home to the Ba'athist elites under Saddam. Nowadays, it is a mix of Shiites and Sunnis, though heavier on the latter. We arrived at the first polling site. Three days earlier and approximately 300 meters (about 985 feet) away, a suicide vest bomber attempted to board and blow up a bus filled with Iraqi Army soldiers who were voting during the

Special Voting Period or Conditional Voting Day on March 4, 2010. This attack backfired. The would-be bomber failed in his attempt to board the bus and detonated the suicide vest against the side of it. He was the only victim.

As we arrived at the polling site, security team soldiers exited our four MRAP vehicles, searching and clearing the immediate area to ensure there were no IEDs or other threats nearby that could harm the UNAMI observers before they dismounted and proceeded to the polling center. In accordance with Iraqi High Electoral Commission (IHEC) policy and the Iraqi prime minister's orders, the U.S. military could not be any closer than 300 meters from a polling site. We could only drop off the UNAMI observer team, and they could walk alone into the polling center.

Once the area was clear, the two team members, along with two armed civilian security personnel, headed into the polling center. At approximately 0730 hours, numerous explosions shook the area around us. It was nothing that directly put us in imminent danger, but the audible signature was heard fairly close by. I thought that all hell and the enemy's fury had been unleashed and that we soon would be in direct contact with them.

Explosions continued for the next hour at a rate of one every five to ten minutes. I provided command and control on the ground and over the radio, and I had a direct link to our brigade TOC back at Victory Base Complex and the 6th IA Division CTOC. As I communicated with Norris, who was collocated with Ahmed, initial reports indicated that the explosions were mortars and rockets raining down on the city. I counted at least twelve to fifteen explosions during the hour and half we were at ground zero. An area that on any normal day was a thriving marketplace with streets full of shoppers and vendors and congested with cars, people, and local police on this day was a ghost town. There were no cars on the streets except for local ISF, and there were very few people. A nationwide no-vehicle ban put in place by the GOI and prime minister had a lot to do with this.

I could count on one hand the number of people I saw who had already voted or were in the process of voting. I feared that this historic election would, in fact, be marred by violence. The nearby explosions did keep many voters at home. So far the enemy's strategy was working. However, we were early in the voting process and, not one attack had occurred at or inside a polling station.

Our greatest fear that day was the threat of a lone suicide vest bomber who might manage to disguise himself amongst the crowd. For all we knew it could have been a woman or even a young child. I would not put anything past al-Qaeda or other extremists. In the past, extremists had used women and children as suicide bombers. Certainly the ISF soldiers on the ground guarding the polling sites were not taking any chances. One Iraqi Army "jundi" body-searched a little Iraqi girl who was no more than five years old. They searched everyone, including elderly men confined to wheelchairs. Nothing on this day was taken for granted; the stakes were too high.

To protect ourselves against threats, my security team placed concertina wire on our vehicles, forming a perimeter that allowed for at least a hundred-meter standoff. No way was this the day any one of us was giving it up.

After about thirty minutes, the UNAMI observer team returned to the vehicles and we departed for the second polling site, which was supposed to be covered after lunch. But due to the low early-morning voter turnout, the team made a hasty assessment and decided to move on to the next site, which was about a kilometer away on the same road. Once we arrived, the same procedures for establishing security and clearing the area were performed by Conley and her squad of military police soldiers. Once the ground was clear, the UNAMI team headed for the second polling center to observe the voting process.

One of the UNAMI team's security guards told me that "The situation in and around Baghdad seems really bad" and that he was getting reports texted over his cell phone that there had been thirty explosions in Baghdad. Chaos had erupted. I disagreed with his assessment; clearly he was not getting the same reports that I was. I told him that they were in good hands and that we had security under control. He needed to do his damn job, just like the rest of us. This was the thought that ran through my head. I remained professional though, and we continued on.

The UNAMI team spent about twenty minutes at the second polling center. Not a lot of voters were present there, either, and there were no long lines, as was anticipated. Explosions could still be heard; some near, and some further off in the distance. All reports indicated, though, that nothing major had occurred. The situation was tense and gut-wrenching, but neither we nor the elections were in grave danger. As the UNAMI team returned to the vehicle, the security guy said that the UNAMI head honcho was scrubbing their mission and that there would be no afternoon portion. "The situation is way too dangerous and we need to return to the UNAMI compound in the International Zone," he said.

The IZ was the safest place. It was where everyone who worked in Iraq wanted to be, and I was more than glad to take them there. An Associated Press reporter was also with us, one of several AP journalists who were covering the elections all across Iraq. As updates came in, she would get on her satellite phone and call New York to provide real-time updates from the ground. As part of our information operations (IO) strategy, we were trying to get her in the right locations to shape the story and write about how well the elections were progressing and to file reports about how voter turnout was overwhelming despite the enemy's effort to derail it through voter intimidation by use of violence such as the bombings that could be heard throughout the city. In this regard, at that given moment in Baghdad (approximately 1000 hours), the enemy was winning. In poker terms, they still held a pair of aces. But it would not last long as the next and final card would soon be dealt.

An intense IO campaign was applied, supported by U.S. forces and executed by the Baghdad Operations Command, headquarters of the IA for all of Baghdad. Messages spread to all commands and subordinate units that the explosions were being perpetrated by al-Qaeda and others as a scare tactic to dissuade voters from turning out to the polls and letting their voices be heard. The bombs were small in nature. The enemy had placed explosives inside two-liter plastic soda bottles and spread thousands of them across the city and elsewhere in the belts surrounding Baghdad. Word of this spread like wildfire, and voter turnout gradually increased throughout the day. In some places, voter turnout remained steady all day as voters were not intimidated at all.

By the end of the day, it was estimated that roughly 62.9 percent of voters cast ballots. The attacks were relatively ineffective; forty-two people were killed and 110 wounded throughout Iraq. Baghdad bore the brunt of attacks. In the largest attack, twenty-five people were killed and twenty injured when a Katyusha rocket struck a flat in the Ur neighborhood in northeastern Baghdad. Also in Baghdad, Katyusha rockets killed four others and wounded sixteen in the neighborhoods of Qreiat and al-Hurriya, while roadside bombs killed seven.

In Mahmoudiyah, a city located approximately 15 meters (9.3 miles) south of Baghdad, a policeman was killed and eleven others were injured when two mortars struck a polling center. One woman was killed and thirty-six people wounded during attacks on polling centers in the insurgent stronghold of Mosul.[2] Events could have been far worse, but the ISF held their ground. Had the vehicle ban not been implemented by GOI, one or two car bombs could have ruined the day.

Al-Qaeda and other insurgent groups failed to meet their objectives. The election went on without any major attacks or disruptions. Al-Qaeda and other extremist groups could not deliver a decisive blow. Their scare tactics had minimal impact on the day that mattered most. As the world watched with baited breath, the Iraqi Army and GOI prevailed. After seven years of struggling for freedom and democracy, on this day, Iraqis braved the fear and violence that surrounded them and let their voices be heard.

Maj. Steve Phillips summed it up this way from a U.S. soldier's perspective:

"The National Elections was one of the proudest days that I witnessed over the course of my time in Iraq. The Iraqis knew that this election was going to be on the world stage, and their attention to the event and preparations leading to it reflected accordingly. U.S. Forces throughout the country could have remained in the truest sense of 'tactical overwatch' on this day—in hindsight we never needed to even leave our bases. The Iraqis believed this, too, I think, but knew that failure was not an option. As a result, ISF were willing to take the lead and to ask us to remain out on the streets, but only in the shadows. I will never forget seeing the masses of people walking to the designated polling stations in Nasir Wa Salam. They wore their best clothes, families held hands, and no one looked fearful of an enemy that could strike at any moment. They looked resolute—and they were."

After the voting had wrapped up and the polling centers closed, I was chosen to speak on behalf of our brigade at a postelection press conference. This meeting was conducted over video teleconference to news outlets from the Seattle and Tacoma, Washington, area to provide a firsthand account of exactly what took place. I led with an opening statement followed by a question-and-answer session. Every question revolved around the reported violence and its impact on the election. Every time I responded with the same answer: The violence was minimal; the most deadly attack was a house bombing that killed six people and wounded four others. The low-yield explosives placed in plastic bottles were more of a scare tactic used by the enemy to create a psychological effect to intimidate or dissuade voters versus being used as a means to damaging buildings or polling sites or killing Iraqi citizens. I stated that the results of this historical day were made possible by the hard work, sacrifice, and efforts of the ISF. Without them on the frontlines, the enemy would have prevailed. In closing, I stated that Iraqi citizens placed their trust in the ISF and no matter the threat would not be deterred. I ended the press conference saying that, "The will of the people triumphed."

Later, President Obama addressed the nation from the White House rose garden, stating that, "Today's voting makes it clear that the future of Iraq belongs to the people of Iraq." He went on to thank all the U.S. military members and civilians for their support and assistance in making the day possible. He ended with a congratulatory message to all Iraqis, stating:

"On behalf of the American people, I congratulate the Iraqi people on their courage throughout this historic election. Today, in the face of violence from those who would only destroy, Iraqis took a step forward in the hard work of building up their country. The United States will continue to help them in that effort as we responsibly end this war, and support the Iraqi people as they take control of their future."[3]

After the Elections

We soon entered a very fragile period. The elections were a success and a historic event, but now the demanding task of forming and seating a government would begin. After all votes had been counted and official results were released at the end of March 2010, the Iraqiyya Party, led by Allawi, was the clear winner, having won ninety-one seats by a very narrow margin over incumbent Prime Minister Maliki's State of Law Party, which had won eighty-nine seats. Neither Allawi nor Maliki possessed the votes or the magic number of 163 seats, the majority required to form the government. Coalitions would have to be formed in order to gain a majority of seats, required to form the government and elect a prime minister.

Meanwhile, the ISF along with support from U.S. forces, were trying to maintain security and stability to provide time for Iraq to seat the government. Although security was relatively calm, it could easily have turned south. It is much like having your finger in a fragile dike that has been breached by rushing water. The ISF had their finger in a gaping hole, and we were behind them holding them up. The obvious question was whether the ISF could keep the dike from bursting open while the political jockeying went back and forth as politicians slugged it out.

All the while, the enemy still loomed large, attacking in all ways possible to try to derail the political process and create further instability. They did this through continued attacks in the form of silenced pistol assassinations and the use of the magnetic car bombs targeting prominent mid- to high-level political figures and ISF leadership. Since election day March 10, 2010, through April 2010, there had been more than fifty such attacks. These attacks continued to undermine security and disrupt the formation of the new government. As if that was not enough to deal with, Prime Minister Maliki, recognizing defeat by Allawi, called for a recount of the votes by IHEC, specifically the votes for Baghdad Province.

Max Boot, a senior fellow in national security studies at the Council on Foreign Relations, criticized Maliki's actions in an editorial, stating that, "Maliki, a sectarian Shiite, won't accept the possibility that Allawi, a secular Shiite who enjoys overwhelming support among Sunnis, could displace him as Prime Minister."[4]

Boot went on to criticize President Obama and his administration for their inaction to get involved and influence Maliki to accept the vote, so Iraq could move on with forming its government: "Senior officials in the Obama administration are reportedly becoming more involved behind the scenes to avert such a disaster, but so far they have made limited progress."[5]

Based on what we were observing on the ground, it appeared that the administration was focused on the drawdown and transition out of Iraq instead of on the long-term development and success of Iraq. This was evident by orders we received before the election that we would reduce the U.S. military footprint from 95,000 to 50,000 by the end of August 2010, which led to the Responsible Drawdown of Forces plan. The original timeline negotiated by the Bush Administration in 2008 was that we would not begin our drawdown until after Iraq had installed its new government. It was expected by all involved that there would be postelection fallout and jockeying from various parties, but with the hope that it would be resolved by June 2010 at the latest. Once Maliki called for a recount, GOI officials forecasted that a government would not emerge until October or November 2010. Based on this timeline, the withdrawal of 45,000 troops by September 1, 2010, was somewhat premature. According to Boot, "Large troop reductions at a time of such political uncertainly will send a dangerous signal of disengagement and lessen America's ability to preserve the integrity of the elections."[6]

Even after arguments like this were made by Boot and several other top military leaders and members of Congress, including Senators Lindsey Graham and John McCain, President Obama did not waiver and was steadfast that we would stay the course with the established drawdown date.

Personally I agree with the position of Senator John McCain in that we as a nation should never publicly announce a timeline of withdraw during wartime. We were tipping our hand to the enemy. It is true that a specific date can be established as a planning tool, but it should be kept secret from the public and, most importantly, from our enemies. In this case, all our enemies had to do was wait it out. Once we withdrew, they would have full reign to exact their violence and destruction. Publishing a timeline is like handing a complete playbook over to an opposing football team, along with all the signals that represent those plays. By doing so, you are assured defeat. At the tactical level, however, we had no choice in this matter; we simply followed the orders of our superiors, namely the commander in chief.

As the days passed, I was afforded some time to continue looking into the whole notion of Shiite Expansionism. I was steadfast on proving that it did exist, even if just to satisfy my own curiosity.

Conley and James examined the demographics and distribution of polling sites. I was looking to see if there was equity between the numbers of polling sites in Shiite neighborhoods compared to the number in Sunni areas. I focused our efforts on examining our OE. We discovered that there were in excess of 400 polling sites in our OE, the majority of which were within the Amanat (city of Baghdad). But west toward Abu Ghraib, the number decreased dramatically. There were ten to twelve polling sites in the Zaidon area, a historic site that dates back to ancient civilization.

According to Iraq Ministry of Interior and IHEC records, the majority of the population is Sunni; approximately 95 percent up of a population of just less than 200,000. Simple math showed that there was one polling site per every 20,000 people (if all 200,000 were registered voters). Toward Baghdad, particularly in the Shiite district of Shulla, which is 99 percent Shiite and has a population of approximately 250,000, there were more than fifty polling sites.

This was incredibly one-sided to say the least. The message was that the Shiite-dominated GOI (though no public official would admit it) would do whatever it took to win the election. This included putting an aggressive Shiite Brigade Commander like Rahim in charge of Sunni areas and limiting the number of polling sites in the areas where Sunnis would vote.

This scenario I laid out is not representative of all of Iraq. This is merely a small sampling from our OE. Despite Shiite efforts to suppress or restrict the Sunni population from turning out for the vote, they overcame the odds and turned out in record numbers. In our OE alone, more than 65 percent of the Sunni population voted. Based on my sampling of Sunni sheiks conducted during key leader engagements following the elections, the majority of them stated that their fellow tribesmen voted for Allawi, a secular Shiite, and his Iraqiyya Party, which had several Sunni candidates in the alliance.

As I look back on the whole election process, it was not fair to the minority Sunnis, even if it was successful overall. Clearly the Shiites had made every attempt to steal the election. I knew that nothing would change based on my findings. It was more to validate my own beliefs and, if anything, at least highlight that this strategy did in fact exist even though everyone inside the GOI would outright deny it. Finally it validated the point that if this country was serious about establishing and serving as a representative democracy in the Middle East, although in its infancy, they still had a ways to go to break down the sectarian barriers that existed. The important takeaway was that this election laid the groundwork for democracy to take shape, and it gave every Iraqi citizen a taste of what democracy and freedom is all about. This was a watershed event for Iraqi citizens that only knew authoritarian rule through sheer coercion and brutality.

The recount of ballots officially started on April 19, 2010. I had recently returned to Iraq from a two-week environmental leave and could not believe what I was told about Prime Minster Maliki challenging the election because it did not turn out as favorably as he had hoped. Regardless of the situation, nothing could break my spirit. Turns out, after being back in theater for approximately two weeks, I received great news from my lovely wife that she was pregnant and we would be expecting our first child together in January 2011. With that news, I was motivated and could endure any challenge that was thrown at me.

As for the ballot recount, this would have a major impact on our brigade as we found out that the ballots would have to be moved from the ballot warehouses, specifically the Karkh Warehouse located in our OE near the Kadimiyah District and the Rusafa Warehouse located on the east side of the Tigris River. Because the Karkh, better known as the Debash warehouse, was in our OE, our brigade would play a prominent role in ensuring the ballots were secured and delivered to the al-Rasheed Hotel without incident to allow for the recount.

The Baghdad Operational Command (BOC) plan for executing the movement of ballots was to conduct one complete ballot box truck movement a night from each warehouse, alternating nights between the two. Our recommendation to the BOC commander was to load them all up and move them in one mass movement, which would allow for all the ballots to get to the Al Rasheed Hotel in one move, thus limiting the exposure and vulnerability of attack. But they were steadfast on their plan to do it their way. As a result, the recount would be extended over an eighteen-day period.

Under the plan, the ballots would be exposed every night for more than two weeks, susceptible to interdiction by al-Qaeda if they chose to attack. There was serious risk assumed by all involved. By chance, if al-Qaeda was successful at targeting a truck loaded with ballots with an IED or RPG, it would cripple the political process and propel Iraq into a tailspin.

During the recount, the U.S. military and our brigade in particular would play a more prominent role than we did during the actual national elections. The reason is because the forming of the new government was the lynchpin behind allowing the U.S. military and U.S. government to meet the timelines for the drawdown of combat forces to the 50,000 threshold by September 1, 2010. Somewhere at the strategic level it was decided by U.S. State Department, USF–I, and GOI, that we would participate by providing the security to ensure the ballots were not compromised. We had a vested interest in seeing that the recount went off without incident. Based upon the mission orders received from Odierno, this was a decisive effort for the brigade, and it was certainly the center of gravity for all of Iraq.

With the orders in hand, Norris and our staff conducted combined planning with the 6th Iraqi Army and federal police and drafted the security plan to accomplish this strategic task. So important was the mission we named it Operation Raider Recount. We would provide the route clearance teams to clear the road leading from the warehouse to the IZ where the Al-Rasheed Hotel was located. We would integrate our vehicles along with the ISF vehicles that escorted the ballot trucks in order to enhance security and prevent any attack. Additional support provided by U.S. forces included attack aviation to watch the movement of the trucks as they proceeded on the route. The same plan was executed by U.S. forces and ISF on the other side of the Tigris River. We would alternate nights, securing and returning counted ballots to and from the respective warehouses.

It seemed as though the planning and staff energy for this simple yet complex operation took more time and energy than it did to plan the Allied Invasion of France. We could not make this shit up. It was an intense period for all of us. But as the decisive strategic operation in theater and importance this mission had on shaping the future of Iraq, it was imperative that U.S. forces and ISF got it right. The stress and intensity associated with the planning and executing was justified in the end.

To execute this task, Norris assigned 2-12 FA Battalion, commanded by Lieutenant Colonel Terry Braley. This was the logical choice being that the warehouse and routes to travel to and from the IZ were in his OE. Major Deric Holbrook, the 2-12 FA, operations officer, planned the operation and was a key participant and facilitator in each movement. He provided a detailed account of the operation from street level:

"The mission given to us from our brigade headquarters was simple; secure the movement of ballots from the Debash Warehouse to the Al Rasheed Hotel combined with the Iraqi Army in order to allow IHEC personnel to recount all Baghdad Ballots. The limitations and directives that accompanied this mission were the difficult factors. They were: 1. Maintain a minimal US presence in the convoy movement (no more than 2 × HMMWVs), 2. There must a Field Grade Officer in each movement, and 3. There must be a Lieutenant Colonel commanding and controlling the movement from a TAC positioned at the Debash Warehouse (ballot storage facility). The actual movement from the Debash Warehouse to the Al Rasheed Hotel (recount location in the Green Zone) was simple and a less than 20 KM straight line movement, all within

2-12 FA's OE. The problem was that this route went through three different Iraqi Army Brigades sectors; 54th, 22nd, and 56th Baghdad Brigade, therefore all three Iraqi Army Brigades wanted to be a part of the movement security plan. Additionally, the Iraqi Police and the Iraqi Traffic Police specifically, were charged with securing the roads itself, as that was their primary function.

The U.S. portion of the mission consisted of a nightly confirmation and synchronization of all the resources including, UAV surveillance, route clearance (US and Iraqi), Close Air Support (CAS), Attack Aviation, Quick Reaction Force (QRF), as well all Iraqi Army and Police elements. This confirmation was coordinated through the operations channels from USF–I to 4-2 SBCT to the 2-12 FA Battalion. Once confirmation was received, a U.S. QRF platoon, the Battalion TAC, and two, M1114s HMMWVs moved to their perspective start points. The TAC was always positioned at the Debash Warehouse, the QRF was positioned along the route in order to provide immediate support to the two M1114s (10 × U.S. Soldiers), and the two security vehicles either went to the Debash Warehouse or the al Rasheed Hotel to pick up ballots and link up with all other security forces.

The TAC Set up command and control of the mission from the warehouse while two security vehicles and I, as well as nine other Soldiers (Platoon Leader, or Platoon Sergeant and 1 × Squad) coordinated with all the Iraqi Security Forces participating in the movement. This coordination typically happened in standard Iraqi fashion (huge gaggle of vehicles and personnel in the street). There were literally 25 Iraqi security vehicles and 75 to 100 Iraqi Soldiers or Police from each brigade and police crammed into one 200 meter section of the road nightly. Typically Iraqi Colonels and Generals would arrive to supervise their Soldiers and ensure the mission was going successfully, and they would of course bring their entourage to add to the head count on the side of the road outside the warehouse. With the use of the translators, I would ensure that all elements were in place and ready prior to start time. The start time was critical as both U.S. Explosive Ordnance Disposal (EOD) and Iraqi EOD were conducting route clearance operations directly in front the convoy nightly. This, along with attack aviation, UAV, and CAS overhead was synchronized to ensure the ballots were watched from the warehouse to the hotel and that any possible indication of an enemy attack was identified and neutralized prior to the ballots moving through an ambush site. Nightly, I would receive direct confirmation from IHEC personnel on site that the ballots were ready to be moved, and he would begin the movement from the warehouse or hotel out through the gates and into a sea of Iraqi Security Forces who were ready to secure the movement. Once outside the *secure compound of the warehouse or hotel, two ballot trucks (small Iraqi Semi Trucks) would fall into the center of the 25 Iraqi Security Vehicles. My vehicle would always take lead and the second U.S. security vehicle (Platoon Leader or Platoon Sergeant from Bravo Battery, 2-12 FA) would stay directly behind the ballots trucks.*

One would think that this operation subtly named "Operation Raider Recount" would be filled with confusion and a synchronization nightmare with all the assets and agencies participating. However, Raider Recount went off successfully every night, without incident and was a complete success. This is not to say that there wasn't confusion, because there was, almost nightly. What can be said is that the Iraqi Security Forces, massed on their objective, fought through any confusion on the ground with their direct leadership style, and made the mission happen with a little help from the U.S. forces and our incisive need to rehearse the operation. Working relationships, tactics, techniques and procedures (TTPs) were established on site nightly between ISF leaders and me. Prior to every patrol we conducted a map or talk through rehearsal with all ISF leadership. Each combined rehearsal, typically on an ISF truck hood ensured all participants knew the route (which never changed), where the ballots trucks were being positioned in the convoy (which changed depending on which IA brigade was 'in charge' that night, and the start time (which changed nightly depending on the IHEC's timeline). Actions on contact were discussed as well, although no set Standard Operating Procedure was established. After rehearsals were complete and TTPs were established, the security convoy executed movement either south or north. Each night the streets were completely blocked from any civilian traffic and Iraqi Police stood vigilant at each intersection. Attack Aviation screened the route ahead of the convoy. UAV video feeds were observed by the 2-12 FA TOC and information was relayed to me and the convoy. I would then pass information from the Attack Aviation and UAV assets through an interpreter to the ISF leadership on hand held radios provided by the ISF. This was the 4-2 SBCTs and 2-12 FA's attempt to provide real time intelligence to the ISF en-route. Whether or not the ISF used it will never be known. What is known is that every night the routes were cleared, civilian traffic was moved off the streets in downtown Baghdad (which is a feat all in itself), and the ballots were moved safely, without incident, for 14 nights."

The mission lasted until May 14, 2010. All ballots from the Baghdad Province were successfully moved without interdiction of any kind. Never once was an attack, either direct fire or IED, attempted against the ballot convoy. The success of this operation served as further testament to the progression and capacity, both in planning and execution, the ISF had obtained. In actuality, they could have planned and executed this all on their own without our support.

Once the recount was complete, IHEC officially announced on May 14, 2010, that all 11,298 ballot boxes had been recounted (more than 3 million votes) and the results ended up being the same as they had been before it was called for by Prime Minister Maliki. The Iraqiyya Party, led by Allawi, was the outright winner obtaining the aforementioned ninety-one seats. Prime Minister Maliki's State of Law Alliance remained at eighty-nine seats. Furthermore, they confirmed that there was no sign of fraud or violations. I suspect the notion or existence of Shiite Expansionism was never considered. (Why would it be when it did not exist, right?) Based on the findings, Maliki reluctantly accepted the outcome.

Our mission and involvement surrounding the elections was complete. It was an overwhelming success for us and our ISF partners, and it provided a perfect segue for us to begin our transition and preparation for departure.

From May 1, 2010, through end of July 2010, we focused all of our efforts on the transition phase. This phase would be as daunting, if not more challenging, as the last. Our brigade first transitioned all of our civil capacity operations, including all projects, to the U.S. Department of State. The plan laid out by the State Department was to consolidate ePRTs down to three total teams: ePRT North, South, and Baghdad. All operations and current projects were passed on to ePRT Baghdad. Major Patrick Hemmer, Captain Talgin Cannon, and their team did an outstanding job of ensuring 100 percent accountability of all funds and confirming that all paperwork was in order, allowing for a seamless transition.

We had one final civil military operation to conduct to serve as a grand finale before closing it out completely. This final operation would become known as the Mother of All Humanitarian/Medical Assistance Missions. It provided the perfect ending to a great tour of duty and closed the chapter on our partnership with 6th IA, Abu Ghraib Sheik Support Council, and community leaders. The most challenging task to execute during the transition phase was the close out and transfer of authority of all our JSSs and COPs over to the ISF. Maj. Dave Voorhies, Major Tony New, and Operations Sergeant Major

Brian Hollis would play a key role in these transfers and closeouts, which were taking place all over theater as units focused on transition.

During the height of the surge, more than five hundred individual FOBs, JSSs, and COPs were spread throughout Iraq. As we entered May 2010, only a hundred were left. From May to July 2010, we successfully completed closeout and transfer of our ten JSSs or COPs, including JSS Tarmiyah, Agur Quf, Nasir Wa Salam, and JSS Justice. When all was said and done, we had accurately accounted for more than $10 million worth of material and equipment such as beds, air conditioners, computers, televisions, audio-visual equipment, and a ton of other material that had been requisitioned and built up during the past eight years. Our brigade was the first in theater of the units remaining that accomplished this task without any issues.

As this transition was underway, there was still a lot of uncertainty surrounding the formation of the Iraqi government. Iraqi parliament leaders, specifically Maliki and Allawi, fought to form alliances to allow their respective parties to achieve the magic number of 163 seats in order to allow the party to form the government and select the new prime minister. This political infighting would last for several months after we had departed. All the while, the enemy threat still persisted and political and military assassinations continued, though on a smaller scale. The enemy continued to use silenced pistols and magnetic car bombs to carry out attacks. The other major threat that existed was the suicide car bombs. These attacks were the most catastrophic and hardest to prevent. These large-scale bombings were the weapon of choice for both Sunni and Shiite extremist groups.

During the two years since the surge, continuing with combined offensive operations between ISF and U.S. forces, the enemy suffered heavy losses and did not have the manpower to carry out large-scale ground attacks. Every attack they planned and executed had to be precise, so they relied on car bombs to kill en masse and undermine the legitimacy of ISG and GOI.

Based on existing conditions, Odierno decided to keep our brigade in theater until the latest possible moment while still allowing the U.S. military to meet its timeline to reduce the number of troops by 50,000 no later than August 31, 2010. Doing so provided him and USF–I with strategic flexibility during a period for potential instability.

The plan was to have us remain in theater for an additional two weeks to serve as an on-call quick-reaction force that could be dispatched wherever needed. In order to achieve this, it would require our brigade to plan and execute a tactical road march out of Iraq commencing on August 15, 2010, in order to meet the official date established by President Obama signifying that the last combat brigade had departed theater. The two weeks that the tactical road march bought us ensured that USF–I maintained the operational flexibility to retain a Stryker Brigade Combat Team's combat power should any enemy actions during the drawdown reach its tipping point and all hell broke loose. This tactical road march was officially coined "The Last Patrol."

CHAPTER 10
THE LAST COMBAT PATROL

Tactical Road March out of Iraq into Kuwait
July–August 2010

❝ We've persevered because of a belief we share with the Iraqi people—a belief that out of the ashes of war, a new beginning could be born in this cradle of civilization. Through this remarkable chapter in the history of the United States and Iraq, we have met our responsibility. Now, it's time to turn the page. ❞

President Barack Obama

On August 1, 2010, we executed our final operation in Abu Ghraib. It wasn't a tactical operation, but rather a civil military operation of goodwill. We had planned this jointly with the ISF, Sheik Support Council, and local leaders months previous. The ISF and sheiks took the lead, advertised it throughout the OE for two months, and coordinated media coverage.

More than 3,000 Iraqi men, women, and children from all over the OE showed up and benefited from the services provided. The most promising aspect of this operation is that it was executed solely by Iraqis; we only provided supplies. Ahmed was on hand walking around with Norris, shaking hands and hugging babies as if the two were on the campaign trail bidding for reelection. We went out of our way to make this the mother of all humanitarian/medical assistance events ever conducted in theater. We emptied out every container we had that were filled with toys, clothes, soccer balls, school supplies, backpacks, and more. All of these items were loaded onto cargo trucks and transported to the event. Included was more than $50,000 of medical supplies, including wheelchairs for disabled children. It was truly the pinnacle of nonlethal operations for our brigade and, more importantly, for ISF and community partners. It was a fitting end to the final chapter.

Planning for the tactical road march out of Kuwait began in earnest in July 2010, based on the decision by Odierno to retain us in theater, thus providing USF–I with operational flexibility whereby they could dispatch us to deal with any enemy-related uprising or attack. Bottom line: we had to be out of Iraq no later than August 31 to meet the requirements of the 50,000-troop reduction deadline mandated by President Obama.

Officially this departure would mark the end to our combat mission in Iraq, bringing an end to Operation Iraqi Freedom and the start of Operation New Dawn. We would be the last official combat brigade to depart Iraq. Our brigade staff, led by Maj. Dave Voorhies along with Operations Officer Maj. Tony New, did a superb job at drafting a succinct plan that would allow the entire brigade to meet this deadline. The plan called for a total of four serials or march units to depart Baghdad, with the first serial departing the evening of August 15, 2010, and each remaining serial following in sequence every twenty-four hours. The last unit was to cross the border into Kuwait on the morning of August 19, 2010. Each serial was comprised of one or two battalions. Serial 1 was 4-9 IN, "Manchus;" Serial 2 was 2-1 Cavalry Squadron, "Blackhawk," and 2-12 Field Artillery Battalion, "Viking;" Serial 3 was 2-23 IN "Tomahawk;" and the final serial was 1-38 IN "Rock."

The 360-mile march would take us south out of Baghdad along Highway 1 with one overnight-stop at Camp Adder, located near Nasiriyah. The following evening, we would depart Camp Adder and end at the Khabari Crossing in Kuwait early the next morning. A total of 360 vehicles, mainly Stryker Combat Vehicles and additional support/recovery assets, would make the trip south. More than 2,200 soldiers participated in this historic journey. Attack aviation and unmanned aerial vehicle assets flying overhead provided route reconnaissance and additional security.

I elected to travel in the first serial with Charlie Company, 4-9 IN commanded by Captain Guy Girouard, a former company commander of mine at JRTC. I felt this would be a fitting end for us since we had both previously fought against this brigade during their MRX at JRTC. Now, a year after fighting with the brigade as a member of the Raider Combat Team, we would close the book on Operation Iraqi Freedom. The brigade commander, Norris, and his TAC opted to travel with the last serial comprised of 1-38 IN. Once the news broke of this historic trip, the brigade immediately started receiving requests from major media outlets from around the world requesting to embed with us to cover the operation. Among the requests was one submitted by NBC News to allow war correspondent Richard Engel to accompany us and provide live video coverage of the road march. USF–I approved the request, and Engel accompanied the last serial, riding shotgun with 1-38 IN Commander Lieutenant Colonel John Leffers.

In order to provide live play-by-play coverage, Engel brought along his high-tech satellite truck, known appropriately as the "Bloom mobile." This vehicle was made famous during the invasion in 2003, when the late David Bloom embedded and traveled with lead elements of the 3rd Infantry Division, the first division to cross the border into Iraq, when he suddenly died due to deep vein thrombosis and pulmonary embolism before reaching Baghdad.

I fully understood Engel's desire for wanting to accompany us: first to honor his former colleague and second to complete the chapter on Iraq from when NBC News first broadcast and covered the initial invasion.

The most challenging task in planning this operation was drafting the media plan to synchronize and distribute embedded journalists across the brigade formation to ensure equal coverage. It was total media frenzy as all the major new outlets jockeyed for position and favor. I give credit to Major Chris Ophardt, our brigade public affairs officer, and his team of great soldiers for honchoing this event and running interference for us. Prior to the departure of the first serial, we provided more than fifty media members a concept brief laying out the ground rules for reporting live during the event.

With the planning for the road march, we also began our transition with the brigade that would assume our OE. This was a unique transition to say the least. The official combat mission in Iraq would end on our watch and subsequent departure from theater. On September 1, 2010, Operation Iraqi Freedom transitioned to Operation New Dawn. With this new operation came a new mission that was exclusively an advise-and-assist mission for remaining U.S. forces. To accomplish this mission, the Army formed and established seven advise and assist brigades (AABs) that would stay behind or deploy into Iraq and execute the vital mission of security assistance.

The AABs were traditional maneuver brigades much like ours; however, they were given additional mission specific assets and resources such as additional MiTTs and other nonorganic assets. Moreover, they were put through special training prior to deploying to theater, including training in city management, civil affairs, and border patrol.

The Army selected brigade combat teams as the unit to build advisory brigades partly because they would be able to retain the inherent capability, combat equipment, and soldiers to conduct offensive operations in the event the situation and conditions in Iraq warranted it. The major difference between them and us was the mission they would conduct. It would strictly be an advisory role. Where we had partnered with ISF units down to the battalion level, the AABs would partner with them starting at the division level and higher. In some circumstances, they would drop down and partner with an Iraqi Army Brigade Headquarters, as was the case with 1-3 AAB, which assumed our OE and had a battalion partner with Rahim and the 24th IA Brigade. This partnership with the 24th IA Brigade was the exception and not the rule. 1-3 AAB, based on their structure and manpower, did not have the manpower and leadership to cover down below the division level to individual brigades.

Our OE was assumed by 1-3 AAB, led by Colonel Roger Cloutier. His brigade was part of the 3rd Infantry Division based out of Fort Stewart, Georgia. They had arrived in theater in February 2010, replacing the 30th "Old Hickory" Infantry Division of the North Carolina National Guard and assuming their OE in southern Baghdad. Next they assumed the OE of 2nd Brigade, 10th Mountain Division based out of Fort Drum, New York, in northeast Baghdad. Finally, they transitioned with us and assumed our OE in August 2010, taking control for all of Baghdad and the surrounding areas.

They had taken complete control of an area that was once occupied and held by three brigades consisting of more than 15,000 soldiers compared to 1-3 AAB's 4,500. It was a tough mission, but the brigade was seasoned, had great soldiers, and was led by great leaders who would step up and meet the challenge.

We completed the transition with them on or around August 10, 2010. The transition itself was easier than previous ones. There were no buildings, JSSs, FOBs, or equipment to transfer. There were no civil capacity projects to handover. All these transfers had already been completed as every base JSS and COP we occupied had been turned over to the GOI and ISF. Most equipment, except for our organic equipment, had been turned in at Victory Base in July. The last remaining task left to accomplish was turning out the lights and locking the doors at Victory Base. We were the last unit to occupy it.

On July 4, we took a break from the planning to celebrate Independence Day. As luck would have it, we got a surprise visit by Dr. Jill Biden, Vice President Joe Biden's wife. Dr. Biden accompanied her husband on this trip to make the rounds and visit with the troops to thank them and their families for their service and sacrifice. She stopped in at brigade headquarters and met briefly with Norris before joining Raider Brigade soldiers for a 4th of July barbeque celebration that I and others had planned. We celebrated by having a Texas-style barbeque cookout behind headquarters. Voorhies helped prepare steaks, hamburgers, and hot dogs as we tried to mimic traditional festivities occurring that day back in the States. While I was slaving away over the grill in the blistering heat, Dr. Biden and her entourage, escorted by Norris, approached the grill. I was honored to meet her as I admire the work she has done serving as an advocate for military families. I shook her hand and welcomed her to Baghdad and the Raider Brigade. I noticed she was looking over my shoulder at the juicy steaks simmering on the grill. I sensed that she and her team was hungry, and I told her that one of those steaks had her name on it. Norris extended an invitation to her and the group to dine with us, which she accepted. I served her the best steak I could find. Over the years, I have cooked a lot of steaks for a lot of people, but this set a new standard.

We chatted for a bit and I thanked her for braving the danger and gracing us with her presence on this special day. I also thanked her for all her work and support that she had done advocating for the troops and their families. After preparing her plate, she sat down and enjoyed her steak. During dinner, she visited with several soldiers of the brigade. Prior to departing, she assisted Norris with cutting our July 4th cake and later addressed the crowd. "I just want to say what an honor it is to spend the 4th of July with my family," she said, explaining that as the mother of a soldier, she considers the military her extended family.

Dr. Biden expressed her appreciation of the deployed soldiers' hard work and thanked them and their families for their service. After that she received an orientation of our Stryker vehicles headed by Huggins and his personal security detachment crew. Soon afterward she departed to visit other units located on Victory Base. Overall, it was a great celebration that afforded everyone a break from the rigors of war.

As the days of the tactical road march neared, we made our rounds saying final goodbyes and farewells to our ISF partners. One night, we assembled at the 6th IA Division Headquarters, located at FOB Constitution, less than a five-minute drive away from our headquarters. Ahmed had summoned Norris, Voorhies, New, Fiol, James, and me to a final meeting. Ahmed had assembled his key staff and commanders to share this special occasion with us. We sat and talked for a couple of hours over hot tea, reminiscing about the past year and all the great accomplishments we had enjoyed together. As we neared the end of the visit, I sensed that the mood in the room was changing. Conversation and laughter began to soften, taking on a sentimental tone. I sensed emotion taking over both Norris and Ahmed, who had forged a great partnership and friendship. The night would end with one final hug and handshake.

In all my years of military service, including two previous tours in Iraq, I had never witnessed or been a part of something as surreal as this. This was much more than a partnership. We were brothers in arms, fighting for a shared cause we all believed in, so much so that we were willing to lay down our lives to obtain it. We had forged an unbreakable bond in the streets of Baghdad and in the alleys of Abu Ghraib, walking side by side in spite of the danger that lurked, never once second-guessing why we were there.

As the meeting concluded, Ahmed presented each of us with a photo collage that displayed all of our pictures, a symbol of the team that had been formed during the past year. As Ahmed called me up and presented the picture, we shook hands and hugged. I said, in my best Arabic, "*shukran sadi, al-humdillah,*" which means "thank you, Sir. thanks be to God." I told him I had a great year and how much of an honor it was to serve with him and his soldiers. I added that his forces were ready and more than capable to provide for the security of Iraq and its people. I wished him all the best in the months and years ahead.

On August 3, our brigade received a visit from Odierno. He came to headquarters to bid us farewell and to commend us for our hard work and success during the past year. During his visit, he presented our brigade staff and the entire command team, including all subordinate battalion commanders and their command sergeants majors, with end-of-tour awards. As he pinned a bronze star on my chest, my mind began to reflect over the years and tours I served under him. The war had come full circle for him, just as it had for me.

Between 2003 and 2004, Odierno, while serving as 4th Infantry Division Commander, received a lot of criticism from journalists, military strategists, and even other officers in the military for his use of heavy-handed tactics while operating in the Sunni Triangle. Most critical of him was Thomas Ricks, senior Pentagon correspondent for *The Washington Post*. In his first Iraq War book, *Fiasco: The American Military Adventure in Iraq*, Ricks hammered Odierno for the lethal stance he took while combating insurgents in the most volatile area in Iraq. He quoted several sources he had interviewed to build his case, most of whom were not mentioned by name. Specifically he stated that:

> "Gen. Odierno, 4th Infantry Division and its subordinate brigades and battalions had earned a reputation for being overly aggressive. He went on to say that the division and its units used 'ham-fisted approaches' that may have appeared to pacify its area in the short term, but in the process alienated the population."[1]

Later in the book, he cited an interview with a general who was serving there during the same time as Odierno. This general, who was not mentioned by name, called out Odierno stating that "The 4th ID— what they did was a crime."[2] Ricks continued unwarranted and unfounded criticism of Odierno throughout the book, implying that all the 4th ID did was kill people and abuse prisoners. Of course, this was patently false and totally unfair to everyone who served with and wore the 4th Division's Ivy Patch during this period. Ricks seemed to have forgotten an important rule of life: Never judge a man unless you have walked in his shoes.

I learned early in life from my father, coaches, and teachers to never judge a man unless you walked in his shoes. I think this life lesson was never taught to Ricks or, if so, it flew over his head. I am a staunch supporter of Odierno and a defender of all that we did in Iraq between 2003 and 2004. While our actions were aggressive, they were not criminal. At that time in Iraq that is what the conditions called for. We could not afford to be weak or timid in the face of the enemy. We were trying to quell and defeat the insurgency before it gained momentum. Moreover, Iraqis responded to force and violence. They may not have liked it, but they respected its use. Whoever had the iron fist was the ruler. Winning the hearts and minds was secondary at the time.

Recall that prior to 2006, the Army did not have doctrine that governed counterinsurgency. Nor did we train tactics or principles for executing a counterinsurgency campaign. The last time we fought one in Vietnam, we lost on the strategic level, and because of that we tried to suppress it and forget it had ever happened. If there had been any lessons learned, they were forgotten.

In Iraq at the time, our aggressive tactics and strategy were working. We were simply executing what we had been trained to do. Once we figured out a better way and learned from the mistakes we had made, we adapted and made the adjustments. I give full credit and praise to Odierno for recognizing the nature of the war at the time and understanding what was required to defeat the enemy. I also have a lot of respect and admiration for his leadership by example and undaunting courage.

I personally escorted Odierno through the streets of Albu Hishma in 2004 as we patrolled the area on foot. He wanted to get a first-hand look and assessment on the ground from a tip-of-the-spear perspective in what was the most troubled and violent village in Iraq at the time. That particular day, we probably walked more than a mile and a half through the narrow, dusty streets. As we walked, locals gathered on the sides of the road and gave us evil stares, stares so evil they could seemingly pierce body armor. I was shocked that we were not attacked that day. It was the norm in this savage village.

Ricks and others like him were much too eager to chastise the military without fully understanding what it was like on the ground. I doubt very seriously that Ricks ever once donned a ballistic helmet or body armor and patrolled the violent streets with soldiers in Iraq or any other theater. Nor had he ever been shot at by a sniper or blown up by an IED. Had he experienced life from the front sight of an M-4 carbine walking along RPG alley, he may have gained a better perspective of why our tactics were aggressive. I personally do not have a lot of respect for the man. Some journalists I do, like *New York Times* war correspondent Dexter Filkins, who earned his spurs while patrolling with soldiers from the great Ivy Division. Through these patrols, he experienced the boredom and abject terror that punctuate the daily life of an infantryman in combat. On the other hand, journalists like Ricks usually fly in for a day or two, get a snapshot, and fly out. Once back in the safe confines of Washington, D.C., they write lies and half truths, misrepresenting the facts and events, such as those surrounding the Samarra Bridge incident by linking them with Captain Eric Paliwoda's death.

Ricks's account of this event missed the mark. I should know: I was there when it all happened. He then published it and turned into a best-seller predicated on the efforts of the warrior in the arena and not his own. Much like the graduate student writing research, the effort is in the data mining, not the actual production. Hail to the man in the arena with the dust on his face, grit in his teeth, and the sweat in his eyes—and not the play-by-play announcer or Monday-morning quarterback.

Using the streets of Albu Hishma as a laboratory for the examination of change during combat operations in the Iraqi theater, we noted the circular bend of change. Events after the invasion led to the insurgency. During the insurgency, events on the streets of Albu Hishma were commonplace for U.S. combat operations. Soldiers fought for the streets of Albu Hishma on a daily basis. Our actions called for more lethality than civil compassion. During the surge, our mission was to end the cycle of sectarian violence, clear the streets of all insurgents, and return them to civil control. Again, tactics used were somewhat lethal in nature. The counterinsurgency strategy allowed U.S. forces and ISF to return the streets, marketplaces, and playgrounds of Iraq to the people. The circle closed with the withdrawal of U.S. forces from the cities and the assumption of a supporting role and partnership with ISF and GOI. The circle closed with the final patrol south.

Odierno experienced firsthand the brutal combat conducted during the postinvastion months. A strong proponent of the surge, he played a key role in shaping the strategy that blunted the blossoming insurgency in Iraq. He then embraced the COIN strategy and implemented it to perfection. Following that, he led U.S. forces out of an Iraqi-controlled Iraq, proving that he had learned the lessons from the past, adapted, and became a leader for all seasons. I was fortunate enough to have served for him during every key phase of this war, and I witnessed first-hand the implementation of his strategic vision as it morphed to defeat a sophisticated enemy and gave hope to the people and nation of Iraq. His vision and art of command proved to be prophetic.

At last it was August 15, 2010. As soon as I awoke, I cleaned the trailer in which I had lived for the past year. That night would be the last I spent in Baghdad. I loaded my personal baggage onto a Stryker Combat Vehicle and departed for breakfast with Voorhies. Over breakfast, we reminisced about the past years and laughed at several exploits that had taken place. Voorhies was not as lucky as I was: He and Hollis would have to stay in Iraq for another week facilitating our departure and ensuring that any last-minute issues were resolved. They would be the last two Raiders in Iraq and would turn over the keys to headquarters to the designated FOB mayor before flying to Kuwait via military aircraft and linking up with us for the redeployment home.

After breakfast ended, Voorhies and I went to the gym for one last workout, which was our standard routine while there. I then headed over to division headquarters and said goodbyes to Major General Terry A. Wolff, USD–B commander, and Colonel Mark Calvert, USD–B chief of staff. I thanked them both for the opportunity to serve under them and for all their support to our brigade over the past seven months. Finally, I wished them success in the remaining four months they had in theater. After that I met Conley and my crew so we could depart for the short drive to Camp Striker that housed 4-9 IN and would serve as the staging base for the tactical road march south. In order to make this trip even more special, I brought along James and Niess. It was only fitting that they make this historical trip with me since they were truly the nucleus of our nonlethal team and had accompanied me on the majority of operations I had conducted outside the wire. Upon arriving at Camp Striker, the entire 4-9 IN Battalion was lined up in march order, as though we were departing immediately. Every soldier was a bit more giddy and motivated than in the past few weeks. They could actually sense the barn door was opening and that it wouldn't be long before we were in it.

I was met at 4-9 headquarters by Major Steve Phillips, who led me back to Beiger's office. I told him we could leave right now and that it would not break my heart to stay in the country any longer than I had to. We talked for a bit then headed into his conference room for the final patrol brief. The conference room was filled with all the key leaders of the battalion and anyone else who had a major role in facilitating the operation. Major Brian Lionberger, who had replaced Phillips as the operations officer, provided the majority of the brief to the assembled group. The plan he laid out was succinct and straightforward.

We would depart prior to midnight in four separate serials comprised of the four assigned companies. I was in serial two with Charlie Company, which would trail Alpha Company by forty-five minutes. It was a simple mission. Everyone knew the route and alternate routes. The most important take-away was knowing where the medical resources were located in the event (God forbid) we were attacked along the route and needed to get any soldiers to emergency care. Call signs and radio frequencies of supporting and adjacent units also were provided.

The threat that existed all along had not changed. IEDs were still the number one killer of U.S. soldiers on the battlefield. However, their frequency had significantly decreased during the past few months to less than one attack a week on average. In most cases, little damage was done. I felt confident that we would execute this operation without any major incidents.

Another threat or risk in this case was an internal one: driver alertness and awareness. We were traveling in the dead of night and had to ensure that our drivers stayed awake and alert and did not venture off the road into a ditch. To mitigate this risk, we implemented a rest plan. A rest-over day would take place at Camp Adder, approximately three quarters of the way to Kuwait.

The final threat we faced was that of Iraqi civilian traffic. Iraqis are terrible drivers. During the hundreds of patrols that I had participated in in Iraq, local drivers were always weaving in and out of our formation, often causing wrecks that did not end favorably for them. (A crazy phenomena follows wrecks in Iraq. For some reason, the civilian car involved would simply be abandoned, depending on the severity of the damage.)

The final countdown was on. We had eight hours left in Baghdad before we headed south. My only remaining fear was the threat of indirect fire. I certainly did not want to lose anybody at this stage in the game. To eat up the remaining time, a rest plan was instituted to ensure all crewmembers, and especially the drivers, were well rested. I was far too anxious and could not sleep, so James, Niess, and I walked the short distance over to the P/X to purchase a few snacks (better known as "pogey bait") for the trip. Over café lattés, we counted down the hours at a nearby picnic table, talking and sharing a thousand laughs about our experiences.

About an hour away from departure, we walked back to the assembly area and conducted final preparations. Shortly after our arrival there, the first serial, Alpha Company 4-9 IN, departed the staging area headed south. We were next in the order of movement.

I took up my position in the commander's hatch, donned my headset, and made a radio check with my crew. I could sense from the tone of their response they were motivated, more than I had ever witnessed. At approximately 2330 hours on August 14, 2010, we departed out of the south gate of Camp Striker, turning south on MSR Tampa. As the Stryker vehicle exited the gate, I felt elated and satisfied, knowing that we were departing Victory Base for the last time.

My crew was focused and determined as ever, weapons at the ready, and everyone was scanning their assigned sectors. This posture would last the entire trip until we crossed the border. Although this tactical road march was not as dangerous as other patrols we had executed, we were taking nothing for granted. An enemy still existed and would like nothing better than to send us off with an IED blast as a parting shot. I was determined to cross the border with my crew and entire patrol intact. Somehow I knew God was riding shotgun with us.

The first and longest leg of the trip lasted about eight hours until we reached Camp Adder, approximately 200 miles away. Once the last vehicle of Charlie Company, 4-9 IN was on the road, Girouard called over the command net and told the lead element pick up the pace.

Within about thirty minutes, we had reached the outskirts of Baghdad. Off in the distance, I could see the urban sprawl. The best view of Baghdad is at night; somehow the darkness combined with limited lighting disguises the filth and neglect. Seven years ago, the scene was much different. As I entered Baghdad then on the same route I was traveling now, the city was on fire and in ruin. Buildings lay in rubble and were smouldering. U.S. and coalition troops littered the landscape. Tanks and BFVs were visible at every major intersection. Gunfire could be heard in the distance. This time, though, there were no U.S. troops occupying the city.

Iraqi Army and police forces occupied key intersections and checkpoints. Devastated buildings had been removed or renovated. The one thing that remained was the horrible stench. I will never forget nor will I miss the horrible smell of burning refuse and raw sewage.

As our patrol moved at a relatively swift pace, we came upon the Rasheed and Dora districts. Five years ago, the streets of these districts were filled with dead Iraqis, both Sunni and Shiites. The bloodshed could have carved another river through the city. We had fought long and hard to stop the sectarian violence and take back the streets from al-Qaeda and Shiite militias. Today, both Rasheed and Dora were once again relatively peaceful and stable. Children were playing soccer in the streets, markets were thriving, restaurants and coffee shops were packed. Many new retail stores had sprouted up. Stores were filled with plasma televisions, satellites, home appliances, furniture, and tons of cell phones and computers.

This progression was years in the making, enabled by the bloodshed and sacrifices of great soldiers and civilians. Something that looked like freedom and democracy was taking shape in Baghdad. I gave a call over the headset to my crew and told them to look back and say goodbye to Baghdad for the last time, and I thanked them for their service in making this day possible.

As the skyline of Baghdad faded in the distance, we entered Momuadiyah and Yousifiyah, referred to on base as the "fiyas." These towns had seen a lot of intense fighting and bloodshed during the past seven years. The stretch of MSR Tampa we were traveling on was one of the most dangerous in all of Iraq. There had been a countless number of IED attacks over the past seven years, several of which were catastrophic, resulting in the deaths of U.S. soldiers. During previous tours, it was not a matter of if but when one would hit you. During my first tour, more than eighteen IED strikes detonated on or near my vehicle. This time around it was different; while IEDs were still a viable threat, they were not as prevalent. For the first time, soldiers were able to relax and ease their nerves a bit while staying guarded. Even more promising, while heading south away from Baghdad, IED strikes were less likely.

We made it out of the fiyas without incident. From there on out, it was clear sailing. The only real threat was the boredom that set in. That far south of Baghdad, the landscape is nothing but wide-open desert, desolate with nothing to draw your interest. On occasion, we saw a few camels and herds of sheep grazing on dirt and random weeds that somehow grow there. To counter the boredom and keep everyone awake and alert, we told jokes and war stories over the internal communications system. Eventually, the soldiers began to sing songs as if they were auditioning for *American Idol*. In our case, no one would have qualified.

In between the chatter, I received situation reports from Girouard on the status of the route ahead, which had been relayed over his battalion command net from the 4-9 IN Scouts who had departed ahead of us. All reports received were positive. The route was clear, and there were no incidents of IEDs. At the same time, I was monitoring the brigade command net, receiving reports from Voorhies, who was running the command and control node at Victory Base Complex. His reports were consistent with those sent by Girouard. What it boiled down to was that if we could withstand the boredom and the dull landscape, the trip would be a success.

We were about 100 miles in to the trip when the sun began to rise. As if it was not hot enough already (100 degrees Fahrenheit), it would soon worsen. I noticed the vehicles in front of us were slowing down. I glanced down at my map: we had arrived at the preplanned refueling site. This planned refuel operation was the most excitement on the trip. For whatever reason, it was one of the most inefficient operations I had ever been a part of.

When it was briefed back at Camp Striker, the concept and plan seemed succinct. But when it came to execution, it could not have been more of a SNAFU. The plan called for each Stryker vehicle to pull up and straddle a 5,000-gallon fuel tanker, receive a splash of fuel (approximately 15 to 20 gallons), and depart, moving ahead while the rest of the vehicles executed the same drill. It was supposed to work like a NASCAR pit stop. But in reality, the Strykers required much more fuel.

Refueling a company's worth of Strykers was supposed to take less than an hour from start to finish. It seemed reasonable, but it was anything but. By the time we arrived, we had caught up to the lead convoy. They were supposed to have been cleared by the time we got there. Civilian traffic was backed up, too, and in some cases, civilian cars were weaving in and out of our formation. This became the immediate threat.

After all was said and done, we waited on the shoulder of the road for two and a half hours before we received fuel. It took two hours to refuel Charlie Company, 4-9 Infantry. By the time we departed, it was almost 1100. The sun had risen, and it was blistering hot. As we sat there, my crew began to become frustrated, as did I. Finally, I told them to enjoy it: in the larger scheme of life and in our profession, SNAFUs like this occur routinely. More importantly we were leaving Iraq for the last time. What was there to complain about? Nothing.

The last 50 miles of the first leg following the refuel debacle were uneventful. I could see the outline of Camp Adder off to our front in the distance. We finally arrived there at approximately 1400 hours, the entire patrol worn out from the blistering heat.

We consolidated all our Stryker vehicles in a large dirt motor pool, posted guards, and departed for lunch. After a quick lunch, the majority of soldiers bedded down for a few hours.

We were scheduled to depart at 2200 hours. The crew mounted and were standing and chomping at the bit to begin the final leg. I donned my radio headset and gave a radio check to Conley, James, Contreras, and Girouard. We filed out of the motor pool and lined up in March Order. At that point, I received a call over the radio from Girouard telling me that the route ahead was clear; no significant incidents had been reported from the patrol that preceded us. As we exited the gate of Camp Adder, we turned southbound onto MSR Tampa. This was it. The only thing that stood between us and Kuwait was time itself, a boring landscape, and a few herds of camels.

Once the last vehicle exited the gate and turned onto MSR Tampa, Girouard gave the order to pick up the pace. We increased our speed to approximately 45 to 50 miles per hour. At this pace, we would be crossing the border into Kuwait around 0400.

We were out of the danger zone. While IEDs were still a threat, they were very unlikely. Hell, there was nothing out here. It was wide-open desert. There were no villages and very little sign of human life. There certainly was no cover for the enemy to hide. When I made the trip north in April 2003 during the invasion, I traversed this same area. At that time, the road and surrounding desert was littered with destroyed Iraqi tanks, artillery systems, and other armored vehicles. Many of these destroyed vehicles still remained.

After hours of boredom, we arrived at the intersection of MSR Tampa and Route Aspen, which ran due south, a straight shot to Khabari Crossing, the border of Kuwait. We were halfway there. We had 60 miles to go. Soon our journey would come to an end.

Once the last vehicle of our serial turned onto Route Aspen, Girouard made a call over the radio to pick up the pace. Without hesitation, the lead vehicle obliged. Everyone could smell the finish line.

By now it was 0230. Back in Baghdad, the second serial had departed; both 2-1 Cavalry Squadron and 2-12 Field Artillery Battalion were on the road behind us. I hoped and prayed that they would have the same luck and fortune as we did. In the back of my mind, I just knew that the enemy had something planned for us and wanted to send us off with a bang. Based on all reports I was receiving from our headquarters, though, there had been no issues. As we continued on Route Aspen, I received a call that the lead element had crossed the border into Kuwait. We were not far behind. The units that trailed us also were progressing without incident. Everything was going as planned.

The final 60 miles seemed like an eternity. The desert landscape was dark and lonely. There were no signs of life anywhere. At last I could see several amber lights, shining bright as if a beacon to guide us in. I alerted all crewmembers and the passengers who were below sleeping to wake up and take in the last 10 miles of this historic trip. As we drew closer and closer, we could sense that civilization was near. The last 2 miles were an all-out sprint to the finish line. Within a half mile of the border, I could see Kuwaiti and U.S. soldiers manning the gate at Khabari Crossing. It was 0330 on August 16, 2010.

As the lead Stryker approached, the gates were pushed back, creating a gap as if the Red Sea had parted, allowing clear passage into Kuwait. We had made it safely without incident.

As I crossed through the gates, Kuwaiti and U.S. soldiers were waving and cheering. Several cameras and journalists had taken up position to capture our departure from Iraq. Suddenly I got a call over from Girouard over the radio: "Raider 8 welcome to Kuwait. It has been an honor to serve with you."

I replied the same, and over my internal communications net, I thanked my crew for their service and sacrifice. I told them that they had a lot to be thankful for. First and foremost was arriving in Kuwait with everyone intact. Second, that we departed Iraq having accomplished our mission with honor, respect, and dignity. Most of all we gave hope to the Iraqi people. Hope for a better and brighter future.

As we cleared the gate, we followed the vehicles to our front and pulled off the main road into a designated staging area. We were required to stop and consolidate all of our ammunition for turn in and to account for all our sensitive items and equipment before moving on to our final destination at Camp Virginia. As my Stryker came to a halt, the ramp was lowered and we dismounted the vehicle. As I stepped onto the ground, I hugged Conley, Niess, James, and my interpreter Johnny, congratulating them for their efforts in making this day possible. It was truly an emotional event.

As I looked around, soldiers were giving each other high fives and shouting, "We made it!" at the top of their lungs. Journalists were scattered throughout the formation trying to capture on camera the perfect images of this historical event. After shaking hands with my crew and other soldiers, I removed my body armor and lit a Cuban cigar I had saved for this special moment. It was the finest cigar I had ever smoked. The only thing missing was a glass of fine cognac. That would have to wait until my return home.

All around me, soldiers continued to celebrate. Many of them were posing for pictures, proudly displaying the U.S. flag. Camera flashes were going off as if we were at a rock concert. Why not? After all, these soldiers deserved to celebrate. They were all rock stars in their own right.

After taking several pictures with my crew, I walked down the line of vehicles, shaking every soldier's hand that I came in contact with, thanking them for their service. Finally, I met up with Girouard. We shook hands and embraced for a quick hug, and I thanked him for his service and all that he had done for me while at Fort Polk and while deployed in theater. It was a surreal moment that captured the essence of what we do as soldiers, leaders, and warriors. As I walked the entire formation, soldiers were being called aside by journalists to give interviews. It was an incredible moment to witness the instant relief and jubilation displayed by these deserving heroes. I was simply proud to have been along for the ride.

It was almost seven years and five months to the date from when I first walked the line at Camp New Jersey prior to my crossing into Iraq for the first time. I remembered it like it was yesterday. Soldiers were nervous—not afraid, but apprehensive about fear of the unknown dangers that lurked beyond the border in Iraq. Many of them, including me, wondered if we would survive and make it home alive. The majority of us had never seen combat. All we had to rely on was our faith and trust in our leaders, our training, and our equipment. The rest would take care of itself.

Seven years and five months later, here I stood on Kuwaiti soil, celebrating as a member of the final combat brigade to have departed Iraq. So many thoughts were racing through my mind that it brought me to the brink of mental exhaustion. I was running on fumes. What once filled my heart with anxiety, stress, and fear of the unknown had been replaced by jubilation, relief, satisfaction, and an overwhelming sense of accomplishment. It was a proud day for me and for all of us. I was just glad it was over.

Niess described it best:

> "After spending a year in Iraq focused on partnership with the Iraqi Army and using Non-Lethal strategies to build the economy and medical infrastructure of the Abu Ghraib province, it was very moving to be part of the Last Patrol and safely arrive in Kuwait. There was a sense of calm, that the full circle of combat operations and re-building from the US Forces has been complete, and now we peacefully leave as the Iraqi people take ownership of their country and work towards a more positive future."

I had seen all sides of this war up close: the good, the bad, and the ugly. As part of the initial wave, we were celebrated and greeted as liberators. In the waning months, we were hated and scorned as occupiers. In the midst of a bloody civil war, we stood strong, focusing our efforts and resources on protecting the population. The surge and the implementation of the new COIN doctrine allowed us to quell sectarian violence and defeat the majority of extremists, both Sunni and Shiite. This success bought us space and time to allow us to focus on training and building capacity for the ISF while we used nonlethal resources to execute nation building.

Through these efforts we rebuilt local markets, restored critical essential services, and reinvigorated an agriculture industry that was left for dead. Finally, we facilitated a successful national election that witnessed record voter turnout of more than 62 percent despite the fear of attacks and intimidation from extremists. The success of these elections was made possible by a trained, capable, and determined ISF, which executed an impenetrable security plan that withstood all enemy attempts to breach it. The skill and competence displayed by the ISF, coupled with the security and civil capacity gains, signaled that the combat mission in Iraq was over.

Through years of trial and tribulation, we had preserved. All the hard work, bloodshed, and sacrifice came at a steep cost. More than $800 billion of taxpayer money was spent to fund this war. The war also cost much in life: more than 4,400 U.S. soldiers and civilian lives and an even greater number of men and women wounded in action. Ultimately the mission was accomplished and the desired end state achieved. Conditions had been established for irreversible momentum. Iraq's fate now rests in the hands of Iraqis, who will have to take ownership and responsibility in order to chart their destiny.

In the words of Norris during his address to the brigade while assembled in Kuwait: "We depart Iraq having accomplished our mission, with honor, respect, our legacy, and our reputation intact."

Iraq had come full circle.

EPILOGUE

❝ Let every nation know, whether it wishes us well or ill, that we shall pay any price, bear any burden, meet any hardship, support any friend, oppose any foe to assure the survival and the success of liberty. ❞

John F. Kennedy

As I move into the twilight of my career as a soldier, I am compelled to review all that has happened during the past twenty years. I have used this book to examine some of the milestones and make sense out of the disorder of the ground combat that has occurred over the past eight years in Iraq.

War on any scale was never a consideration when I was commissioned in 1988 and even after the First Gulf War. The thought of war was not even a distant consideration in 1991 when I entered active duty. Prior to my commissioning, I had enlisted in the Texas Army National Guard in 1985. During that timeframe, we were engaged in the arms race with the former Soviet Union during the Cold War. Every training exercise focused on defeating the Russian horde at the Fulda Gap. The most historical event of this period was the tearing down of the Berlin Wall in 1989, allowing for German reunification. Essentially, when the wall came down, the world changed. Our immediate adversary no longer posed the significant threat that it had since the end of World War II.

From 1988 to 2000, the Army continued to focus its tactics and preparation on large-scale conventional wars and small-scale contingency operations such as Grenada and the invasion of Panama. The only major war to be fought during this period was Desert Storm, when coalition forces ousted Saddam and the Iraqi Army out of Kuwait. If anything, though, that war did more to create a false reality about the future of warfare and the eventual enemies that threatened America and our allies. In September 2001, reality hit home, and the world we lived in changed overnight. What I remember most is the courage and bravery of the first responders, specifically the firemen from New York City Fire Department, Battalion 11, led by their commander, Richard Picciotto, who rushed to the aid of their fellow men. These brave and courageous men ascended smoke-filled staircases without hesitation or even the thought that their life could end minutes later.

Following the aftermath, I remember the national unity and pride that was displayed by the American public. For a moment, this country set politics and everyday worries aside, uniting behind a cause that would ultimately exact justice in the rugged mountains of Afghanistan and the blistering desert sands of Iraq. It was in Iraq that I discovered the same fighting spirit, bravery, and courage displayed by soldiers who were mirroring the spirit of the first responders that tragic day. I was there in the very beginning and watched as the invasion of Iraq unfolded. Soon after, I made the advance north out of Kuwait into Iraq and traveled as far north as Kirkuk. I witnessed Iraqi citizens greeting us as liberators and heroes. During the postinvasion period, I witnessed the war shift in monumental proportions as the insurgency gained momentum and the population turned against us.

No longer were we liberators. Instead we were reviled as occupiers. During my first deployment, I saw the best that America has to offer in taking the fight to the enemy. The likes of Bolyard, who always led his men into harm's way, put himself up front in the "fatal funnel," never once thinking of himself. It was leadership by example in the truest sense of the slogan.

I also witnessed the brave and courageous feats of Specialist Jason Testa, who dodged numerous IED attacks, rocket propelled grenade attacks, and other direct-fire ambushes while driving an unarmored Humvee with no doors.

Never once did these soldiers complain or seek an easier path. They were always beside me on every mission.

Then there was Captain Eric Paliwoda, the "Gentle Giant," an engineer by trade but an infantryman at heart. He and his company alone cleared countless kilometers of dangerous roads and trails throughout Balad and Albu Hishma of mines and IEDs, ensuring freedom of maneuver for our troops. In a lot of cases, these engineer soldiers did it by walking the shoulders of roads with mine detectors in austere conditions while the threat of snipers loomed large. Daily temperatures often exceeded 120 degrees Fahrenheit. Never once did these soldiers complain or shun the danger.

I spoke some of the last words ever said to Paliwoda before he was killed in action on January 2, 2004. Since that tragic day, I wear a bracelet engraved with his name to honor and remember my comrade and friend. This bracelet has served as inspiration for two subsequent tours and will never be removed until I link-up with him and my fellow warriors in heaven.

During subsequent tours, I watched as the war changed again with the rise of sectarian violence that brought the country to the brink of civil war. Soon after, the surge would follow. During my final trip, I witnessed the Iraqi Army come of age. Furthermore, I also witnessed a country rebuild from the ground up and conduct historic national elections.

Finally it ended where it all began for me, as I took the same route out of Iraq that I entered the country some seven years earlier. At that point, the war had come full circle, for me and a lot of others.

During these tours, I was fortunate enough to have spent time with extraordinary young men and women, America's treasure, who braved the elements and danger all to make Iraq a better place than when they found it. Because of them, and thousands of others, Iraq is truly a free and sovereign nation with an opportunity for a better and more prosperous future (see Appendix A).

Only those who have served in the gravest of conditions can know what I am talking about. The American soldier is the currency of diplomacy. No single group of Americans understands the cost of vital national interests like a soldier does. We all swore an oath to uphold and defend the Constitution and obey the orders of the president. When ordered to do so, we sally forth to do battle with the enemies of the state.

As I complete these final thoughts, it is only fitting and somewhat ironic that our mission in Iraq ended with the final 4,500 troops departing Iraq on December 18, 2011, bringing an official end to Operation New Dawn and closing the door on our military involvement in Iraq.

As our military mission has ended, we depart with our heads held high, knowing we changed those things that we could and that we defeated the enemy that opposed us. The only regret I have was that we could not narrow the gap of sectarian divide, which would have been virtually impossible. That is a daunting task that Iraqis will have to overcome. I fear that the new free Iraq will crumble under the weight of the people who populate it. There will be continued trouble and violence as extremists seek to derail democracy. These same struggles occurred in our country after we defeated the British Army and forced them out so our democracy could take shape. But Americans were united to the cause of forming a union. This same will exists among the Iraqi people. I have seen it up close in their eyes, particularly in the eyes of children. It is time for Iraq to seize the moment, put aside sectarian issues, and form a government that is balanced and representative of all Iraq. A national identity must be established for this to occur. Someone like Thomas Jefferson with a vision of the future must emerge from the ancient desert sands to chart their destiny and lead them forward to capitalize on their potential. The foundation exists, but the will of the people must step forward in order to triumph. If not, the circle will be broken.

Even as we speak Iraq remains a volatile place, suicide bombings occur daily at an alarming rate. This violence will continue until the Iraqi government and Iraqi Security Forces answer the call and put an end to it as they are trained, equipped, and more than capable of doing so. The framework for peace and stability was established by the American soldier who spent the last eight years forging a free nation from the rubble left by an oppressive despot and his Ba'athist regime.

For the foreseeable future, Iran will shape events in the region unless they are dealt with accordingly. America must be hesitant and calculate its drawdown and reorganization of its armed forces to ensure we have the combat power to respond decisively. Diplomacy must be the national tool of choice, but the U.S. must be prepared for a military solution as a last resort. If and when this option is exercised it will once again require the sum of America's military might.

Given the geographical location, lessons learned, and scope of our withdrawal, the next event will not be exclusively high-technology-centric but again will require boots on the ground to ensure victory.

I look forward to the next several years and hope they do not include another wartime deployment to Iraq. I say this not because I will not be ready but because it would mean that Iraq had failed and all our efforts and sacrifice to this date would have been in vain. We sacrificed far too much in the bloodshed of great Americans for our efforts to be viewed as anything other than heroic and triumphant.

I look forward to the U.S. Army as an institution healing itself and opening up the aperture on training by ensuring that we are proficient across the full spectrum on conflict. I hope that we take and apply the lessons learned from the past, right or wrong, good or bad. This will only make us stronger in our next battle. I pray that our wounded warriors heal and get the resources and treatment they deserve for all that they gave us. Finally, I hope during this period of economic uncertainty that we make a strong defense our nation's priority commitment. We cannot be weak in the face of our adversaries. If we cut or hollow out our military as we have in years past, it will be at great risk to our national security. Likewise if we fail to take care of our veterans, current soldiers, and their families, we should be ashamed of ourselves. They represent less than 1 percent of the population and deserve everything they get and more. It was said by Calvin Coolidge that "a nation that forgets its defenders will itself be forgotten." May we never forget those past and present who answered the call to defend us and provide the blanket of freedom we sleep under every night.

My time as a warrior is ending. The sun is setting on a career full of experiences that could only be summarized by one word: phenomenal. I am forever indebted to all those with whom I have served for or alongside. They truly made me the officer and person I am today. I, too, have stood on the shoulders of giants. Any credit or accolades due are theirs and theirs alone. We are and forever will be a band of brothers and sisters.

Finally, I am blessed to have the love and untiring support of a great wife and family. They are my rock and have remained grounded ensuring the home front was secured throughout my service to our nation.

As a colonel, I will transition to more staff jobs and plan for the next phase of my life. After retirement, I want to serve as a teacher and a coach to give back what was given to me. As I lay down my rucksack for the last time, I look forward to supporting my lovely wife Wendy as she continues her military career. I look forward to watching my son Dillon graduate from college and pursue an Army career as he has chose to follow in my footsteps. I look forward to seeing my precious daughter Chloe graduate high school and pursue her career dreams. I pray that I have taught them well through years of personal example. Also, I will have time to spend with my youngest son Kyle, teaching him the values of integrity, service, sacrifice, and honor much like I taught his brother and sister. That's all I can do: ensure that he never takes for granted one breath of precious freedom that so many have fought and died to preserve.

APPENDIX A
HEROES

Let it be known that the following men and women are heroes of Operation Iraqi Freedom. Soldiers (representing less than 1 percent of the U.S. population) stepped up to the challenge and took the oath to defend our great nation against enemies who sought to do us harm. These men and women are warriors whose determination, steadfast loyalty, bravery, and sacrifices brought freedom and hope to a country that knew only tyranny and oppression. Never once did these soldiers complain or seek an easier path. While this list is not all-inclusive, it is representative of all soldiers and civilians who served in Iraq for a cause bigger than themselves. They are the best that America has to offer. While they will never admit to it, nor accept it, the credit due is theirs. I am honored and humbled to have had the opportunity to lead and serve alongside of them.

Operation Iraqi Freedom 01–02, (2003–04)

SPC Jason Testa, HHC 1-8 Infantry Battalion
SPC Matthew Francis, HHC 1-8 Infantry Battalion
SPC Jonathan Brown, HHC 1-8 Infantry Battalion
SSG Cory Blackwell, HHC 1-8 and Bravo Company 1-8 Infantry Battalion
SSG Tim Bolyard, Scout Platoon Sergeant, HHC 1-8 Infantry Battalion
SSG Dale Panchot, Bravo Company 1-8 Infantry Battalion (KIA, November 17, 2003)
1SG Daniel Dailey, HHC 1-8 Infantry Battalion
1LT Patrick Bradley, Chemical Officer and ICDC coordinator, HHC 1-8 Infantry Battalion

CPT Jonathan Harvey, Adjutant, HHC, 1-8 Infantry Battalion

CPT Todd Brown, Commander, Bravo Company "War Machine,"
1-8 Infantry Battalion

CPT Eric Paliwoda, "Beast 6," Commander, Bravo Company
4th Engineer Battalion better known as Delta Company
1-8 Infantry Battalion (KIA, January 2, 2004)

CPT Matt Cunningham, Commander, Alpha Company, "Attack"
1-8 Infantry Battalion

CPT Kevin Ryan, Commander, HHC 1-8 Infantry Battalion

CPT Alex Williams, Intelligence Officer, (S-2), HHC 1-8 Infantry
Battalion

CPT Frank Blake, Signal Officer, (S-6), HHC 1-8 Infantry
Battalion

CPT Gregory Ralls, Assistant Operations Officer,
HHC 1-8 Infantry Battalion

CPT Timothy Knoth, Assistant Operations Officer,
HHC 1-8 Infantry Battalion

MAJ Rob Gwinner, Battalion Executive Officer (XO),
HHC 1-8 Infantry Battalion

LTC Nate Sassaman, Commander 1-8 Infantry Battalion

Operation Iraqi Freedom 05–07 (2006–07)

1SG Robert Leimer, HHC 4th Brigade, 4th Infantry Division

SGM Michael Bennett, Brigade Operations SGM,
HHC 4th Brigade/4th Infantry Division

SGM Charles Geiswite, Brigade Operations SGM,
HHC 4th Brigade/4th Infantry Division

CSM John Moody, Brigade CSM, HHC 4th Brigade/4th Infantry
Division

CPT Bobby Ball, HHC 4th Brigade/4th Infantry Division

CPT Will Horton, Brigade Chaplain, HHC 4th Brigade/4th Infantry
Division

MAJ Paul Taylor, Assistant Operations Officer,
4th Brigade/4th Infantry Division

MAJ Scott Coulson, Brigade Plans Officer, HHC
4th Brigade/4th Infantry Division

MAJ Rick Applehans, Brigade Intelligence Officer,
HHC 4th Brigade/4th Infantry Division

MAJ Gary Martin, Support Operations Officer (SPO),
 HHC 704th Brigade Support Battalion
MAJ Mark Cheadle, Brigade Public Affairs Officer,
 HHC 4th Brigade/4th Infantry Division
LTC Troy Smith, Brigade Deputy Commanding Officer,
 HHC 4th Brigade/4th Infantry Division
LTC Rick Morales, Brigade Operations Officer, (S-3),
 HHC 4th Brigade/4th Infantry Division
COL Mike Beech, Commander, 4th Brigade/4th Infantry Division

1st Battalion (Airborne), 509th Infantry Regiment, JRTC, Fort Polk, Louisiana, 2007–09

PFC Bobby "Koelsch," HHC, 1-509th Infantry
SGT Jose Pilot, Bravo Company, 1-509th Infantry

Operation Iraqi Freedom 09–10, 2009–10

PFC Denisha Gilmore, Military Police Platoon, HHC,
 4th Stryker Brigade, 2nd Infantry Division
PFC Andrew Toppin, Military Police Platoon, HHC,
 4th Stryker Brigade, 2nd Infantry Division
PFC Chris Terrell, Military Police Platoon, HHC,
 4th Stryker Brigade, 2nd Infantry Division
PFC Tiffany Austin, Military Police Platoon, HHC,
 4th Stryker Brigade, 2nd Infantry Division
SGT Ian Ralston, Medic, 2nd Battalion, 23rd Infantry
 Regiment
SSG Marc Eltringham, Military Police Platoon, HHC,
 4th Stryker Brigade, 2nd Infantry Division
SGT Martin Contreras, Military Police Team Leader, HHC,
 4th Stryker Brigade, 2nd Infantry Division
SFC Jonathon Wagner, Scouts, HHC, 4th Stryker Brigade,
 2nd Infantry Division
SSG Eric Brew, HHC, 4th Stryker Brigade, 2nd Infantry Division
SFC Virgil Valentine, HHC, 4th Stryker Brigade, 2nd Infantry
 Division

1LT Ryan Grace, Key Leader Engagement Coordinator, HHC, 4th Stryker Brigade, 2nd Infantry Division

CPT Caitlin Conley, Military Police Platoon Leader, HHC 4th Stryker Brigade, 2nd Infantry Division

CPT Gabi Niess, Brigade Non-lethal Planner, HHC 4th Stryker Brigade, 2nd Infantry Division

CPT Talgin Cannon, Assistant Joint Projects Management Officer, HHC, 4th Stryker Brigade, 2nd Infantry Division

CPT Clarke Brown, Brigade Operations Planner, HHC 4th Stryker Brigade Combat Team, 2nd Infantry Division

CPT Guy Girouard, Brigade Operations Officer and Commander, Charlie Company, 4th Battalion, 9th Infantry Regiment

CPT Josh Betty, Commander, Charlie Company, 1st Battalion, 38th Infantry Regiment, and Commander, HHC, 4th Stryker Brigade, 2nd Infantry Division

CPT Christopher Ophardt, Brigade Public Affairs Officer, HHC, 4th Stryker Brigade, 2nd Infantry Division

CPT Brian Forester, Brigade Operations Planner, HHC, 4th Stryker Brigade, 2nd Infantry Division

CPT Denny Dresch, Brigade Operations Planner, HHC, 4th Stryker Brigade, 2nd Infantry Division

CPT Keith Roberts, Commander, Alpha Company, 4th Battalion, 9th Infantry Regiment and Brigade Operations Officer, HHC, 4th Stryker Brigade, 2nd Infantry Division

CPT Kevin Molloy, Brigade Operations Officer, HHC, 4th Stryker Brigade, 2nd Infantry Division

CPT Reed Markham, Brigade Operations Officer, HHC, 4th Stryker Brigade, 2nd Infantry Division

CPT Luke Calvert, Brigade Operations Officer, HHC, 4th Stryker Brigade, 2nd Infantry Division

CPT Corbett Baxter, Brigade Comptroller, HHC, 4th Stryker Brigade, 2nd Infantry Division

CPT John Olson, Brigade Legal Team, HHC, 4th Stryker Brigade, 2nd Infantry Division

CPT Chris Blaha, Commander, HHC, 4th Stryker Brigade, 2nd Infantry Division

CPT Cynthia Ling, HHC, 4th Stryker Brigade, 2nd Infantry Division

CW3 Wayne Grimes, aviation airspace manager, HHC, 4th Stryker Brigade, 2nd Infantry Division

CW3 Gus McKinney, Brigade Intelligence Specialist, HHC,
 4th Stryker Brigade, 2nd Infantry Division
MAJ Sam Fiol, Brigade Intelligence Officer, (S-2), HHC, 4th Stryker
 Brigade, 2nd Infantry Division
MAJ Dave Voorhies, Brigade Executive Officer (XO), HHC,
 4th Stryker Brigade, 2nd Infantry Division
MAJ Jarett Broemmel, Brigade Operations Officer, HHC, 4th Stryker
 Brigade, 2nd Infantry Division
MAJ Patrick Hemmer, Joint Projects Management Officer (JPMO),
 HHC, 4th Stryker Brigade, 2nd Infantry Division
MAJ Mike Harding, Brigade Engineer, HHC, 4th Stryker Brigade,
 2nd Infantry Division
MAJ Kevin James, Brigade Information Operations Officer, (S-7),
 HHC 4th Stryker Brigade, 2nd Infantry Division
MAJ Tony New, Operations Officer, (S-3), 4-9 Infantry and Brigade
 Operations Officer, HHC, 4th Stryker Brigade, 2nd Infantry
 Division
MAJ Eric Stafford, Brigade Staff Judge Advocate, HHC, 4th Stryker
 Brigade, 2nd Infantry Division
SGM Brian Hollis, Brigade Operations SGM, HHC 4th Stryker
 Brigade, 2nd Infantry Division
CSM Jeff Huggins, CSM, 4th Stryker Brigade, 2nd Infantry Division
COL John Norris, Commander, 4th Stryker Brigade, 2nd Infantry
 Division

Civilians

Farouk
Johnny Albazi
Amro Shadi

APPENDIX B
RULES OF ENGAGEMENT
(ROE)
March 2003

Coalition Forces Land Component Command (CFLCC) Rules of Engagement, (ROE) issued to Soldiers prior to invasion of Iraq in March 2003.

CFLCC Rules for Use of Force
Nothing in these rules limits your inherent authority and obligation to take all necessary and appropriate action to defend yourself, your unit, and others US Forces

1. **HOSTILE FORCES:** NO forces have been declared hostile.

2. **HOSTILE ACTORS:** You may engage persons who commit hostile intent with the minimum force necessary to counter the hostile act or demonstrated hostile intent and to protect US Forces.

   Hostile act: An attack or other use of force against US Forces or a use of force that directly precludes /impedes the mission/duties of US Forces.

   Hostile intent: The threat of imminent use of force against US Forces or the threat of force to preclude/impede the mission/ duties of US Forces.

3. You may use force, up to and including deadly force, against hostile actors:
   a. In self defense;

   b. In defense of your unit, or other US Forces;

   c. To prevent the theft, damage, or destruction of firearms, ammunition, explosives, or property designated by your Commander as vital to national security. (Protect other property with less than deadly force).

4. **ESCALATION OF FORCE:** When possible, use the following degrees of force against hostile actors:

   a. SHOUT; verbal warnings to HALT or "QIF" (pronounced "COUGH")

   b. SHOVE; physically restrain, block access, or detain

   c. SHOW; your weapon and demonstrate intent to use it

   d. SHOOT; to remove the threat of death/serious bodily injury or to protect designated property. IF YOU MUST FIRE:

      1. Fire only aimed shots. NO WARNING SHOTS

      2. Fire no more rounds than necessary

      3. Fire with due regard for the safety of innocent bystanders

      4. Take reasonable efforts not to destroy property

      5. Stop firing as soon as the situation permits

5. **CROWDS:** Control civilian crowds, mobs, or rioters interfering with US Forces with the minimum necessary force. When circumstances permit, attempt the following steps to control crowds:

   a. Repeated warnings to HALT or "QIF" (pronounced "COUGH")

   b. Show of force, including riot control formation

   c. Blocking of access, or other reasonable use of force necessary under the circumstances and proportional to the threat

6. **DETAINEES:** You must stop, detain, search, and disarm persons as required to protect US Forces. Detainees will be turned over to the Military Police or Kuwait Police ASAP.

7. **Treat all persons with respect and dignity.**

APPENDIX C
MILITARY DECISION MAKING PROCESS (MDMP)
FM 101-5, Chapter 5

Decision making is knowing *if* to decide, then *when* and *what* to decide. It includes understanding the consequence of decisions. Decisions are the means by which the commander translates his vision of the end state into action. Decision making is both science and art. Many aspects of military operations—movement rates, fuel consumption, weapons effects—are quantifiable and, therefore, part of the *science* of war. Other aspects—the impact of leadership, complexity of operations, and uncertainty regarding enemy intentions—belong to the *art* of war. The military decision-making process (MDMP) is a single, established, and proven analytical process. The MDMP is an adaptation of the Army's analytical approach to problem solving. The MDMP is a tool that assists the commander and staff in developing estimates and a plan. While the formal problem-solving process described in this chapter may start with the receipt of a mission, and has as its goal the production of an order, the analytical aspects of the MDMP continue at all levels during operations. The MDMP helps the commander and his staff examine a battlefield situation and reach logical decisions. The process helps them apply thoroughness, clarity, sound judgment, logic, and professional knowledge to reach a decision. The full MDMP is a detailed, deliberate, sequential, and time-consuming process used when adequate planning time and sufficient staff support are available to thoroughly examine numerous friendly and enemy courses of action (COAs). This typically occurs when developing the commander's estimate and operation plans (OPLANs), when planning for an entirely new mission, during extended operations, and during staff training designed specifically to teach the MDMP. The MDMP is the foundation on which planning in a time-constrained environment is based. The products created during the full MDMP can and should be used during subsequent planning sessions when time may not be available for a thorough relook, but where existing METT-T factors have not changed substantially.

APPENDIX D
1-8 INFANTRY (M)
Task Organization, April 2003–March 2004

A/1-8 IN	**Task Force Control**
1/A/1-8 IN	Scouts/HHC/1-8 IN (4 × sections)
2/A/1-8 IN	Mortars/HHC/1-8 IN (3 × 120mm)
3/A/1-8 IN	Maintenance Platoon/HHC/1-8 IN
	Medical Platoon/HHC/1-8 IN
B/1-8 IN	Support Platoon/HHC/1-8 IN
1/B/1-8 IN	Tactical Psyop Team 1684 TPD/362 TCP
1/B/1-8 IN	Communications Team G22/124th SIG BN
3/B/1-8 IN	A/TM 9/443 Civil Affairs BN
	B/TM 7/443 Civil Affairs BN
C/1-8 IN	Ambulance Company/Treatment Squad/C/64th FSB
1/C/1-8 IN	
2/C/1-8 IN	
3/C/1-8 IN	

Total Personnel in Task Force: approximately 925

B/4th ENG
1/B/4th ENG
2/B/4th ENG

APPENDIX E

4TH BRIGADE/4TH INFANTRY DIVISION

Task Organization from OIF 05-07 from November 2005 to October 2006

Headquarters & Headquarters Company (HHC): includes all key Brigade Staff elements, Command Group, and admin sections.

1st Battalion – 12 Infantry Regiment: (Mechanized Infantry Battalion made up of 5 × Companies, broken down into an HHC, 2 × Mechanized Infantry Companies and 2 × Armor Companies that are M1A1 Tanks and M2A3 Bradley Fighting Vehicle equipped)

8th Squadron – 10th Cavalry Regiment: (Mechanized Cavalry Squadron with 4 × Troops, broken down into an HHC and 3 × Cavalry Troops that are M2A3 Bradley Fighting Vehicle and HMMWV equipped)

2nd Battalion – 77th Field Artillery Regiment: (Field Artillery Battalion made up of 3 × Batteries broken down into a Headquarters and Service Battery and 2 × Firing Batteries that are 155mm Self Propelled Howitzer equipped)

4th Special Troops Battalion: (included all slice elements listed below)

    Signal Company

    Military Intelligence Company

    Military Police Platoon

    Chemical Recon Platoon

704th Support Battalion: (Logistics Battalion that includes all Classes of Supply/Services and Maintenance assets including the 3 companies listed below)

Transportation/Supply/Fuel Company
>   Maintenance Company
>   Medical Company

Attached (units that were not organic to 4th Brigade/4th Infantry Division)

2nd Battalion – 506th Airborne Infantry Regiment: (Light Infantry cross attached from 101st Airborne Division broken down into 4 × Companies consisting of an HHC, and 3 × Rifle Companies)

1st Battalion – 26th Infantry Regiment: (Mechanized Infantry Battalion cross attached from 1st Armored Division, Germany made up of 4 × Companies consisting of an HHC and 3 × Rifle Companies)

425th Civil Affairs Company

US Navy Explosives Ordnance Disposal (Platoon equivalent)

615th Military Police Company

21st Military Police Company

C/1-147 Military Police Company

441st Tactical Human Intelligence Teams (x 3 teams)

1440th Tactical Psychological Operations (PSYOPS) Team

US Air Force – 11th ASOS: Tactical Air Control Party (Provided Close Air Support communications/targeting)

21st Georgian Infantry Battalion: (provided interior Green Zone/International Zone Security)

5 × K9 US Army Military Working Dog Teams

Host Nation Forces (partnered Iraqi Army Forces)

5th Brigade – 6th Iraqi Army Division

Note: Total count of personnel assigned was more than 5,000 U.S. soldiers; when combined with nonorganic units and host nation forces, the total was more than 8,000.

4TH STRYKER BRIGADE COMBAT TEAM/ 2ND INFANTRY DIVISION (4-2 SBCT)

(Task Organization for OIF 09-10 from September 2009 to August 2010)

1st Battalion – 38th Infantry Regiment: (Stryker equipped Battalion with 4 × Companies consisting of an HHC and 3 × Stryker Companies)

4th Battalion – 9th Infantry Regiment: (Stryker equipped Battalion with 4 × Companies consisting of an HHC and 3 × Stryker Companies)

2nd Battalion – 23rd Infantry Regiment: (Stryker equipped Battalion with 4 × Companies consisting of an HHC and 3 × Stryker Companies)

2nd Squadron – 1st Cavalry Regiment: (Stryker equipped Squadron with 4 × Troops consisting of an Headquarters and Headquarters Troop and 3 × Stryker Cavalry Troops)

2nd Battalion – 12th Field Artillery Regiment: (A Field Artillery Battalion with 4 × Batteries consisting of an Headquarters and Headquarters Battery, and 3 × firing Batteries equipped with 155mm towed Howitzers)

702nd Brigade Support Battalion: (A logistics support battalion that provides all Classes of Supply/Services including transportation, ammunition, maintenance and medical support. The Battalion is made up of 4 × companies as listed below)

> Headquarters and Headquarters Company
> Alpha Company (Transportation Company)
> Bravo Company (Maintenance Company)
> Charlie Company (Medical Company)

Separate Companies: (often referred to as enablers that are typically found in a Special Troops Battalion, within the Stryker Brigade these companies are assigned to each of the Stryker Battalions to provide Training, Readiness and Administration [TRA] oversight for). The 5 separate companies are:

> Headquarters and Headquarters Company (HHC) (includes all key Brigade Staff elements, Command Group, and admin sections)
>
> 45th Military Intelligence Company
>
> 38th Engineer Company
>
> 472nd Signal Company
>
> Fox/52 Anti-Tank Company: (equipped with Anti-Tank Guided Missile Vehicle)

Attached Units not organic to 4-2 SBCT (units were attached to 4-2 SBCT but were not organically assigned as permanent units to the Brigade)

U.S. Air Force Joint Tactical Air Control Team (coordinates close air support/targeting)

U.S. Air Force Tactical Control Party (coordinates close air support/targeting)

2 × Department of States embedded Provincial Reconstruction Teams (ePRTs):

> ePRT (West)
>
> ePRT (North)

Bravo Company 422nd Civil Affairs Company

2 × Combat Camera Detachment

6 × Human Intelligence Collection Teams (assigned 1 × per Stryker Battalion)

1 × Human Terrain Team

1 × Law Enforcement Training Team

3 × U.S. Army Military Working Dog Teams

8 × Military Training Teams (MiTTs) (1 × MiTT Team assigned to every Iraqi Army Brigade that we were partnered with as listed below)

> 6th Iraqi Army (IA) Division MiTT
>
> 24th Brigade/6th IA Division MiTT
>
> 22nd Brigade/6th IA Division MiTT
>
> 54th Brigade/6th IA Division MiTT
>
> 36th Brigade/9th IA Division MiTT
>
> 37th Brigade/9th IA Division MiTT
>
> 9th Iraqi Army Logistics MiTT
>
> 9th Iraqi Army TAC MiTT

1 × Federal Police Training Team (FPTT)

> 6-2 FPTT

1 × Counter-Intelligence (CI) Team

Host Nation Forces (partnered Iraqi Security Forces, includes Iraqi Army, Iraq Police, and Federal Police Forces)

6th Iraqi Army Division

> 22nd Brigade/6th Iraqi Army Division
>
> 24th Brigade/6th Iraqi Army Division
>
> 54th Brigade/6th Iraqi Army Division

9th Iraqi Army Division
>   9th Iraqi Army Division TAC

36 Brigade/9th Iraqi Army Division
>   37th Brigade/9th Iraqi Army Division

Iraqi Police (7 × local district Police Departments)
>   Abu Ghraib Police
>
>   Mansour Police
>
>   Khadra Police
>
>   Khadamiyah Police
>
>   Salhiya Police
>
>   Tajo Police
>
>   Tarmiyah Police

Federal Police
>   6-2 Federal Police (made up of 3 × Battalions, 1st through 3rd Battalions)

Note: Total combined strength of 4-2 SBCT organic assets was in excess of 5,000 soldiers. When combined with other direct support units and our Iraqi Partners, the combined strength totaled more than 10,000 soldiers and civilians.

APPENDIX G
IRAQI SECURITY AGREEMENT

Agreement
Between the United States of America and the Republic of Iraq
On the Withdrawal of United States Forces from Iraq and the
Organization of Their Activities during Their Temporary
Presence in Iraq

Preamble

The United States of America and the Republic of Iraq, referred to hereafter as "the Parties":

Recognizing the importance of: strengthening their joint security, contributing to world peace and stability, combating terrorism in Iraq, and cooperating in the security and defense spheres, thereby deterring aggression and threats against the sovereignty, security, and territorial integrity of Iraq and against its democratic, federal, and constitutional system;

Affirming that such cooperation is based on full respect for the sovereignty of each of them in accordance with the purposes and principles of the United Nations Charter; Out of a desire to reach a common understanding that strengthens cooperation between them;

Without prejudice to Iraqi sovereignty over its territory, waters, and airspace; and Pursuant to joint undertakings as two sovereign, independent, and coequal countries;

Have agreed to the following:

Article 1: Scope and Purpose

This Agreement shall determine the principal provisions and requirements that regulate the temporary presence, activities, and withdrawal of the United States Forces from Iraq.

Article 2

Definition of Terms

1. "Agreed facilities and areas" are those Iraqi facilities and areas owned by the Government of Iraq that are in use by the United States Forces during the period in which this Agreement is in force.
2. "United States Forces" means the entity comprising the members of the United States Armed Forces, their associated civilian component, and all property, equipment, and materiel of the United States Armed Forces present in the territory of Iraq.
3. "Member of the United States Forces" means any individual who is a member of the United States Army, Navy, Air Force, Marine Corps, or Coast Guard.
4. "Member of the civilian component" means any civilian employed by the United States Department of Defense. This term does not include individuals normally resident in Iraq.
5. "United States contractors" and "United States contractor employees" mean non-Iraqi persons or legal entities, and their employees, who are citizens of the United States or a third country and who are in Iraq to supply goods, services, and security in Iraq to or on behalf of the United States Forces under a contract or subcontract with or for the United States Forces. However, the terms do not include persons or legal entities normally resident in the territory of Iraq.
6. "Official vehicles" means commercial vehicles that may be modified for security purposes and are basically designed for movement on various roads and designated for transportation of personnel.
7. "Military vehicles" means all types of vehicles used by the United States Forces, which were originally designated for use in combat operations and display special distinguishing numbers and symbols according to applicable United States Forces instructions and regulations.
8. "Defense equipment" means systems, weapons, supplies, equipment, munitions, and materials exclusively used in conventional warfare that are required by the United States Forces in connection with agreed activities under this Agreement and are not related, either

directly or indirectly, to systems of weapons of mass destruction (chemical weapons, nuclear weapons, radiological weapons, biological weapons, and related waste
of such weapons).

9. "Storage" means the keeping of defense equipment required by the United States Forces in connection with agreed activities under this Agreement.

10. "Taxes and duties" means all taxes, duties (including customs duties), fees, of whatever kind, imposed by the Government of Iraq, or its agencies, or governorates under Iraqi laws and regulations. However, the term does not include charges by the Government of Iraq, its agencies, or governorates for services requested and received by the United States Forces.

Article 3 Laws

1. While conducting military operations pursuant to this Agreement, it is the duty of members of the United States Forces and of the civilian component to respect Iraqi laws, customs, traditions, and conventions and to refrain from any activities that are inconsistent with the letter and spirit of this Agreement. It is the duty of the United States to take all necessary measures for this purpose.

2. With the exception of members of the United States Forces and of the civilian component, the United States Forces may not transfer any person into or out of Iraq on vehicles, vessels, or aircraft covered by this Agreement, unless in accordance with applicable Iraqi laws and regulations, including implementing arrangements as may be agreed to by the Government of Iraq.

Article 4 Missions

1. The Government of Iraq requests the temporary assistance of the United States Forces for the purposes of supporting Iraq in its efforts to maintain security and stability in Iraq, including cooperation in the conduct of operations against al-Qaeda and other terrorist groups, outlaw groups, and remnants of the former regime.

2. All such military operations that are carried out pursuant to this Agreement shall be conducted with the agreement of the Government of Iraq. Such operations shall be fully coordinated with Iraqi authorities. The coordination of all such military operations shall be overseen by a Joint Military Operations

Coordination Committee (JMOCC) to be established pursuant to this Agreement. Issues regarding proposed military operations that cannot be resolved by the JMOCC shall be forwarded to the Joint Ministerial Committee.

3. All such operations shall be conducted with full respect for the Iraqi Constitution and the laws of Iraq. Execution of such operations shall not infringe upon the sovereignty of Iraq and its national interests, as defined by the Government of Iraq. It is the duty of the United States Forces to respect the laws, customs, and traditions of Iraq and applicable international law.

4. The Parties shall continue their efforts to cooperate to strengthen Iraq's security capabilities including, as may be mutually agreed, on training, equipping, supporting, supplying, and establishing and upgrading logistical systems, including transportation, housing, and supplies for Iraqi Security Forces.

5. The Parties retain the right to legitimate self defense within Iraq, as defined in applicable international law.

Article 5 Property Ownership

1. Iraq owns all buildings, non-relocatable structures, and assemblies connected to the soil that exist on agreed facilities and areas, including those that are used, constructed, altered, or improved by the United States Forces.

2. Upon their withdrawal, the United States Forces shall return to the Government of Iraq all the facilities and areas provided for the use of the combat forces of the United States, based on two lists. The first list of agreed facilities and areas shall take effect upon the entry into force of the Agreement. The second list shall take effect no later than June 30, 2009, the date for the withdrawal of combat forces from the cities, villages, and localities. The Government of Iraq may agree to allow the United States Forces the use of some necessary facilities for the purposes of this Agreement on withdrawal.

3. The United States shall bear all costs for construction, alterations, or improvements in the agreed facilities and areas provided for its exclusive use. The United States Forces shall consult with the Government of Iraq regarding such construction, alterations, and improvements, and must seek approval of the Government of Iraq for major construction and alteration projects. In the event that the use of agreed facilities and areas is shared, the two Parties shall bear the costs of construction, alterations, or improvements proportionately.

4. The United States shall be responsible for paying the costs for services requested and received in the agreed facilities and areas exclusively used by it, and both Parties shall be proportionally responsible for paying the costs for services requested and received in joint agreed facilities and areas.

5. Upon the discovery of any historical or cultural site or finding any strategic resource in agreed facilities and areas, all works of construction, upgrading, or modification shall cease immediately and the Iraqi representatives at the Joint Committee shall be notified to determine appropriate steps in that regard.

6. The United States shall return agreed facilities and areas and any non-relocatable structures and assemblies on them that it had built, installed, or established during the term of this Agreement, according to mechanisms and priorities set forth by the Joint Committee. Such facilities and areas shall be handed over to the Government of Iraq free of any debts and financial burdens.

7. The United States Forces shall return to the Government of Iraq the agreed facilities and areas that have heritage, moral, and political significance and any non-relocatable structures and assemblies on them that it had built, installed, or established, according to mechanisms, priorities, and a time period as mutually agreed by the Joint Committee, free of any debts or financial burdens.

8. The United States Forces shall return the agreed facilities and areas to the Government of Iraq upon the expiration or termination of this Agreement, or earlier as mutually agreed by the Parties, or when such facilities are no longer required as determined by the JMOCC, free of any debts or financial burdens.

9. The United States Forces and United States contractors shall retain title to all equipment, materials, supplies, relocatable structures, and other movable property that was legitimately imported into or legitimately acquired within the territory of Iraq in connection with this Agreement.

Article 6 Use of Agreed Facilities and Areas

1. With full respect for the sovereignty of Iraq, and as part of exchanging views between the Parties pursuant to this Agreement, Iraq grants access and use of agreed facilities and areas to the United States Forces, United States contractors, United States contractor employees, and other individuals or entities as agreed upon by the Parties.

2. In accordance with this Agreement, Iraq authorizes the United States Forces to exercise within the agreed facilities and areas all rights and powers that may be necessary to establish, use, maintain, and secure such agreed facilities and areas. The Parties shall coordinate and cooperate regarding exercising these rights and powers in the agreed facilities and areas of joint use.
3. The United States Forces shall assume control of entry to agreed facilities and areas that have been provided for its exclusive use. The Parties shall coordinate the control of entry into agreed facilities and areas for joint use and in accordance with mechanisms set forth by the JMOCC. The Parties shall coordinate guard duties in areas adjacent to agreed facilities and areas through the JMOCC.

Article 7 Positioning and Storage of Defense Equipment

The United States Forces may place within agreed facilities and areas and in other temporary locations agreed upon by the Parties defense equipment, supplies, and materials that are required by the United States Forces in connection with agreed activities under this Agreement. The use and storage of such equipment shall be proportionate to the temporary missions of the United States Forces in Iraq pursuant to Article 4 of this Agreement and shall not be related, either directly or indirectly, to systems of weapons of mass destruction (chemical weapons, nuclear weapons, radiological weapons, biological weapons, and related waste of such weapons). The United States Forces shall control the use and relocation of defense equipment that they own and are stored in Iraq. The United States Forces shall ensure that no storage depots for explosives or munitions are near residential areas, and they shall remove such materials stored therein. The United States shall provide the Government of Iraq with essential information on the numbers and types of such stocks.

Article 8 Protecting the Environment

Both Parties shall implement this Agreement in a manner consistent with protecting the natural environment and human health and safety. The United States reaffirms its commitment to respecting applicable Iraqi environmental laws, regulations, and standards in the course of executing its policies for the purposes of implementing this Agreement.

Article 9 Movement of Vehicles, Vessels, and Aircraft

1. With full respect for the relevant rules of land and maritime safety and movement, vessels and vehicles operated by or at the time exclusively for the United States Forces may enter, exit, and move within the territory of Iraq for the purposes of implementing this Agreement. The JMOCC shall develop appropriate procedures and rules to facilitate and regulate the movement of vehicles.

2. With full respect for relevant rules of safety in aviation and air navigation, United States Government aircraft and civil aircraft that are at the time operating exclusively under a contract with the United States Department of Defense are authorized to over-fly, conduct airborne refueling exclusively for the purposes of implementing this Agreement over, and land and take off within, the territory of Iraq for the purposes of implementing this Agreement. The Iraqi authorities shall grant the aforementioned aircraft permission every year to land in and take off from Iraqi territory exclusively for the purposes of implementing this Agreement. United States Government aircraft and civil aircraft that are at the time operating exclusively under a contract with the United States Department of Defense, vessels, and vehicles shall not have any party boarding them without the consent of the authorities of the United States Forces. The Joint Sub-Committee concerned with this matter shall take appropriate action to facilitate the regulation of such traffic.

3. Surveillance and control over Iraqi airspace shall transfer to Iraqi authority immediately upon entry into force of this Agreement.

4. Iraq may request from the United States Forces temporary support for the Iraqi authorities in the mission of surveillance and control of Iraqi air space.

5. United States Government aircraft and civil aircraft that are at the time operating exclusively under contract to the United States Department of Defense shall not be subject to payment of any taxes, duties, fees, or similar charges, including overflight or navigation fees, landing, and parking fees at government airfields. Vehicles and vessels owned or operated by or at the time exclusively for the United States Forces shall not be subject to payment of any taxes, duties, fees, or similar charges, including for vessels at government ports. Such vehicles, vessels, and aircraft shall be free from registration requirements within Iraq.

6. The United States Forces shall pay fees for services requested and received.
7. Each Party shall provide the other with maps and other available information on the location of mine fields and other obstacles that can hamper or jeopardize movement within the territory and waters of Iraq.

Article 10 Contracting Procedures

The United States Forces may select contractors and enter into contracts in accordance with United States law for the purchase of materials and services in Iraq, including services of construction and building. The United States Forces shall contract with Iraqi suppliers of materials and services to the extent feasible when their bids are competitive and constitute best value. The United States Forces shall respect Iraqi law when contracting with Iraqi suppliers and contractors and shall provide Iraqi authorities with the names of Iraqi suppliers and contractors, and the amounts of relevant contracts.

Article 11 Services and Communications

1. The United States Forces may produce and provide water, electricity, and other services to agreed facilities and areas in coordination with the Iraqi authorities through the Joint Sub-Committee concerned with this matter.
2. The Government of Iraq owns all frequencies. Pertinent Iraqi authorities shall allocate to the United States Forces such frequencies as coordinated by both Parties through the JMOCC. The United States Forces shall return frequencies allocated to them at the end of their use not later than the termination of this Agreement.
3. The United States Forces shall operate their own telecommunications systems in a manner that fully respects the Constitution and laws of Iraq and in accordance with the definition of the term "telecommunications" contained in the Constitution of the International Union of Telecommunications of 1992, including the right to use necessary means and services of their own systems to ensure the full capability to operate systems of telecommunications.
4. For the purposes of this Agreement, the United States Forces are exempt from the payment of fees to use transmission airwaves and existing and future frequencies, including any administrative fees or any other related charges.

5. The United States Forces must obtain the consent of the Government of Iraq regarding any projects of infrastructure for communications that are made outside agreed facilities and areas exclusively for the purposes of this Agreement in accordance with Article 4, except in the case of actual combat operations conducted pursuant to Article 4.
6. The United States Forces shall use telecommunications systems exclusively for the purposes of this Agreement.

Article 12 Jurisdiction

Recognizing Iraq's sovereign right to determine and enforce the rules of criminal and civil law in its territory, in light of Iraq's request for temporary assistance from the United States Forces set forth in Article 4, and consistent with the duty of the members of the United States Forces and the civilian component to respect Iraqi laws, customs, traditions, and conventions, the Parties have agreed as follows:

1. Iraq shall have the primary right to exercise jurisdiction over members of the United States Forces and of the civilian component for the grave premeditated felonies enumerated pursuant to paragraph 8, when such crimes are committed outside agreed facilities and areas and outside duty status.
2. Iraq shall have the primary right to exercise jurisdiction over United States contractors and United States contractor employees.
3. The United States shall have the primary right to exercise jurisdiction over members of the United States Forces and of the civilian component for matters arising inside agreed facilities and areas; during duty status outside agreed facilities and areas; and in circumstances not covered by paragraph 1.
4. At the request of either Party, the Parties shall assist each other in the investigation of incidents and the collection and exchange of evidence to ensure the due course of justice.
5. Members of the United States Forces and of the civilian component arrested or detained by Iraqi authorities shall be notified immediately to United States Forces authorities and handed over to them within 24 hours from the time of detention or arrest. Where Iraq exercises jurisdiction pursuant to paragraph 1 of this Article, custody of an accused member of the United States Forces or of the civilian component shall reside with United States Forces authorities. United States Forces authorities shall

make such accused persons available to the Iraqi authorities for purposes of investigation and trial.

6. The authorities of either Party may request the authorities of the other Party to waive its primary right to jurisdiction in a particular case. The Government of Iraq agrees to exercise jurisdiction under paragraph 1 above, only after it has determined and notifies the United States in writing within 21 days of the discovery of an alleged offense, that it is of particular importance that such jurisdiction be exercised.

7. Where the United States exercises jurisdiction pursuant to paragraph 3 of this Article, members of the United States Forces and of the civilian component shall be entitled to due process standards and protections pursuant to the Constitution and laws of the United States. Where the offense arising under paragraph 3 of this Article may involve a victim who is not a member of the United States Forces or of the civilian component, the Parties shall establish procedures through the Joint Committee to keep such persons informed as appropriate of: the status of the investigation of the crime; the bringing of charges against a suspected offender; the scheduling of court proceedings and the results of plea negotiations; opportunity to be heard at public sentencing proceedings, and to confer with the attorney for the prosecution in the case; and, assistance with filing a claim under Article 21 of this Agreement. As mutually agreed by the Parties, United States Forces authorities shall seek to hold the trials of such cases inside Iraq. If the trial of such cases is to be conducted in the United States, efforts will be undertaken to facilitate the personal attendance of the victim at the trial.

8. Where Iraq exercises jurisdiction pursuant to paragraph 1 of this Article, members of the United States Forces and of the civilian component shall be entitled to due process standards and protections consistent with those available under United States and Iraqi law. The Joint Committee shall establish procedures and mechanisms for implementing this Article, including an enumeration of the grave premeditated felonies that are subject to paragraph 1 and procedures that meet such due process standards and protections. Any exercise of jurisdiction pursuant to paragraph 1 of this Article may proceed only in accordance with these procedures and mechanisms.

9. Pursuant to paragraphs 1 and 3 of this Article, United States Forces authorities shall certify whether an alleged offense arose during duty status. In those cases where Iraqi authorities believe the circumstances require a review of this determination, the Parties shall consult immediately through the Joint Committee, and United States Forces authorities shall take full account of the facts and circumstances and any information Iraqi authorities may present bearing on the determination by United States Forces authorities.

10. The Parties shall review the provisions of this Article every 6 months including by considering any proposed amendments to this Article taking into account the security situation in Iraq, the extent to which the United States Forces in Iraq are engaged in military operations, the growth and development of the Iraqi judicial system, and changes in United States and Iraqi law.

Article 13 Carrying Weapons and Apparel

Members of the United States Forces and of the civilian component may possess and carry weapons that are owned by the United States while in Iraq according to the authority granted to them under orders and according to their requirements and duties.

Members of the United States Forces may also wear uniforms during duty in Iraq.

Article 14 Entry and Exit

1. For purposes of this Agreement, members of the United States Forces and of the civilian component may enter and leave Iraq through official places of embarkation and debarkation requiring only identification cards and travel orders issued for them by the United States. The Joint Committee shall assume the task of setting up a mechanism and a process of verification to be carried out by pertinent Iraqi authorities.

2. Iraqi authorities shall have the right to inspect and verify the lists of names of members of the United States Forces and of the civilian component entering and leaving Iraq directly through the agreed facilities and areas. Said lists shall be submitted to Iraqi authorities by the United States Forces. For purposes of this Agreement, members of the United States Forces and of the civilian component may enter and leave Iraq through agreed facilities and areas requiring only identification cards issued for

them by the United States. The Joint Committee shall assume the task of setting up a mechanism and a process for inspecting and verifying the validity of these documents.

Article 15 Import and Export

1. For the exclusive purposes of implementing this Agreement, the United States Forces and United States contractors may import, export (items bought in Iraq), re-export, transport, and use in Iraq any equipment, supplies, materials, and technology, provided that the materials imported or brought in by them are not banned in Iraq as of the date this Agreement enters into force. The importation, re-exportation, transportation, and use of such items shall not be subject to any inspections, licenses, or other restrictions, taxes, customs duties, or any other charges imposed in Iraq, as defined in Article 2, paragraph 10. United States Forces authorities shall provide to relevant Iraqi authorities an appropriate certification that such items are being imported by the United States Forces or United States contractors for use by the United States Forces exclusively for the purposes of this Agreement. Based on security information that becomes available, Iraqi authorities have the right to request the United States Forces to open in their presence any container in which such items are being imported in order to verify its contents. In making such a request, Iraqi authorities shall honor the security requirements of the United States Forces and, if requested to do so by the United States Forces, shall make such verifications in facilities used by the United States Forces. The exportation of Iraqi goods by the United States Forces and United States contractors shall not be subject to inspections or any restrictions other than licensing requirements. The Joint Committee shall work with the Iraqi Ministry of Trade to expedite license requirements consistent with Iraqi law for the export of goods purchased in Iraq by the United States Forces for the purposes of this Agreement. Iraq has the right to demand review of any issues arising out of this paragraph. The Parties shall consult immediately in such cases through the Joint Committee or, if necessary, the Joint Ministerial Committee.

2. Members of the United States Forces and of the civilian component may import into Iraq, re-export, and use personal effect materials and equipment for consumption or personal use. The import into, re-export from, transfer from, and use of such imported items in

Iraq shall not be subjected to licenses, other restrictions, taxes, custom duties, or any other charges imposed in Iraq, as defined in Article 2, paragraph 10. The imported quantities shall be reasonable and proportionate to personal use. United States Forces authorities will take measures to ensure that no items or material of cultural or historic significance to Iraq are being exported.

3. Any inspections of materials pursuant to paragraph 2 by Iraqi authorities must be done urgently in an agreed upon place and according to procedures established by the Joint Committee.

4. Any material imported free of customs and fees in accordance with this Agreement shall be subjected to taxes and customs and fees as defined in Article 2, paragraph 10, or any other fees valued at the time of sale in Iraq, upon sale to individuals and entities not covered by tax exemption or special import privileges. Such taxes and fees (including custom duties) shall be paid by the transferee for the items sold.

5. Materials referred to in the paragraphs of this Article must not be imported or used for commercial purposes.

Article 16 Taxes

1. Any taxes, duties, or fees as defined in Article 2, paragraph 10, with their value determined and imposed in the territory of Iraq, shall not be imposed on goods and services purchased by or on behalf of the United States Forces in Iraq for official use or on goods and services that have been purchased in Iraq on behalf of the United States Forces.

2. Members of the United States Forces and of the civilian component shall not be responsible for payment of any tax, duty, or fee that has its value determined and imposed in the territory of Iraq, unless in return for services requested and received.

Article 17 Licenses or Permits

1. Valid driver's licenses issued by United States authorities to members of the United States Forces and of the civilian component, and to United States contractor employees, shall be deemed acceptable to Iraqi authorities. Such license holders shall not be subject to a test or fee for operating the vehicles, vessels, and aircraft belonging to the United States Forces in Iraq.

2. Valid driver's licenses issued by United States authorities to members of the United States Forces and of the civilian component,

and to United States contractor employees, to operate personal cars within the territory of Iraq shall be deemed acceptable to Iraqi authorities. License holders shall not be subject to a test or fee.

3. All professional licenses issued by United States authorities to members of the United States Forces and of the civilian component, and to United States contractor employees shall be deemed valid by Iraqi authorities, provided such licenses are related to the services they provide within the framework of performing their official duties for or contracts in support of the United States Forces, members of the civilian component, United States contractors, and United States contractor employees, according to terms agreed upon by the Parties.

Article 18 Official and Military Vehicles

1. Official vehicles shall display official Iraqi license plates to be agreed upon between the Parties. Iraqi authorities shall, at the request of the authorities of the United States Forces, issue registration plates for official vehicles of the United States Forces without fees, according to procedures used for the Iraqi Armed Forces. The authorities of the United States Forces shall pay to Iraqi authorities the cost of such plates.

2. Valid registration and licenses issued by United States authorities for official vehicles of the United States Forces shall be deemed acceptable by Iraqi authorities.

3. Military vehicles exclusively used by the United States Forces will be exempted from the requirements of registration and licenses, and they shall be clearly marked with numbers on such vehicles.

Article 19 Support Activities Services

1. The United States Forces, or others acting on behalf of the United States Forces, may assume the duties of establishing and administering activities and entities inside agreed facilities and areas, through which they can provide services for members of the United States Forces, the civilian component, United States contractors, and United States contractor employees. These entities and activities include military post offices; financial services; shops selling food items, medicine, and other commodities and services; and various areas to provide entertainment and telecommunications services, including radio broadcasts. The establishment of such services does not require permits.

2. Broadcasting, media, and entertainment services that reach beyond the scope of the agreed facilities and areas shall be subject to Iraqi laws.

3. Access to the Support Activities Services shall be limited to members of the United States Forces and of the civilian component, United States contractors, United States contractor employees, and other persons and entities that are agreed upon. The authorities of the United States Forces shall take appropriate actions to prevent misuse of the services provided by the mentioned activities, and prevent the sale or resale of aforementioned goods and services to persons not authorized access to these entities or to benefit from their services. The United States Forces will determine broadcasting and television programs to authorized recipients.

4. The service support entities and activities referred to in this Article shall be granted the same financial and customs exemptions granted to the United States Forces, including exemptions guaranteed in Articles 15 and 16 of this Agreement. These entities and activities that offer services shall be operated and managed in accordance with United States regulations; these entities and activities shall not be obligated to collect nor pay taxes or other fees related to the activities in connection with their operations.

5. The mail sent through the military post service shall be certified by United States Forces authorities and shall be exempt from inspection, search, and seizure by Iraqi authorities, except for non-official mail that may be subject to electronic observation. Questions arising in the course of implementation of this paragraph shall be addressed by the concerned Joint Sub-Committee and resolved by mutual agreement. The concerned Joint Sub-Committee shall periodically inspect the mechanisms by which the United States Forces authorities certify military mail.

Article 20 Currency and foreign exchange

1. The United States Forces shall have the right to use any amount of cash in United States currency or financial instruments with a designated value in United States currency exclusively for the purposes of this Agreement. Use of Iraqi currency and special banks by the United States Forces shall be in accordance with Iraqi laws.

2. The United States Forces may not export Iraqi currency from Iraq, and shall take measures to ensure that members of the United States Forces, of the civilian component, and United States contractors and United States contractor employees do not export Iraqi currency from Iraq.

Article 21 Claims

1. With the exception of claims arising from contracts, each Party shall waive the right to claim compensation against the other Party for any damage, loss, or destruction of property, or compensation for injuries or deaths that could happen to members of the force or civilian component of either Party arising out of the performance of their official duties in Iraq.

2. United States Forces authorities shall pay just and reasonable compensation in settlement of meritorious third party claims arising out of acts, omissions, or negligence of members of the United States Forces and of the civilian component done in the performance of their official duties and incident to the non-combat activities of the United States Forces. United States Forces authorities may also settle meritorious claims not arising from the performance of official duties. All claims in this paragraph shall be settled expeditiously in accordance with the laws and regulations of the United States. In settling claims, United States Forces authorities shall take into account any report of investigation or opinion regarding liability or amount of damages issued by Iraqi authorities.

3. Upon the request of either Party, the Parties shall consult immediately through the Joint Committee or, if necessary, the Joint Ministerial Committee, where issues referred to in paragraphs 1 and 2 above require review.

Article 22 Detention

1. No detention or arrest may be carried out by the United States Forces (except with respect to detention or arrest of members of the United States Forces and of the civilian component) except through an Iraqi decision issued in accordance with Iraqi law and pursuant to Article 4.

2. In the event the United States Forces detain or arrest persons as authorized by this Agreement or Iraqi law, such persons must be handed over to competent Iraqi authorities within 24 hours from the time of their detention or arrest.

3. The Iraqi authorities may request assistance from the United States Forces in detaining or arresting wanted individuals.

4. Upon entry into force of this Agreement, the United States Forces shall provide to the Government of Iraq available information on all detainees who are being held by them. Competent Iraqi authorities shall issue arrest warrants for persons who are wanted by them. The United States Forces shall act in full and effective coordination with the Government of Iraq to turn over custody of such wanted detainees to Iraqi authorities pursuant to a valid Iraqi arrest warrant and shall release all the remaining detainees in a safe and orderly manner, unless otherwise requested by the Government of Iraq and in accordance with Article 4 of this Agreement.

5. The United States Forces may not search houses or other real estate properties except by order of an Iraqi judicial warrant and in full coordination with the Government of Iraq, except in the case of actual combat operations conducted pursuant to Article 4.

Article 23 Implementation

Implementation of this Agreement and the settlement of disputes arising from the interpretation and application thereof shall be vested in the following bodies:

1. A Joint Ministerial Committee shall be established with participation at the Ministerial level determined by both Parties. The Joint Ministerial Committee shall deal with issues that are fundamental to the interpretation and implementation of this Agreement.

2. The Joint Ministerial Committee shall establish a JMOCC consisting of representatives from both Parties. The JMOCC shall be co-chaired by representatives of each Party.

3. The Joint Ministerial Committee shall also establish a Joint Committee consisting of representatives to be determined by both Parties. The Joint Committee shall be cochaired by representatives of each Party, and shall deal with all issues related to this Agreement outside the exclusive competence of the JMOCC.

4. In accordance with paragraph 3 of this Article, the Joint Committee shall establish Joint Sub-Committees in different areas to consider the issues arising under this Agreement according to their competencies.

Article 24 Withdrawal of the United States Forces from Iraq

Recognizing the performance and increasing capacity of the Iraqi Security Forces, the assumption of full security responsibility by those Forces, and based upon the strong relationship between the Parties, an agreement on the following has been reached:

1. All the United States Forces shall withdraw from all Iraqi territory no later than December 31, 2011.
2. All United States combat forces shall withdraw from Iraqi cities, villages, and localities no later than the time at which Iraqi Security Forces assume full responsibility for security in an Iraqi province, provided that such withdrawal is completed no later than June 30, 2009.
3. United States combat forces withdrawn pursuant to paragraph 2 above shall be stationed in the agreed facilities and areas outside cities, villages, and localities to be designated by the JMOCC before the date established in paragraph 2 above.
4. The United States recognizes the sovereign right of the Government of Iraq to request the departure of the United States Forces from Iraq at any time. The Government of Iraq recognizes the sovereign right of the United States to withdraw the United States Forces from Iraq at any time.
5. The Parties agree to establish mechanisms and arrangements to reduce the number of the United States Forces during the periods of time that have been determined, and they shall agree on the locations where the United States Forces will be present.

Article 25 Measures to Terminate the Application of Chapter VII to Iraq

Acknowledging the right of the Government of Iraq not to request renewal of the ChapterVII authorization for and mandate of the multinational forces contained in United Nations Security Council Resolution 1790 (2007) that ends on December 31, 2008;

Taking note of the letters to the UN Security Council from the Prime Minister of Iraq and the Secretary of State of the United States dated December 7 and December 10, 2007, respectively, which are annexed to Resolution 1790;

Taking note of section 3 of the Declaration of Principles for a Long-Term Relationship of Cooperation and Friendship, signed by the President of the United States and the Prime Minister of Iraq on November 26, 2007, which memorialized Iraq's call for extension of the above-mentioned mandate for a final period, to end not later than December 31, 2008:

Recognizing also the dramatic and positive developments in Iraq, and noting that the situation in Iraq is fundamentally different than that which existed when the UN Security Council adopted Resolution 661 in 1990, and in particular that the threat to international peace and security posed by the Government of Iraq no longer exists, the Parties affirm in this regard that with the termination on December 31, 2008 of the Chapter VII mandate and authorization for the multinational force contained in Resolution 1790, Iraq should return to the legal and international standing that it enjoyed prior to the adoption of UN Security Council Resolution 661 (1990), and that the United States shall use its best efforts to help Iraq take the steps necessary to achieve this by December 31, 2008.

Article 26 Iraqi Assets

1. To enable Iraq to continue to develop its national economy through the rehabilitation of its economic infrastructure, as well as providing necessary essential services to the Iraqi people, and to continue to safeguard Iraq's revenues from oil and gas and other Iraqi resources and its financial and economic assets located abroad, including the Development Fund for Iraq, the United States shall ensure maximum efforts to:
   a. Support Iraq to obtain forgiveness of international debt resulting from the policies of the former regime.
   b. Support Iraq to achieve a comprehensive and final resolution of outstanding reparation claims inherited from the previous regime, including compensation requirements imposed by the UN Security Council on Iraq.
2. Recognizing and understanding Iraq's concern with claims based on actions perpetrated by the former regime, the President of the United States has exercised his authority to protect from United States judicial process the Development Fund for Iraq and certain other property in which Iraq has an interest. The United States shall remain fully and actively engaged with the Government of Iraq with respect to continuation of such protections and with respect to such claims.
3. Consistent with a letter from the President of the United States to be sent to the Prime Minister of Iraq, the United States remains committed to assist Iraq in connection with its request that the

UN Security Council extend the protections and other arrangements established in Resolution 1483 (2003) and Resolution 1546 (2003) for petroleum, petroleum products, and natural gas originating in Iraq, proceeds and obligations from sale thereof, and the Development Fund for Iraq.

Article 27 Deterrence of Security Threats

In order to strengthen security and stability in Iraq and to contribute to the maintenance of international peace and stability, the Parties shall work actively to strengthen the political and military capabilities of the Republic of Iraq to deter threats against its sovereignty, political independence, territorial integrity, and its constitutional federal democratic system. To that end, the Parties agree as follows:

In the event of any external or internal threat or aggression against Iraq that would violate its sovereignty, political independence, or territorial integrity, waters, airspace, its democratic system or its elected institutions, and upon request by the Government of Iraq, the Parties shall immediately initiate strategic deliberations and, as may be mutually agreed, the United States shall take appropriate measures, including diplomatic, economic, or military measures, or any other measure, to deter such a threat.

The Parties agree to continue close cooperation in strengthening and maintaining military and security institutions and democratic political institutions in Iraq, including, as may be mutually agreed, cooperation in training, equipping, and arming the Iraqi Security Forces, in order to combat domestic and international terrorism and outlaw groups, upon request by the Government of Iraq.

Iraqi land, sea, and air shall not be used as a launching or transit point for attacks against other countries.

Article 28 The Green Zone

Upon entry into force of this Agreement the Government of Iraq shall have full responsibility for the Green Zone. The Government of Iraq may request from the United States Forces limited and temporary support for the Iraqi authorities in the mission of security for the Green Zone. Upon such request, relevant Iraqi authorities shall work jointly with the United States Forces authorities on security for the Green Zone during the period determined by the Government of Iraq.

Article 29 Implementing Mechanisms

Whenever the need arises, the Parties shall establish appropriate mechanisms for implementation of Articles of this Agreement, including those that do not contain specific implementation mechanisms.

Article 30 The Period for which the Agreement is Effective

1. This Agreement shall be effective for a period of three years, unless terminated sooner by either Party pursuant to paragraph 3 of this Article.
2. This Agreement shall be amended only with the official agreement of the Parties in writing and in accordance with the constitutional procedures in effect in both countries.
3. This Agreement shall terminate one year after a Party provides written notification to the other Party to that effect.
4. This Agreement shall enter into force on January 1, 2009, following an exchange of diplomatic notes confirming that the actions by the Parties necessary to bring the Agreement into force in accordance with each Party's respective constitutional procedures have been completed.

Signed in duplicate in Baghdad on this 17th day of November, 2008, in the English and Arabic languages, each text being equally authentic.

FOR THE UNITED
STATES OF AMERICA

FOR THE
REPUBLIC OF IRAQ

APPENDIX H
U.S. ARMY DRAWDOWN AND TRANSFORMATION

Things move slowly throughout the military and do not take effect overnight. Although the new revised *FM 100-5* published June 1993 recognized that the Soviet Army was no longer our threat, as late as November 1993, the Army was still teaching Soviet tactics, and there still was no mention of fighting an insurgency or counterguerrilla campaign or defending against an asymmetric threat.

I learned this first hand while attending the Infantry Officer Advance Course at Fort Benning, Georgia, better known as "Home of the Infantry," in November 1993. The entire course curriculum and tactics centered on Soviet tactics. I wrote several operations orders that strictly dealt with opposing the Soviet Army or a third-world army that was modeled and equipped after the Soviet military. All students were issued a set of enemy doctrinal manuals that covered Soviet equipment, tactics, and organizational make-up. We were repeatedly tested on our knowledge of Soviet tactics, equipment, and order of battle. One test question asked how many lug nuts were on a Soviet T-72 Main Battle Tank.

By the end of the course, I could recite by memory the entire Soviet Army order of battle, starting with the composition of the Advance Guard followed by the main body, second- and third-echelon forces, including the number and types of vehicles in each of these formations, weapons systems, and all the ranges from their artillery systems down to their individual weapons such as the AK-47. Upon graduation, infantry captains were experts on Soviet doctrine, tactics, and equipment. Problem was there was no Soviet Army to fight.

At no time during the course was there ever a block of instruction or even a mention of counterinsurgency or counterguerrilla warfare. There were certainly no reviews or discussion of lessons learned from past Vietnam battles. I learned nothing about winning the hearts and minds of a given population or nation building. Instead, it was my job to close with and destroy the enemy. The Vietnam War was so unpopular that the Army and our nation wanted to forget it ever happened. But we should have learned from the lessons of Vietnam. Going forward they would have helped make operations in Iraq easier to plan and execute and most likely we could have ended the war years earlier.

U.S. Army Structure, 1990–99

In 1990 as we entered Operation Desert Storm, the Army was designed and built around the division base structure. A typical division such as the 82nd Airborne Division consisted of three maneuver brigades, an artillery, or fire brigade, aviation brigade, support brigade, and all associated supporting elements including military intelligence, cavalry, military police, signal battalion, and an engineer battalion for a total strength ranging from 12,000 to 17,000 soldiers. Heavy or mechanized divisions were much larger based on the sustainment footprint. The maneuver brigades stood alone and were made of three maneuver battalions, either infantry or armor or a combination of both. All additional combat enablers such as the artillery battalion, engineer battalion, and the support battalion were subdivided and assigned a habitual support relationship to a respective maneuver brigade to form a brigade combat team (BCT). Typically, a brigade would not train on a daily basis with its enabler units. The only time they would all come together was for major field training exercises or for culminating training events at one of three National Training Centers: Joint Readiness Training Center, Fort Polk, Louisiana; National Training Center, Fort Erwin, California; or Combined Maneuver Training Center, Hohenfels Germany. Units would deploy to combat or other regional conflicts as a complete force package.

The Army had a total of eighteen divisions, along with several separate combat brigades and numerous combat support and combat service support organizations for a total active military strength of more than 730,000. The majority of these were heavy divisions made of armor and mechanized forces equipped with M1 Abrams Tanks and Bradley Fighting Vehicles. These heavy forces were left over from the Cold War as the Army had built them to confront the Soviet Army in Europe. Four of the eighteen divisions were stationed in Germany. The remainder we scattered throughout the continental United States, Hawaii, Alaska, and Korea.

Army Postwar Drawdown (1992–96)

From 1992 through 1996, the Army and military in general underwent a massive drawdown, most of which occurred in fiscal year 1992. Starting with the end of Operation Desert Storm, the Army drafted and executed a drawdown plan that took us from eighteen active duty divisions to ten. By the time President George H. W. Bush's term ended, the active Army had cut more than 200,000 troops. President Bill Clinton entered office in January 1993 with an Army end strength of approximately 575,000. By the time he left office in 2000, the Army was reduced to 482,000. This was the active duty combat strength, less National Guard and Reserve units, that strategic planners used to plan the invasion of Afghanistan and Iraq.

Army Transformation: U.S. Army Structure, (1999–2005)

As part of the Army drawdown, it was decided by Army Chief of Staff General Eric K. Shinseki, who assumed the post in June 1999, that we needed to reorganize and transform the Army to meet the demands of the new contemporary operating environment for the twenty-first century. It was the belief of Army and other strategic defense planners that a window of opportunity existed whereby America would not face a major adversary thus allowing for breathing room to reorganize and reequip the Army to better meet security needs heading into a world of uncertainty.

Shinseki gave his first speech on October 12, 1999, officially launching Army Transformation while attending the Association of United States Army Annual Convention held in Washington, D.C. In attendance were several thousand soldiers, including numerous high-ranking military officers and Department of Army civilians. In introducing Army Transformation, Shinseki stated that:

"To adjust the condition of the Army to better meet the requirements of the next century, we articulate this vision. Soldiers on point for the nation, transforming this, the most respected force that is dominant across the full spectrum of operations. With that overarching goal to frame us, the Army will undergo a major transformation ..."

The transformation plan had seven broad goals: to make the Army more responsive, deployable, agile, versatile, lethal, survivable, and sustainable. The overall transformation plan was to take thirty years to achieve its end state, commencing in 2000 and ending in 2030. The primary focus of transformation was to switch the Army from a division-centric force to a modular brigade combat team-focused force. The goal of transformation was to give the Army the ability to deploy a combat-capable brigade anywhere in the world within ninety-six hours, a full division in 120 hours, and five divisions on the ground within thirty days. This would be a remarkable feat if the Army could pull it off, considering that it took more than thirty days to get one heavy division deployed to Saudi Arabia during Operation Desert Storm.

The plan was a three-prong attack focused on sustaining the legacy force, bridging the gap with the interim force, and ultimately reaching the end state of establishing the objective force.

The legacy force centers on the major weapons systems that the Army has in its inventory at the time, principally the Army's primary ground combat vehicles, M1 Abrams tanks, and M2/M3 Bradley Fighting Vehicles, armored field artillery systems, and combat-support vehicles. This force is widely known and recognized as the Army's heavy force, comprising the Army's armored and mechanized divisions such as the 1st Armored Division located in Germany. Within the overall transformation concept, the Army would continue to sustain and upgrade the heavy force while developing the other paths: interim and objective force. The fact remains that the legacy force would continue to be the Army's primary war fighting maneuver force for the foreseeable future and was the force we would deploy into Iraq in 2003.

The interim force was primarily a stopgap force in several ways and a leap-ahead force in others. The plan was to use existing technology to reequip and enhance brigade-sized maneuver units to adapt them to meet many of the Army's missions. Doing so would enable these units to deploy more rapidly than heavy forces but also have more combat lethality, ground mobility, and soldier protection than the Army's light infantry forces (airborne, air assault, and other light infantry units). The interim force had another purpose, too. While interim force units handle missions, they also would be used to develop much of the doctrine and training aspects for the objective force capitalizing on lessons learned from training exercises and real world deployments.

The objective force represents the art of the possible: what can be done to organize, equip, and train units to assimilate the best aspects of the light, heavy, and interim forces. Strategists believed that the line distinguishing the light and heavy force would progressively blur. The objective force path was designed to provide the Army the means to make that blur possible while retaining current legacy force capabilities—the full spectrum capabilities that are the nucleus of the army vision. The objective force is the science and technology phase, which focuses on the equipment to be used by the force. Research and development is underway throughout the Department of Defense to create a new family of armored fighting vehicles called the future combat system. The main goal is to produce fighting vehicles that are lighter than the armored vehicles in service today but that offer the same if not greater lethality and provide soldiers better protection.

Inevitably, we would be transforming the Army while engaging in major combat operations in Afghanistan and Iraq. In layman's terms, we would be building an aircraft while in flight. This would certainly challenge the Army and stretch us thin in the years ahead.

Some would argue that this was more than a simple overhaul of the Army. Top leaders contend that Army Transformation is one of the most drastic changes ever envisioned by the Army. It is not simply about replacing old equipment with newer equipment, vehicles, basing, doctrine, tactics, and training that have undergone incremental changes since the battles of Lexington and Concord and after every battle since. It is a complete overhaul and redesign of training, equipment, manning, doctrine, and institutional thinking—a burnishing of the Army down to bare metal, piece by piece, and rebuilding it while never taking it offline.[1]

The main focus for future operations was establishing the interim force. The Army plan was to build and create a total of six to eight

Interim Brigade Combat Teams (IBCTs); eventually these brigades would transition from IBCTs to become known as Stryker Brigade Combat Teams (SBCTs). The first two IBCTs were established at Fort Lewis, Washington. The IBCTs were born of necessity based on more than ten years of Army deployment experience, and most notably from the lessons learned from the deployment to Saudi Arabia during Operation Desert Shield.

The 82nd Airborne Division deployed first and established the first line of defense, more popularly known as the "line in the sand." While there they faced a substantial Iraqi heavy armored force. The ability to get there first does not mean that soldiers had the right military equipment and capabilities for the job. Although the 82nd was never tested, had the Iraqi Army decided to attack, it had the potential to turn out badly for us. It was evident from this operation and subsequent operations in Albania and Kosovo that the Army needed a lighter force that could deploy rapidly that still packed a punch and provided adequate protection for soldiers.

This would become even more evident once we invaded Iraq in 2003 with the introduction of improvised explosive devices (IEDs). IEDs were lethal, with catastrophic results, so much so that our legacy armor vehicles, specifically M1A1 Tanks and M2/M3 Bradley Fighting Vehicles, could not withstand or defend against the blast and effects of these crude devices. Moreover, once the interim force Stryker Combat Vehicle was introduced into theater, it too was penetrable and did not provide adequate protection. As a result, the Army worked to produce and field Up-Armored High Mobility Multi-Wheeled Vehicles (HMMWVs [Humvees]) followed by the production and fielding of the Mine Resistant Ambush Protected (MRAP) series of vehicles that drastically reduced and mitigated the threat posed by IEDs. Depending on the nature and composition of the IED strike even these vehicles were not foolproof.

From October 1999 through June 2002, two designated IBCTs were established at Fort Lewis, Washington: 3rd Brigade, 2nd Infantry Division and 1st Brigade, 25th Infantry Division. On March 7, 2000, 3rd Brigade, 2nd Infantry Division accepted the first four of thirty-two loaner Generation III Light Armoured Vehicles (LAV IIIs) from Canada. These were the original test vehicles for the newly formed brigade. Testing would take place for nine months as the vehicles were put through the paces by soldiers assigned to the brigade.

Finally on November 17, 2000, a decision was made by the Army to award a contract to General Motors and General Dynamics Land Systems to build the Army's new combat vehicle based on the LAV III prototype. These new vehicles would eventually be named the Stryker Combat Vehicle, in honor of two soldiers whose valiant sacrifice is a proud symbol of U.S. Army heroism: Private First Class Stuart S. Stryker was killed in action during World War II, and Specialist 4th Class Robert F. Stryker was killed in action during the Vietnam War. The new Stryker Vehicle began showing up at Fort Lewis, Washington, on June 6, 2002. On July 1, 2002, the IBCTs officially changed their unit designation to SBCT.

From June 2002 to May 2003, both units would execute several high-visibility training validation and certification exercises. 3rd Brigade, 2nd Infantry Division completed its certification ahead of 1st Brigade, 25th Infantry Division and upon completion, the unit received orders that it would deploy to Iraq in support of Operation Iraq Freedom in November 2003. I was there in Iraq and watched as the Army reached this historical milestone. After the deployment of 3-2 SBCT, 1-25 would follow in October 2002. From there the Army would continue to deploy Stryker Brigades to Iraq as they came on line. This was the wave of the future, paving the way toward the objective force.

I was fortunate to have had the opportunity to execute my third and final tour to Iraq with one of the Army's premier Stryker Brigades, 4th Brigade, 2nd Infantry Division from September 2009 to August 2010. I witnessed up close the awesome capability of the Army's future force. This last tour of duty with the Stryker Brigade put a stamp on my career as an infantry officer. I had served in every type infantry unit the Army has: airborne, mechanized, light, and Stryker unit. A career that started out in the Texas Army National Guard as a Mechanized Platoon Leader maneuvering in old Vietnam relic M1113s Armored Personnel Carriers, then to M2/M3 Bradley Fighting Vehicles, and finally concluding as I traversed the ancient sands where civilization began in the Army's premier infantry fighting vehicle. My time in the infantry had truly come full circle.

As the Stryker Brigades were coming online, the Army, as part of the overall transformation plan, focused on the institution and began revising and updating all of its doctrinal manuals. The revision started with the capstone operations doctrine, *FM 100-5, Operations*.

The manual was completely overhauled to reflect the current and future environment we would be fighting in and was officially published in June 2001 under a new title, *FM 3-0, Operations*. No longer were we simply conventionally focused on large-scale battles against a uniformed adversary. Rather, it outlined the missions and requirements for conducting operations across the full spectrum of conflict. This basically classified Army operations into two categories: war or military operations other than war (MOOTW). Within this spectrum of conflict, the Army determined that units will execute a range of military operations, either offense, defense, stability, or support:

- **Offensive operations** aimed at destroying or defeating an enemy, their purpose is to impose U.S. will on the enemy and achieve decisive victory.
- **Defensive operations** to defeat an enemy attack, buy time, economize forces, or develop conditions favorable for offensive operations. Defensive operations alone normally cannot achieve a decision. Their purpose is to create conditions for a counteroffensive that allows Army forces to regain the initiative.
- **Stability operations** to promote and protect U.S. national interests by influencing the threat, political, and information dimensions of the operational environment through a combination of peacetime developmental, cooperative activities, and coercive actions in response to crisis.
- **Support operations** employing Army forces to assist civil authorities, foreign or domestic, as they prepare for or respond to crisis and relieve suffering. Domestically, Army forces respond only when the National Command Authority (NCA) directs them to. Army forces operate under the lead federal agency and comply with provisions of U.S. law, to include the Posse Comitatus and Stafford Acts.

The new FM prescribed that Army commanders at all echelons, may combine different types of operations simultaneously and sequentially to accomplish missions in war and during MOOTW. For each mission, the Joint Force Commander and the Army Component Commander determines the emphasis Army forces place on each type of operation. Offensive and defensive operations normally dominate military operations in war and some during Small-Scale Contingencies (SSC).

Stability and support operations predominate during MOOTW that include certain SSCs and Peacetime Military Engagements (PME).

Embedded within this concept of units doing several operations simultaneously, it was also recognized that tactical operations need to be more decentralized to the lowest levels possible. In the past, operating under and within the framework of the AirLand Battle Doctrine, tactical operations were centralized; in other words, tactical decisions were being made by division- and brigade-level leadership and staffs versus decentralized operations which the decisions are made by the units and soldiers on the ground at the tip of the spear. As we entered the twenty-first century, it was inevitable that we would eventually face some type of asymmetrical threat, although no one anticipated it happening this soon as it did in September 2001. As operations unfolded in Afghanistan and Iraq, it became more apparent that the nature of this fight across a noncontiguous battlefield was a decentralized fight.

Based on this assertion, it was imperative that young squad and platoon leaders must be trained and proficient in related skills and be empowered to make snap decisions during the heat of combat in the absence of orders. These decisions could have strategic consequences depending on the decision made and the outcome. It was an awesome responsibility that now rested on their shoulders, and, based on the quality of soldiers in our ranks, they were clearly up to task.

The other significant change in *FM 3-0* was the recognition that the Army will not operate exclusively while conducting full spectrum operations. Rather, all operations would be as part of a joint force, often within a multinational and interagency environment. Within the new doctrine, the Army classified this as a unified action. Under unified action, commanders integrate joint (all services), single service, special, and supporting operations with interagency, nongovernmental, and multinational, including U.N. operations.

The only other changes were more in terminology when defining the operational environment and establishing the framework for operations. "Area of Operations" switched to "Operational Environment." What used to be known as the main and supporting efforts changed to decisive, shaping, and sustaining efforts. These terms are used to identify a unit's role in the operation and to allocate resources. Typically a unit, for instance a brigade that is designated as the main or decisive effort for an attack as the lead element, will get the majority of resources dedicated to it for its operation such as having priority of fires, attack aviation, or fixed wing close air support more so than units designated as the supporting or shaping effort.

The constant in the new manual that was carried over from the one were the elements of combat power: maneuver, firepower, leadership, and protection. The new manual added one more element: information. Also the nine principles of war were retained: objective, offensive, economy of force, mass, maneuver, unity of command, simplicity, surprise, and security. The tenets of Army operations remained unchanged: initiative, agility, depth, synchronization, and versatility. Essentially these were classified together as the fundamentals of Full Spectrum Operations.

FM 3-0 was a sound architecture upon which the invasion of Iraq was based. However, it was not perfect. Just after September 11, 2001, the Army had yet to fully digest it and its impact at the operational and tactical level. The ink was still wet as it was implemented. In hindsight, the doctrine was lacking. The manual did address combating and countering asymmetric threats in future conflicts; however, it was lacking in the fact that it did not address fighting and prosecuting the protracted counterinsurgency campaign that we would soon dominate combat operations in Iraq. A conventional doctrine to combat insurgency operations at the operational and tactical levels did not exist. This doctrinal gap would prove to be the genesis of COIN doctrine several years later.

As the independent gears associated with transforming the Army meshed, the face of the free world changed forever. On September 11, 2001, al-Qaeda terrorists attacked our homeland by hijacking andflying planes into the Twin Towers in New York City and the Pentagon in Washington, D.C. Another hijacked plane most likely destined for the White House or U.S. Capitol was overtaken by passengers on board and crashed in a remote field in Pennsylvania. This tragic act perpetrated by cowards changed the world we lived in forever and set our nation on a war footing for the foreseeable future.

The force structure that was available to the NCA was in a state of flux: legacy brigades, interim brigades, and other modularized forces. The entire Army institution was focused on transforming when called to combat in the Middle East. American soldiers and the brigades they belonged to sallied forth to battle as they were manned and equipped. Some brigades such as the legacy brigades looked like brigades from the 1990s. Others had transformed to the twenty-first century model. Each brigade would morph and reorganize to fight the enemy it was confronted with in its designated battle space. This allowed the Army as a whole to execute the directives of the Secretary of Defense and Chief of Staff of the Army to continue to transform while in direct combat.

NOTES

Chapter 1

1. Department of the Army. *Field Manual 100-5 (FM 100-5).* Author: Washington, D.C., August 1982.

2. An asymmetric threat simply means that we would no longer face a conventional Army who wore uniforms and had an order of battle as it did in the past. Our future enemies will use whatever tactics they can, such as IEDs or massive suicide bombings or civilian jets as missiles, as a means to destroy U.S. national will and our capability to wage war.

3. Krulak, General Charles C. "The Strategic Corporal: Leadership in the Three Block War." *Marines Magazine,* January 1999.

4. Cohen, Michael A. "The Powell Doctrine's Enduring Relevance." New American Foundation: Washington, D.C., July 22, 2009. The Powell Doctrine was a carry-over from the Weinberger Doctrine following the Vietnam War and other small regional conflicts such as Grenada in 1983 and our involvement in Lebanon in 1986, which resulted in the death of 241 Marines.

    The doctrine was built on six principles:

    1) The United States should not commit forces to combat overseas unless the particular engagement or occasion is deemed vital to our national interest or that of our allies.

    2) If we decide it is necessary to put combat troops into a given situation, we should do so wholeheartedly, and with the clear intention of winning.

    3) If we do decide to commit forces to combat overseas, we should have clearly defined political and military objectives.

    4) The relationship between our objectives and the forces we have committed—their size, composition, and disposition—must be continually reassessed and adjusted if necessary.

    5) Before the United States commits combat forces abroad, there must be some reasonable assurance we will have the support of the American people and their elected representatives in Congress.

    6) The commitment of U.S. forces to combat should be a last resort.

5. The United States and the Coalition Provisional Authority introduced money as a weapon before combat had ended. We started to execute nation-building tasks before the fighting had ceased. Iraq was not stable at the time; it was still an unstable and hostile environment. I argue that we should have continued to fight and concluded operations before we began nation building. The declaration made by President Bush that major hostilities were over was a premature declaration from my vantage point on the ground.

Chapter 2

1. *St. Augustine Times*, September 16, 2001.
2. The observer controllers are the external set of eyes that watch over you and critique how you are doing. They are usually experienced officers and NCOs who help coach, teach, and mentor units when they are executing their Mission Rehearsal Exercise.
3. The four phases were:
   a. Phase I: Alert, Marshall, and Deploy to Theater
   b. Phase II: Air Campaign
   c. Phase III: Ground Offensive
   d. Phase IV: Post Invasion
4. Gibson, Major David R. "Casualty Estimation in Modern Warfare," *Army Logistician*, November–December 2003.

Chapter 3

1. Murray, Williamson and Scales, Major General Robert H. *The Iraq War: A Military History*. Harvard University Press: Boston, 2003, pp. 72–73.
2. According to the *New World Encyclopedia*, Bedouin, derived from the Arabic word *badaw*, a generic name for a desert-dweller, is a term generally applied to Arab nomadic pastoralist groups, who are found throughout most of the desert belt extending from the Atlantic coast of the Sahara via the Western Desert, Sinai, and Negev to the eastern coast of the Arabian desert. It is occasionally used to refer to non-Arab groups as well, notably the Beja of the African coast of the Red Sea. They constitute only a small portion of the total population of the Middle East, although the area they inhabit is large due to their (formerly) nomadic lifestyle. Reductions in their grazing ranges and increases in their population, as well as the changes brought about by the discovery and development of oil fields in the region, have led many Bedouin to adopt the modern urban, sedentary lifestyle with its accompanying attractions of material prosperity all while maintaining their traditions. The majority of Bedouin families in Kuwait who live in the city stake a claim in the desert and setup their elaborate tents using them as a weekend retreat.
3. Mujahedin-e Khalq Organization (MEK or MKO)
   National Liberation Army of Iran (NLA)
   People's Mujahidin of Iran (PMOI)
   National Council of Resistance (NCR)
   National Council of Resistance of Iran (NCRI)
   Muslim Iranian Student's Society

The fall of Saddam Hussein's regime affected the circumstances of the designated foreign terrorist organization, the MEK. The MEK was allied with the Iraqi regime and received most of its support from it. The MEK assisted the Hussein regime in suppressing opposition within Iraq, and performed internal security for the Iraqi regime. The NLA was the military wing of the National Council of Resistance of Iran.

Mujahedin-e-Khalq [MEK] facilities in Iraq included:

- Camp Ashraf, the MEK military headquarters, is about 100 kilometers west of the Iranian border and 100 kilometers north of Baghdad near Khalis.
- Camp Anzali near the town of Jalawla (Jalula), about 120 to 130 km (70 to 80 miles) northeast of Baghdad and about 40 to 60 km (20 to 35 miles) from the border with Iran).
- Camp Faezeh in Kut
- Camp Habib in Basra
- Camp Homayoun in Al-Amarah
- Camp Bonyad Alavi near the city of Miqdadiyah in Mansourieh (about 65 miles northeast of Baghdad)

On May 10, 2003, V Corps accepted the voluntary consolidation of the Mujahedin-E-Khalq's forces, and subsequent control over those forces. This process was expected to take several days to complete. Previously, V Corps was monitoring a cease-fire brokered between the MEK and special forces elements. The MEK forces had been abiding by the terms of this agreement and are cooperating with Coalition soldiers.

By mid-May 2003 coalition forces had consolidated 2,139 tanks, armored personnel carriers, artillery pieces, air defense artillery pieces, and miscellaneous vehicles formerly in the possession of the Mujahedin-E Khalq (MEK) forces. The 4th Infantry Division also reported they have destroyed most of the MEK munitions and caches. The voluntary, peaceful resolution of this process by the MEK and the coalition significantly contributed to the coalition's mission to establish a safe and secure environment for the people of Iraq. The 4,000 MEK members in the Camp Ashraf former Mujahedeen base were consolidated, detained, and disarmed and were screened for any past terrorist acts.

The United States, which lists National Council of Resistance of Iran as a terrorist organization, closed the NCRI's Washington office in 2003.

Source: Global Security http://www.globalsecurity.org/military/world/para/mek.htm

Chapter 4

1. Operation Provide Comfort

Following Desert Storm, the entire Kurdish population of Iraq attempted to flee the country to the north out of fear that Saddam Hussein would attempt to exterminate their entire population. Because of political concerns, Turkish officials refused to allow these desperate people permission to cross the border into Turkey. The result was that hundreds of thousands of Kurds were trapped on barren and rocky hillsides, vulnerable not only to Hussein's forces, but to the harsh elements as well. Without basic necessities such as water, food, and medical supplies, hundreds of Kurds were dying each week. In April 1991, President George H. W. Bush made the decision to provide relief and protection for these beleaguered people. Smith was given the task of rapidly establishing and deploying a Joint Force whose mission was to "stop the dying." Literally overnight, Operation Provide Comfort was born. In less than forty-eight hours from receiving the order to "do something," cargo and fighter aircraft were redeployed to bases in southern Turkey, where they began delivering humanitarian supplies. Over a period of a few weeks, a U.S.-led coalition force was deployed into northern Iraq, resettlement areas constructed, and a demilitarized zone established for the protection of the Kurds.

Source: GlobalSecurity.org: http://www.globalsecurity.org/military/ops/provide_comfort.htm

2. Sources:
   a. *The Iraq Study Group Report*. United States Institute of Peace: Washington, D.C., December 2006. Retrieved from http://www.usip.org/isg/index.html
   b. ISG Final Report dated September 30, 2004. Retrieved from http://www.globalsecurity.org/wmd/library/report/2004/isg-final-report/
   c. DCI Special Advisor Report on Iraq's weapons of mass destruction. Retrieved from https://www.cia.gov/library/reports/general-reports 1/iraq_wmd_2004/index.html#sect1

3. Brown, Todd S. *Battleground Iraq, Journal of a Company Commander*. Department of the Army: Washington, D.C., 2007. Retrieved from http://www.history.army.mil/html/books/070/70-107-1/CMH_70-107-1.pdf. Reprinted with permission.

4. Filkins, Dexter. *The New York Times*, Sunday, December 7, 2003.

5. Retrieved from http://www.globalsecurity.org/military/world/iraq/baqir-hakim.htm

6. op. cit. (Todd Brown)

7. op. cit. (Todd Brown)

8. Phares, Walid. *The Coming Revolution: Struggle for Freedom in the Middle East*. Threshold Editions: New York, 2007.

9. Negus, Steve. "The Insurgency Intensifies, Middle East Research and Information Project," Vol. 34, Fall 2004, MER 232—The Iraq Impasse. Retrieved from http://www.merip.org/mer/mer232

10. Trudeau, Garry B. *The War in Quotes*. Andrews McMeel Publishing: Riverside, New Jersey, 2008.

11. *Ibid.*

12. Bacevich, Andrew J. "The Petraeus Doctrine," *The Atlantic Magazine*, October 2008.

13. Schmitt, Eric. "Army Chief Raises Estimate of G.I.'s Needed in Postwar Iraq," *New York Times*, February 28, 2003.

14. Vest, Jason. "The War After the War," *Village Voice*, March 19, 2003, page 1.

Chapter 5

1. Filkins, Dexter. *The Forever War*. Knopf: New York, 2008.

2. Moore, Harold G. and Galloway, Joseph Lee. *We Were Soldiers Once ... and Young: Ia Drang—The Battle That Changed the War in Vietnam*. Harper Perennial: New York, 1993.

3. op. cit. (Filkins)

4. op. cit. (Todd Brown)

5. op. cit. (Todd Brown)

6. op. cit. (Todd Brown)
7. Right seat ride/left seat ride (RSR/LSR) occurs during the transition of two units; the incoming and outgoing unit. The incoming unit rides passenger in the right seat while the outgoing unit drives them around. Once complete, the incoming unit takes over the driver's seat with the outgoing unit riding shotgun or in the passenger seat. After this is complete, the outgoing units departs theater as the incoming or new unit assumes responsibility for the area.

Chapter 6

1. McGeough, Paul. "The World's Most Dangerous Road," *The Sydney Moring Herald*, June 8, 2005.
2. Woodhouse, Major Dale B. "MRAP's Future With the Army," *Army Sustainment, ALU*: Fort Lee, Virginia, PB 700-11-02 Volume 43, Issue 2, March–April 2011. Retrieved from http://www.almc.army.mil/alog/issues/MarApr11/mraps_future.html

   Feickert, Andrew (Specialist in Military Ground Forces). *Mine-Resistant, Ambush-Protected (MRAP) Vehicles: Background and Issues for Congress*. Washington, D.C.: Congressional Research Service 7-5700, April 27, 2009.
3. Knickmeyer, Ellen and Ibrahim, K. I. "Attack on Shiite Shrine Sets Off Protests, Violence," *Washington Post Foreign Service*, February 23, 2006.
4. "United States Condemns Bombing of Important Shia Mosque in Iraq," The White House, Office of the Press Secretary, February 22, 2006.
5. op. cit. (*Washington Post*, February 23, 2006.)
6. Warrick, Joby. "Lacking Biolabs, Trailers Carried Case for War," *Washington Post*, A01, April 12, 2006.
7. Associated Press, June 8, 2006.
8. "UNHCR Worried About Effect of Dire Security Situation on Iraq's Displaced." The UN Refugee Agency, October 13, 2006. Retrieved from http://www.unhcr.org/452fa9954.html
9. Refugees International (website). Retrieved from http://www.refintl.org/where-we-work/middle-east/iraq
10. Raddatz, Martha. "Gen. George Casey: Iraq Civil War 'Possible,' Troop Reductions Less Likely," ABC News, July 8, 2006.
11. "Baghdad Morgue Revises August Death Toll Upward 300 Percent," ABC News, September 6, 2006.
12. I met John for the first time in our dining facility located at FOB Prosperity. He had arrived days removed from Mosul and was visiting with Beech and our staff to get an orientation of the operation prior to his troops returning to theater. First impressions are always lasting, I knew instantly from talking to him for a brief minute the caliber of officer he was. His reputation clearly preceded him. I would link up with him three years later in June 2009. He was selected to command the 4th Stryker Brigade Combat Team based at Fort Lewis, Washington. After I completed battalion command at Fort Polk, I was assigned to his brigade and had the distinct honor of serving with him in Iraq from September 2009 to August 2010 as his deputy brigade commander during my third tour.
13. *The Iraq Study Group Report*. United States Institute of Peace: Washington, D.C., December 2006. Retrieved from http://www.usip.org/isg/index.html

Chapter 7

1. Brookings Institution. "Iraq Index: Tracking Variables of Reconstruction and Security in Post Saddam Iraq." October 7, 2007.

2. "Fact Sheet: The New Way Forward in Iraq." The White House, Office of the Press Secretary: Washington, D.C., January 10, 2007.

3. Sanger, David E., et al. "The Struggle for Iraq: A Year at War—Evolving Strategies; Chaos Overran Iraq Plan in '06, Bush Team Says," *New York Times*, January 2, 2007. Sandalow, Marc. "Election 2006: America's Referendum on War," *San Francisco Chronicle*, January 23, 2007.

4. Wright, Robin and Tyson, Ann Scott. "Joint Chiefs Advise Change in War Strategy," *Washington Post*, December 14, 2006.

5. *Ibid.*

6. op. cit. (*Washington Post*, December 14, 2006.)

7. King, Larry. CNN News, December 14, 2006.

8. Kagan, Fredrick. "Choosing Victory: A Plan for Success in Iraq," *Phase I Report*. Washington, D.C.: American Enterprise Institute, January 5, 2007.

9. "Iraq: A Turning Point." Washington, D.C.: American Enterprise Institute. Retrieved from http://www.aei.org/events/eventID.1446/event_details.asp

10. Odierno, Lieutenant General Raymond. *The Surge in Iraq: One Year Later*, Heritage Lectures No. 1068, The Heritage Foundation, Washington, D.C., March 13, 2008. Reprinted with permission.

11. Roggio, Bill. "Operation Phantom Thunder: The Battle of Iraq," *The Long War Journal*, June 27, 2007. Retrieved from http://www.longwarjournal.org/archives/2007/06/operation_phantom_fu.php#ixzz1eSfmDeQd).

12. Gilbert, Michael. "Operation Phantom Thunder: The Battle of Iraq," *News Tribune*, June 21, 2007.

13. op. cit. (Odierno, Lieutenant General Raymond. *The Surge in Iraq: One Year Later*, March 13, 2008.)

14. Galula, David. *Counter Insurgency Warfare: Theory and Practice*. Hailer Publishing: St. Petersburg, Florida, 2005.

15. Nagl, LTC John A. *The Evolution and Importance of Army/Marine Corps Field Manual 3-24, Counterinsurgency*. Retrieved from http://www.press.uchicago.edu/Misc/Chicago/841519foreword.html

16. Johnston, David and Broder, John M. "F.B.I. Says Guards Killed 14 Iraqis Without Cause," *New York Times*, November 13, 2007.

17. *Ibid.*

18. op. cit. (*New York Times*, November 13, 2007.)

19. op. cit. (Odierno, Lieutenant General Raymond. *The Surge in Iraq: One Year Later*, March 13, 2008.)

20. op. cit. (Odierno, Lieutenant General Raymond. *The Surge in Iraq: One Year Later*, March 13, 2008.)

21. Cloud, David S. "Ex-commander Calls Iraq War 'Nightmare;' Hits Bush, Aides on 'Flawed' Strategy," *New York Times*, October 12, 2007.

22. Cave, Damien. "2007 Is Deadliest Year for U.S. Troops," *New York Times*, November 7, 2007.

23. "U.S. Military Says Iraq Troop 'Surge' Has Ended," Reuters, July 22, 2008.

24. op. cit. (Odierno, Lieutenant General Raymond. *The Surge in Iraq: One Year Later*, March 13, 2008.)

Chapter 8

None

Chapter 9

1. Iraqi Deaths. iCasualties.org. March 2010. http://icasualties.org/iraq/index.aspx
2. Washington, D.C.: White House, Office of the Press Secretary, March 7, 2010.
3. Boot, Max. *Los Angeles Times*, May 9, 2010.
4. *Ibid.*
5. op. cit. (*Los Angeles Times*, May 9, 2010)

Chapter 10

1. Ricks, Thomas E. *Fiasco: The American Military Adventure in Iraq.* The Penguin Press: New York, 2006.
2. *Ibid.*

Appendix H

1. Transformation Handbook published by Association of United States Army [AUSA], Dennis Steele, 2001.

ACKNOWLEDGEMENTS

I knew within months of departing Iraq for the first time that I wanted to tell our story—a story of the brave men and women who fought so gallantly against an enemy that flat-out hated us and everything we stood for. Our sole purpose for being there was to rid Iraq and the Middle East of a brutal dictator and in doing so establish a representative democracy in Iraq, one in which the citizens of Iraq could let their voices be heard as they charted their destiny and choose who would govern them.

When I first set out on this journey, I was overcome by events that halted any and all progress in bringing the story to life. Plus, at the time, the market was flooded with memoirs; another book on Iraq would simply gather dust and make for a solid paperweight on someone's desk. Then came my second tour, during which I was removed from planning and executing lethal combat operations and served as a brigade executive officer focused on command and controlling the fight from inside a well-protected palace in the heart of Baghdad. Simply put, there would be no more door kicking; rather, I became a facilitator of operations and synchronized the resources needed for our forces on the ground. From this tour I gained a new perspective and understanding of the strategic picture and what the U.S. government and military were trying to accomplish in Iraq as a whole.

I could have written this book following that tour, but the timing was not right. Iraq was marred by sectarian violence and on the brink of if not already engulfed in civil war. There was still a lot of work to be done. We, the U.S. Military, were partly to blame as our actions on the ground and our lack of understanding the war we were fighting led us to this point. After departing Iraq the second time, I had an opportunity to right the ship and made an impact training our soldiers and units about the right way to prosecute the war in hopes of turning it around. At the same time, our new COIN doctrine was unveiled and implemented in Iraq along with the surge of troops. The combination of these two events provided the resources—both intellectual and manpower—necessary to quell the violence and return Iraq to somewhat of a state of normalcy.

After departing battalion command from the Joint Readiness Training Center at Fort Polk, Louisiana, I returned to Baghdad to see the final chapter play out. Through adaptation and learning from past mistakes, we turned the corner. The surge and COIN had proven effective. Attacks in Iraq were at an all-time low. Meanwhile, the Iraqi Security Forces (ISF) had grown leap years in their capacity to provide security for the population. So evident were these changes that the Government of Iraq (GOI) and the United States brokered a deal and signed the Iraqi Security Agreement that ultimately gave total control of security and all facets of operations to GOI and ISF. For us it meant that we would no longer serve in a lead role; rather, we would take a back seat and provide tactical, operational, and strategic oversight as required.

During my final tour in Iraq, my brigade took an active step, reaching out to the ISF to establish an enduring partnership that would be the envy of all Iraqi and U.S. units serving in Iraq. Because the violence was low and conditions were relatively calm, it provided a window to focus on capacity building for the ISF, as well as on nation building. Moreover, we were aided by enhanced Provincial Reconstruction Teams (ePRTs) provided by the U.S. State Department to assist us in these tasks. As the year unfolded, I watched as the ISF continued to grow in capacity. As each day passed, they required less and less assistance and mentorship. The climax came with their performance during the National Parliamentary Elections in 2010. Through their determined efforts alone, they withstood the onslaught of attacks and intimidation from al-Qaeda and other insurgent groups, thus providing a safe environment that enabled a record number of Iraqis to vote.

Meanwhile, civil capacity efforts and associated projects kick-started the local economy, providing jobs and local economic growth to a starving community. Also, the agriculture industry was reinvigorated, and once again the fertile land between the Euphrates and Tigris rivers was enriched with crops.

A relatively secure environment, a strong and capable ISF, a newly elected GOI in transition, and an economy on the (albeit slow) rise were all signals that it was time for us to depart. Our combat mission in Iraq was complete. We had laid the groundwork for irreversible momentum, and Iraq's future clearly rested in the hands of its people. For the common Iraqi citizen, there was hope—hope for a better and brighter future far different from the decades they spent under oppression.

I had a front-row seat to either experience or personally witnessed every major turning point in this war. By the time we crossed the border into Kuwait on August 16, 2010, I knew it was time to tell the story of Operation Iraqi Freedom in a holistic way; the unvarnished truth of how the war came full circle from the time we first invaded.

Upon my return, I sat down with Colonel John Norris and sketched out a rough road map focused on four distinct periods: the invasion; the postinvasion, including the emerging insurgency and sectarian violence; the surge; and, finally, post-Security Agreement period, concluding with the last patrol. Without his support and visual depiction in charting a way forward, this work would not have been possible. I am forever indebted to him for his leadership by example, his personal and professional mentorship, and most of all his friendship.

Thanks also go to my point man, contributing editor, and dear friend, Mike Walling, without whose vision, expertise, dedication, and encouragement this journey would have been lonely as I embarked into uncharted waters, and the project would have never sat sail. Thanks for taking garbled comments and turning it into a book that tells the true story of our heroic deeds in Iraq that the American people can read and enjoy for years to come. Thanks for Keeping the Faith, always!

To my good friend, Major Steve Phillips, thanks for serving as my ghost editor and as a sanity check when I ventured off azimuth. Your input was sound and thought provoking. You accompanied me on a journey from beginning to end. Your fingerprints are embedded in every section of this work. You clearly deserve more credit for your contributions; this small paragraph does little to justify your impact. You are clearly one of the finest officers that I have ever served with and are one the "good guys." Best of luck in your future assignments— there are no limits for you.

Thanks to my chief editor Kelli Christiansen and marketing director John Tintera of Osprey Publishing for taking a chance on this book. I appreciate the faith, trust, and confidence you had in us to see this through.

A special thanks to Colonel (Ret.) Mark Lisi, Lieutenant Colonel Nick Mullen, Major Todd Brown, Major Dave Voorhies, Major Kevin James, Captain Gabi Niess, and Captain Caitlin Conley. Thanks for the memories and inspiration you gave me to pursue this project. Without your friendship, counsel, and dedication, this would not have been possible. Thanks for being there when I needed an azimuth check. You are the finest officers and noncommissioned officers with whom I have ever served. Any success that I enjoy, the credit is yours.

I owe a debt of thanks to my lifelong pastor at Macedonia Baptist Church in Mesquite, Texas, Brother John Livaudias, who provided me with comfort and reassurance through readings of scripture prior to my first deployment into Iraq. Your sound counsel and advice got me through some tough times. I am truly a better person and officer for having you in my corner. I will forever be indebted to you for your teachings and unconditional support.

To my family, Wendy, Dillon, Chloe, and little Kyle, thanks for your love and support as I embarked on this journey. For a year I have been deeply involved and consumed with this project, so much so that you guys often came second. While my reasons seem selfish, it was more to provide you a lasting record of a period in my life that defined me as a career officer and let you gain an inside view and understanding of what really went on in Iraq outside of the occasional short letters and e-mail. Simply put, I could not accomplish anything I set out do without your love and support. Dillon, Chloe, and Kyle, you guys are the love of my life. You have been through so much at such a young age. I am amazed every day at the resiliency and courage you display. You are the true inspiration in my life, and I get my strength from you to do what I do. Wendy, thanks for your love, support, and patience during this period of absence. It was almost as if I was deployed all over again. Thanks for being the rock that holds our relationship and home together. Thanks for being both parents to our precious son Kyle during my time away. Most of all, thanks for coming into my life at the right time and place.

Finally, to the soldiers and leaders with whom I have served, most notably the soldiers of 1-8 Infantry Battalion, 3rd Brigade–4th Infantry Division, 4th Brigade–4th Infantry Division, 1-509th Airborne Battalion, and 4th Stryker Brigade Combat Team–2nd Infantry Division, thanks for your dedication, service, and most of all your sacrifice. I have learned something from each and every one of you. I am certainly a better leader and a better man for having served with you. Through your efforts alone, Iraq is a better place with a future that is still to be determined. But you have laid the ground work for democracy to flourish. You are America's treasure. I am both humbled and honored to have served with you, my Band of Brothers.

ABOUT THE AUTHOR

Colonel Darron L. Wright has served in the U.S. Army for twenty-six years. He was first assigned to active duty in 1991, when he served as a platoon leader, company executive officer, and company commander with the 3rd Battalion, 17th Infantry Regiment, Fort Ord, California. His next assignment was as a company commander of C Company, 3-325 Airborne Infantry Regiment and E CO 313th Military Intelligence Battalion, Long Range Surveillance Detachment (LRSD), Fort Bragg, North Carolina from 1996–2000. From 2000–01, Col. Wright served as the Chief of Operations for 7th Infantry Division, Fort Carson. Colorado. Later, Col. Wright was assigned to 1st Battalion, 8th Infantry Regiment, Fort Carson, Colorado, and upon arrival, the unit deployed to Iraq in support of Operation Iraqi Freedom where he served as the Battalion Operations Officer. Following his second tour of combat, Col. Wright served as the battalion commander for 1st Battalion (Airborne), 509th Infantry Battalion located at Fort Polk, Louisiana. After completion of battalion command, Col. Wright deployed with 4th Stryker Brigade, 2nd Infantry Division as the Deputy Brigade Commander during OIF 09–10, operating in Northwest Baghdad. Col. Wright is the recipient of the Bronze Star with "V" device, the Bronze Star Medal, the Meritorious Service Medal, the General Douglas MacArthur Leadership Award, and numerous other awards and commendations. He earned his Master's degree in Strategic Studies and National Security Decision Making from the Naval War College.

INDEX